S0-AZO-780

Shakespeare's
Metrical Art

Shakespeare's
Metrical Art

GEORGE T. WRIGHT

UNIVERSITY OF CALIFORNIA PRESS

Berkeley   Los Angeles   London

University of California Press
Berkeley and Los Angeles, California
University of California Press, Ltd.
London, England
© 1988 by
The Regents of the University of California

Printed in the United States of America
1   2   3   4   5   6   7   8   9

Library of Congress Cataloging-in-Publication Data

Wright, George Thaddeus.
  Shakespeare's metrical art.

  Includes index.
    1. Shakespeare, William, 1564–1616—Versification.
2. English language—Early modern, 1500–1700—
Versification.   I. Title.
PR3085.W75   1988   822.3'3   87-10931
ISBN 0-520-06057-1 (alk. paper)

For Norma and Bob Weaver

Lovers, like me, lifelong, of measured tones

Contents

Contents

Preface

Poetry is language composed in verse, that is, language of which an essential feature is its appearance in measured units, either as written text or in oral performance. Although other units, larger or smaller, play an important part in poetry, in literate cultures the *line* is the indispensable unit of verse and the one by which we recognize its nature. Paragraphs of prose lack this essential feature: in different printed versions the separate lines may end at different words without injury to meaning or form; different printed versions of poems must retain the lines as they are. If a line is too long to print on a narrow page or column, the printer must use some conventional means to show that the leftover words belong with the ones they follow. Even when the sense of one line runs over to the next, it is important to the form of a poem that the lines be preserved intact.

If the line is the basic unit of a poetic text, meter and stanza measure the line in respect to units smaller or larger than the line. The *meter* of a line is its inner rhythmical structure, which in English we understand as a relationship between stressed and unstressed syllables. Since poems do not normally change their meter in every line but establish and confirm repetitive rhythmical patterns, often we must read several lines of a poem before we can hear a pattern of stressed and unstressed syllables that inheres in all of them, with or without variation. Once we can hear the basic pattern, we can recognize it as it is realized differently in all the succeeding lines; we listen for the returning pattern. Although the term *stanza* usually designates a particular arrangement of lines (a certain number of them in a design that may mix long lines and short, and with a specific patterning of rhymes), it is probably the best word we have to signify our more general interest in the way lines combine to form larger prosodic units. Meter lets us hear the line's inner relations, stanza its outer connections.

This book is chiefly concerned with the verse lines of Renaissance poems and plays and with the way poets of this period, and Shakespeare in particular, structured their lines (meter) and connected them with each other (stanza)—a dry subject that might seem hardly worthy of interest, but it is out of such structures and relations that poets like Wyatt and Shakespeare, Donne and Milton, achieved their powerful and passionate poetry. The intensity with which they or their characters speak, an intensity we can still hear in their written texts and in stage performances, owes much of its special force to its having been expressed in verse. The verse form springs the feeling, enables it to leap from the speaking voice or text to the listening reader. Many who have been moved by these poems or plays will acknowledge that the patterned verse has something to do with their experience, but a more detailed study of the deeper structures and motions of this verse can help to show more specifically how the whole verse system these poets use—principally, the iambic pentameter system—works to produce such extraordinary effects in their poetic speech.

Many scholars have written about poetic meter in the Renaissance, but their interest has usually been technical, not aesthetic, and the subject has constituted a corner of poetic studies that has not much attracted literary critics. In the nineteenth century it became a matter of concern to Shakespeareans only as a means of settling problems of chronology; metrical style, of little interest in itself, provided clues to dating and authorship. Similarly, the study of Chaucer's verse has been more concerned with whether or not certain syllables were pronounced than with aesthetic effects in the verse. Such concerns were natural when the establishment of texts was necessary to provide a foundation for further literary study. Unfortunately, one result of the primitive statistical methods used in those early days to study rhyme, feminine endings, deviant lines, and similar matters was to render these subjects dry and dull. When New Critics focused attention on poetic detail, they often cited particularly felicitous phrases, lines, or passages in which the poet's metrical skill contributed to fine effects. But the expressive metrical technique of only a few major poets has been described at length by critics whose interest has been equally in prosodic structure and aesthetic purpose—for example, Donne by Arnold Stein, Pope by Jacob Adler, Milton by Edward Weismiller. Except for early studies that focused on syllabic structure and not on expressive function, the meter Shakespeare used over his whole career has hardly been treated at all. Two recent exceptions are books by Henri Suhamy and Marina Tarlinskaja, whose modes of study (linguistic and statistical in the second, analytical and encyclopedic in the first) are less directly concerned than mine with metrical expressiveness.

My main purpose here is to describe the metrical system Shakespeare uses, particularly in his plays—the basic forms of his iambic pentameter line, its relation to other patterns (such as short lines, long lines, and prose), its changes over his career, and, most of all, the expressive gestures and powers this system provides for Shakespeare and his dramatis personae. To describe these matters fully, it has seemed necessary to place Shakespeare's practice in historical perspective, specifically in the context of the decasyllabic line he inherited and strongly influenced. To understand Shakespeare's metrical art, one has to appreciate the new freedom with which this line had just begun to be written as he started his career; that freedom, to which Sidney and Spenser (and Marlowe) contributed much, emerged from the mid-Elizabethan rigor of Gascoigne and his contemporaries as they developed the line they inherited from Surrey. But the smooth Surrey is most intelligible in contrast to the rough Wyatt, and Wyatt's strange meters are best approached through the bizarre system he derived from Lydgate, who in turn makes no sense apart from Chaucer. Chaucer constitutes a distinct beginning of the long tradition that culminates in Shakespeare and takes extravagant turns in Donne and Milton. Although Shakespeare's metrical practice can be described in its own terms (and Chapters 5–16 try to do so here), it becomes fully coherent only as we grasp, link by link, the chain that runs back to Chaucer.

If this backward-moving rationale, this curiosity to trace the historical sources, strikes any reader as excessive, it seems modest enough to me. My teaching and scholarly work has been mainly in twentieth-century poetry, and my interest in poetic style first focused chiefly on contemporary or modernist verse. It was partly in order to grasp the issues of free verse, to understand what it was free *from,* that I became absorbed in the technical study of earlier iambic writing. The breakdown of the iambic pentameter tradition seemed most intelligible if one studied its early triumphant development. As this book tries to suggest, the free verse line is not so much a departure from iambic pentameter as the inevitable next step in a centuries-long process that has followed its own strong logic. Only part of that process is described here—from its beginnings in Chaucer to the great confluence of English phrase and metrical line in Shakespeare and some of his contemporaries and successors. Some later stages—especially the crisis of accentual-syllabic meter in nineteenth- and twentieth-century poetry—I hope to trace more briefly in another book.

Writing about iambic pentameter involves a critic in complex problems of interpretation and procedure, questions about how a poet writes, how a reader reads, how a listener in the theater hears, and on what evidence and following what procedures a critic classifies and interprets. In studying earlier English verse, one encounters textual problems of every sort: In the absence of any speaker of Middle English, how can we know how Chaucer's verse sounded—to Chaucer, to Lydgate, or to Wyatt? To what extent were the poems of Chaucer, Wyatt, and Donne (among others), and to what extent should they be, conceived of as oral poetry for which graphic representation in a written text is merely a necessary convenience that guarantees its continued accessibility? Most perplexing, if even the text of a printed poem raises profound problems of interpretive procedures, what about the text of a play? Is it a script for actors, a dramatic poem, or a contrivance of a hundred editors? Is it the written text (and which one?) or the patterned language we listen to in the theater (and in which performance)? For a blind poet, what constitutes a text?

Convinced that the present study should broach but cannot resolve such theoretical questions, I have tried to stay sensitively aware of the processes through which Renaissance poetic texts have been enabled, by their authors, by an antecedent metrical history, and by contemporary and later readers and listeners, to come into existence. My aim is not to arrive at true readings, but to show the extraordinarily vast range of metrical resources English poets of this period found and nurtured in the iambic pentameter line. For one reason or another, readers and critics have usually had little understanding of these resources, and the chapters of this large book try to treat this heroic subject with something of the passion for system, for pattern, and for expression that marks the poets themselves.

The study of meter is always to some extent intrusive. Like most intense experiences, verse moves too fast and is too seamless for us to discern its segments as they pass or to hear, with full consciousness, its collecting and dissolving structures. Analysis slows down the beautiful current in order to help us understand the principles of its flow. The reader who is already deeply sensitive to the sound of verse lines and their movement in time may justly feel offended at any minute analysis that stops the verse and directs our rapt attention to this or that part of its design. But when I hear students, innocent of dissection, murdering the verse; when I hear learned scholars at professional meetings quote Shakespeare's lines without any apparent sense of their difference from ordinary speech, without any effort to convey with their voices, even in passing, the grace and force of those words that move us so in the theater; and when I hear gifted actors, blessed with the ability to speak the speech trippingly or, when appropriate, with due gravity, mislay the accents, omit words or change keys, and ignore the metrical clues to the meaning of the verse because they are unaware of the metrical principles on which it rests, I cannot help believing that a better understanding of those principles may encourage some readers, scholars, and actors to listen more closely to the meter, to hear how much of human feeling is involved in its structures, and, when the occasion calls, to speak the verse with a finer sense of its rise and flow.

In citing lines from Shakespeare's *Sonnets,* I have usually followed Booth's edition, except when the original punctuation has seemed to offer a metrical hint. In the same way, I have used *The Riverside Shakespeare* as the principal source of quotations (and of all line numbers) from the plays and from other poems by Shakespeare, but have sometimes preferred the Folio (or, rarely, a Quarto) reading for specific passages. I have kept the original spelling for some poets, like Wyatt, Spenser, and Donne, where it sometimes provides metrical hints, but have used modernized-spelling texts (like Booth's) for most other poets and passages; in certain cases (*The Riverside Shakespeare* sometimes and Ringler's edition of Sidney always), I have modernized the spelling. In every case I have normalized *u* to *v* and *v* to *u* in accordance with modern orthography.

I am conscious of many tangled threads that have led to the making of this book. The lifelong habit of writing verse, often metrical verse, has helped me understand meter from the point of view of the poet who composes it as well as from that of the reader. Music from my sister's piano filled the homes I grew up in. Singing in the Columbia University choir for several years under the sensitive direction of Lowell P. Beveridge taught me much about the expressive articulation of Renaissance and Baroque music. I owe more specific debts to many friends, relatives, colleagues, and students,

especially to those who have encouraged me in this enterprise from the
beginning, have written letters of support in my behalf, and have helped
me master various sides of my subject: to Percy G. Adams, Jacob H. Adler,
John F. Andrews, Joel Conarroe, Calvin Kendall, Andrew MacLeish,
Susan McClary, Karen Murdock, Marina Tarlinskaja, E. Paul Werstine,
and to two friends who would have been pleased to see it brought to
completion, John Macoubrie and Josephine Miles. I acknowledge with a
certain awe two more particular debts: Helen Vendler has generously
given me important help and encouragement at several stages of this work;
and T. V. F. Brogan, whose stupendous bibliography has wonderfully fa-
cilitated work in this field, kindly read the original, rather bloated manu-
script and saved it from many blunders of substance and blemishes of style.

I have also benefited from talk about verse and prose in seminars of
the Shakespeare Association of America. Several colleagues at the Univer-
sity of Minnesota (in addition to those already mentioned) have encour-
aged and supported this work, notably Kent Bales, Norman Fruman,
Michael Hancher, and J. Lawrence Mitchell. Our English Department
staff have also been extremely helpful, especially Greg Holupchinski,
Deborah Steinmetz, and, for many valiant years, Dorothy Conlan. It is
hard to imagine how this book could ever have been completed without
fellowships from the John Simon Guggenheim Memorial Foundation
and the National Endowment for the Humanities (as well as a Summer
Stipend from the NEH). I am very grateful to Doris Kretschmer, Rose
Vekony, and Jane-Ellen Long for their intelligence, tact, and industry in
shepherding a difficult manuscript through the several stages of review
and revision to publication. I owe a great deal also to my students, both
graduate and undergraduate, who have suffered through and reveled in
the meter of English poems for many years; and to my wife, Jerry, whose
patience during this and other critical enterprises has been of much longer
date. Finally, I thank *Studies in Philology* and *Shakespeare Quarterly* for
permission to reprint or adapt material from essays that first appeared in
their pages; and Scribner's for allowing me to use some short passages
originally written for an article in *William Shakespeare: His World, His
Work, His Influence* (1985).

Darwin revolutionized our study of nature by taking the actual variation among actual things as central to the reality, not as an annoying and irrelevant disturbance to be wished away.

R. C. LEWONTIN (27)

And in spite of all the pains I had lavished on these problems, I was more than ever stupefied by the complexity of this innumerable dance, involving doubtless other determinants of which I had not the slightest idea. And I said, with rapture, Here is something I can study all my life, and never understand.

SAMUEL BECKETT, *Molloy* (169)

CHAPTER 1

The Iambic Pentameter Line

When Shakespeare and Marlowe and Ben Jonson sat around the Mermaid Tavern and talked like we are doing, iambic pentameter was wonderfully new and timely.

(WILLIAM CARLOS WILLIAMS, 29)

How to Read It

Iambic pentameter has often been called the most speechlike of English meters, and this is undoubtedly true, especially of its blank verse form. Whether it is true because English is a naturally iambic language is a more questionable claim. A language that insistently pushes the stresses on words to the front, to the first syllable, as all Germanic languages do, would seem to be distinguished by an impulse toward the trochaic, and certainly large numbers of English words, such as *window, table, swimming,* and *laughter,* are in themselves natural trochees. Natural iambs, on the other hand, are easily provided not only by iambic words (*alone, submit*) but also by combining *a* or *the* or prepositions with monosyllabic nouns, which are also numerous in English, or by combining pronouns with monosyllabic verbs: *I doubt, you see, he went.* But which of these impulses, iambic or trochaic, is stronger in English speech generally is hard to say. What seems beyond dispute is that the trochaic and iambic currents of our speech find an appropriate arena in meter that is iambic rather than trochaic, and this is because iambic verse accommodates a wide range of metrical variations and trochaic verse does not, though why this should be so is again mysterious.[1]

I

Patterns we find in poetry always derive from patterns we discern or intuit in the world around us.[2] The arrangement of words and phrases in poetic lines reflects our custom of speaking, and of hearing each other speak, in a succession of rhythmic units; if the lines are metrical, if they make patterns out of series of lightly or strongly stressed syllables, they reflect the fact that when we speak we speak a succession of syllables with greater and lesser degrees of stress. If verse is iambic, that means that it assumes as a fundamental feature of our speech the frequent—and some-times regular and rhythmic—alternation of unstressed and stressed syl-lables, and that it mirrors our occasional tendency to use several of those two kinds of syllables in that order—a climactic order perhaps, a rising rhythm (as it is often called), in which the movement is repeatedly (and even noticeably) from the less prominent syllable to the more prominent. Within the line we will usually be more aware of a quick succession of syllables with contrasting degrees of stress than of an insistent series of iambs; it is easier to notice the alternation than to say whether at any point the rhythm is iambic or trochaic. The first "foot" in iambic verse, too, is frequently reversed, so that we start the line with a stressed syllable. The last foot, however, is rarely reversed, and the pattern we come to know as we keep listening to iambic meter is one that moves inexorably, through several different modes of passage, to a final confirmation of iambicity. On the other hand, poems that use many feminine endings tend to undermine this feature of iambic verse and may have some expressive reason for do-ing so.

Although the English syllables we speak can be spoken with many degrees or shades of emphasis (of loudness, sharpness, duration, and other ways of signaling importance), it seems likely that in most English speech we perceive two major levels of stress, and that we hear (and learn to produce so that others may hear) a continuous series of relatively stressed and relatively unstressed syllables. In any sustained string of spoken English words, the syllables uttered at one of these levels serve as background to the syllables uttered at the other. Whatever the actual loudness of a syllable, its place in a series (as stressed or as unstressed) will depend on its difference from the other sort of syllable with which it composes the series.

This Saussurean observation is a crucial one. Syllables are not stressed (´) or unstressed (ˇ) in any absolute sense, but only in relation to the essentially dual levels of stress established by each word-string.[3] This is not to say, however, that every syllable is spoken with a degree of stress that makes immediately clear to which of these two levels it belongs. Stressed syllables may vary in strength, and unstressed syllables may vary in weakness, and a third group may strike us as uncertain, as falling into a range that seems stronger than unstressed but weaker than stressed (here marked as ˅). In the most regular meters, such syllables are relatively rare; but their frequent appearance in English iambic pentameter helps to make this meter sound more speechlike than any other. In effect, iambic pentameter recognizes and incorporates an intermediate kind of syllable that may appear either in a stressed or in an unstressed "position," and that acquires interest and emotional resonance by being different from syllables we can more readily identify as either stressed or unstressed.

Because the syllables we speak usually fall into one or the other of the two main kinds, stressed or unstressed, we are likely not only to listen for the stressed syllables but to perceive them as coming at fairly regular intervals. As one group of scholars has suggested: "it is the recognition of a pattern of recurrent stressed syllables against a background of unstressed syllables that accounts for the fact that widely different intervals between stressed syllables appear to the listener to be 'approximately' equal" (Faure et al., 77). This feature of English speech is also reflected in English poetic meters, most of which are isochronous. That is, the intervals between stressed syllables are perceived as fairly uniform. This uniformity can be kept in two ways. *If the meter is accentual,* it measures the interval between stressed syllables by the time that elapses between them, without specifying how many unstressed syllables appear in that interval. In looser forms (nursery rhymes, for example), the number of syllables that intervene between stressed ones may be extremely variable, from zero to six or so. *But if the meter is not only accentual but also syllabic,* then the interval between its accented syllables is marked not by a measured time-lapse but by the occurrence of a fixed number of unaccented syllables (usually one). In such a meter we hear a pulsation (see Halpern, 185) in each stressed syllable, but the intervals between stressed syllables are not so regular. In the most daring such meter, iambic pentameter, one or more pauses may occur in midline, but to the trained ear what counts is that the pattern of alternation which is structurally essential to the line will be resumed after each pause. As we know from many productions, when Othello says, "Put out the light, and then put out the light" (*Othello,* 5.2.7), the actor may make a pause of some length after the fourth syllable, but the iambic pattern of the line is not disturbed, only suspended. This capacity for internal delay distinguishes poetic from musical meter.

The nature of iambic poetry in English, then, is largely determined by its sources in English speech, and these are, in summary, of two kinds: (1) our perception of two levels or ranges of stress, with a third, complicating range between them; (2) our perception of a series of pulsations, the intervals between which are in verse measured by the occurrence of one unstressed syllable. This sequence will be complicated by several standard kinds of variation from the regular pattern. But the effect of these complicating factors is both to bring iambic poetry nearer to spoken English and, for purposes of emotional intensification, to jeopardize our perception of the strict accentual-syllabic pattern.

It is especially when iambic poetry is cast in pentameter that these sources of complexity fully emerge. This is largely because pentameter is itself the most problematical line-length, and the mark of this is its resistance to simple division: it does not divide readily into two shorter rhythmical units. We tend to perceive other long lines as breaking in two: six- or eight-beat lines into two equal parts, seven-beat lines into one segment of four beats and one of three followed by a pause which is felt as a fourth beat:

6 beats

> When I was fair and young, | and favor graced me
> Of many was I sought, | their mistress for to be
>
> (Poem by Queen Elizabeth I, in Hebel and Hudson, 54)

7 beats

> As I in hoary winter's night | stood shivering in the snow,
> Surprised I was with sudden heat | which made my heart to glow
>
> (Southwell, "The Burning Babe," in Hebel and Hudson, 238)

8 beats

> Do not, to make your ladies game, | bring blemish to your worthy name,
> Away to field and win renown! | with courage beat your enemies down!
>
> (Humphrey Gifford, "For Soldiers," in Hebel and Hudson, 101)

In the last quoted passage, the internal rhymes make doubly clear how decisive the midline break is. It appears that lines of more than five stresses have only a provisional reality.[4] Even when the midline break is accorded minimal value, we are still likely to perceive the lines as compound in nature and to hear distinctly the shorter lines of which they are composed.

Four-foot iambic lines, on the other hand, though they constitute a significant resource for poets writing in English, lack the amplitude of the five-foot line and seem as a rule unable to survive the absence of rhyme, a defect which partly limits their power to seem convincingly speechlike. The same is even truer of forms made up entirely of shorter iambic lines.

Pentameter, then, is the most speechlike of English line-lengths, especially when it appears without rhyme. Long enough to accommodate a good mouthful of English words, long enough too to require most of its lines to break their phrasing somewhere, it also resists the tendency to divide in half. In fact, it *cannot* do so. A midline pause, wherever it appears, leaves two stressed syllables on one side and three on the other. For iambic pentameter, however highly patterned its syntax, is by nature asymmetrical—like human speech. If we divide a ten-syllable line "in half," we do not get two equal segments but two unequal ones:

To witness duty, | not to show my wit   (Shakespeare, Sonnet 26:4)

Five syllables on either side of the break, but different numbers of stressed and unstressed syllables, so that, though we may hear a syllabic symmetry, the line resists giving us a metrical balance to accompany it. The result is very different in feeling from, say, Browning's shorter line, "So might I gain, so might I miss" ("The Last Ride Together," line 40), where the metrical break and balance match the phrasal break and balance. Poets have sometimes set themselves the exercise of writing an iambic pentameter line with the balance that is natural to a more symmetrical line:

I shall find time, Cassius; I shall find time   (*Julius Caesar*, 5.3.103)

Twelve year since, Miranda, twelve year since   (*The Tempest*, 1.2.53)

Take your own time, Annie, take your own time

(Tennyson, "Enoch Arden," line 463)

Only the second of these is perfectly symmetrical, but at the cost of being headless. All of them are tours de force and work against the grain of a meter that characteristically resists such balances. Even in the highly ordered poetry of Pope, where line is set against line in the couplet, and phrase against phrase in the antithesis, the pentameter line keeps these oppositions from being worked out too simply. The meter of Pope's poetry is impressive just because the frame within which its binary oppositions are achieved is itself both binary (being iambic) and resistant to binary pattern (being pentameter).

It is probably because of these numerical oddities and our perceptual response to them that iambic pentameter, except in the hands of its dullest practitioners, keeps the most highly patterned language from sounding trivial. It can lend gravity, dignity, portentousness, even grandeur to statements and utterances; and where rhymed tetrameter couplets often evoke a feeling of ease, of elegance, of achieved simplicity, iambic pentameter, whether in rhymed stanzas, heroic couplets, or blank verse, usually conveys a sense of complex understanding, as if the speakers of such lines were aware of more than they ever quite say, or as if there were more in their speeches than even they were aware of. If the language of everyday life or even the language of other forms of poetry seems usually to leave untouched, unsounded, certain depths of human experience, iambic pentameter has seemed to centuries of poets and listeners the poetic form most likely to reach these depths and to make their resonances audible.

The iambic pentameter line, then, has amplitude and asymmetry sufficient to carry significant English speech. What makes it even more speechlike is its uncanny capacity to vary the metrical norm without fundamentally violating it. Over the centuries poets have experimented with different variations and their combinations, and the results suggest that this line can enter into pacts with almost any metrical devil and still keep its soul intact. By the nineteenth century most poets were willing to try an occasional anapest as an agreeable means of relieving a perceived monotony in the standard line, and some twentieth-century poets (for example, Stevens, Lowell, and Larkin) have gone much further in the direction of transforming it into a loosely accentual five-stress line, even into a kind of shadow norm that we sense in poems, such as those of Ashbery, that pointedly steer clear of it. But from Shakespeare's time to the early nineteenth century (and, except for the anapestic variant, to the early twentieth), poets writing iambic pentameter habitually permitted themselves to diverge from the meter in three conventional ways in order to give variety, interest, grace, and sometimes expressive character to their lines. Most poets used other means as well—midline pauses and endline enjambments—but these are the three metrical variations that almost every poet writing in English has understood to be standard and permissible.

These three variations, with perhaps a fourth that has not been much noticed, are inherent in the structure of iambic meter. At a length as long as pentameter but no longer (not so long as to *have* to break repeatedly into smaller segments), poets soon found that they could not persistently write lines in which all five stressed syllables were equally stressed and the unstressed syllables equally unstressed. "Of hand, of foot, of lip, of eye, of brow" (Shakespeare, Sonnet 106:6) represents only an extreme possibility, not an average pattern for English iambic pentameter, and even this line's rhythm can be shaded by a resourceful voice. On the contrary, when lines are devised that "fit" the meter without notable wrenching of accent, it will be found that some of the strong syllables are stronger than others, some weak ones weaker than others. To take a line at random from Spenser's *The Faerie Queene*:

But he is old, and withered like hay   (III.ix.5.1)

Even with the poet's implied directive to pronounce the *-ed* of "withered" (or the line will fall short of its ten syllables), we will not give it so strong an emphasis as we give "old," "with-," and "hay." Probably, too, "he" is somewhat more lightly stressed. On the other hand, "like" would probably, in anyone's recitation of the line, receive more emphasis (be said louder, or more sharply, or at a higher pitch, or take longer to say, or a combination of these) than the other "unstressed" syllables of the line. Such variations of stress among stressed or among unstressed syllables do not alter the iambic character of the line: every even syllable still receives at least a shade more stress than the syllable it follows. But they suggest that the art of iambic verse, especially of iambic pentameter, is an art requiring continuous negotiation of the stress-values of syllables. Even if, as we said earlier, English syllables mainly alternate between two general levels of

7

stress, as they appear in English words and phrases the degree of emphasis we give them varies greatly, depending on necessities of local sense as well as on conventions of lexical and phrasal stress.[5]

If there is, in fact, a characteristic pulse for iambic poetry, which we recognize crudely by such formulas as ti-TUM, ti-TUM, ti-TUM, ti-TUM, ti-TUM, we also know that so exact a repetition is *always* violated by the particular words that appear in actual lines (this could be avoided only by using the crude formula itself as a line), for different vowels differently enclosed by consonants will not be given the identical value in speech. Again, this does not mean that from the point of view of scansion, a mildly varied line is not "regular." But "regularity" in iambic meter denotes only the uniform recurrence of a *relative* superiority of stress in every second syllable (or in most of them) over the one it follows; it does not denote an equality of stress among the strong or among the weak syllables.

In a meter so constituted, where variation is inevitable, the degree of variation in each of a line's five feet will determine the contour of the line. So long as the variation is minimal, hardly perceptible, and does not change the basic relationship between the two syllables of any so-called foot, the reader is likely to take it in stride, will probably not much notice the small differences between strong or between weak syllables and will keep on hearing the iambic current. But when a syllable that appears to be in one of the strong positions is substantially weakened or a syllable in a weak position notably strengthened, a listening reader will become aware that one of the major traditional variations in iambic meter is taking place.

When ĭn | disgrace with for|tŭne ănd | mĕn's ēyes

This opening line of Shakespeare's twenty-ninth sonnet includes three feet that appear to violate the expected iambic pattern: a trochee in the first foot, a pyrrhic in the fourth, a spondee in the last. Nevertheless, when the line is spoken or heard silently by a reader with some auditory experience of the tradition, it does not violate the pattern: enough of the line is still iambic to sustain the iambic feeling, especially when earlier lines (from the previous sonnets in the sequence) and later ones in this poem adhere more unambiguously to the iambic design, so that our experience of this line is influenced by our iambic set. But the line is less divergent than it appears. For one thing, the so-called pyrrhic and spondaic feet do

8

not run counter to the basic iambic requirement that the second syllable in the foot be pronounced more strongly than the first. It is only that the differences here seem minimal, that "-tune and" seem almost equal in value, though both are lightly stressed, and that "men's eyes" seem almost equal, though both are quite strongly stressed. Since absolute equality of syllable stress rarely occurs, however, it seems likely that in both cases the second syllable is somewhat more strongly stressed than the first (or is so perceived) and that what we have in the last two feet of the line are, essentially, a pyrrhic iamb and a spondaic iamb. For clarity's sake, some critics avoid these terms; many who retain them do so with the understanding I have just described.

The trochaic pattern in the opening foot is also a standard variation for iambic pentameter. Trochees occur elsewhere in some lines, too, but Renaissance poets used them especially often at the beginning of the line or at midline following a pause, where they were welcome as a metrical flourish that could enliven the usual pattern. The initial variation was so common that the sequence of trochee and iamb must often have been perceived as a double foot (equivalent to a form of the Greek ionic), one of the rare such forms in English verse.

All three variations work not only to give an attractive variety to the iambic line but to convey a greater complexity, to hint at a wider range of feeling and a more richly patterned world of social eventfulness than a stricter meter would register. If the line had read, for example,

* In deep disgrace with fortune, eyes of men

its straightforward meter would not have caught the uneasiness, the uncertainty, about "men's eyes" that in Shakespeare's line is conveyed not only by the phrase itself but by the more deeply inflected meter as well.

At first these variations may appear peculiar, since they to some degree challenge the stability of iambic meter itself. But the very pattern of iambic verse and the variability of stress in the language insure that they will occur. So long as the iambic foot remains in place and does not accept trisyllabic or monosyllabic "substitutions," the natural flexibility of English stress will inevitably result in the weakening or strengthening of stressed or unstressed syllables here and there in most lines. In practice, the poet may produce the following changes in the normal iambic foot:

9

1. Increase the difference in stress between ˘ and ´ (strong iamb).
2. Increase the stress on the unstressed syllable (spondee).
3. Diminish the stress on the stressed syllable (pyrrhic).
4. Combine 2 and 3 (trochee).

In a different analysis, there are two principal kinds of variation from iambic rhythm. If the term *iambic* designates an increase of stress from the first to the second of a pair of syllables, the possible variations are decrease of stress (trochee), or level stress. Level stress may be found in any degree of stress: weak, intermediate, or strong. Weak level stress is pyrrhic, strong is spondaic; for intermediate we have no traditional name, but it frequently occurs (see Chapter 13), as we will hear in this line if we give it a natural reading:

Ay, that's the fírst | *thǐng thǎt* | we have to do   (*3 Henry VI*, 4.3.62)

These variations, commanded by a skillful poet, can go a long way toward making iambic pentameter carry a strong flavor of natural English speech. Shakespeare's use of them to convey a great variety of states of mind, Donne's to suggest the stumbling, precise discourse of a lover or arguer feeling his rhetorical way, Milton's to shadow forth the grand motions of his epic narrative, all exemplify ways of manipulating the counters of this expressive system so that it answers these poets' different purposes. Later, we shall see how these variations from the strictly regular iambic foot are used in specific passages and how effectively they can "represent" the speech of characters under stress or the feelings appropriate to different states of mind or visions of reality.

The Two Orders

Simple as this system seems, critics and scholars sometimes take radically opposed views of its principles or its practice. This is not the place to enter into lengthy theoretical dispute with metrists of different persuasions. Later passages and notes will do so occasionally. But the view of iambic meter pursued in these pages differs strongly from those held by three groups of contemporary analysts of meter, whom we may conveniently identify here as Counterpointers, Four-stressers, and Phrasalists.

Counterpointers understand lines of verse to exhibit two separate patterns at once—the prose rhythm of the words and the metrical norm—and what they find interesting is the divergence of the rhythm from the meter. This is not, on first view, an unreasonable position, but it has frequently become so when, under the influence of structural linguists, it maintains that these two forces, the rhythm and the meter, remain quite separate and that what we enjoy is the abstract difference between them.[6] My own view, briefly, is that best enunciated by W. K. Wimsatt (1970a): that we must often in practice, in performance, "tilt" (785) the phrasing in the direction of the meter and that if we fail to do so the divergence is likely to be so extreme that we hear a hodgepodge, not a counterpoint. In fact, we hear, not two lines, but one—one actual rhythmic line that *realizes* the meter in its own idiosyncratic way. Variant lines depart not from a form we hear but from a form we *expect* to hear. The distinction is crucial. (See below, Chapter 4, note 5, and Chapter 13, pp. 186–88.)

Four-stressers, noticing that one of the major points of stress in an iambic pentameter line is often weaker than the others, have speculated that an undercurrent of the four-stress meter of Old English may still be perceived under later iambic pentameter.[7] But a line of verse cannot be two meters at once—it is either one thing or another; and even in a pyrrhic foot (that is, in a foot that lacks a speech stress) we continue to hear a pulse, a metrical stress, just as in a foot that harbors two strong speech stresses we can distinguish the one that receives a metrical pulse from the one that does not.

Thus, we do not read this line as a four-stress one:

When to the sessions of sweet silent thought

If we do, the line cannot still be understood as iambic pentameter. If it is something else, it is not that. Rather, we recognize that the pyrrhic and spondee in the third and fourth feet involve a pulse on "of" but not on "sweet," though "sweet" is stressed more strongly than "of":

When to | the ses|sions of | sweet si|lent thought

Phrasalists maintain that poets from Chaucer to Shakespeare frequently wrote loose combinations of rhythmical phrases rather than metrical lines.[8] This theory comes dangerously close to imposing an anachro-

11

nistic free-verse structure on poetry of a much earlier period than our own. The view presented here is that poets do not compose verse in phrases rather than in lines, but in both at once; it is in the play *between* the metrical line and the rhythmical phrase that the great interest of meter lies.

These three dubious doctrines diminish English poetry by reducing its formidable polyphonic music to an abstract exercise, to a rattling dogtrot, or to a meager harmony of rhythms-without-meter. Their partisans all misunderstand the nature of metrical counterpoint and the place of phrasing in the metrical system of iambic pentameter. Some old-time prosodists had an exaggerated reverence for metrical correctness and were insufficiently sensitive to the natural rhythms of English phrasing. But these newer schools, in their zeal to correct the excessive strictness of traditional prosodists, have gone so far as either to discard or to neutralize meter in favor of the infinitely various freestanding rhythms of spoken English. Some of them seem essentially hostile to iambic pentameter, finding it tedious and mechanical and hoping to rescue from what they see as its dead hand the lively literature it once roused to exuberant life. The belief on which this book rests is that there are always at least two structural orders simultaneously audible in iambic pentameter—the metrical and the phrasal (actual lines and stanzas, and actual phrases and sentences)—and their varied rhythmic interplay constitutes the great beauty of the form.

The disposition to read metrical lines as composed of phrases is in itself eminently sensible. Although the phrasal organization of a line is not its meter, anyone can see or hear that a line of verse is composed of words in phrases. We regularly group together successive words that can conveniently form a unit of breath or a rhythmic unit:

> How with this rage   shall beauty hold a plea
> Whose action   is no stronger   than a flower?
>
> (Shakespeare, Sonnet 65 : 3–4)

Even lines like these, without internal punctuation, seem to fall naturally into two or three syntactical groupings, although a reader certainly need not pause at the phrase boundaries.

Of all English meters, iambic pentameter makes the most of divergences between the stress pattern of a line and the phrasal pattern. As we have already seen, the stresses need not be equal in weight or come at equal intervals, but the variety of ways phrases of different lengths and shapes may be fitted to the line is almost infinite. Pauses may appear after any internal syllable; the line itself may be cut into several distinct segments, as in Shakespeare's

> Where is thy head? Where's that? Ay me! where's that?
>
> (*Cymbeline*, 4.2.321)

or in the line Ben Jonson distributes among six speeches spoken by three characters:

Face.	Bawd!				
Subtle.		Cow-herd!			
Face.			Conjurer!		
Subtle.				Cutpurse!	
Face.					Witch!
Doll.					O me!

(*The Alchemist*, 1.1.107)

The ingenuity with which Renaissance English playwrights fit the phrase to the line is dazzling. Clearly, they mean us to hear two orders of language at once: a metrical order, in which the stresses alternate five times from weak to strong (with variations), and the order of the phrase or sentence, an order that seems to move along, to say what it has to say, without noticing the metrical pattern. But we as listeners have the opportunity to observe and to hear *both orders of language alive in the same words*.

If this counterpoint contributes such variety to single lines, we feel it even more strongly in extended passages. One important feature of any poet's prosody is the way successive lines move together so that we perceive a stanza or a couplet or a passage of blank verse as a significant union of lines that flow into one another and compose a rhythmical unit larger than the isolated line. The Renaissance English poet habitually composed long poems in stanzas, which required a skill in persuading readers that a series of rhymed lines belong together semantically and syntactically as well as metrically. In stanzas or quatrains like the following, poets tried not only to make effective single lines but to give each passage a continuity, an ease, that testifies to a command of line-flow:

13

When in the chronicle of wasted time
I see description of the fairest wights
And beauty making beautiful old rhyme
In praise of ladies dead and lovely knights   (Shakespeare, Sonnet 106:1–4)

> As when the mast of some well timbred hulke
> Is with the blast of some outragious storme
> Blowne downe, it shakes the bottome of the bulke,
> And makes her ribs to cracke, as they were torne,
> Whilest still she stands as stonisht and forlorne:
> So was he stound with stroke of her huge taile.
> But ere that it she backe againe had borne,
> He with his sword it strooke, that without faile
> He joynted it, and mard the swinging of her flaile.
>
> (Spenser, *The Faerie Queene*, V.xi.29)

> For every houre that thou wilt spare mee now,
>   I will allow,
> Usurious God of Love, twenty to thee,
> When with my browne, my gray haires equall bee;
> Till then, Love, let my body raigne, and let
> Mee travell, sojourne, snatch, plot, have, forget,
> Resume my last yeares relict: thinke that yet
>   We'had never met.   (Donne, "Loves Usury," lines 1–8)

In the first two examples, most lines are endstopped, but parallel phrasing or forceful syntax facilitates the easy movement from one line to the next, and we are likely to take in each set of lines as an especially melodious and integral group. Donne's stanza has a comparable ease of movement, but it conveys a headlong excitement partly through its use of run-on (or enjambed) and short lines. The sense of Donne's breathless sentence spills over lines 5–6 and 7–8; not even the rhyme can hold back the voice; it seems, on the contrary, to be powering its way past rhymes to its highly animated and outrageous assertion. Much of the metrical interest of the lines (and of Donne's lines generally) derives from the tension we feel between the strictness with which he observes the metrical requirements and the urgency of a passion that speaks as if it wanted to knock down all such irritating barriers.

For, despite critics' interest in isolating and defining "the iambic pentameter line," a line of verse does not stand alone. We may recognize a set of ten English syllables as exhibiting an iambic pentameter pattern, but it does not normally become a line of verse until it appears among others similar in syllabic structure. And the specific character of a line depends a great deal on whether it appears in a rhyming stanza, as one of a pair of rhymed lines in a sequence of couplets, or in a passage of blank verse. It also depends on the degree to which it and its surrounding lines are end-stopped or enjambed—that is, on how much and how frequently the sense of a line runs over into the next line without punctuation or notable pause. Even syntactical patterns—rhetorical figures of repetition or contrast—will significantly affect the movement and emphasis of metrical lines. When Macbeth tells his wife, in a trenchant figure,

> I dare do all that may become a man;
> Who dares do more is none,   *(Macbeth,* 1.7.46–47)

the assertion acquires a special force from the fact that the phrasing is parallel but the meter is not. Pope's parallel ideas proceed very differently—in metrically matched lines:

> True wit is Nature to advantage dressed,
> What oft was thought but ne'er so well expressed
>
>   *(An Essay on Criticism,* II.297–98)

These ways of accommodating the rhetorical balance to the metrical measure are radically different in effect. Rhymed verse sets up an expectation of pattern; in stanzas the expectation is usually fulfilled after an interval; in couplets, much sooner. The waiting time is shorter, and the matching rhyme must come with comparative rapidity. The anxiety with which we wait for it is therefore more intense, and its release is much more of a relief. To be disappointed of that rhyme would be shocking or comic, a failure to meet the terms of the virtual contract which the poet has negotiated with the reader. (See Hollander, 1975, 187–211.)

In blank verse, too, especially when it is severely enjambed, we hear a music composed of the two simultaneous orders of meter and rhetorical period:

Not poppy, nor mandragora,
Nor all the drowsy syrups of the world
Shall ever medicine thee to that sweet sleep
Which thou ow'dst yesterday.   (*Othello*, 3.3.330–33)

Our revels now are ended. These our actors
(As I foretold you) were all spirits, and
Are melted into air, into thin air   (*The Tempest*, 4.1.148–50)

Long time in even scale
The battle hung, till Satan, who that day
Prodigious power had shown, and met in arms
No equal, ranging through the dire attack
Of fighting Seraphim confused, at length
Saw where the sword of Michael smote, and felled
Squadrons at once   (Milton, *Paradise Lost*, VI.245–51)

In the first passage, the full middle lines can be heard quite distinctly as lines; in the second, because line 149 does not possess the same syntactical integrity as the others, we may lose a little the sense of line and only regain it when the lines that follow meet the metrical pattern more audibly (see Chapter 14). The third passage exhibits Milton's unusually complex sentence patterns, which drive through the metrical lines with an astonishing mixture of authority and deference.

Renaissance readers of verse (and even listeners in the theater) were expected to follow the twin authorities of meter and sentence, to feel the tension in their divergence and the harmony in their congruence. Different poets would take different views of how far that divergence might be carried and what kinds of harmonies the poet should aim at—certainly the verse of the English Renaissance progressively educated the reader in the range of these harmonies—but it was clear to everyone that the writing of poetry meant more than the creation of splendid single lines. The single line extends into couplets, stanzas, passages, speeches, even cantos and scenes, and the test of a poet's powers lies largely in his ability to master the arts of line-flow and strophic construction. It follows that any useful account of iambic pentameter must attend not only to the variant structure of the single line but to the ways lines are combined into larger prosodic and dramatic structures.[9]

Individual and Historical Differences

The efforts of scholars and critics to offer a true account of English iambic pentameter are further complicated by the facts that different poets use it very differently and that it may change its character from one literary era to another. It appears that there is not just one iambic pentameter but many. Among later poets, Browning, Hopkins, Yeats, Frost, Eliot, Stevens, Lowell, and Merrill have developed highly distinctive pentameter lines; in earlier centuries, too, there are often striking differences between one poet's meter and another's or even between a poet's early and late metrical styles: Shakespeare and Milton are vivid examples. To say only that a poet writes iambic pentameter or blank verse tells little about that poet's work.

Iambic pentameter itself, as the most prominent English meter for more than five centuries, has passed through several more or less distinct historical stages,[10] so that at different times audiences have entertained somewhat different expectations as they read or listened to blank or rhymed pentameter. Audiences are always diverse and usually include some members who listen intently to the rhythm and some who largely ignore it; but an audience trained on Marlowe's dramatic blank verse will not have the same experience of verse or the same expectations of it as an audience trained by Dryden's dramatic rhymed couplets. No account of iambic pentameter can be accurate that does not recognize how radically its procedures have changed from one period to another and at the hands of different, especially of eccentric, practitioners. In certain periods—in the Renaissance, for example—a "standard" iambic pentameter develops, a form whose features can be described with confidence. But the iambic pentameter of some great poets and playwrights—Wyatt, Shakespeare (in his later plays), Donne, Webster, and Milton—is often extremely idiosyncratic. It is characteristic of this meter that strong poets of every period have not merely learned to use it efficiently, refining their knowledge of it into a skill which they come to manipulate almost instinctively, but that they wrestle with it, compel it to perform new work, and tune it to their own distinctive energies. Even those poets whose iambic pentameter is notable rather for smoothness and ease than for oddity—Chaucer, Spenser, Shakespeare in his sonnets, Jonson, and others—have sometimes struggled to achieve those harmonies later readers have justly admired.

Probably any great meter or poet must develop in this way. A great meter is no mere implement, like pen or typewriter, but a keyboard a young poet learns to master, exploring its range and subtleties, stretching its capabilities of harmony and expressiveness. Merely to accept the meter as given by one's predecessors, to write one's verses "in" iambic pentameter, is to assist at the death of a metrical form and perhaps of one's own poetry. The demise of iambic pentameter as the chief meter of English poetry probably owes much to its coming to be understood even by poets themselves as an available prosodic form, a meter to write poems "in," a Roman road, rather than as a kind of heroic adventure or even a haunted house. To be sure, the restoration of iambic meter in the twentieth century—by Yeats, Eliot, Stevens, Lowell, and others—has constituted an impressive and relatively unnoticed achievement in an age of free verse. But for all these poets the meter has consistently included a strong retrospective element, and from this point of view their iambic verse has often seemed, despite its energy, a tremendous elegiac homage to a meter of the past.

Renaissance iambic pentameter, in contrast, appeared as a new discovery. Chaucer had virtually invented it; since his time it had been lost or fumbled, then reinvented as a somewhat rigid meter, used in rime royal narratives, and declaimed rather woodenly on stage. Far from being the school meter it later became, the English ten-syllable line[11] was widely regarded as a poor provincial cousin to the much more expressive meters of Latin quantitative poetry. Then, with an extraordinary suddenness, several remarkably able poets and playwrights—Sidney, Spenser, Marlowe, Shakespeare, Donne, and Jonson—saw what a flexible and adaptable meter it was, how much could be said with it, how much feeling, passion, and power could be expressed through it. In Sidney's sonnets of the early 1580s (not known to most of his contemporaries till 1591) and in poems and plays written mainly from 1590 to 1610, these writers explored the harmonies and dissonances of the new meter. They did so without feeling (as later poets, especially after Milton or Pope, had to feel) oppressed by the weight of its greatness, by its canonical status, by its reverential position as "the meter of Shakespeare and Milton." Milton was not yet born, and Shakespeare, in Colette's phrase, had not yet become Shakespeare. For the writers of the Renaissance, the meter was at least fairly new, certainly new in its force, its range, its power; and every line they wrote was not at all (as the lines of nineteenth- and twentieth-century poets often are) an invocation of a sacred tradition. They could play with it, enjoy it, twist it, thwart it, make music with it, dress their own living speech in its expressive folds.

Many later poets have done skillful work in iambic pentameter, but they have never recovered that early excitement, which can probably only be felt when a meter (or any aesthetic mode) with extraordinary expressive possibilities first bursts upon the awareness of artists. In English poetry this happened twice with iambic pentameter: once with Chaucer; and once when, after the meter had been rediscovered, its full capacities came to be seen and heard, in the 1590s and subsequent years, perhaps extending all the way to Milton. The excitement of renewing and refining the meter can be felt even in so late a poetry as Pope's. When in later centuries young poets first feel the excitement of poetic creation, it is often derived from poets two hundred years their seniors, and it is usually somewhat polite and secondhand. Keats learned his meter from Spenser, Shakespeare, and Milton, Byron from Pope, Browning from Donne and Shelley, Yeats from Shelley and Spenser. But however gifted the pupils, the meter they mastered rarely had the spirit and animation of its original. Except for some modern poets engaged in restoring or extending the form, it is fair to say of almost all the most brilliant poetry written in the last two hundred years that its iambic pentameter is not its most striking achievement. Whatever the truth about other aesthetic modes and instruments, it appears to be true of iambic pentameter that the most interesting and powerful work in it has been done by poets who, whether inventing, extending, refining, or restoring, were in some sense in on it from the beginning.

The beginning, of course, was Chaucer, whose iambic pentameter initiates the English history of the form—which after him, however, is strangely mishandled until Wyatt's imaginative reconstruction reveals some of its hidden powers (Chapter 2). Chapters 3 and 4 are concerned with its rise to prominence in the sixteenth century. From that point on, the book focuses on Shakespeare: on his *Sonnets* (Chapter 5), on the problems of dramatic blank verse (Chapter 6), and on the unusual instrumentation that makes up Shakespeare's metrical, syllabic, and expressive keyboard (Chapters 7 through 16). Two concluding chapters (17 and 18) point to further metrical innovation in Donne and Milton and draw the study to a close.

CHAPTER 2

Chaucer and Wyatt: Early Expressive Pentameters

Chaucer

If iambic pentameter has taken different forms in its long history, and in some degree varies with every mature practitioner, the forms it took before Shakespeare's time differ from one another quite remarkably. After Shakespeare, the meter in a sense settled down, became tame or domesticated: except for Milton, whose verse style in his own time ran sharply against the current, iambic pentameter became relatively fixed in its procedures, going through a strict Augustan phase, a more flexible Romantic phase, and finding strong variant forms in Tennyson, Browning, Hopkins, Yeats, and some persistent twentieth-century poets. It is still capable of surprising variety. But the changes in decasyllabic style between 1370 and 1610 are in retrospect even more astonishing. The metrical systems of Chaucer, Lydgate, Wyatt, and early Tudor poets can be summarized here only briefly; they typically include both a metrical norm and techniques of expressive variation.

For readers who master enough Middle English to read Chaucer with facility, his iambic pentameter is likely to seem the most distinctive in the language. This is not only because of the change from Middle to Modern English, but because Chaucer's rhythm and pace are unique. Quick, smooth, lively, melodious, his verse avoids awkward consonant clusters and turgid sequences of monosyllabic adjectives, nouns, and verbs. It does this largely by making use of the final -e of many words as an optional syllable for the meter. The result is a line that moves repeatedly from one strongly stressed word-stem to another over unstressed syllables that are hardly more than grace notes:

And smalë fowelës maken melodye   (*GP*, 9)[1]

Not that all the even syllables come in for strong stress. Many lines include one or two weaker syllables in stress positions:

It snewëd *in* his hous of mete and drinke   (*GP*, 345)

And *of* his port as meeke as *is* a mayde   (*GP*, 69)

He *was* as fressh as *is* the month of May   (*GP*, 92)

In many lines, consequently, the voice speeds over the unstressed syllables to light with special strength on the relatively rare stressed ones:

Upon an *amb*lere *es*ily she *sat*,
Y*wym*pled *wel,* and on hir *heed* an *hat*
As *brood* as is a *bok*eler or a *targe*   (*GP*, 469–71)

The pyrrhic feet can still be heard as feet, but their effect is usually to make the line move quickly and to direct emphasis to a small number of strongly stressed syllables.

In the lines just quoted we can see Chaucer using a high proportion of small words whose rhetorical function is to highlight the more substantial content words (usually nouns, verbs, and adjectives): "As . . . as is a . . . or a . . ."; "And of his . . . as . . . as is a . . ."; "He was as . . . as is the . . . of . . . ." This is a stylistic feature especially familiar to readers of Chaucer; he invites the reader to race comparatively swiftly over the minor words to get to the words of greatest importance. This method is not entirely foreign to later poets; some write lines as rapid in movement as any of Chaucer's. But the combination of rapid movement and unusually strong stress contrasts helps to give Chaucer's verse its zestful pace and tone. With so few points of stress in the typical line, the narrative speeds along, dashing past minor words and syllables and hitting the major ones sharply.

In addition, Chaucer, as the first fashioner of iambic pentameter lines, developed a repertoire of expressive variations—the same standard ones that most later poets use, except that, as the current of this verse is different, the metrical variations seem also a little different, both in sound and function. Because the current is quick and light, there is a tendency, enforced by Chaucer's characteristic tone, for the sudden accesses of extra stress in the form of spondees and trochees to sound exaggerated, hyperbolic, and ironic. The narrator's customary stance in such lines is to pretend to be mightily impressed:

> And foughten for oure feith at Tramyssene
> In lystës thriës, and *ay slayn* his foo (GP, 62–63)

That is, he killed his enemy every single time!

> *Wo was* his cook but if his saucë were
> Poynaunt and sharp, and redy al his geere (GP, 351–52)

Or for purposes of grave emphasis, Chaucer can slow down the steady current of his verse with a series of spondees and strongly stressed major syllables:

> *Swich fyn* hath, lo, this Troilus for love!
> *Swich fyn* hath al his gretë worthynesse!
> *Swich fyn* hath his estat real above,
> *Swich fyn* his lust, *swich fyn* hath his noblesse!
> *Swich fyn* hath falsë worldës brotelnesse! (TC, V.1828–32)

Yet, even as we admire Chaucer's metrical resourcefulness in such passages, we have to acknowledge that they are exceptional and that his variations are used for limited purposes. As Eleanor Prescott Hammond pointed out eighty years ago, there is a range of metrical subtlety, involving the use of such variations, which Chaucer does not essay (1908, 488–90). It is not to disparage Chaucer's masterly control of meter to suggest that the exaggerated stress-contrasts in his syllables do not form a congenial metrical setting for Miltonic or even Shakespearean sound effects. Where Wyatt and later poets can quicken a phrase composed of monosyllabic adjective and noun:

> And softly said, '*dere hert,* how like you this?' (XXXVII.14)

Chaucer finds different means:

> Ywis myne owenë *deerë hertë* trewe (*TC,* V.1401)

The difference is characteristic. The availability of the *-e* enables Chaucer to place what would later be a monosyllabic adjective ("der-") in a stressed position of its own. The voice can linger on it there and make as much of it as the interpreter wishes. Wyatt's spondaic phrase is a later convention and a key resource of most iambic poetry written at least from Sidney's time to our own, for it not only appears in single feet but combines with other kinds of feet to provide a rich storehouse of differently shaped and sounded phrases.[2] The rareness of this kind of spondee in Chaucer, which is directly attributable to his phonetic treatment of *-e,* helps to give his verse a special character of its own. It is not less expressive but differently expressive.[3]

Chaucer also uses trochaic "inversions" somewhat differently from later poets. Like them, he frequently deploys initial trochees for variety and grace: "*Hath in* the Ram" (*GP,* 8); "*Redy* to wenden" (*GP,* 21); "*Bold was* hir face" (*GP,* 458). But later poets also use trochees, both initial and medial, as an appropriately energetic means of signaling some violent, sudden, or momentous action:

> And perjurde wights *scalded* in boyling lead
>
> (Kyd, *The Spanish Tragedy,* 1.1.70)

> *Shatter* your leaves before the mellowing year (Milton, "Lycidas," 5)

Such lines can be found in Chaucer, but infrequently:

> *Wondrynge* upon this word, *quakyng* for drede ("Clerk's Tale," 358)

> *Swyvëd* the milleres doghter bolt upright ("Reeve's Tale," 4266)

> And seye hym thus, "God woot, she slepeth softe
> For love of the, whan thow *turnest* ful ofte! (*TC,* I.195–96)

Chaucer also uses what has been called a hovering accent on lightly stressed disyllabic prepositions: "And heeld *after* the newe world the space" (*GP,* 176). The same uncertainty of stress characterizes Romance words in lines like the following:

Of which *vertu* engendred is the flour $\qquad$ (*GP*, 4)

On this *lady,* and now on that, *lokynge* $\qquad$ (*TC*, I.269)

Romance words often appear in the final foot of a line, and in Chaucer's verse, as in that of later poets, the final foot is usually the one least visited by trochaic variation. The presumption is therefore strong that such words in Chaucer's verse (if not in his own spoken English) retained the dominant stress on the second syllable. Attempts like Ian Robinson's (123) to read rather bouncy trochees into such lines ("On this lády, and now on that, lókynge") seem anachronistic and unconvincing. We can be sure that in such combinations the first syllable was not completely negligible, for that would be contrary to its well-documented position as the syllable in process of assuming the major stress in its word. But if the first is stronger than most unstressed syllables, the second probably remains the metrically dominant one.

Chaucer uses other metrical variations—that is, phrasal combinations that result in some modification of the iambic current—some of which are familiar to later poets and some not. Unlike his contemporary Gower, he is not committed to the virtual repetition of iambic rhythm in every foot of an iambic line,[4] nor is he content, like his successor Lydgate, to break the phrasing of his lines almost always after the fourth syllable.[5] On the contrary, Chaucer makes decasyllabic lines out of phrases of unusually various lengths; and even when he writes in rhymed couplets, he is willing on occasion to let the sense of his sentence run over the line-ending. The result is an attractively various line-flow, all the more remarkable when we reflect that Chaucer had no English models to follow but was making up his variant lines and rhythms as he went along.[6]

Another source of variety in Chaucer's verse, one that will make for trouble later on, is his use of a few odd line-types, which, though they range from occasional to rare for him, will in his English successors constitute major paradigms of the fifteenth-century decasyllabic line. The three principal deviant lines are the headless, the broken-backed, and the line with an epic caesura. Of these the commonest is the headless line (carets show where an expected syllable is missing):

∧Twenty bookës, clad in blak or reed $\qquad$ (*GP*, 294)

∧Gynglen in a whistlynge wynd als cleere   (*GP,* 170)

It is nat honest, it may nat avaunce
∧For to deelen with no swich poraille   (*GP,* 246–47)

These examples show how skillfully Chaucer can use the line without an initial upbeat. The first expresses awe, the second freedom from care, the third impatience. We cannot find a strong mimetic justification for its every appearance, but as a rule Chaucer used it much more purposefully than his wayward successors, for whom it was evidently a mere metrical crutch.

The same is true of the line with the so-called epic or lyric (or feminine) caesura, which gives us an extra unstressed syllable before the midline break. The extra syllable often seems a mere extension of the previous stressed one (like Gerard Manley Hopkins' "outride"), and the pattern usually invites a pause before the second half-line resumes a more regular meter. In Chaucer's verse this extra syllable and pause are sometimes used for effects of expansiveness:

Wyd was | hĭs părĭsshe, | and houses fer asonder   (*GP,* 491)

or dramatic gesture:

And in | hĭre bŏsŏme | the lettre doun he thraste   (*TC,* II.1155)

or lightness of touch:

Than robës riche, | ŏr fĭthĕle, | or gay sautrie   (*GP,* 296)

The so-called broken-backed (or Lydgate) line, which omits an unstressed syllable after the midline break, is rare in Chaucer; some scholars have denied that he uses it at all. When it occurs, its chief effect is to throw extra stress on the strong syllable that begins the second half-line. If such strong stress is not justified by some meaning in the words, the broken-backed line will appear to be the limp resource of an ungifted poet, as it often does in the fifteenth century. But Chaucer does have an occasional line that appears to use this metrical pattern to good expressive effect:

My tale is doon, ∧for my wit is thynne. ("Merchant's Tale," 1682)

These three odd line-types have often troubled scholars and critics, especially those with strict ideas about the proprieties of iambic pentameter verse, who have interpreted them as blemishes on the stately heroic line. Sometimes such critics have apparently taken the view that no poet in his senses would ever deliberately compose such lines and that wherever they appear they betray the poet's incompetence or carelessness. Textual editors of Chaucer have tried to emend, elide, or syncopate such lines out of existence. But that Chaucer resorted to lines of the first two types seems clearly established, and some of his fifteenth-century successors evidently thought he used the third type, too. Unlike them, he apparently never combines them to form even odder lines. (See below, pp. 28ff.) But Chaucer's iambic pentameter had not hardened its rules, and his ear evidently enjoyed the occasional line with an exceptional structure as a pleasing variation from the more frequent decasyllabic pattern.

That Chaucer could handle the marriage of meter and phrasing with a masterly touch may be illustrated briefly by two lines (760–61) from "The Pardoner's Tale." The mysterious old man, badgered by the three rioters, agrees to tell them where Death can be found:

"Now, sires," quod he, "if that yow be so leef
To fyndë Deeth, turne up this croked wey

The language is perfectly ordinary except that the final phrase has high symbolic overtones. The first line, like so many in Chaucer, is full of minor words that demand at most middling stress; the second is crammed with words of more significant content. The first is segmented twice, the second once, but the central assertion is divided into three consecutive and climactic parts: an address, a condition, and a direction. The second of these runs over the line, so that the tripartite structure of the speech is gracefully (but with a certain tension) comprehended in only two lines. Both lines are obediently iambic, but several phrases offer a variety of options to the skilled performer. The first syllable of "Now, sires" might be drawn out with ominous effect; the voice may run quickly over "if that," emphasize its first syllable, or linger somewhat on or after "that"; "so" may be given extra weight, and "leef" slowed slightly; the second line's midline pause may be expressive; the phrasal verb "turne up" retains the iambic stress on its second syllable, but "turne" offers opportunities for rich enunciation; and "this" may be pronounced in such a way (the *s* drawn out and the voice hesitating after it) as to suggest the enigma that is buried deep in the final phrase. Everything leads to this phrase: the quick small words of the first line, the periodic syntax, the speech-act of respectful compliance, the naturalistic tendering of directions, and the equivocal stressing of several metrically paired syllables. No one else for almost two hundred years would be writing lines of such subtlety and force.

What nedeth it to sermone of it moore? Chaucer led English poets to the decasyllabic line and discovered for himself an abundant array of techniques for varying not only the line but also the stanza. Later poets discovered further refinements and procedures that permitted the line to achieve levels of expressiveness that Chaucer rarely touched, partly because the tenor of his verse rarely needed them. Certainly Chaucer's work served as a model for his successors, but apparently as an increasingly enigmatic model, as their own verse wandered from his simpler principles of line and hardly pretended to follow his varied play of line and phrase, his subtle modulations, and his masterly control of the line-flow of couplet and stanza.

Wyatt

By the second quarter of the sixteenth century, when Sir Thomas Wyatt began to write poems in iambic pentameter, the ease and grace which had characterized Chaucer's line had long been lost, at least by English poets. The Scottish Chaucerians—notably, Henryson, Dunbar, and James I—continued to write in metrically regular stanzas, but something peculiar and nearly unaccountable occurred in the verse of Chaucer's English followers. In Hoccleve, Lydgate, and other English poets of the fifteenth century, the art of Chaucer's iambic pentameter disintegrated. Lydgate's lines are often monotonously regular; Hoccleve's frequently appear to insist on stressing unlikely syllables. Whether the loss of final -*e* was largely responsible for throwing their lines into disorder or whether, as seems likely, the odd character of their verse results from the conscious adoption of some bizarre species of decasyllabic line, the century and a quarter of versification between 1400 and about 1525 left iambic pentameter in so strange a state that, instead of taking off from where Chaucer had left it, poets from Wyatt on had, in effect, to begin all over again.

Among the English poets who wrote between Chaucer and Surrey, Wyatt is easily the most gifted and interesting, but the metrical system he uses in his apparently pentameter poems is an odd one that has baffled critics for centuries.[7] Even though his poems written in shorter meters are metrically deft, sometimes brilliant, his longer-line poems seem perplexingly rough. Their syllables exceed or fall short of the expected number, and it often looks as if Wyatt were somehow incompetent as a composer of longer-line verse.

But Wyatt probably developed his puzzling decasyllabic lines from two different sources: the fifteenth-century heroic line of Lydgate and his successors, and the contemporary Italian hendecasyllable. The Lydgate tradition exploited those three aberrant lines Chaucer had apparently used sparingly—the headless line, the broken-backed line, and the line with an epic caesura—and combined their odd features to form still more deviant lines. In Lydgate's work, too, there is almost always a strong midline pause—a caesura—after the fourth syllable, and the constancy of this pause has the effect of dividing the line into two halves. The full line stitched together its two halves, and the half-lines had several different optional structures:

First half

a.	˘ ´ ˘ ´	(normal)
b.	˘ ´ ˘ ´ ˘	(epic caesura)
c.	´ ˘ ´	(headless)
d.	´ ˘ ´ ˘	(headless and epic caesura)

Second half

e.	˘ ´ ˘ ´ ˘ ´	(normal)
f.	˘ ´ ˘ ´ ˘ ´ ˘	(feminine ending)
g.	´ ˘ ´ ˘ ´	(broken-backed)
h.	´ ˘ ´ ˘ ´ ˘	(broken-backed and feminine ending)

Any of the first-half patterns could be linked to any of the second-half patterns to form a verse line. Some of the sixteen possible line-patterns might not be strictly decasyllabic (they might have as few as eight or as many as twelve syllables), but five of the syllables in every such line would still receive metrical stress. The basic combinations (omitting the ones with feminine endings) are eight in number:

1. ˘ ´ ˘ ´   ˘ ´ ˘ ´ ˘ ´
2. ˘ ´ ˘ ´   ´ ˘ ´ ˘ ´
3. ˘ ´ ˘ ´ ˘   ˘ ´ ˘ ´ ˘ ´
4. ˘ ´ ˘ ´ ˘   ´ ˘ ´ ˘ ´
5. ´ ˘ ´   ˘ ´ ˘ ´ ˘ ´
6. ´ ˘ ´   ´ ˘ ´ ˘ ´
7. ´ ˘ ´ ˘   ˘ ´ ˘ ´ ˘ ´
8. ´ ˘ ´ ˘   ´ ˘ ´ ˘ ´

Each of these eight line-types may be varied with a feminine ending or with a late caesura (after the sixth syllable). Each of the first four line-types may also be varied by an additional unstressed syllable at the beginning (*double onset*). The eight basic line-types with their variants could thus generate as many as forty different line-patterns.[8]

This is a calculus of lines which may have extra or missing unstressed syllables on either side of a midline break, or at the beginning or end of a line. Because the line is so palpably made up of two half-lines, the epic caesura may seem like a feminine ending of the first half-line, and the broken-backed line may seem like a headless second half-line. In any case, half-lines may link with each other to form an extremely varied set of possible line-forms. Here are some examples from the works of poets in this tradition:

1. Ănd wáke ăll nýghte / ănd slépe týll ĭt bĕ nóne

                                      (Skelton, "The Bowge of Courte," 382)

2. Fŏre wél thŏu wóst / ĭf Ī shăll nŏt féine   (Lydgate, *Temple of Glas*, II.911)

3. Fŭll súbtýll pérsŏnes / ĭn nómbrĕ fóure ănd thrĕ́

                                      (Skelton, "The Bowge of Courte," 133)

4. By tasted swetenes / make me not to rew (Wyatt, LXXIX.3)

5. With a clerke / that connynge is to prate

(Skelton, "The Bowge of Courte," 454)

6. 'Ay,' quod he, / 'in the devylles date (Skelton, "The Bowge of Courte," 375)

7. Sol and Luna / were clypsyd of ther liht

(Lydgate, "Letter to Gloucester," in Hammond, 1927, line 29; virgule in text)

8. He was trussed / in a garmente strayte

(Skelton, "The Bowge of Courte," 505)

An example of double onset:

Who so list to hounte / I know where is an hynde (Wyatt, VII.1)

For Lydgate this system was sufficient. He uses the line-types for variety but varies little within them. Some line-types he uses more than others, and for long passages he hardly diverges at all from the basic type-1 line, divided after the fourth syllable. But whether he repeats or diverges, his lines seldom make much use of trochaic variations within an iambic context. Spondees are also rare, and we may suspect that his unstressed syllables in stressed positions did not signal a pyrrhic foot so much as a pounded beat. In the following lines, for example (admittedly more various than most), Lydgate's phrasing conforms exactly to the meter and never exerts against it any pressure worth mentioning. The seven lines belong to five different line-types; but, whatever the line-type, the phrasing sits down neatly within it:

	Line-Type
And on the wallys / of Thebes lay her fon,	3
Reioysing hem / of this unhappy eure,	1
wenyng therby / gretly to recure.	8
And on her toures / as they loken oute,	4
They on Grekys / enviously gan shoute,	8
And, of despit / and gret enmyte,	2
Bad hem foolys / gon hom to her contre	7

(*Siege of Thebes*, lines 4088–94)

30

Wyatt uses the same basic keyboard, but with a much greater deli-
cacy and resourcefulness. He evidently developed his unusual long-line
meter when he set out to translate poems, usually sonnets, from the Italian.
Whatever his earlier skill in lyrics written in shorter meters, he must have
sensed, as he started to translate Petrarch, that in the Italian sonnet form he
had touched a deeper current of poetry. Whereas the rime royal stanzas
common among Chaucer and his successors were an admirable form for
continuous stately narrative or for the expression of public sentiments, the
Italian sonnet, with its interweaving rhymes and flowing, yet segmented,
sentences, its multiple elisions (which hurry the line) and its lingering
feminine endings, seems fitted for a much more private utterance, espe-
cially for the tracing of half-hidden, debating, contradictory, and ironic
feelings that course within the troubled breast of a lover.

Southall argues convincingly that Wyatt's best verse is "a psychologi-
cal drama of inner perturbation and distress" (67); it "expresses the doubts,
anxieties, trials and tribulations of an unusually sensitive mind confront-
ing a perplexing and dangerously insecure world" (69). The poems in
octosyllabic meters, with their sharp rhythms, portray this perilous realm
through formal pairings and confrontations, half-line matching half-line,
rhymed line matching rhymed line. The effect is that of formal jousting or
dancing, the oppositions well-lit and precisely set up, even though we
know that beneath them lurk questions about love and court that are
deliberately left unresolved. But the sonnets are darker altogether, the
balances (between two-foot and three-foot segments) less precise, less pre-
dictable. The longer line lends itself to a greater variety of internal ar-
rangements; its ambiguous oppositions must be posed more problemati-
cally within or between half-lines, between line and line, quatrain and
quatrain, though even here, in the management of the sonnet's segments,
Wyatt the master of balanced phrases rarely lets his periods correspond to
his quatrains. The long but faintly out-of-step procession of self-judging,
self-condemning utterances conveys the troubled turning of a mind in
anguish or uncertainty. The mystery of love's insecurity, its incessant be-
wilderments, can be intimated through the obscurity of the rhythms, the
obsessive hesitations, quickenings, and tightenings of the jointed line.

It seems likely, therefore, that as he wrote out his versions of Pe-
trarch's poems, with the Italian texts constantly before him, Wyatt was
trying to provide in English a poetic texture similar to Petrarch's. One way

to do this was to make frequent use of elisions, of lengthenings and short-enings of syllables within the line, in order to render in an English equiva-lent the Italian manner of racing over some syllables and pausing impor-tantly on others. The Lydgatian decasyllabic was an obvious model, and he used it for these translations. For a sensitive metrist the eight-line sys-tem provided opportunities to imitate the Italian system of alternately speeding and slowing syllable-groups. The extra unstressed syllable at the beginning of the line, or at the caesura, or at line's end might recall the tumbling trochaic rhythms of the Italian hendecasyllable, even at the risk of occasionally losing the iambic feeling. Furthermore, the shortening of syllables by elision or syncope and the syllabic ambiguity of English *-es, -ed, -eth,* and *-en,* especially in the metrical setting of the Lydgate line, afforded him the most promising opportunities.

Wyatt's use of the traditional line, then, is far more purposeful and intelligent than that of his post-Chaucerian predecessors, who for the most part adopt it automatically, and without any thought about its inher-ent capacities, as a narrative or celebratory instrument—the poet's fife and drum. Even if their lines, too, can be seen, with the aid of the eight-line system, as more often regular than we have been used to finding them, they seem to drift from one line-type to another for no expressive purpose, and they rarely introduce metrical variations to reflect meaning in shifts of sound. They understand meter purely as a frame, not as an expressive instrument.[9] But Wyatt, no doubt because of his wider acquaintance with Continental models, especially Petrarch, is utterly different from these predecessors in regarding meter as an expressive medium in which depar-tures from exact metronomic repetition can reflect the changing emotions of a troubled speaker and recall the syllabic texture of Italian verse. What we can discern in his extraordinary sonnets is an able and inventive metrist struggling to invest a brisk and racy metrical system with a flexible expres-siveness that is at this point literally foreign to it.

Wyatt's well-known poem "They fle from me," though it is not a sonnet, can illustrate these points briefly. Here is the first stanza, with an indication of its line-types (f = feminine ending; a = caesura after the sixth syllable):

	Line-Type
They fle from me | that sometyme did me seke	1
with naked fote | stalk|ing in my chambre	2f

I have | sene theim | gen|till tame | and meke   8
that nowe are wyld | and | do not | remembre   2f
that | sometyme | they put theimself in daunger   5f
to take | bred at | my hand | & nowe they raunge   1a
bese|ly seking | with a | conti|nuell chaunge   3

(XXXVII.1–7)

In this stanza and the two that follow, Wyatt is really using a metrical system, not just composing poetry in phrases, though phrases are important to him. He has a keyboard, which authorizes coherent lines of basically iambic verse; and although some of his lines, like some of Donne's, may puzzle us, we need not feel baffled. The system he uses in almost all his verse is a four-part system, the parts of which can be clearly distinguished:

1. Metrical forms: for the decasyllabic line, an array of Lydgatian line-types with strong midline breaks, which sometimes appear elsewhere than after the fourth or fifth syllable.

2. Metrical variations, similar to those used later on: trochees, some spondees and pyrrhics, a very occasional anapest; and some combinations that never became standard for iambic pentameter (for example, a monosyllabic third foot; a pyrrhic foot followed by a trochee).

3. Syllabic procedures: elision, synaloepha, syncope, expansion of monosyllables into disyllables, and so forth. Some of these techniques remained available to poets for centuries.

4. Accentual conventions: especially, near-spondaic pronunciation of some disyllabic words or phrases; shifting or level stress in many words, notably Romance words, for which a definitive pronunciation, at least in verse, had evidently not yet become established (*fortune, vertue*); and occasional use of "thwarted stress" (unspeechlike stress on minor syllables of polysyllabic words).

The phrasing arrangements Wyatt uses are a further level of organization. They work with and through the others to secure effects of balance, opposition, intensification, crispness—sometimes of speechlike authenticity. Phrase joined to phrase composes the Wyatt line. The phrases, normally two to a line, are themselves usually different in character and feeling (that is, composed of different kinds of grammatical units, though often with sharply contrasting features). The skill required to write such a line appears to consist in deploying phrases that combine this difference with this capacity for contrast. As we read these poems, we have a strong sense of the phrase and of the line, a much weaker sense both of the sentence and of the quatrain (or tercet). The struggle of the agonizing lover seems reflected in the difficulty with which the distinctive phrases combine to form a patterned line, and perhaps also in the awkwardness with which the lines sometimes combine to form larger prosodic units. In his longer-line poems generally, Wyatt appears to be absorbed much more deeply in the problems of assembling phrases into lines than in the problems of arranging those lines into groups that flow melodiously and please the ear with the larger patterns of quatrain or stanza.

This preoccupation with the line, to the injury of the line-flow, was more than compensated for by the next two generations of sixteenth-century poets, who, abandoning Wyatt's complex decasyllabic system, found easier terms on which to make single lines and interested themselves instead in the problems of composing harmonious stanzas or sonnets that course more fluently from quatrain to quatrain than these difficult poems of Wyatt's ever do. But he himself may have come round to this position—or at least part way. Those sonnets that were evidently composed later take two crucial steps in the direction of smoothness: they avoid problematical rhymes, and they stick very largely to the 1 (or 1a) or 4 (or 4a) line-types. The surer rhymes and more regular meter help us to feel as well a greater quatrain- (and tercet-) integrity.

Inventive and resourceful as the metrical system Wyatt used in these poems may have been, it was even then too difficult for his readers. It takes considerable metrical sophistication to hear what is happening around a Wyatt caesura, and even someone who grasps the system may not see how individual lines are meant to be read. Several lines in "They fle from me" offer the reader alternative choices—for example:

> Thȧnked bḗ | fȯrtúne / it hath ben othrewise   (XXXVII.8)

or

> Thȧnkĕd | bĕ fȯrtŭne / it hath ben othrewise

In the most intriguing of Wyatt's sonnets, several or most or sometimes almost all the lines present perplexing problems of interpretation. The

34

system he is using probably has too many variables for a casual reader to tolerate. But when, in what appears to be his later verse, he began to moderate the freedom with which he varies the line, he could use the line-types eloquently, along with trochees, pyrrhics, and spondees, as expressive resources—for example, in this passage from Satire I:

		Line-Type
	I am not he suche eloquence to boste,	1
	To make | the crow | sing|ing as the swanne,	2
45	Nor call the lyon of cowarde bestes the moste,	3
	That cannot take a mows | as the | cat can:	1a
	And he that diethe for hunger of the golld	1 or 3
	Call him | Ales|saundre, | and say that Pan	7a
	Passithe | Apollo in musike manyfold;	3 or 4a
50	Praysse Syr Thopas for a noble tale,	8
	And skorne the story that | the kny|ght tolld	4

(CV.43–51)

The variety of line-types here (perhaps eight in nine lines) does much to enforce Wyatt's irony. Wherever there is an extra or an omitted syllable, the tone is sharpened: we feel the sarcasm in "the crow \| singing as the swanne" because of the two successive stressed syllables, and the extra little catch at the center of lines 45 and 49, and perhaps of 47, makes the argument sound more headlong. The unusual 7a-pattern in line 48 seems likewise energetic, for it appears to begin the line with three successive trochees; the line ends iambically, but the next one has several features that revive the trochaic feeling. The headless line 50 *sounds* clipped and caustic. These striking effects, which Wyatt uses skillfully here and can call up at will when he needs them, work in conjunction with metrical substitutions to give the passage its strength of movement: the pyrrhic-spondee combination at the end of line 46 (unusual before Sidney), and the trochee that begins line 49. Finally, the disyllabic pronunciation of "knyght" in line 51 (which lets it rhyme with Wyatt) gives a special intensity to the poet's scorn for these scorners.

In these enterprising poems, then, Wyatt appears to be forging a distinctive decasyllabic style comparable to those of later masters. The line-types here function not as alternative paradigms in the manner of Lydgate et al. or of his own early sonnets (shifting from one type to another so that we get little sense of a single norm), but as metrical variations on the basic type-1 or type-4 line, the line of iambic pentameter. When Wyatt presents David's self-blame in the first of the Penitential Psalms, he largely abandons the French polysyllabic words of aureate verse and develops a monosyllabic style that joins a steadier iambic meter to emphatic and expressive phrasing. In this style, repeated words and phrases, internal rhymes, expressive trochees and spondees, an epic caesura (type 3), alliteration, assonance, and consonance, and similar devices intensify the feeling in a way that is characteristic of poems of the later sixteenth and of the seventeenth century and utterly beyond the reach of such earlier poets as Lydgate, Hoccleve, and the rest:

		Line-Type	
I lord ame *s*trayd: *I,* *s*ek withowt recure,		I	
Fele a*l* my *l*yms, that have rebe*lld for fere,*		I	
*Sha*ke in di*s*payre, onle*s* thou me a*s*sure.		I	
100	*Mye flesshe* is tro*u*bl*ed,* *my* h*art d*oth *feare* the *speare*;	3	
	That dread *of death, of death that ev*er la*s*tes,	I	
	Threateth ǀ *of* right and drawe*th neare* and *neare.*	I	
	*M*oche *more* *my* *sowle* is tro*w*bl*ed* *by* the *blastes*	I	
	Of *th*eise a*s*sa*w*lte*s,* that *come* as *thick* a*s* hayle,	I	
	Of worldl*ye* vā*ny̆*tie, that *temptacion* ca*s*te*s*	4	105
	Agayn*st* the *wey*ke bu*lwar*ke ǀ of the ǀ *flesshe frāyle*	Ia	

(CVIII.97–106)

In the generation after Wyatt, poets went further in the direction of standardizing the iambic line, but they did not much advance the development of its expressive resources, which remained latent for forty years while poets learned to write the measured line. The development of a simpler metric than the multi-type jointed line had several important results. It assured a wider audience, and it encouraged a larger number of writers to try their hand at an art that promised success on easier terms. It made possible, too, the development of smoother melodic currents throughout a quatrain, tercet, or couplet. Its simpler metrical base offered exactly the opportunities for expressive variation that would later form the peculiar wealth of a great metrical tradition. For it was only after the Tudor poets had simplified the poetic line that Sidney, Shakespeare, and Milton could make those spondaic, pyrrhic, and trochaic departures from it that

36

give it much of its force and character. Their line is not so multiform as Lydgate's, but it is much more economical; it permits fewer variations from the norm (and the norm is more definite), but those few (along with a more mobile midline pause) allow it to bring into play an immense range of quickly recognizable speech-patterns.

In the last analysis, the jointed line, brilliant as it is in the hands of a master, is inherently too subservient to the spoken phrase, too deficient in predictable musical pattern. Since the basic pattern is variable, we may not be sure what the variations vary from, so our sense of them as variations is diminished and confused. Or, to put it differently, the formal side of the struggle between line and phrase, between life-conditions and the immediate life that they test, is underrepresented. We do not feel this, of course, in the strong meters of Wyatt's octosyllabic poems nor, to the same extent, in the Satires and Penitential Psalms; but in the early sonnets it is as if the power that constrains human action and struggle is too shapeless to serve as a convincing antagonist to the dark inner turmoil of the speaker. In a few of these poems Wyatt makes this situation, this existential incoherence, wonderfully moving, but its force rests on a precarious metric. The metric of Shakespeare—thanks largely to Wyatt himself—was to be more solidly constructed.

CHAPTER 3

The Sixteenth-Century Line:
Pattern and Variation

Old and New Directions

By 1564, the year of Shakespeare's birth, iambic pentameter was still a clumsy and lumbering meter. In contrast to Chaucer's mastery of a serviceable and expressive pentameter line, the achievement of metrical grace and strength in the sixteenth century was an arduous and painful struggle, a heroic quest of a sort, in the pursuit of which poets appear to have been, like Spenser's courtly knights, all too frequently distracted and irresolute. We have learned to think of this meter as a remarkably rich and subtle one, capable of the most delicate or powerful effects in the hands of a master. But, apart from Wyatt himself, whose expressive experiments were far in advance of his time, hardly any poet before the 1580s would have regarded such a view as sensible. Almost all the verse produced in this meter before 1575 or so could lay little claim to richness and subtlety, only at most to a certain energy that was usually neutralized by the monotony of the beat. The best literary minds of the day understandably regarded such verse, especially when rhymed, as crude and trivial, not at all comparable in expressiveness and complexity to the classical quantitative meters. As Edmund Waller still could put it a century later: "Poets that lasting marble seek, / Must carve in Latin, or in Greek" (198).

In *Well-Weighed Syllables,* Derek Attridge has told, with clarity and understanding, the story of sixteenth-century quantitative verse. By his account, although the Romans may have heard the apparent disparities between the stress-accents of words and the durational quantities of syllables in verse lines (and this subject is very obscure), changes in the pronunciation of Latin by the fifth century A.D. "meant . . . that the quantities on which Latin verse was based ceased to be a property of the spoken language and had to be learned for the purpose of scanning and writing poetry in classical metres" (21). Medieval scholars, of course, dutifully learned them and taught them to dutiful schoolboys in England as elsewhere. But even though Latin verse was probably pronounced in a normal way by stressing the syllables that in a prose passage would receive accent, the trained reader would see a pattern of quantitative values running partly counter to the prose rhythm. Thus in the famous opening line of the *Aeneid*, the first syllable of *cano* receives speech-stress, but in the quantitative scheme it functions as short:

Arma virumque cano Troiae qui primus ab oris

As Attridge points out: "The effect of [the] rules . . . is to prevent the coincidence of stress and ictus in the centre of the line" (14). The reader is expected to register intellectually (and perhaps perceptually) the tension generated by this conflict. In addition, the Latin hexameter could fulfill its metrical requirements with an enviable versatility, for each of the first four feet could consist either of two long syllables or of one long one and two short ones. The line's final syllable, too, might be either long or short; if it was short, the final foot would register a difference from all the other feet in the line.

Such wide and subtle options, it was held, made it possible for Latin poets to achieve the grandest poetic effects. In contrast, English poetry could make no claim to greatness so long as it lacked a meter capable of such variety. And what did it have? A "rustick rythmery" (104), produced by "the uncountable rabble of ryming Ballet makers and compylers of sencelesse sonets" (103), "wooden *rythmours*" (102), a "Gotish kinde of ryming," "rude versifying" (100), "our rude beggerly ryming" (93).[1] Even George Gascoigne, though he is willing to make the best of it, is ashamed of the English system of versification:

> And surely I can lament that wee are fallen into suche a playne and simple manner of wryting, that there is none other foote used but one; wherby our Poemes may justly be called Rithmes, and cannot by any right challenge the name of a Verse. (G. Smith, vol. 1, 50)

In such a state of affairs, Attridge imagines, an Elizabethan humanist might have found "the rhythmic beat of English verse . . . crude and distasteful, so different from the sound of Latin verse, with its accentual irregularity, leavened only occasionally by bursts of rhythmicality" (92). End-rhyme, too, would provide further evidence of English barbarism, and the English language itself "would seem crude and disorganised, without rules, without constant orthography, and (most important as far as verse was concerned) without any agreed division of syllables into long and short" (92).

Not one of the poets or commentators on poetry before Sidney appears to have had an inkling of the potential splendor of English pentameter as a medium for some of the greatest poetry ever written in any language. They would probably all be astonished to hear that it could be so, that one of their own countrymen then living—not a university humanist, but a grammar-school boy from the provinces—would take this crude meter and, building on hints provided by other poets even closer in age to the doubters, construct a series of magnificent literary works in an iambic pentameter fully as brilliant as the verse of Virgil or Homer. Such a result would have seemed delusory to them, for nothing in the practice of iambic pentameter in their day could have led them to imagine a verse accomplishment of such magnitude in so poor and trivial a meter: a meter with only two syllables per foot, lacking the extensive possibilities of variation offered by the Latin hexameter, and without the intellectually perceived structure of long and short syllables that gives every line of Latin verse its differently devious way of fulfilling the metrical paradigm. For Elizabethan readers, in fact, iambic pentameter was perceived essentially as a line whose pattern was entirely defined when you stated that it had ten syllables. Although they understood that the line was iambic, not until late in the eighteenth century did prosodists begin to talk about the alternating accent that seems to us so palpable a feature of iambic pentameter practice and that poets and readers had obviously aimed at and responded to from Surrey on. The critical emphasis on the *number* of syllables, however, becomes understandable when we realize how much the humanists and scholars admired the capacity of the Latin verse line to *vary* the number of syllables and, by so doing, to achieve expressive effects. In comparison with these, an unvarying ten-syllable meter of regularly alternating stresses seemed poor indeed.[2]

In desperation, some Elizabethan poets, including Sidney and Spenser, tried to devise an English quantitative verse that would function on the same principles as the Latin. Essentially, the system regards as long any vowel (and syllable) which is followed by more than one consonant, and it permits the composition of such memorable lines as the following (quoted from Attridge, 1974, 136, 166):

All travel|lers do̅ | gla̅dlȳ re̅|po̅rt great | pra̅yse o̅f Ŭ|ly̅s se̅s
This cre̅eke | with ru̅n|ning pas|sadge the̅e | channe̅l in̆|hauntĕth

The first of these lines has an unusual spriteliness, but clearly this way of writing is, for an accentual language like English, a dead end.

If quantitative Latin verse offered some poets an alluring example, what has usually been called "the native tradition"—that is, accentual alliterative verse—presented an alternative model. Many Old English and Middle English masterpieces (from *Beowulf* to *Piers Plowman* and *Sir Gawain and the Green Knight*) belong to this tradition, and a more homely version of it could still be heard in the rhymed "tumbling verse" of the popular stage in the sixteenth century (see below, Chapter 6, for examples). If in quantitative verse a varying number of syllables in the foot and in the line were thought to produce harmony and a pleasing flexibility, the same uncertainty about numbers of syllables in tumbling verse produced the entirely different effects of roughness and an exaggerated emphasis on stressed syllables. By the same token, poets who by writing in strict iambics fixed the number of syllables in foot and line, while conceding a loss in subtlety when compared to Latin quantitative verse, could reduce the thumping that necessarily results when several unstressed syllables precede a stressed one, especially when the stressed ones alliterate. When only one unstressed syllable precedes each stressed one, the need to pounce on each stressed one is materially lessened. At first, however, as poets became accustomed to a new sort of verse in which both the number of syllables and the number of accents mattered, the syllables occupying the stressed positions had to be firmly accented in order for the verse to be heard as verse. In effect, the accentual character of accentual-syllabic verse had to be heavily audible for a time, and this necessity temporarily hooded the new meter's capacity for variety and difference—specifically, its capacity for expressive and pleasing metrical variation.

Given this situation, Glenn S. Spiegel may be right in suggesting that the main problem for poets (lyric as well as dramatic) in the generation or so before Shakespeare began to write was to mitigate the force of the native tradition. To do this, to soften the pounding accentualism that was characteristic of most forms of early Tudor verse, Spiegel claims, they reduced excessive alliteration on stressed syllables, regularized the number of syllables in a line, and varied their stanza forms. All of these steps were means of asserting the difference of iambic pentameter from the hypnotically repeated series of (frequently alliterating) stressed syllables, with an indeterminate number of unstressed syllables between the stressed ones.[3]

If this is true, then what we perceive as the excessive regularity of the iambic pentameter written by poets of this period must be understood both as a necessary response to an audience (whether private or public) who insisted on hearing regular beats and as a means of escaping (by providing a fixed number of weak syllables with each strong one) the tumbling feeling of the less disciplined accentual forms. The "smoothness" that poets aimed at in their meter could be achieved by two related but apparently opposed means: on the one hand, the poet had to be sure that the five beats of his line were heard as such, that every second syllable was audibly more prominent than the one it followed (though the availability of some metrical variations made this a flexible requirement); on the other hand, he had also to make the successive beats neither too consistent in their stark contrast to the weak syllables nor exactly isochronous. As readers, we must measure a lapse of syllables as well as a lapse of time. And, though we must hear the beat insistently enough to establish it as a recurrent pattern, we must enjoy as well a repertoire of variations, of departures from the pattern.

It took a long time for these variations to become established, no doubt partly because the need for an audible beat was at first so imperious. This need may help to explain the popularity of other iambic meters like poulter's measure and fourteeners, with their long lines that trip from beat to beat with little subtlety or capacity for expressive variation. One decisive advantage of iambic pentameter over such meters lay in its readiness to combine into stanza forms, as the longer-line measures could not conveniently do. Every stanza-shape gave a somewhat different feeling, and even though poets at first usually preferred to write in such time-tested forms as rime royal, the versatility of iambic pentameter—its adaptability to many different functions and forms—must have recommended it strongly to writers. It could be written in continuous lines or molded into quatrains, seven-line stanzas, sonnets, or stanzas of anyone's devising, and even be mixed with shorter or longer lines. It could be rhymed or blank, and it could be used on the stage or in the study—for dramatic productions or for heroic, tragic, or satiric poetry. All these capacities were not shared by the more single-minded poulter's or fourteeners, and they helped to insure a privileged position for iambic pentameter even at a time when its full potentialities were not yet audible to the innocent Elizabethan ear.

Constitutive Features of Iambic Pentameter

By 1590, then, when Shakespeare began to write the works we know, the chief features of his central meter had already been set: (1) the ten-syllable iambic line; (2) a conventional midline break in phrasing; (3) line-integrity (most lines were endstopped); and (4) a "smooth" reconciliation of English phrasing and the metrical pattern. The regular pentameter line comprised these features, along with the standard variations (trochaic, pyrrhic, and spondaic) which poets used with increasing skill to make their lines more graceful, varied, and expressive.

SYLLABLE-COUNT AND STRESS-PATTERN

Sixteenth-century writers speak of the line as having ten syllables (or, occasionally, an eleventh that constitutes a "feminine ending"). Although they do not discuss the stress-pattern in detail, it is understood that the pattern is iambic, a two-syllable pattern that occurs five times (pentameter). By the nineteenth century, poets had begun to admit anapests into pentameter lines for the sake of variety, but here at the beginning it was important to the poets to keep the strict syllable count. Anapestic variations leaned in the direction of the crude tumbling rhythms of folk verse, and composers of iambic pentameter evidently aspired to a more dignified species of composition.[4] After 1600, writers of dramatic blank verse, including Shakespeare and Webster, loosened this requirement in the service of a more expressive dramatic meter, but, with rare exceptions, nondramatic iambic pentameter adhered to the nonanapest rule for two more centuries.

The regular beat, of course, did not always make for authentic dignity. Here, for example, is one of the contemporary versions of the Pyramus and Thisbe story which Shakespeare doubtless had in mind when he wrote *A Midsummer Night's Dream:*

> Beholde (alas) this wicked cruell wall,
> Whose cursed scyte, denayeth us perfect sight:
> Much more the hap, of other ease at all.
> What if I should by force, as well one might:
> And yet deserves, it batter flat to ground,
> And open so, an issue large to make:
> Yet feare I sore, this sooner will redownde,
> To our reproche, if it I undertake:
> As glad I would, then us to helpe or ayde

> ("The History of Pyramus and Thisbie, Truely Translated," in
> *A Gorgeous Gallery of Gallant Inventions,* 110)

The insistent stress on every second syllable is maintained at exorbitant cost to sensible grammar. This foot-by-foot progress is matched by an equally obsessive phrase-by-phrase and line-by-line accumulation.

A remarkable proportion of the iambic verse between Surrey and Sidney is written in just such regular iambs; and even when, unlike this passage, it has other poetic virtues to recommend it, it is likely to grow wearisome to our later, more accomplished ear. It nevertheless seems probable that the aim of the best versifiers in this tradition was not merely to drum out the beats but to compose a sequence of words which, while establishing a definite rhythm, would still permit actors or reciters to speak them with some impassioned feeling. Certainly much of the verse written in this style has for its subject the strong emotion of the speaker, and there is no reason to believe that the Elizabethans thought any more than we do that a mechanical delivery was an effective resource for a despairing lover.[5]

MIDLINE BREAK

From Surrey to Sidney all poets break most of their lines after the fourth syllable, with either a strong pause (signaled by punctuation) or a

44

weaker one, so that the line appears to be buckled into unequal segments of two and three feet. We have seen already how invariable this pattern was in Lydgate and how common in Wyatt. In Wyatt's successors it again becomes habitual. Chidiock Tichbourne's "Elegy," for example, composed, it is said, on the eve of his execution, pursues an implacable beat. The phrasal break after the fourth syllable relentlessly splits every line identically into two segments:

> My prime of youth is but a frost of cares,
> My feast of joy is but a dish of pain,
> My crop of corn is but a field of tares,
> And all my good is but vain hope of gain;
> The day is past, and yet I saw no sun,
> And now I live, and now my life is done. (Hebel and Hudson, 196)

Two further stanzas follow the same obsessive design.

But to the sixteenth-century ear (and perhaps to ours) this four-syllable and six-syllable pattern was an agreeable sound and the poet's skill lay in his ability to find fairly natural but also fairly eloquent phrases to fit the syllabic requirements. To gauge the appeal of this art, we must enjoy the two-step move to the pause, and then the three-step sweep to line's end. To hear this effect repeatedly in lines made up of phrases that in ordinary speech showed no such obvious pattern evidently gave distinct pleasure to Elizabethan listeners. The words move in waves toward the phrase-ends, which are often marked by commas, even when no real break in thought occurs.

Certainly few poems are so unblinkingly regular as Tichbourne's, and even Surrey and his most slavish imitators occasionally vary the placement of the midline pause. They become aware that a break in phrasing may appear after the fifth, the sixth, or the seventh syllable without disturbing the metrical structure of the line:

> And with remembraunce of the greater greif (Surrey, 70)

> Whan with the unwonted weyght, the rustye keel
> (Sackville, "Induction," in *A Mirror for Magistrates*, line 492)

> Such spight yet showes dame fortune (if she frowne,)
> (Gascoigne, *Works*, vol. 1, 329)

Although their preference remains strong for a break after the fourth, this rudimentary flexibility in placing the midline break must have struck some poets as a useful way to vary the line and counter its tendency to rhythmic monotony. Even as early as 1579, Spenser had learned to break his lines softly at the fifth or sixth syllable, with a strikingly original rhythmic result:

> 'Where I was wont to seeke the honey bee,
> Working her formall rowmes in wexen frame,
> The grieslie todestoole growne there mought I se,
> And loathed paddocks lording on the same:
> And where the chaunting birds luld me a sleepe,
> The ghastlie owle her grievous ynne doth keepe.'
>
> ("December," *The Shepheardes Calender,* lines 67–72)

The freedom with which later Elizabethan poets vary the position of the midline break has several consequences, two immediate and one delayed: it admits into the line great numbers of natural English phrases that are not themselves naturally iambic ("The grieslie todestoole," "And loathed paddocks"); it solves the problem of monotony by giving successive lines different rhythmic contours; but it also undermines the predictability, and hence the stability, of the line. As we shall see in detail further on, when a pause comes late in the line the likelihood of enjambment is increased, the phrasing is more apt to spill over the line-ending into the next line, and the phrasal integrity of the line may be compromised by the reader's or listener's sense that another structural authority—the sentence—is competing for prominence with the metrical line. Early Elizabethan versification is essentially an art of congruence, a fitting of phrase to metrical pattern; by Shakespeare's time it has become as well an art of counterpoint, an art in which the rhythmic phrase may work either with or against the metrical current. (See Chapter 14, below.)

LINE-INTEGRITY

The line was normally endstopped. Even when no punctuation appeared at the line-ending, a syntactical unit was usually complete at this point and poets rarely ended a line in the middle of a phrase.

46

And as the knyght in fyeld among his foes,
Beset wyth swurdes, must slaye or there be slayne:
So I alas lapt in a thousand woes,
Beholding death on every syde so playne,
390　I rather chose by sum slye secrete trayne
To wurke his death, and I to lyve thereby,
Than he to lyve, and I of force to dye.

(Sackville, "The Complaynt of Henrye Duke of Buckingham,"
in A Mirror for Magistrates, lines 386–92)

In this rime royal stanza the characteristic pause after the fourth syllable is maintained, and every line except the fifth ends in punctuation. But even the enjambment of lines 390–91 is of the kind that at least permits a pause between "by sum slye secrete trayne" and "To wurke his death."

Such lines are likely to be apprehended very much as lines, especially when the end of the line is also marked by rhyme. There is a congruence between the line and the segment of thought or speech. The stanza's complex assertion comes to us in line-long segments, joint participants in a common enterprise.

Perhaps nowhere in Elizabethan poetry is this made clearer than in Sir John Davies' poem "Orchestra, or a poem of dancing" (1596). Davies' subject here is the galliard, but it might be our own—iambic pentameter:

But for more divers and more pleasing show,
A swift and wandring daunce he did invent,
With passages uncertaine to and fro,
Yet with a certaine aunswere and consent
To the quick musick of the Instrument.
　Five was the number of the Musicks feete,
　Which still the daunce did with five paces meete.　　　(Davies, 108)

Reading this silently or aloud, one easily gets a sense of the egalitarian integrity of each line and of the way all of them, despite their interior rhythmic and verbal differences, their "passages uncertaine to and fro," nevertheless act in concert to produce the finished stanza. The rhymes "answer and consent" to each other; and, along with "the number of the Musicks feete," they fix the length and end-point of each line. Later, when blank-verse poets spill the phrasing into the next line—as Shakespeare habitually does in his later plays, and Milton in *Paradise Lost*—the sense of the line as one in a series of equal metrical and semantic units will be imperiled. The loss of rhyme and of our sense of stanza will work with enjambment to make the line-ending increasingly hard for the ear to mark, and we may follow the windings of the sentence more easily than the steps of the line—unless we have the page before us, though in this case, too, the ear may fall out of practice.

The joy that Elizabethans evidently could feel in the coming together of English phrases and regular meter is evident in single lines as well—in Spenser's "One day I wrote her name upon the strand" (*Amoretti*, 75:1) or in Drayton's "Since ther's no helpe, come let us kisse and part" (*Idea*, 31:1). Shakespeare and other dramatists provided plenty of lines that could give this pleasure: "Tell her I am arrested in the street" (*The Comedy of Errors*, 4.1.106); "I thank my God for my humility" (*Richard III*, 2.1.73). Totally natural, and yet iambic pentameter: this is likely to be our pleased response to such lines. And even longer sentences which string out their phrases over several lines, each of which constitutes a significant segment exactly five feet long, apparently gave pleasure to Elizabethan ears:

> Smile, stars, that reign'd at my nativity,
> And dim the brightness of their neighbor lamps;
> Disdain to borrow light of Cynthia,
> For I, the chiefest lamp of all the earth,
> First rising in the east with mild aspect,
> But fixed now in the meridian line,
> Will send up fire to your turning spheres,
> And cause the sun to borrow light of you.
>
> (Marlowe, *Tamburlaine the Great* Part I, 4.2.33–40)

Our own preference is usually for sentence segments of unequal length that result from frequent midline breaks and generous enjambment; but Marlowe's mighty line is mighty in its insistence not only on the beat but also on the integrity of the five-foot segment of thought.

ENGLISH PHRASING AND THE METRICAL LINE

The basic aim of most poets who wrote in iambic pentameter up to at least 1575 was to find language that would be compatible with the meter, natural phrasing that would fit into the system of five alternating stressed and unstressed syllables without notable wrenching of accent. This is not easy for everyone to do, and hardly anyone can do it for long stretches without becoming trivial or ridiculous. All phrases in English are not iambic; when we speak naturally, stresses do not automatically occur where iambic meter wants them, and it takes some managing to arrange the verse so that, in Gascoigne's words,

> even in this playne foote of two syllables you wreste no woorde from his natural and usuall sounde . . . that all the wordes in your verse be so placed as the first sillable may sound short or be depressed, the second long or elevate, the third shorte, the fourth long, the fifth shorte, etc. (*Certayne Notes of Instruction,* in G. Smith, vol. 1, 50–51)

He gives two lines as examples: "*I understand your meanying by your eye,*" which works, and "*Your meaning I understand by your eye,*" which does not, because two of its stressed syllables ("un-" and "stand-") fall in the wrong places. Or, more precisely, because (he says) the meter forces stress on "-der-." In Gascoigne's metrical world, the meter is strong enough to do so, stronger therefore than the natural phrase. He implies that in any conflict between the two the meter must prevail.[6] But he is arguing against provoking such conflict. As Elizabethan poets became more adept in the art of writing iambic pentameter, they came to understand more explicitly that their aim must be to seek harmony between these two potential antagonists, iambic meter and English phrases.

More specifically, in order to reconcile what the poets recognized as an attractive meter with the natural rhythms of English phrasing, they resorted to conventional practices of two kinds: *those which alter the language in order to normalize the meter, and those which allow for variations in the meter in order to accommodate patterns of emphasis that are natural to the language.* This mutual alteration, effected at first in small ways, is basic to the art of English iambic verse generally and is essential to its grandest expressive achievements.

First, in order to fit English speech more successfully to iambic pentameter, the poets began to allow themselves the license of letting their language diverge from that of normal spoken English, chiefly in four respects.

1. *Variable pronunciation of minor syllables.* It should be understood that in Elizabethan times there was no very precise understanding of what constituted a syllable. (See Chapter 10, below.) Furthermore, the same word could be pronounced differently in different dialects. To compound the problem, it is likely that even in the same person's speech variant pronunciations—doublets, like *fancy* and *fantasy, courtesy* and *curtsey, ignomy* and *ignominy, poesy* and *posy*—might exist side by side. Finally, Modern English was still in the course of change, and hardly any pronunciation, at least of a minor syllable, can be thought of as having been established as standard. Linguistic scholars have written at length about the problems of syllabification in the poetry of this period, and especially in Shakespeare's (see Kökeritz, 1953, 1969, Partridge, 1964, and Cercignani), and there has been considerable dispute as to whether apparent anapestic feet really occur in Shakespeare's verse or are to be accounted for by his tendency to fuse or compress minor syllables, as in "It is the star to ev'ry wand'ring bark." (See Chapter 10, below.) But whether such combinations as *-ion* or *-uous* were normally pronounced as monosyllabic or disyllabic by Shakespeare's contemporaries, they appear to have been capable of functioning as fused syllables when the meter required it ("You had but that opinĭon of yourself," *Julius Caesar*, 2.1.92) and as distinct syllables on other occasions ("Will purchase us a good opiniŏn," *Julius Caesar*, 2.1.145). Similarly, words like *heaven, seven, either, spirit, whether* may fit the meter either as monosyllables or disyllables; words like *cardinal, temporal, innocent, wandering,* either as disyllables or as trisyllables. In sum, these poets treated uncertain combinations of syllables variously, according to their metrical convenience. When modern readers come upon such combinations, they would be well advised to let the meter influence their pronunciation and to compress or elide to the extent that graceful or forceful reading permits.

2. *Pronunciation of -ed.* Some of the variations in syllabification may have been artificial inventions adopted for the sake of the meter; for most of them it is hard to be sure because we cannot know for certain how the Elizabethans actually pronounced these syllables. But there can be no doubt about the deliberate sounding of the *-ed* suffix in words where linguistic evidence clearly shows that it was not pronounced in speech. Probably this device was adopted in imitation of Chaucer and other earlier poets, whose verse often requires the pronunciation of *-e, -es,* and *-ed.* Although,

in an effort to be deliberately archaic, Spenser sometimes sounds what would normally be a silent *-es*, Elizabethan poets as a rule do not sound the first two endings, probably because few words then current sounded them (and they did not understand Chaucer's use of them); but the sounded *-ed* survived (and still survives) in the past and past-participle forms of verbs ending in a dental consonant (*added, noted*), in a few adjectives such as *aged, learned, beloved, blessed,* and *cursed,* and in others like *rugged, jagged, naked,*[7] which might be troublesome to pronounce without a vowel intervening between the guttural stop and the final *d* (though we manage *begged, sagged, jogged,* and many other such words). But even when the silent assimilation of *-ed* presented no articulatory problem, Elizabethan poets frequently resorted to the *-ed* suffix if the meter required an additional syllable. The more than occasional appearance of this device remained a mark of poetic language for several decades; it was employed with considerably more restraint in late-seventeenth- and in eighteenth-century poetry, was revived by Romantic poets (especially Keats) who wished to sound antique, and remained a mark of old-fashioned and even bad poetry at least until very recently.

3. *Exaggerated use of the auxiliary verbs* do *and* did. Although in sixteenth-century speech these words may well have been used for emphasis more often than they are now, it is clear that many poets used them in poems principally for metrical reasons. Spenser, for example, in Sonnet 81 from *Amoretti,* uses such pleonastic forms in five different lines: "does sparke" (4), "doth lay" (6), "doth dark" (7), "doth display" (9), and "do make" (11). Such words serve little purpose other than to fill up the meter. This gratuitous introduction of unneeded auxiliary forms also remained a feature of poetry for centuries and indeed became one mark of a poetical style.[8]

4. *Inversion of natural word order.* Although—to judge from Elizabethan prose, including letters and representations of conversation—inversion of normal word order was more frequent than it is with us, it became especially characteristic of poetic speech. Again Spenser offers egregious examples of the lengths to which poets could go in displacing words and phrases from what seem their most natural positions. *The Faerie Queene* is full of remarkable passages of this kind. In the following stanza, every line but one contains at least one syntactical inversion:

Ne *stayd he,* till he came unto the place,
Where late *his treasure he entombed had;*
Where when he *found it not* (for *Trompart bace*
Had *it purloyned* for his *maister bad*)
With extreme fury he became quite mad,
And ran away, ran *with him selfe away:*
That who so straungely had *him seene* bestadd,
With upstart haire and staring *eyes dismay,*
From Limbo lake him late escaped sure would say.   (III.x.54)

In the last line, even if the three three-word phrases were idiomatic En-
glish, as the second one certainly is not, they would have to appear in
reverse order to sound anything like normal speech. Spenser is willing
to distort the natural language quite severely in order to keep his lines
metrical; frequently, as here, the inversions serve rhetorical purposes as
well. Except for Milton, whose style owes much to Spenser, and Gerard
Manley Hopkins, whose syntactical distortions are enlisted in the service
of intense speech, no later poet inverts the normal order of English words
as much as Spenser. For centuries, syntactical inversion was a common
resource of poets and for many readers a characteristic sign of poetic style.
Indeed, poetry that did not make use of this device would have seemed
to many readers of poetry from 1550 to 1920 strangely unpoetical, even
crude.[9]

Variation in Tudor Poetry

Along with these ways of adjusting the language to fit the meter,
poets also began to vary the meter to accommodate a wider range of English
phrasing. They learned to use the basic metrical variations that make up
the iambic pentameter keyboard from the middle of the sixteenth century
to at least the beginning of the twentieth: the trochaic "inversion," espe-
cially in the opening foot of a line, and the pyrrhic and spondaic "substitu-
tions." It appears that at first they tolerated these variations and regarded
them as imperfections best avoided. The smooth and regular line was best.
But as time went on, they noticed that such variations do not interfere with
our continued perception of a line as iambic, and that, far from constitut-

ing a blemish, they could be used for important purposes: to enliven and diversify the metrical pattern, to contribute to the formal symmetry and grace of a poetic stanza or movement, and to intensify moments of significant lyrical or dramatic feeling.

As poets felt their way into the new metrical system they were collectively devising, they began to see, among other things, that English phrasal rhythms behaved differently from Latin quantitative patterns. Gascoigne, in particular, observed that English stress does not always come in two weights, strong and weak. He realized that certain words had a kind of middle stress value and were capable without awkwardness of occupying either stressed or unstressed positions in the line: for example, *all, both, can, do, each, full, may, much, must, might, my, no, none* (as adjective), *such, that, this, these, too, which,* and *yet.* Words of this kind evidently puzzled the Elizabethan, who derived from Latin poetry the belief that individual syllables—monosyllabic words as well as the syllables of polysyllabic words—were inherently long or short, hence inherently stressed or unstressed. But English includes many more monosyllables than Latin, and in actual speech monosyllabic words like those above may or may not receive stress. In his *Certayne Notes of Instruction,* Gascoigne distinguishes "three maner of accents, *gravis, levis,* et *circumflexa.*" The first two, heavy and light, are drawn from traditional descriptions of Latin quantitative verse and correspond to our *stressed* and *unstressed;* "the circumflexe accent is indifferent, sometimes short, sometimes long, sometimes depressed and sometimes elevate" (G. Smith, vol. 1, 49). Although he does not carry his analysis beyond the point of deciding on the relative stress of syllables within the same word, Gascoigne is evidently struggling toward some understanding of phrasal rhythm and its capacity to treat the same word sometimes as strong and sometimes as weak. But he could recognize this variability only in words like those that appear in the list above, not as a potential feature of *all* monosyllables. He apparently continued to believe that the kind of accent a word receives in poetry (and presumably in speech) is inherent in the word rather than a function of the rhythmic phrase in which it figures.[10]

As they became more sensitive to the rhythmic subtleties of English and more open to the attractions of metrical variation, the poets developed a much more natural line, one that can accommodate many more English phrases than the strictly alternating pattern could ever do. Instead of the "poor," inflexible meter of five consecutive unalterable feet, which early critics thought impoverished when compared with the resourceful and various Latin hexameter line, iambic pentameter with its three standard variations became an extraordinarily flexible metrical form. Poets such as Sidney and Shakespeare soon realized—their practice tells us more than all the critical commentary written in their time and for centuries afterward—that these three kinds of variation could, in skillful combination, produce an inexhaustible register of possible English lines using all the familiar and imaginable tones of English speech.

In practice they discovered that the iambic pentameter line may be composed of four different kinds of iambic feet—the normal iamb, the spondaic iamb, the pyrrhic iamb, and the inverted iamb (trochee); that speech junctures may occur before, after, or between the syllables in any of these kinds of feet; that all of them represent, not a fixed ratio of weak and strong, but a range of possible relative strengths as various as the language can provide; and that these kinds of feet may appear in a given line in many (but not all possible) combinations. There must, of course, be enough normal iambs to establish the basic rhythm; the last foot, and almost always the second foot, must avoid trochaic variation; pyrrhic feet cannot follow one another; successive trochees imperil the iambic pattern; a pyrrhic foot preceding or following a trochaic foot has an awkward sound. But with these restraints, none of which is absolute, virtually any arrangement of the four basic types of iambic foot will result in a line that an experienced listener or reader can perceive as iambic.

Here, as examples, are numerous lines in which the iambic patterning is composed and varied in notably different ways. I have divided the lines into feet to show how variously the foot-divisions cut into the phrasing. And I have used a stress system of three levels to show of what different kinds of stresses iambic or trochaic feet can be composed. (In general, throughout this book, a foot is called spondaic [or a spondaic iamb] when its first syllable has a secondary [ˇ] degree of stress and its second syllable receives a primary [ˊ] or secondary stress. Only very rarely will we encounter two successive primary stresses.)

1. Of hand, of foot, of lip, of eye, of brow (Shakespeare, Sonnet 106:6)

2. Mȁkes blȃck | nȋght beaȗ|teȍus, ȁnd | hẽr ȍld | fȃce nȇw
    (Shakespeare, Sonnet 27:12)

54

3. Age rules | my lines | with wrin|kles in | my face   (Drayton, *Idea*, 22:2)

4. Now at | the last | gaspe, of | loves la|test breath   (Drayton, *Idea*, 31:9)

5. Feare, sick|nesse, age, | losse, la|bour, sor|row, strife

     (Spenser, *The Faerie Queene*, I.ix.44.6)

6. Shall with | his owne | blood price | that he | hath spilt

     (Spenser, *The Faerie Queene*, I.v.26.4)

7. While grace|full pit|ty beau|ty beau|tifies   (Sidney, *A and S*, 100:4)

8. Do thou | then (for | thou canst) | do thou | complaine

     (Sidney, *A and S*, 94:5)

9. How long | a time | lies in | one lit|tle word!
10. Four lag|ging win|ters and | four wan|ton springs
11. End in | a word: | such is | the breath | of kings.

     (Shakespeare, *Richard II*, 1.3.213–15)

12. Here's a | young lad | fram'd of | ano|ther leer

     (Shakespeare, *Titus Andronicus*, 4.2.119)

This system is so flexible, and so well adapted to the patterns of English intonation, that we cannot always say precisely whether a given foot is spondaic or normal, pyrrhic or normal, trochaic or iambic. It is in the nature of this pattern, as the poets of this generation developed it, to allow some discretion to the speaking voice, just as in English speech the same set of words may be spoken differently even by the same person in different moments or moods. In the foregoing list "Shall with" (6) and both instances of "Do thou" (8) might well be given various readings, and there is hardly any limit to the changes a skillful actor might ring on "one" in 9. The weaker-stronger pattern admits of almost infinite variability, especially when it allows occasional divagations into stronger-weaker and tolerates phrasal combinations of syllables that freely spill over the foot-divisions.

Further contributing to the variability of iambic pentameter lines are four other sources of flexibility, each of which will be treated later in detail. First, feminine endings, rare from Surrey to Sidney, are used more often by later poets, and their effect is to provide another variant that makes the pattern a little less rigidly iambic. Second, poets more and more come to see the attractiveness of using a distinctively trochaic phrasal rhythm within the iambic framework to break up, or to provide a kind of counterpoint for, the basic iambic movement of the line (for example, 7 above). Third, the midline break is treated with increasing freedom as the poets explore its possibilities; it appears much more often after the fifth, sixth, or seventh syllable, or earlier than the fourth, or even later than the eighth; sometimes it vanishes entirely. Fourth, the increasing and more radical use of enjambment extends the line's phrasal connections beyond the line itself and results in another kind of counterpoint between the line and the sentence (or at least the sizable clause). All of these devices have two far-reaching effects: they enormously increase the range, vitality, and expressive capacity of the iambic pentameter—and they begin to undermine it.

To see more graphically how poets of the sixteenth century gradually became aware of the expressive resources of the iambic pentameter line, we can look more closely at some verse techniques of Surrey, Gascoigne, Spenser, and Sidney. Even so regular a metrist as Surrey could, as the occasion required, resort to purposeful variations. Gascoigne, at his best, writes a speechlike verse that flows through long series of highly regular lines with energy and ease. Spenser fashions a melodious metrical art not closely tied to speech but elegant in sound and vigorous in movement. But it is Sidney's verse that, for the first time in English, succeeds in adapting impassioned speech to iambic meter.

CHAPTER 4

Flexibility and Ease in Four Older Poets

Surrey

Yt was the night that sownd & quiet rest
Had throwgh the erth the wearied bodies caught;
700   The woodes, the raging seas war fallen to rest;
When that the starrs had half ther course declinde;
The feldes whiste, beastes, & fowles of dyvers hwe,
& what so that in the brode slowghes remaine,
Or yet amonges the busshie thickes of bryer,
705   Laid downe to slepe by sylence of the night,
Gan swage ther cares, mindles of travailes past.
Not so the sprite of this Phenician,
Unhappie she, that on no slepe coold chaunce,
Nor yet nightes rest in eie nor brest coold entre;
710   Her cares redowble; love rise & rage againe,
& overflowes with swelling stormes of wrathe.
Thus thinkes she then, thus rowles she in her minde:
"What shuld I do? shall I now beare the skorne
For to assaye myne old wooers againe,
715   Or humblie yet a Numyde spouse require,
Whose mariage I have so ofte disdainde?"   (*Aeneid*, IV.698–716)

Surrey is writing before the rules Gascoigne was to codify had so
narrowed poetic practice that major syllables all found their way to
stressed positions and minor ones to unstressed, with circumflex syllables
occupying either kind. Surrey's original verse is highly regular, though
never quite so formulaic as Gascoigne's, Googe's, and Turbervile's. But in
translating Virgil he feels obliged to capture some of the mysterious and

ominous atmosphere of Virgil's Latin. He is also writing in blank verse, the form he devised for this occasion, and the absence of rhyme permits a flow of the sentence pattern over the line-endings that is unprecedented in English verse. This is most notable in lines 702–6, where one main clause takes three syllables—"The feldes whiste" (hushed)—and the next is developed through four-and-a-half lines with great deliberateness.

The importance of these lines is signaled as well through skillful metrical touches. After four quite regular iambic lines, in line 702 the variations begin to mark moments of tension:

> The feldes | whiste, beastes, | & fowles of dyvers hwe,
> & what | so that | in the | brode slowghes | remaine,
> Or yet amonges the busshie thickes of bryer,
> 705   Laid downe | to slepe by sy|lence of | the night,
> Gan swage | their cares, | mindles | of travailes past.

The unusual break in line 702 between the short clause and the long one is made all the more striking by its occurring so early as after the third syllable and in the middle of a spondee. In the next line we find what look like two successive pyrrhic feet ("that" is redundant; "what so that" means "whatsoever") followed by a slow spondee. Line 704 is regular, with some strong iambs, but the initial spondees of the next two lines, the pyrrhic in 705, and the medial trochee in 706 all invite a portentous reading of these impressively Virgilian lines. The rest of the passage is more conventional: most of the stresses fall on strong nouns, adjectives, and verbs; circumflex words like *not, no, nor, coold* (could), and *thus* occupy unstressed positions and permit the feet that include them to be heard as variously iambic or spondaic. Where *nightes* and *love* occupy the unstressed position, the result is more unambiguously spondaic. Pyrrhic feet, on the other hand, result when stress falls on syllables like *on* (708) and *in* (712).

In his translation of the *Aeneid* especially, but in some other poems as well, Surrey shows himself a resourceful metrist, experimenting with expressive possibilities. Far from being a mechanical filler-up of beats, he seems aware that what he wishes to say can be intensified by metrical variations in diverse combinations, by varying the position of the midline break, and, now and again at least, by permitting the segments of complex sentences to establish a rival interest to that of the line. But this does not happen often. Surrey's usual procedure is to keep the matter contained within the quatrain. "The Poets Lament for His Lost Boyhood" is organized this way in elegiac quatrains most of which enlarge on some remembered aspect(s) of Surrey's boyhood at Windsor: "The large grene courtes," "The statelye sales: the ladyes bright of hewe," "The palme playe," "The graveld ground," "the medes yet spredd for rewthe," "The secret groves," "The wyld forest," "The voyd walles eke," and so on. The lengthy elegy on Wyatt proceeds similarly from topos to topos, its seven central stanzas beginning with "A hed," "A visage," "A hand," "A toung," "An eye," "A hart," and "A valiant corps." Indeed, Surrey's mastery of the sonnet depended on his sensitivity to the organization of its parts. It is only occasionally, when the energy of Virgil's syntax forces him to it, that Surrey's phrasal units exceed the line and we feel the power of the sentence as an alternative authority to that of the well-behaved metrical line:

> With this the yong|mens cou|rage did encrease,
> And through the dark, | like to | the ravening wolves
> Whom raging fu|rie of | their empty mawes
> Drives from | their den, | leaving | with hungry throthes
> Their whelpes behinde, among our foes we ran,
> Upon | their swerdes, | unto | apparant death;
> Holding | alway the chiefe | strete of | the town,
> Coverd | with the | close sha|dowes of | the night.   (*Aeneid,* II.455–62)

The unusually complex sentence structure seems to encourage more than the usual number of metrical variations (marked above), presumably to register both the violence of the first lines and the furtiveness of the last. This is an impressive early instance of a tradition whose grander metrical departures would come later.

Gascoigne

The mid-century return to strict regularity, animated now and then only by an initial trochee or a weak spondee, implies that the poets interpreted the variations of Wyatt and Surrey not as expressive but as metrical blemishes. They *liked* the regular 4 + 6–syllable line and the way English phrases could be arranged to fit line-segments of just these sizes. Gascoigne, the best poet of this period, is clearly interested in bringing together natural English and the verse line by finding ordinary phrases that fit the pattern and combining them smoothly into passages that do not violate our sense of the way English flows. He is willing to tolerate small distortions, "but not so hardly as some use it" (*Certayne Notes of Instruction,* in G. Smith, vol. 1, 53). Gascoigne is not likely ever to write four lines as contorted as these, which Nicholas Grimald addresses to his mercifully dead mother:

> Me, brought to light, your tender arms sustained,
> And with my lips your milky paps I strained.
> You me embraced, in bosom soft you me
> Cherished, as I your only child had be. (Hebel and Hudson, 51)

Gascoigne will not pay so high a price to keep the metrical pattern (and the rhyme); he will keep it, but by means of a more astute selection of phrases and sentence patterns:

> This is the *Queene* whose onely looke subdewed,
> Her prowdest foes, withowten speare or sheeld/
> This is the *Queene,* whome never eye yet viewed,
> But streight the hart, was forst thereby to yeelde/
> This *Queene* it is, who (had she satt in feeld,
> When *Paris* judged, that *Venus* bare the bell,)
> The prize were hers, for she deserves it well/
> ("The Vanities of Bewtie," *Works,* vol. 2, 526)

Neither the superfluous commas (mainly to signal the midline break and the line-ending) nor the grammatical anomaly in the last three lines impedes the speechlike flow of the passage. The only word that sounds at all out of place is the archaic "withowten," but this is a minor license compared to the distortions forced on the language by Grimald.

Such poetry is lively, resourceful, even elegant. It negotiates convincingly the marriage of English phrasing and metrical pattern. It says nothing especially interesting, but it says it with commendable grace, and it may have set a pattern for gracious verse compliments paid to the queen and other patrons. Shakespeare may have intended a parody of such passages when he has Mercutio say of Queen Mab:

This̄ is̆ | that very Mab
That plats the manes of hor|ses̆ in̄ | the night,
And bakes the elf|-lŏcks in̄ | foul̄ slŭt|tish hairs. . . .
This̄ is̆ | the hag, when maids | lĭe ŏn | their backs,
That press|ĕs thĕm | and learns them first to bear,
Mák̄ing | them wŏ|mĕn ŏf | gŏod cár̆|rĭ age.
This̄ is̆ | she—   *(Romeo and Juliet,* 1.4.88–95)

Shakespeare's passage is much freer with spondees, pyrrhics, and trochees
(marked above); it locates the break more variously, and it begins and ends
in midline. These devices, along with the richer and more playful imagery,
help to portray the mercurial excitement of the character Mercutio. Com-
pared with Shakespeare's lines, Gascoigne's seem relatively unenterpris-
ing, but the ease and naturalness of the earlier poet's work, its masterly
joining of phrase and line, was a necessary step in the development of the
iambic line. Probably a generation of poets and listeners had to hear with
pleasure the falling together of the natural accent and the metrical beat
before the creative departures from the norm could provide more extrava-
gant pleasures.

Spenser

The mellifluous line and stanza of Spenser fall essentially within this
tradition. Despite his odd-sounding experiments in quantitative verse and
in the more wayward meters of *The Shepheardes Calender,* Spenser's tens of
thousands of iambic pentameter lines are notable for their regularity, flu-
ency, and grace. Perfectly willing, as we have seen, to distort natural word
order, he rarely writes a line whose daring metrical variations imperil our
sense of the iambic norm. In *The Faerie Queene,* line after line, stanza after
stanza, canto after canto, book after book, the art of iambic pentameter
unfolds smoothly and swiftly. Neither the grammatical inversions nor the
occasional spondees, pyrrhics, and trochees slow down the lively pro-
cession of lines. Here is a representative stanza, selected almost at random.
(Una, accompanied by her attendant lion, is seeking aid from two helpless
women, mother and daughter, who are too frightened to grant her
"entrance.")

Which when | none yield|ed, her | unruly page
With his | rude clawes | the wicket open rent,
And let her in; | where, of | his cruell rage
Nigh dead | with feare, and faint astonishment,
5   Shee found them both in darkesome corner pent;
Where that | old wo|man day and night did pray
Upon | her beads, devoutly pen|itent:
    Nine hun|dred *Pater nosters* every day,
And thrise | nine hun|dred *Aves,* she was wont to say.   (I.iii.13)

A number of technical points should be noticed about this passage. First, the midline breaks usually occur after the fourth syllable (five times in the eight pentameter lines), but—and this distinguishes Spenser's lines sharply from those of Gascoigne and his contemporaries—even in that position they do not have a uniform strength: line 3 pauses at a semicolon, lines 4 and 7 after commas, but line 5 can easily be read without a pause. Furthermore, these lines that break at the fourth syllable, and thus emphatically enforce the iambic segmentation of the line, are balanced by lines that, breaking at the fifth syllable (like line 1 and perhaps line 6), follow a more trochaic inner rhythm. Line 8 uses only trochaic words between its first and last syllables, and the ninth line delays the usual break in the middle of the alexandrine until after the seventh syllable, confirming the contrary rhythm of the stanza's last two lines. For Spenser and for most good poets after him, one proof of the craftsman's skill lies in the graceful combining of lines like these—lines that pause in one place with lines that pause in another, lines that pause decisively with those that pause weakly or not at all, lines that follow an internal iambic pattern with those that follow a contrary trochaic structure. (See Chapter 14, below.)

Second, despite a few grammatical inversions (lines 2, 3–5, 5, 8–9) and an unnecessary auxiliary verb (line 6), despite what in other poets might seem the awkwardness of beginning a long sentence with "Which," Spenser's management of the complex sentence is authoritative and unambiguous. Even the change of focus from the pictured scene to the old woman's devotions presents no problems of logical or syntactic continuity. Spenser's syntax is almost always strong and perfectly controlled, and Paul Alpers' rule for reading it is a wise one: "Follow the path of least resistance" (84). Although the connectives are sometimes a little obscure (for example, "where, of" in line 3), they present no serious difficulty to the reader caught up in the developing design. Stanzas often consist, as here, of several independent clauses; but whether they are combined into one composite sentence or separate into closely related sentences, we are likely to feel that, together, they constitute one phase of the poem's insistent forward movement. The sense of the stanza is compelling, and our curiosity about the sentence and what it will reveal as it unfolds drives us through the lines to each stanza's end.

Third, metrical variations in Spenser are used conservatively, for the sake of variety and for the momentary marking of significant actions or images. Although a modern reader is tempted to hear possible trochees in "Which, when" (line 1) and "where, of" (line 3), these and all other feet in the stanza can sustain an iambic reading. In line 2, "rude clawes" and, in line 4, "Nigh dead" seem likely spondees, along with "old wo-" and "Nine hun-," but they do not keep the stanza's rhythm from seeming dependably regular. Only line 2 makes any notably expressive metrical gesture. Its initial pyrrhic-spondee combination puts emphasis on the lion's murderous equipment, but the actual rending of the door is performed in three perfectly regular iambic feet: "the wicket open rent." The violence of this action is conveyed not through any alteration of the iambic pattern but through a quickening of it that results from Spenser's employment of trochaic words and of vowels and consonants that somehow sound appropriate: the short vowel *i* followed rapidly by the guttural stop *k*, a quick vowel, and another stop *t*; then, after a tense *o*, by another stop *p*, another obscure vowel, then a nasal, a liquid, a short vowel, a nasal again, and a stop. It is hard to claim that such a combination would always produce the kind of effect that Spenser manages here, but here the disruptive grammatical inversion and the succession of clipped syllables appropriately mirror the lion's violent action. The four syllables that follow, "And let her in," are still iambic, still quick in their movement, but the earlier tension is gone, replaced by this simplicity, as Una steps through the broken door and looks around. What she sees—the two terrified women, one old and blind, the other a deaf-mute, understandably cowering in a corner—is still conveyed through regular iambic lines. The workmanship is remarkably skilled, but Spenser's mind is always intent on the next thing in the story. Nothing is dwelt on too long, and the metrical effects are always kept subordinate to the advancing sentence, the unfolding fable.[1]

To be sure, Spenser does, on one occasion or another, compose lines that are striking for their metrical expressiveness. He can use medial trochees effectively:

As budding braunch | rént frŏm | the native tree   (II.ii.2.6)

A sea of blood | gúsht frŏm | the gaping wownd   (I.viii.16.6)

He frequently employs the pyrrhic-spondee combination:

Wĭth hĭs | lòng taýle . . .   (I.xi.16.9)

Ănd wĭth | stròng flíght . . .   (I.xi.18.3)

Wĭth hĭs | bròad saýles . . .   (I.xi.18.7)

His trusty sword he cald | tŏ hĭs | làst aíd   (I.xi.42.2)

He even uses this figure twice in one line to represent, by its pattern of increasing stress through four syllables (see below, p. 69), the appearance of the dragon in Book I:

Where stretcht he lay upon the sunny side
Ŏf ă | grèat híll, | himself | lĭke ă | grèat híll   (I.xi.4.6)

Spenser's spondees are usually composed of monosyllables, typically an adjective and a noun—"fìrst treé" (I.xi.48.1), "làte fíght" (I.xi.52.7), "deàre kníght" (I.xi.1.7), or these five from a single stanza (49) in Book II, Canto i: "drỳ dróps," "sàd wórdes," "dèad córpse," "greène grás," "Gày steéd"—but in the pattern of three successive stressed syllables that occurs when a spondee follows an iamb, any of the stressed positions may be occupied by a noun, a verb, or an adjective (and sometimes by other important words):

And in her ríght | hànd bóre | a cup of gold   (I.x.13.2)

All keepe the bróad | hìgh wáy, | and take delight   (I.x.10.5)

Loe wher your fóe | lìes strétcht | in monstrous length   (I.viii.45.3)

That threé | yàrdes deépe | a furrow up did throw   (I.viii.8.6)

And take away this lóng | lènt loáth|ed light   (II.i.36.7)

64

When Spenser gives us monosyllabic verbs or nouns in unstressed positions, with rather unimportant words following, we may be tempted to hear a trochaic pattern, but often the lines can (and if so, probably should) be read as iambic:

Gan her | admire, and her sad sorrowes rew   (I.vi.31.4)

That good | Knight of | the Red|crosse to | have slain   (I.vi.41.4)

'Henceforth, sir knight, | take to | you wonted strength   (I.viii.45.1)

Clearly, such lines must be read quietly and quickly to avoid making much of the unstressed noun or verb, but that is exactly the kind of reading that Spenser's stanzas, with their long, flowing periods, impose on the reader. Certainly, to read most such phrases as trochaic would scar the smoothness of Spenser's melodious verse. (See Chapter 13, below, especially pp. 190–97.)

In such lines Spenser is following closely the accentual patterns of English phrasing, which permit stress to fall on words not ordinarily considered important. Similarly, in lines like these he lets the metrical pattern direct stress to just those syllables which, once accented, reveal the particular meaning of the phrase:

Ah deare Sansjoy, next dearest to Sansfoy,
Cause of | my new | griefe, cause | of my | new joy   (I.iv.45.4–5)

The first foot of the second line must be trochaic, but later in the line the iambic pattern requires that we stress *new* rather than *griefe* in the first phrase but *joy* more than *new* in the second, and this requirement brings out meanings that would be lost in a more complacent reading—for example (as if the line were prose):

Cause of my new griefe, cause of my new joy

Sidney

Sidney's variations are quite another story, his concerns almost the reverse of Spenser's, for he cares much more about the expressive phrase than about the forward-flowing current of sentence, stanza, or sonnet. In

Astrophil and Stella, where his handling of iambic pentameter appears at its most innovative, his theme is not the adventurous progress of a model knight but the intense inner suffering of an unsuccessful lover. Accordingly, he tries to render the lover's anguish with an immediacy not often aimed at in literature of this period, when vividness, as Rosemond Tuve long ago assured us, was not nearly so essential a consideration as appropriateness. But Sidney's is an art of the foreground, as compared to Spenser's more distant, panoramic tableaux. Each sonnet in *Astrophil and Stella* is a portrait of the agitated lover, whose agitation is registered most forcibly in the voice—that is, in the syntax and meter.[2]

In fact, Sidney is the first poet in English to give us consistently, throughout a long poem, a verse in which the emotion of the speaker is indicated both by the variety of his sentence forms—exclamations, imperatives, questions, self-interruptions, repetitions, impassioned short sentences, long logical ones—and by the extent to which he permits these energetic constructions to impose their excitement on the meter. Every reader of Sidney must be aware of his lively syntax, his extravagant apostrophes and exclamations: "O Love" (11), "O eyes" (42), "Fly, fly, my friends" (20), "What he?" (54), "Fie, school of Patience, fie" (56), "O voice, O face" (58), "I, I, O I may say, that she is mine!" (69), "but lo, lo, where she is" (79), "O fate, O fault, O curse, child of my bliss" (93), "But, but (alas)" (96); and

> Guess we the cause: 'What, is it thus?' Fie no:
>   'Or so?' Much less: 'How then?' Sure thus it is   (74)

And the lustful outburst:

> 'But ah,' Desire still cries, "give me some food."   (71)

Most of these examples retain the iambic pattern; indeed, if we imagine the words spoken with appropriate feeling, most of the phrases widen the disparity between stressed and unstressed monosyllables. One does not say "O Love" or "O voice, O face" or "O fate, O fault, O curse" as quietly and matter-of-factly, or with as little difference in stress, as one normally says, "The grass is green." On the other hand, in this context "give me some food" presumably asks us to give all four syllables a high degree of

66

tension-generated stress. The animated syntax thus has the effect not only of forcing on the meter spondaic and trochaic variations but also of strengthening some iambs and increasing the range of stress available to an impassioned speaker.

And, in fact, one of the striking features of Sidney's verse is its strong iambic character. The sonnets in *Astrophil and Stella* contain many lines that are not only metrically regular but divide naturally into two-syllable iambic segments:

I may, I must, I can, I will, I do   (47:10)

Her eyes, her lips, her all, saith *Love* do this   (52:3)

'What now sir fool,' said he. 'I would no less   (53:7)

That lap doth lap, nay lets, in spite of spite   (59:10)

O how for joy he leaps, O how he crows   (17:12)

Even when one or more of the unstressed syllables is intensified, we still often hear the same five-unit pattern, different now only in that it accommodates spondees among the more conventional iambs:

It is | mŏst trúe, | that eyes are form'd to serve   (5:1)

Mìlk hánds, | rŏse chĕeks, | or lips | mŏre swĕet, | mŏre rĕd   (91:7)

From this regular base the lines vary in patterns that can be easily distinguished. There is the line in which the two-syllable unit is not always kept phrasally intact; instead, a trochaic word (or more than one) spills over the foot-division:

Fair eyes, sweet lips, dear heart, | thăt fŏol|ĭsh Ī   (43:1)

I might, | ŭnháp|py̆ wŏrd, | O me, I might   (33:1)

Brake bow, brake shafts, | whĭle Cú|pĭd weĕp|ĭng sáte   (17:8)

Lines like these may incorporate pyrrhics:

My mouth doth wă|tĕr, ănd | my breast doth swell   (37:1) or both pyrrhics and spondees, in different parts of the line:

Wĭt leárns | in thee perfĕc|tiŏn tŏ | express   (35:12)

or trochees, initial or medial:

Beáutĭes, | which were of many carats fine   (16:2)

Into your rimes, | rúnnĭng | in rattling rows   (15:6)

or trochees and pyrrhics:

Rích ĭn | the treas|úre ŏf | deserv'd renown   (37:9)

In all these examples, the metrical variations stand out in strong relief from lines that are otherwise very regular. This is typical of Sidney's practice and distinguishes it sharply from that of Shakespeare and most later poets, who do not feel so constrained, when they vary some feet, to make the others perfectly iambic.

Among the other metrical figures that Sidney uses frequently, and always within the framework of a strong iambic line, are some that involve two successive feet:

TROCHEE-SPONDEE

Stélläs fàir háir, | her face he makes his shield   (13:10)

My wits, | quíck ĭn vàin thoúghts, | in virtue lame   (21:4)

SPONDEE-IAMB

Flȳ, flý, mȳ friénds, | I have my death wound; fly   (20:1)

Rích fòols thĕre bè, | whose base and filthy heart   (24:1)

In all these, the four syllables in question are set apart syntactically from the others and seem to compose a double foot. Although spondees are often followed by iambs later in the line, it is when this combination appears in the first two feet that they seem most decisively separated from the words that follow.

PYRRHIC-SPONDEE

Otto Jespersen pointed out nearly a century ago (264) that English poets frequently use this combination and that the pattern requires us to stress each successive syllable more strongly than the last. (See also Winters, 1957, 94.) This 1–2–3–4 pattern may seem to violate the iambic scheme, but since 2 is stronger than 1, and 4 stronger than 3, it conforms exactly to the requirement that the second syllable of each pair be pronounced more strongly than the first. In practice, this combination becomes a chief resource for all later poets who want to vary the iambic line. As with the double-foot variations cited above, we can hear in the following examples how very regular the other feet are:

In her cheek's pit | thou didst thy pitfold set   (11:11)

That busy arch|er his sharp ar|rows tries   (31:4)

That giv'st no better ear | to my just cries   (65:2)

IAMB-SPONDEE

This combination places three strongly stressed syllables together. When the phrase in which this happens is set off from the rest of the line or appears at the end, the emphasis it receives is likely to be especially strong.

My young mind marred, | whom *Love* doth windlass so   (21:2)

To show her skin, lips, teeth | and head so well   (32:11)

Sweet lip, you teach my mouth | with one sweet kiss   (80:14)

PYRRHIC-IAMB

This combination is not often noticed, for usually the pyrrhic functions simply as a weak iamb. Yet in lines like the following the effect of the weakly stressed foot can be to hurry the voice on to the more strongly stressed one that follows and thus to give it more emphasis, or to throw into relief the stressed syllables of the feet that precede and follow it, or at least to speed up that part of the line, or the whole line, in preparation for some more emphatic word or phrase to come.

And as a Queen, | who from her pre|sence sends   (107:9)

Such coltish gyres, | thăt tŏ mў bírth | I owe   (21:6)

And then descried the glist|rĭng ŏf his dárt   (20:13)

TROCHEE-IAMB

This combination is familiar to all readers of iambic pentameter, especially when it appears in the first four syllables of the line. The initial trochee occurs so frequently, and so often in combination with a pause after the fourth syllable, that we may hear these four syllables as a kind of double foot, though the same metrical figure may also appear later in the line, usually after a pause; it may also appear more than once.

Vírtŭe ălás, | now let me take some rest   (4:1)

And I, | mád wĭth dĕlíght, | want wit to cease   (81:13)

By love were made | ápt tŏ cŏnsórt | with me   (95:11)

Stella | foód ŏf mў thoúghts, | heárt ŏf mў heárt   (87:2)

TROCHEE-TROCHEE

This unusual metrical figure, the double trochee, is regarded as "un-metrical" by some generative metrists (see Chapter 13, below, pp. 197–98 and note 10), but it appears occasionally in the work of many poets, from Sidney on, who evidently feel comfortable with it. The last example below may even be a "triple trochee."

With sword of wit, | gívĭng woúnds ŏf | dispraise   (10:10)

That her clear voice | lífts thў fáme tŏ | the skies   (12:8)

Stellă foód ŏf | my thoughts, heart of my heart   (87:2)

Deár, whў máke yŏu móre ŏf | a dog than me?   (59:1)

PYRRHIC-TROCHEE

This is an even more unusual combination, which many readers will feel subverts the iambic pattern. It probably occurs, however, in

Thăt tŏ wín ĭt, | is all the skill and pain   (12:14)

SPONDEE-PYRRHIC

Not a common figure, but it occurs:

Poor passenger, | pass now thereby I did   (20:9)

Copartner of | the riches of that sight   (48:6)

Most of the examples listed above exhibit their patterns in phrases somewhat isolated from others in the line, but the same patterns may be incorporated without phrase-breaks into a more continuous line:

trochee-spondee	Grief but *Love's* winter livery is, the Boy	(70:7)
spondee-iamb	Girt fast by memory, and while I spur	(49:10)
pyrrhic-spondee	That her Grace gracious makes thy wrongs, that she	(12:6)
iamb-spondee	And strange things cost too dear for my poor sprites	(3:11)
pyrrhic-iamb	Why dost thou spend the treasures of thy sprite	(68:5)
trochee-iamb	Gone is the winter of my misery	(69:7)

And several of these combinations may overlap, as in the following line, which includes a spondee-pyrrhic, pyrrhic-iamb, iamb-spondee, and spondee-iamb:

Cry, 'Vic|tory, | this fair | day all | is ours.'   (12:11)

Such a line, freed from what is in most of Sidney's lines a quasi-obligatory iambic segmentation, looks forward to the much more flexible line-making of Shakespeare and other poets.

For in no poet later than Sidney do these variations seem stretched so consciously, as a rule, on so definite an iambic frame. He seems more aware of the line's segments than any competent later poet, so that where they apparently have a gestalt for the whole line and know instinctively whether a given line fits the meter, without any conscious counting of syllables or checking of feet, he seems almost to proceed foot by foot with the same painstaking attention to each segment as Gascoigne.

Still, Sidney's readiness to try out a greater variety of metrical patterns constitutes a crucial step in the history of iambic pentameter. His purpose is clear: to find a metrical language suited to the anguished meditations of a tormented lover who speaks to himself, to his beloved, to sleep, to his eyes, to various implicated entities, always in tones that express or betray his emotional agitation. We can see how this works in Sonnet 39:

> Cŏme sleép, | Ō sleép, | the certain knot of peace,
> The baiting place of wit, the balm of woe,
> The poor | man's weálth, | the prisoner's release,
> Th'indifferent Judge between the high and low;
>   With shield of proof | shiĕld mĕ | from out the prease
> Of those | fĭerce dárts, | despair at me doth throw:
> O make in me those civil wars to cease;
> I will | goŏd trí|bute pay if thou do so.
>   Tăke thoú | of me | smooth píl|lows, sweetest bed,
> A chamber deaf to noise, and blind to light:
> A rosy gar|lănd, and | a weary head:
> And if these things, as being thine by right,
>   Mŏve nŏt | thy heavy grace, thou shalt in me,
>   Livĕlĭer | than elsewhere, *Stella's* image see.

Here we can find the firm iambic base, unvaried in lines 2, 4, 7, 10, and 12, and in many segments of other lines, from which the most telling phrases make their expressive departures. Whereas in reading Spenser our interest is likely to be in the onward progress of the action or thought, here the spondaic phrases invite us to linger over some images and to take them at their full value: "Come sleep, O sleep," "man's wealth," "fierce darts," "good tribute," "smooth pillows." The trochees register sudden accesses of passion—"shield me," "Livelier"—that lift the tone of the poem into a higher dimension of emphasis. The framework within which this higher emphasis records its passionate sound is still, in most respects, conservative, even stiff. The strong iambic beat, the insistent break after the fourth syllable (in ten of the fourteen lines), and the grammatical inversions ("with shield . . . shield me," "at me doth throw," "make in me those . . . ," "Take thou of me," "thou shalt in me . . . see") suggest that, despite the metrical variations, the formal variety of the verse is still subject to strict conventions. Nevertheless, again and again in this sonnet, and throughout the sequence, phrases and lines strike us as genuinely speechlike. The set phrases that compose Sidney's catalogs (lines 1–4 on sleep, lines 9–11 on the things that minister to it) do not clog the lines and are periodically freshened by those impassioned phrases ("Come sleep . . . shield me . . . O make in me," and so on) that carry the speaking frame of the poem forward.

In other poems, too, Sidney succeeds remarkably well, largely through the intelligent application of his variant metrical patterns as they respond to his flexible syntax, in persuading us of the authenticity of Astrophil's cries, curses, prayers, and resolutions.

> But while I thus with this | young li|on played,
> Mine eyes (shall I say curst or blest) beheld
> *Stella*; now she is nam'd, need more be said?　　　　(16:9–11)
>
> Fly, fly, | my friends, I have | my death | wound; fly　　(20:1)
>
> With how | sad steps, | O Moon, thou climb'st the skies,
> How si|lently, | and with how wan a face,
> What, may | it be that . . .　　　　(31:1–3)
>
> Fie, school | of Patience, fie, your les|son is
> Far far | too long to learn | it with|out book　　(56:1–2)
>
> I, I, | O I may say, that she is mine.　　(69:11)[3]
>
> Curst be | the page from whom | the bad | torch fell　　(105:11)

Sidney's interest in verbal patterning is always strong, but extreme examples are usually not very speechlike, as some of his critics have observed. In these two lines, for example,

> Most sweet|-fair, most | fair-sweet, | do not alas,
> From coming near those Cherries banish me,　　(82:7–8)

"alas" does not seem the most apt ejaculation, and the patterning in the first line is certainly precious. Nevertheless, the enjoyment that Sidney and his readers could take here from the reversal of *sweet* and *fair* that still leaves *sweet* stressed both times and *fair* unstressed while *most* moves from unstressed to stressed could easily lead to effects in which the meter makes more significant choices. In, for example, "Do not, O do not from poor me remove" (42:7), the second *do,* falling in a stressed position, receives stronger emphasis than the first and makes the appeal more intense.[4]

Through such arrangements of meter and phrasing, Sidney finds a convincing tonal correlative for the psychological states of the Petrarchan lover and opens up iambic pentameter to a whole new order of English speech.[5] Compared with the earlier uses of iambic pentameter for narrative, dramatic, and even lyric verse, Sidney's discovery of the meter's powers is revolutionary. The next step, as we can see in retrospect, will be taken by Shakespeare, who pours new life into the relatively inert dramatic poetry of his age by adapting and developing to a much finer pitch and for incomparably grander purposes Sidney's art of expressive metrical speech.

"Expressive speech," however, implies that what is spoken must be plausible as words delivered by someone under imaginable circumstances, not just a series of phrases that might as well come out of one person's mouth as another. Expressive language animates its point of view, changes the speech from that of a puppet, an icon, to that of a person, a character who seems a believable representation of a human being. From this point on—say, 1591, when Sidney's sonnets became widely known—the criterion of dramatic plausibility, of mimetic speech, will be an important one for poetry. Even where certain locutions are stylized or otherwise implausible, readers will usually require some kind of verisimilitude in the tone of poems; they will want to feel that the words of the poem could imaginably be spoken by someone under real circumstances.[6] Before this time, that was evidently not a requirement: the words of a poem could be taken as telling something but this might mean telling as a sign or a proclamation tells, not necessarily as a person speaks. So narrative could falter; early dramatic characters could expound as if they were written histories, or philosophize like tracts; the criterion of verisimilitude hardly came into play. The introduction of that criterion, with the special pleasure that accompanies it, the pleasure of recognizing tones of voice that we have used ourselves or heard others use, is sometimes observable in Chaucer, in Wyatt, or in Gascoigne, but it seems not to constitute a primary aesthetic end for English poets until we arrive at Sidney's love poetry. From then on, English poetry is different, and iambic pentameter plays a central role in that difference.

CHAPTER 5

An Art of Small Differences:
Shakespeare's *Sonnets*

All three of Shakespeare's major poems contribute something to Shakespeare's dramatic verse art. The contribution of the *Sonnets,* on which this chapter will focus, is of special importance, for in these poems Shakespeare learned, presumably in the early 1590s, after he had written a few plays and the narrative poems, to fashion a reflective verse whose resonances would thereafter be heard in the speeches of his dramatic characters. But the long poems, too, show Shakespeare learning to pull the thread of the descriptive and narrative sentence through the rhymed metrical stanza. In *Venus and Adonis,* for example, the opening quatrain often expands a theme with description and imagery; the narrowing couplet shepherds it toward its conclusion:

> Hot, faint, and weary, with her hard embracing,
> Like a wild bird being tam'd with too much handling,
> Or as the fleet-foot roe that's tir'd with chasing,
> Or like the froward infant still'd with dandling,
>   He now obeys, and now no more resisteth,
>   While she takes all she can, not all she listeth.   (559–64)

To develop a stanza is very different from developing a speech or a scene, but the poet who has learned how to do the first will have learned much about the second. In these early poems, to be sure, the lines are still all rhymed, equal in length, and spoken (almost always) by the same narrative voice. The greater metrical freedom of the plays (see Chapters 7–14) will permit Shakespeare to make a much more complex and richly expressive dramatic verse art.[1]

The metrical art of Shakespeare's *Sonnets* is not radically different from that of *Astrophil and Stella*. At their best, these poems exhibit greater smoothness and flexibility; the midline break is more variously located; the movement of the verse is more frequently varied by feminine endings and enjambments; the arguments are marked by less exclamation and self-interruption and by more continuous and more philosophical reflection; and the treatment of feeling finds phrases that convey still more subtle nuances. Sidney's varieties of agitation give place to a richer array of troubled feelings expressed in a wider range of metrical designs. But it is basically the same kind of verse—iambic, pentameter, using the by now standard metrical variations to portray the diverse intensities of a lover's protracted and continually changing obsession (or to compose hymns to sources of power). Sidney's sonnet sequence was published in 1591, and its direct influence on Shakespeare's is clear.

The greater agitation of Sidney's speaker is marked by a considerably more emphatic tone of voice, one measure of which is the more enthusiastic punctuation in Sidney's sonnets. Ants Oras has provided convenient counts of the number of times Elizabethan poets have placed commas or stronger punctuation after the different syllables in their lines. It turns out that in their respective sequences Sidney and Shakespeare use exactly the same number of punctuation marks (686), and they place them after the successive syllables as shown in Table 1.

These figures are fairly close and support the suggestion that Shakespeare's metrical practice in the sonnets is not very different from that of Sidney. Shakespeare uses more punctuation (and, presumably, pauses) after the sixth, seventh, and especially the fifth syllables, Sidney more after the second and eighth, and generally after even syllables, which is what we would expect from so iambic a poet. Sidney, however, uses considerably more strong punctuation ("punctuation marks other than commas" [3]), especially after the even syllables (see Table 2). When we observe that all these calculations are made for Sidney's 102 pentameter sonnets as against Shakespeare's 153, it is clear that (if they, or their editors, are using punctuation marks in more or less the same way) Sidney's work seems far more heavily punctuated, hence far more heavily emphatic, and Shakespeare's more smooth and gentle in its discourse: a conclusion likely to be borne out by anyone's reading of the poems.

TABLE 1.

All Internal Punctuation Marks

	1	2	3	4	5	6	7	8	9	Total	First Half[a]	After Even Syllables
Sidney	16	111	23	315	37	134	11	34	5	686	71.7%	86.6%
Shakespeare	14	61	17	312	90	154	20	14	4	686	67.8%	78.9%

[a] Here, and in Table 2, "First Half" means the ratio of pauses after the first four positions to pauses after the last four.

TABLE 2.

Strong Pauses (all punctuation except commas)

	1	2	3	4	5	6	7	8	9	Total	First Half	After Even Syllables
Sidney	2	21	4	51	1	26	1	11	1	118	66.7%	92.4%
Shakespeare	1	15	5	23	10	8	1	1	1	65	80%	72.3%

Like other Elizabethan poets, Shakespeare must have been struck, when *Astrophil and Stella* was published in 1591, by Sidney's appropriation of natural speech-tones to convey the anguished moods of a courtly lover. As the feelings in Shakespeare's sonnets are, on the whole, more subtle and quietly ambivalent, the meter is more restrained and yet more flexible; it proceeds by way of small differences, quiet additions or withdrawals of emphasis. The phrasing is extremely various; that is, we hardly ever find the same phrasing-patterns in successive lines (except for deliberate echoes), and the movement from line to line and quatrain to quatrain permits us to savor a great many line-forms. The midline break appears in different places, and the successive phrases establish remarkably varied groupings of syllables and stresses. For example:

> How like a winter hath my absence been
> From thee, the pleasure of the fleeting year!
> What freezings have I felt, what dark days seen!
> What old December's bareness everywhere!　　　(Sonnet 97:1–4)

Each of the first two lines has a third-foot pyrrhic, but the lines have very different rhythms because of the initial trochee in the first line and the enjambment at the end of it, which lets the phrase run over into the second line, carving the lines into two phrases of different lengths. Although "my absence been" and "the fleeting year" are phrases of similar syllabic structure, they sound quite different because "been" is lightly stressed and the phrase of which it is part continues over the line-ending, whereas "year" ends an emphatic phrase. The next two lines vary the music further: spondees in line 3 slow the movement, and the fourth line makes its unhurried way through tense vowels and clustered consonants that invite the voice to delay the line through seven syllables, then to pause perhaps, and to finish with a more swiftly moving "everywhere!" The midline breaks are muted; to the extent that they occur, they may be felt between phrases as follows: in line 1, after the fifth syllable; line 2, after the second; line 3, strongly after the sixth; line 4, marginally after the seventh. Such "breaks," however, may amount to nothing more than hesitations, and the spondaic and trochaic intensifications require not so much an increase in volume as full and slow articulations of the normally unstressed syllable. The phrasing, too, invites us to voice the contrasts between *fleeting* and *freezing, felt* and *seen,* and to give extra emphasis to the stressed syllable of some iambic feet: *win-, freez-, dark, old, -cem-, bare-,* and *ev-*. If we arrange the lines into a scansion that inserts spaces between its component phrases, we get something like this:

```
  ⁄ ⌣ ⌣ ⁄ ⌣      ⌣ ⌣ ⁄ ⌣ ⁄
  ⌣ ⁄    ⌣ ⁄ ⌣     ⌣ ⌣ ⁄ ⌣ ⁄
  ⌇ ⁄ ⌣    ⌣ ⌣ ⁄    ⌣ ⁄ ⌇ ⁄
  ⌣ ⁄ ⌣ ⁄ ⌣ ⁄ ⌣    ⁄ ⌣ ⌣
```

The duration of the spaces will no doubt vary with the reader. But almost any reading must show how diversely the syllables of this quatrain combine into phrases, and the phrases into iambic lines.

Like Sidney, Shakespeare occasionally writes lines composed stolidly of iambic feet:

Of hand, of foot, of lip, of eye, of brow   (106:6)

But his usual practice is to vary the pattern from one line to the next, to rise to a height of expressive variation in one line and then subside in the next, or to follow such a scheme of excitement, aroused and then allayed, through a whole quatrain or sonnet. Shakespeare is not prodigal of medial trochees in either his poems or his plays; initial trochees appear at least once in all but nine sonnets, but medial trochees are reserved for more special uses and places. They frequently appear late (in the last six lines) and serve as signals of a heightened intensity that must then subside quickly or slowly, depending on how many lines the sonnet has yet to go.

And see thy blood *warm when* thou feel'st it cold   (2:14)

Yet do thy worst, old time; despite thy wrong,
My love shall in my verse *ever* live young.   (19:13–14)

Or, if they sing,'tis with so dull a cheer,
That leaves look pale, *dreading* the winter's near.   (97:13–14)

In some of the sonnets, the metrical patterning achieves a truly remarkable complexity and subtlety—in Sonnet 29, for example:

Whén ĭn | dĭsgráce | wĭth fór|tŭne ănd | mèn's éyes,
Ĭ áll | ălóne | bĕwéep mў óut|căst státe,

And trou|ble deaf | heaven with | my boot||less cries,
And look | upon | myself | and curse | my fate,
Wishing | me like | to one | more rich | in hope,
Featur'd | like him, | like him | with friends | possess'd,
Desi|ring this | man's art, | and that | man's scope,
With what | I most | enjoy | content|ed least;
Yet in | these thoughts | myself | almost | despising,
Haply | I think | on thee, | and then | my state,
Like to | the lark | at break | of day | arising
From sul|len earth, | sings hymns | at hea|ven's gate,
   For thy | sweet love | remem|b'red such | wealth brings,
   That then | I scorn | to change | my state | with kings.

Throughout this poem the meter tends to depart from the normal pattern in the odd lines and to return in the even lines, especially in the lines that end the quatrains and the final couplet. In the first quatrain, line 1 incorporates an initial trochee, a pyrrhic, and a spondee, but line 2 returns us to normal, varying the regular rhythm only with a final spondee; line 3 goes further afield than line 1, rising to a height in the monosyllabic "heaven," which concludes one phrase while the other syllable in its foot begins the next phrase. This trochaic pattern that links two phrases is not unusual: Shakespeare uses it more than two hundred times in his poems and plays. (See below, Chapter 13, pp. 199–202.) Nevertheless, it stretches the foot, momentarily jeopardizes our sense of the meter, and thus serves to represent in metrical form the emotional disturbance Shakespeare is describing in this line. The return of line 4 to a very regular rhythm seems, in contrast and in context, expressive of the speaker's despair. But the sentence continues: through line 5, with its initial trochee and its expressive spondee; through line 6, with its echoing initial trochee but a more regular conclusion; through line 7, which echoes the spondee of line 5 (and perhaps of line 2) in two of its own. By this time the metrical pattern of three successive stressed syllables (usually ⌣ ⌣ ⌣) has become an audible motif. Line 8, the most regular in the poem, continues the practice of returning us to a norm so far associated with the speaker's forlorn and lonely state.

The sentence, however, which all this while has been elevated in pitch, drifting through one modifying phrase after another, waiting for the main clause and especially for the verb that will resolve it, at last in line 9 breaks through to the significant conjunction "Yet"; and as we arrive at a string of words that promises shortly some grammatical resolution of the growing syntactical tension, we find a medial trochee followed by a feminine ending and an initial trochee in line 10. The whole effect of this sequence (especially after line 9's initial trochee, though the meter is temporarily restored in the next two feet) is to give us the momentary illusion of having shifted to another, a falling, meter:

Yĕt ĭn | these thoughts myself | almŏst | dĕspīsĭng,
Hăplў . . .

This turn of metrical events brings the self-dissatisfaction to a troubled climax, but the resumption of regular meter in the last four feet of line 10 no longer carries the tone of melancholy we saw earlier in even lines; rather, it seems on the verge of something imminent and admirable, which does indeed materialize in the spirited line 11. This line, with its initial trochee, feminine ending, and enjambment, swings speedily into line 12, regular except for its midline spondee. Here the pattern of three consecutive stressed syllables reappears, not in the least obscured by the comma after "earth." All these three-syllable figures stand out from the more usual pattern: "one more rich," "this man's art," "that man's scope," "earth, sings hymns." And the same pattern reappears twice in line 13 (as in line 7)—here (as in line 12) no longer expressive of grief and sadness but full of intense joy and celebration, and yielding finally to a more blessedly regular concluding line. But even this one faintly echoes the three-syllable pattern, as though with a muted contentment, in "then I scorn" and "change my state."

In effect, Shakespeare has provided a metrical structure whose most significant component figures change color as the poem changes its tone; like most sound effects in poems, they reinforce whatever mood or feeling the poet is expressing, but what is remarkable here is the poet's power to make the same metrical effects convey quite opposite feelings as the poem's outlook alters.

As this discussion suggests, one of the striking sources of Shakespeare's art is its power to make the most of small differences—of stress, of pattern, of feeling. This power makes itself felt especially in the faint increases or fallings-off of stress that we hear in a string of words, so that we sometimes hardly know which of two syllables in a foot receives greater stress:

> *Shall I* | compare | *thee to* | a summer's day?
> *Thou art* | *more love*|ly and | *more tem*|perate (18:1–2)

However we resolve these choices, the phrasal delicacy forbids thumping. The speech-tones imitated in the sonnets are almost always those of quiet, intimate speech, so that it is hard to imagine even those poems in which the poet's voice is raised being given a really thunderous delivery:

> Take all my loves, my love, yea take them all:
> What hast thou then more than thou hadst before?
> No love, my love, that thou mayst true love call;
> All mine was thine, before thou hadst this more. (40:1–4)

This is still quiet speech, inflected by feeling, and the distinctions of force, of volume, of emphasis, that we observe between stressed and unstressed syllables are made within a smaller register of loudness and softness. Nowhere in the sonnets do we find the roaring speech of Sidney's "O how for joy he leaps, O how he crows" (17:12) or "Fly, fly, my friends, I have my death wound; fly" (20:1) or even that of Hotspur's "Till fields, and blows, and groans, applaud our sport" (*1 Henry IV*, 1.3.302) and certainly not of Lear's "Blow winds, and crack your cheeks; rage, blow" (*King Lear*, 3.2.1). The register is smaller; it omits the louder reaches of speech. But within this register the subtlety with which English inflection can convey feeling is explored perhaps more fully than any other English poet has ever even tried to do.[2]

If Shakespeare learned from Sidney the art of emphatic speech as a medium for troubled feeling, from Spenser he probably learned the softness and musical grace that result from the skillful use of pyrrhic feet. The strong iambs and spondees rise from a base in which some of the feet have yielded their claims to speech-stress (though they still retain their position as feet that count in a string of five metrical feet):

> Nor did I won|der at | the lily's white,
> Nor praise the deep vermi|lion in | the rose;

They were but sweet, but fi|gures of | delight,
Drawn after you, you pat|tern of | all those.   (98:9–12)

In such lines the weakness of one foot is likely (though not certain) to be redressed by strength in another. The first three pyrrhics cited above, for example, by their very weakness direct attention to "lily," "rose," and "delight"; the fourth recedes from the special emphasis given to the first syllable of the key word "pattern" and leads to the important spondaic phrase "all those." Pyrrhic feet in Shakespeare or Spenser thus function as elements in a system in which any two-syllable segment may have almost any rhythmic contour and degree of emphasis, so long as the basic pattern (weaker-stronger) continues to be heard in most of the feet in a passage and usually in most of the feet in a line. Furthermore, the system accommodates pauses, usually at the ends of phrases; and these pauses or hesitations, often signaled by punctuation, may occur between feet (1, 2, 3) or between the syllables of any sort of foot—iambic (4, 5), pyrrhic (6, 7), spondaic (8, 9), or trochaic (10, 11):

1. Lo thus by day my limbs, by night my mind   (27:13)

2. Than this rich praise, that you alone, are you   (84:2)

3. As his triumphant prize—*proud of* this pride   (151:10)

4. If thou couldst answ*er*, "*This* fair child of mine   (2:10)

5. To witness du*ty, not* to show my wit   (26:4)

6. Hath mo*tion, and* mine eye may be deceived   (104:12)

7. Pitiful thri*vers, in* their gazing spent   (125:8)

8. Shaking their scratch'd *ears, bleed*ing as they go   (*V and A*, 924)

9. Ere beauty's dead *fleece made* another gay   (68:8)

10. And the firm soil *win of* the wat'ry main   (64:7)

11. By praising him *here who* doth hence remain   (39:14)

Within his essentially quiet register, Shakespeare makes full use of the possibilities: the reticent pyrrhics, the assertive spondees, and the energetic trochees. These terms do not describe closed categories which two-syllable units always either do or do not enter, but tendencies of stress which though sometimes obligatory (as in first-foot occurrences of trochaic words like "Roses," "Gentle," "Featur'd") are usually more in the nature of invitations to the performing reader (whether the performance is public or silent) to distribute stress according to these patterns: to lean somewhat heavily, say, on the characterizing adjective or adverb to form a spondee ("And with *old* woes *new* wail . . ." [30:4]); to stress the even syllables very distinctly where the sense calls for it ("But if the while I think on thee . . ." [30:13]); or to vary from one kind of foot to another as the sense and phonemic constitution of the syllables require ("Àll lóss|ĕs ărĕ | rĕstóred . . ." [30:14]).

No sonnet exhibits Shakespeare's metrical art more tellingly than Sonnet 116, in which all the usual varieties of feet occur and sometimes in unexpected combinations. Here, with some problematical phrases unmarked for the moment (along with the normal iambic feet), is one way the poem might be scanned:

> Lét mĕ | nŏt tŏ | the mar|riăge ŏf | trŭe mínds
> Admit imped|imĕnts, | love is not love
> Which al|tĕrs when | it alteration finds,
> Or bends | wĭth thĕ | remŏ|vĕr tŏ | remove.
> O no, | ĭt ĭs | an ever fixed mark
> That looks on tem|pĕsts ănd | is never shaken;
> Ĭt ĭs | the star to every wand'ring bark,
> Whose worth's unknown, | althŏugh | his height be taken.
> Love's not Time's fool, though rosy lips and cheeks
> Within his bending sickle's compass come,
> Lŏve al|tĕrs not | wĭth hĭs | brĭef hoŭrs | and weeks,
> But bears it out | ĕvĕn tŏ | the edge of doom:
>   If this be er|rŏr ănd | upon | mĕ próved,
>   I never writ, nor no | man ĕ|ver loved.

The unusually large number of pyrrhic feet—at least one appears in each of the first eight lines and in two later lines—indicates the quiet, confidential tones in which this sonnet, or most of it, is meant to be uttered. The delicacy of lines 3–4, for example—of their thought as well as their sound—could not survive a noisy delivery. This quietness of manner suggests that other phrases, too, that might elsewhere be granted heavier stress are muted to the level of pyrrhics: "not to" (1), "it is" (5, 7). The pyrrhic feet, however, help other phrases to stand out in bolder relief: "it is" performs this service for the decisive iambs of "an ever fixed mark"—the tone is resolute, absolute, certain, and is echoed two lines later in "It is the star." The contrast between the muted pyrrhics and the positive iambs contributes to the impression of very clean and distinct assertions being made in the poem (there can be no doubt: love is like this). The pyrrhics also set off some spondees ("-riage of true minds") and "with his brief hours"); in both these instances the force of the monosyllabic adjective is enhanced by the preceding pyrrhic. The effect is to intensify the feeling with which the speaker is testifying to the truth and passion of love.

And yet these contrasts, these absolutes, nag at the mind a bit; something in the fit of meter, rhetoric, and theme is not quite right. The metrical irony of "brief" is inescapable; "brief hours" takes much longer to say than "and weeks" and seems to describe longer moments of time. The line in which the poet says "Love alters not" is full of metrical accelerandos and retards. If "brief" invites such ambiguous reading, the only other monosyllabic characterizing adjective, "true," may do the same. The very form of the opening statement casts doubt on the speaker's certainty: not "the marriage of true minds allows of no impediments," but "Let me not . . . Admit" them. Whatever you or others say about obstacles to lasting love, I deny that they can trouble true lovers. But if the wording here enforces an uncertainty, so does the meter. Along with the pyrrhics, iambs, and spondees we have so far noted, the poem includes three phrases whose meter is highly problematical.

1. "Let me not to": The trochee-pyrrhic beginning is very unusual in Shakespeare's poems or in Elizabethan poetic practice generally. For the iambic meter to be kept at all after such a beginning is not too easy, so the whole sonnet begins on a metrical razor's edge, as if the poet were conceding at once: this is going to be a difficult argument. The first line and a half then recover the iambic thread.

2. But "love is not love" presents more problems. How are these words to be said? Perhaps "lóve ĭs | nŏt lóve" or "lóve ĭs | nŏt lóve" or "lóve ĭs | nŏt lóve" or "lóve ĭs | nŏt lóve." If we were not constrained by the rhyme to keep the last foot iambic, we might even imagine "lóve ĭs | nŏt lŏve," etc. The difficulty of deciding among such alternatives may have the effect of casting some doubt on the speaker's certainty about love. Coming

as it does just after he has refused to admit impediments, the phrase impedes the line.

3. "Love's not Time's fool." Here, too, we may feel that the stresses could fall on any or all of the four syllables: "Lŏve's nŏt | Tĭme's fŏol" or "Lóve's nòt | Tĭme's fóol" or "Lóve's nŏt | Tĭme's fòol," and so on. Whatever we decide, the tone here, as in line 2, can hardly escape sounding to some degree tormented, scarred with true feeling; the competing stresses reflect competing views of love.

These three problematical phrases contrast markedly with the metrical ease of the rest of the poem. The first one gets us off to a shaky start, but the phrases that follow establish the meter again; the second leads into a notably graceful passage of muted iambs and pyrrhics; and the third gives place to the most sustained series of iambic feet in the poem (within which, however, in line 10 the major words are trochaic). In lines 11–12, the claim that "Love alters not" seems faintly belied by the metrical alteration in line 11 and perhaps by the rhetorical climax of line 12, which is signaled by the poem's only medial trochee. Love, by this time, is something to be endured till doomsday, which seems a strange way to speak of the same love that in lines 1–8 found such lyrical imagery. Lines 13–14 are unexceptional metrically, but their extravagant and illogical claim may serve to reinforce the perception that the poem is being spoken from a point of view deeply involved. After all, the truth or error of these statements about love has nothing to do with whether or not the poet has "writ"; and if the definition of love is mistaken, it does not follow that "no man ever loved"; if love is not like this, the poet seems to say, then there is no such thing as love; this is the only way love can be. The extravagance of such a proposition may cast doubt on the reasonableness of its proponent, especially when other elements of the poem draw us in the same direction.

What we find, then, in Sonnet 116 is a remarkably eloquent presentation of the view that love is absolutely constant, reinforced by numerous metrical indications of constancy but undermined by several metrical counterindications and also by some peculiarities in the form and reasoning that the argument takes. Working against the argument, too, is the evidence of most of the other sonnets—what they say and what they intimate about the complexity and ambivalence of passionate feeling. In view of all this, "true love," understood as an immovable constant, appears to be only a wished-for ideal, a mark, a star, not a realized state of affairs in human experience. Indeed, between line 4 and line 10 the poem's very argument seems to say this, to set an abstract "Love" above the reach of human loves, a Love whose quality and character ("worth") are not intimately understood by most wandering barks, by most lovers, although they love in its name (take its "height"). There seem, in fact, to be three orders of love: (1) Love, remote and ideal, under whose star all lovers love; (2) "the marriage of true minds," constant and eternal, faithful till doom to something more enduring than "rosy lips and cheeks"; (3) ordinary sublunary passion that "is not love" if it "bends with the remover to remove," if it "alters when it alteration finds." Despite the opening suggestion of a "marriage" between "true minds," the poem soon begins to focus on the constancy of one lover who remains constant even though the other is untrue (lines 3–4), and it never returns us to a view of two constant lovers, never again seems to regard that as possible.

Of the three kinds, the poet contends that only the second kind, not the third, is "love"; and he says, in effect, "I am absolutely certain that this is the way love is." His absolute assurance, however, is asserted in the face of his own knowledge that most human loves are not like this; it is not the carefree, self-assured statement of a man perfectly secure in his belief, but an insistence against all the evidence, and the meter's strong problematical passages reflect the problematical character of this absolute view of love.

We can meet in Shakespeare's histories and tragedies characters equally absolute. When Hamlet hears from the Ghost that his father has been murdered, he is eager to know just how:

Haste me to know't, that I with wings as swift
As meditation, or the thoughts of love,
May sweep to my revenge.   (*Hamlet*, 1.5.29–31)

Lysander, in *A Midsummer Night's Dream,* ought to know better; it is he, after all, who dimly perceives that truth which Sonnet 116 tries not to admit: "The course of true love never did run smooth" (1.1.134). But, not long after, on going to sleep a few paces from Hermia, Lysander swears, "end life when I end loyalty" (2.2.63), only to wake, a few lines later, in love with Helena. The pattern is common in Shakespeare, and no playwright is better at presenting resolute subscribers to faiths that the light of day is not kind to.

And the *Sonnets*, though not dramatic,[3] are inherently dynamic; the speaker is constantly contending, either with an intractable world and its ways of frustrating his affections, or with his own mixed feelings. Sonnet 116 is not different in this respect from most of the others; it only seems more noble for its explicit defense of a view of love that is often implicitly admired but is not borne out by all the rest. Above all, the doom of mortality is a perpetual threat, even in Sonnet 116. The strategies used to thwart it—love, children, poetry—are sometimes said to be entirely successful, but the truth of organic aging, withering, decaying, dying is at least as prominent in these poems. Poetry, children, love may do much, but the picture we derive from the *Sonnets,* as from the plays, is of human beings, beautiful and energetic, achieving and lost, asserting their bright resistance to a determined mortality. Sonnet 116 presents the case for believing that human feeling might partake of a permanence and purity that are outside nature. The case is a strong if hopeless one, and no one has argued it more eloquently than Shakespeare; but the *Sonnets* as a group work against it, and even within Sonnet 116 the equivocal meter and the extravagant argument cast doubt on the speaker's claim. These are deep waters, to be sure, and different readers will navigate them differently; what seems clear and certain is that, whatever subtle views the *Sonnets* develop, the equally subtle meter plays a crucial role in reinforcing, undermining, or modifying them.

If this discussion has ranged beyond metrical matters, it is because questions of style and meaning bear largely on meter. The complex figurative language Shakespeare uses—especially his strong imagery—continually magnifies the intensity and emphasis with which his characters' words must be spoken. The *Sonnets* use these figures to convey feelings more intimate, more private, and more problematical than Shakespeare had usually treated in his early plays. Complex turns of argument reveal a speaker often divided in his feelings, but only some of the divisions are explicitly recognized. Undertones of ambiguity haunt these poems, whose ingenious exploration of paradox and antithesis has seemed to most readers to betray more than mere ingenuity. In addition, the association of the speaker's feelings with imagery of the sea, of growing things, with natural cycles of day, season, and year, and with many other ranges of reference suggests that the intricate arguments and clever wordplay are being used to address affections and forebodings that are linked with a larger world.

The plays Shakespeare wrote from the middle 1590s on show how skillfully he could involve the characters' complex inner feelings (and the softer tones of private reflection) in their public actions and conflicts presented on the stage. Instead of merely announcing decisions, characters from Richard II to Olivia to Hamlet to Othello often take us into the psychic council chambers in which they are reached. Their feelings take form on the stage or give signs of having been anxiously arrived at. The language in which they admit to divided feelings or disturbing passions is the language of "silent thought," now for the first time conveyed from the sonnet to the theater, in dialogue as well as in soliloquy. That is, something of the tone and movement we "hear" in the silent sonnet read from the page enters and inflects those voices of rant and passion we hear from the living stage. It is the difference between the beautifully rendered stylish debates of *Love's Labor's Lost,* in which the characters successively take up formal positions, and the more casual remarks of Hippolyta on hounds' voices or Theseus on the imagination, in *A Midsummer Night's Dream:*

> Never did I hear
> Such gallant chiding; for besides the groves,
> The skies, the fountains, every region near
> Seem all one mutual cry. I never heard
> So musical a discord, such sweet thunder. (4.1.114–18)

> I never may believe
> These antic fables, nor these fairy toys. . . .
> And as imagination bodies forth
> The forms of things unknown, the poet's pen
> Turns them to shapes, and gives to aery nothing
> A local habitation and a name. (5.1.2–3, 14–17)

The quiet voice of reminiscence or experience, the muted tones, the pyrrhic dips, the spondaic gravity, the metaphorical and figurative surface, all the stylistic regalia of troubled reflection familiar from the *Sonnets* make their presence deeply felt in the plays that follow, and contrast sharply with the more declamatory self-appraisals of Tamburlaine or Richard III.

The effect of these devices—variously developed and combined during the rest of Shakespeare's career—is greatly to increase the range of what is happening on stage, by giving even to a villainous character such as

Claudius a language and tone inaccessible to characters invented only a few years earlier. What Claudius says to Laertes as he draws him into his plot to kill Hamlet seems to spring from personal reflection on the dynamics of love and resolution:

> Not that I think you did not love your father,
> But that I know love is begun by time,
> And that I see, in passages of proof,
> Time qualifies the spark and fire of it.
> There lives within the very flame of love
> A kind of wick or snuff that will abate it,
> And nothing is at a like goodness still,
> For goodness, growing to a plurisy,
> Dies in his own too much. That we would do,
> We should do when we would; for this 'would' changes,
> And hath abatements and delays as many
> As there are tongues, are hands, are accidents,
> And then this 'should' is like a spendthrift's sigh,
> That hurts by easing.   (*Hamlet*, 4.7.110–23)

This is not to suggest that Claudius is a more deeply meditative and therefore more sympathetic character than we have usually thought. The style he uses is a common resource of Shakespeare's characters in this period, not an indication of his particular sensibility. As one critic puts it: "We cannot judge the degree of a character's imagination by the quality of his utterance" (Bethell, 1952, 64). The style, nevertheless, suggests a reserve of private observation and insight on the part of any character who can use it and thus contributes to our sense of the character and of human beings generally as harboring unrevealed depths and contradictions. This illusion of quiet depths, which is secured in large part by the metrical delicacy we have been reviewing, is the chief gift of the *Sonnets* to the plays.[4]

90

CHAPTER 6

The Verse of Shakespeare's Theater

Invisible, Spoken, Patterned

If English poems of this period assume readers who know and care about love, mortality, fortune, adventure, power, authority, and verse form, plays cast spectators in a somewhat different role. Spectators *see* the action with their eyes, *hear* the verse (and prose) with their ears, and *imagine* the rest; readers see nothing but text and imagine all the action and all the sound. Verse form in English is realized aurally and visually (though all too often it is seen and not heard). Having read many sonnets, we can spot another by its shape on the page and by reading a line or two to recognize its accentual pattern. Similarly, after reading a few stanzas of *The Faerie Queene,* we take it on faith that all the rest of them for hundreds of pages would, if we were to inspect them more closely, turn out to have the same meter. Surveying a poem visually, we do not have to check more than a few lines aurally. Of course, we may be wrong about part of it: some of the lines may be unmetrical or written in a different meter. But our procedure is not meant to be foolproof, only to serve as a practical guide, a source of probably reliable information, a way of scanning the ground before we examine it more precisely. It is what we do when we look at poems.

But verse heard from a stage is different. Early writers of tragic verse for the theater were insufficiently aware of the distinction, and they saw no harm in transferring didactic verse, with all its nondramatic features, to the English stage. The long, stolid speeches function like extended stanzas or sections to advance the action (which is often only an argument). But, sooner or later, playwrights are bound to absorb two inescapable facts about dramatic verse. First, the paradox that in the theater, a world in which action and characters are almost miraculously made visible, verse becomes *in*visible, unmeasured by the eye. Second, it comes to us not in silence from a page we read with our eyes or imagine ourselves speaking, but sounded by human voices other than our own.

These differences are fundamental, both for iambic pentameter and for prose, the two main formal modes of dramatic speech in this period. We cannot *see* the difference between these modes as we watch the drama unfold, and even the clues of rank and genre (for example, prose as a vehicle for comic low persons) become less and less trustworthy; the actors must help us *hear* the difference. So long as the verse is rhymed or at least endstopped, and we hear the actors pause at the end of a line, we can follow the invisible verse even when it builds up sentences as elaborate as Marlowe's. We learn to hear the lines as lines of verse, as measures of spoken language, not as words transferred from a paragraph, from a page. But we never know what is coming next—not, at least, the first time through. We have to keep listening if we want to register when the verse is shifting to prose, when a series of iambic feet is not going to become a full line, when the meter halts or expands, when the usual alternation of weaker and stronger syllables is modified for variety or grace or to show agitation or tenderness. We cannot glance ahead or back, and unless the actors keep helping us, from time to time we may lose the metrical thread.

To be sure, most of us do not follow the verse lines consciously. Iambic pentameter—especially when it is blank—is too subtle and variable to encourage us to stamp our feet in obedience to the beat, but if the actors will keep the meter, our nervous systems can register the continuing metrical pattern even while our more conscious attention is being directed to the action, the characters, and the substance of their words and sentences. Occasionally some metrical phrase or line may stand out with special clarity, and those who enjoy hearing such lines may listen for them or for the continuing iambic rhythm more attentively than the rest of the audience. But one way or another the iambic pattern, measured out in lines that are usually pentameter, will make itself felt in the speeches if the actors do not betray it. The different dimensions of phrase and line, and of line and sentence, can be made audible only if the actors convey to our ears not just the logic and syntax of phrase and sentence, but also the suitably varied and frequently muted meter of the line.

If they do so, we may hear their speeches as verse. But a verse speech in a play is always an odd species. As Coburn Freer has pointed out (25), no dramatic speech has the completeness of a lyric poem. When one speech is concluded, another must ensue; the play is made up of speeches; but "speech" is a term that describes no particular verse form. Although characters in plays may on occasion speak quatrains or sonnets, as Shakespeare's do in *Romeo and Juliet* and in *Love's Labor's Lost,* a speech (or the sequence of speeches that compose a scene) may normally be of almost any length, may be couched in verse or prose (or both), and may or may not embody the formal characteristics we expect of stanzaic poems. In fact, the dramatic terms *speech* and *scene* are not at all descriptive of the form language will take when it is spoken on the stage. Like *line* or *stanza,* they measure language, but the way they measure it is radically different. And, although we can usually see as well as hear when each actor begins and ends a speech, it is only by listening carefully that we can hear, along with the meter in the words, the larger rhythmic curves of emotion that are realized in individual scenes and in the play as a whole.

As we watch a play in the theater, we are also aware that the voices we hear are human voices. Whatever the conventions of our theater, the language spoken by the actors has to be recognizable as human speech. As T. S. Eliot warns (1961, 21): "There is one law of nature more powerful than any of these varying currents, or influences from abroad or from the past: the law that poetry must not stray too far from the ordinary everyday language which we use and hear." The actors must speak intelligible words, phrases, and sentences. In certain traditional types of drama, the utterances presented may be narrow in range and severely stylized, but this was not the case with the English drama. On the contrary, although some conventions still limited the kinds of language characters could speak, the main movement of Elizabethan dramatic dialogue was toward natural speech-tones—indeed, toward a spoken language of the stage that combined natural phrasing and intonation with a high degree of metrical and figurative patterning.

Such natural phrasing had not been an essential ingredient in non-dramatic verse during most of the sixteenth century. What we typically hear in the poetry written between Wyatt and Sidney (as, for example, in *A Mirror for Magistrates* or in many love poems and translations of psalms) is a complaint, a mournful wail spoken by a sufferer who casts a despairing eye over his own discouraging experience or argues for more complaisant treatment on the part of his reluctant lady. The subtle and poignant variations of voice that accompany human emotions, the vocal gestures, are rarely presented with notable complexity. We more often witness an unrelieved outpouring of grief, remorse, or devotion than the modulated utterance in which feelings of different strands participate and which marks a high point of Shakespeare's own presentation of human ambiguity. The speaker of narrative poems takes a long retrospective look at the human events he relates but rarely turns to address anyone, reader or character, who appears as an immediately apprehensible presence. As a result, the voice of most narrative or lyric verse of this period is a single, continuous voice, which says what it has to say briefly or at length but is almost never interrupted or answered; and because it never has to be answered it is normally not held to a common speech.

Drama, by its nature, cannot proceed in this way; it typically involves more voices than one, and these voices must talk to each other. Their idiom must therefore, as Eliot says, not stray too far from believable English tones and syntax. Archaisms, pleonasms, inversions, and other such devices widely used to adjust the phrases of Elizabethan nondramatic verse will sound out of place on a stage in the mouths of native speakers of English. The tendency of dramatic writing actually produced for the stage will be to resist such devices, and Elizabethan drama clearly does so. Although the same words and phrases may, in Shakespeare, have different syllabic values in different lines, and although the syntax of many sentences is probably more elaborate or elusive than the usual sentence spoken by even an especially articulate Elizabethan, the syllabic and syntactical practices of Shakespeare's drama appear, by and large, not to violate but rather to extend the norms of Elizabethan speech. The syllables of some words or phrases *could,* after all, be sounded or heard by Shakespeare's contemporaries in more than one way; the syntax of some spoken sentences *could* be complex or grandiose. These features of English speech that find their way into nondramatic poems can survive as well—perhaps better—in dramatic dialogue. But what about the features that are more specifically verse features? What about rhyme and meter? Since no one talks in verse, what business have they on the stage?

The realistic modern theater (in English at least) would answer these questions decisively. Verse does not belong on the stage. It is too distracting, artificial, estranging, to suit a theater of illusion and empathy. At best it may fit a Brechtian drama of alienation and deliberate challenge. Even Eliot recognized how strongly an audience is likely to resist verse drama. Casting his own plays in a verse whose rhyme soon disappeared and whose meter grew less and less identifiable, he believed that a modern writer of dramatic poetry had to proceed by disguising, possum-like, the fact that he was writing in verse at all.[1]

But the Elizabethan theater was different; its plays were traditionally in verse. Throughout the fifteenth century and most of the sixteenth, English drama, whether play or interlude, folk or court, was mainly written in rhyming forms—in loose tetrameter couplets, rime royal, rime couée, ballad measure, poulter's measure, and the like. The lines were often crude and irregular, and the rhymes roughly measured exuberant strips of language:

> See! here is all the thought that the foolysh urchyn taketh!
> And Tyb, me thinke, at his elbowe almost as mery maketh!
> This is all the wyt ye have, when others make their mone.
> Come downe, Hodge! Where art thou? And let the cat alone!
>
> (*Gammer Gurton's Needle*, 1.5.28–31, in Adams, 474–75)

> Is he gone? Now, by the gods, I will doo as I say!
> My lord, therefore fill me some wine, I hartely you pray;
> For I must drinke to make my braine somewhat intoxicate.
> When that the wine is in my head, O, trimly I can prate!
>
> (*Cambises*, lines 525–28, in Adams, 651)

For unsophisticated spectators, the rhymes must have come down with a pounce. Much of this verse, true to the name later given it, has the same effect as clowns tumbling at a circus. The first rhyme sets us up for a pratfall, and the second meets this expectation with mindless good nature. Experienced readers or viewers may tire of such an empty-headed game. But for an illiterate or barely literate audience, the rhymes make it possible to take pleasure in persistently patterned speech.

And highly patterned speech was congenial to the Elizabethan audience. Rhyme and meter belonged to the class of rhetorical devices they expected to meet in public places. Whether or not they understood that rhyme, meter, and other formal rhetorical schemes had their sources in common speech (we all fall into such patterns now and then), they evidently found them agreeable to listen to. Nevertheless, the movement during Shakespeare's early life is unmistakably toward a verse with diminished rhyme, a less blatant meter, and an increasingly speechlike line-flow. The verse written by Gascoigne for his predominantly prose play *The Glass of Government* (1575) is stanzaic and regular; Peele's *The Arraignment of Paris* (1584) uses rhymed iambic couplets of various line-lengths (and some blank verse). Such playwrights conducted their rhymes with considerable iambic propriety, and by the 1580s the looser tumbling meters had lost their vogue.[2] The preferred verse is much more restrained; combining the gravity of disciplined meter with the pleasure of patterned rhyme, it fashions a dramatic speech that meets the needs of stage dialogue. The extensive rhymed portions of Shakespeare's plays show that such verse, in the hands of a gifted poet, could seem both speechlike and beautifully patterned. The further steps—of doing without rhyme for the greater part of an iambic play, and of writing large segments of a predominantly verse play in prose—would give to a Shakespearean play an even more speechlike texture. But the way was already prepared.

Blank

Until late in the sixteenth century, a play without rhyme would have seemed very odd to an English audience. Rhyme was a necessary embellishment, and only a few enterprising authors at first began to break away from the accustomed practice: Gascoigne by writing a play entirely in prose (*The Supposes,* 1566), and Sackville and Norton by writing one in blank verse (*Gorboduc,* 1561). Both plays forgo the pleasure of rhyme for greater prizes. For Gascoigne, prose permits a much more natural dialogue than verse.[3] For Sackville and Norton, the principal motive for using blank verse may not have been to make their language more natural, though that was to be its ultimate effect for the stage. They may have wished primarily to give their play something of the foreign feeling appropriate to plays of Seneca or to the work of contemporary Italian tragedians, who wrote their Senecan plays in Italian blank verse.

A similar motive prompted writers of nondramatic blank verse, which had been a minor Elizabethan mode, far less often employed than poulter's measure and generally regarded as a "straunge meter."[4] As Tucker Brooke notes, "it was consciously as a strange or foreign metre that blank verse was employed in England throughout the period before Marlowe. It seems to have been valued chiefly as a proper means of translating or simulating the exotic grace of Latin quantitative verse" (187–88), which of course was also unrhymed. Surrey, who introduced it in his translation of Books II and IV of the *Aeneid,* was evidently following the model of a contemporary translation of the second book of the *Aeneid* into *versi sciolti,* the Italian equivalent of blank verse; and most subsequent users of the English form chose it as an appropriate medium in which to translate or imitate Latin originals—either particular authors or "the cool dignity of Latin declamation" (188).[5]

When the shift to dramatic blank verse came, however, its effects exceeded the playwrights' intentions. For one thing, the spectator's relatively frivolous delight in rhyme was replaced by the more austere pleasures of meter. If the viewer was to take in the metrical pattern in this new form, probably the verse had to be endstopped and, in performance, the actors had to make clear where the stresses fell. This was less necessary in the irregular meters of earlier plays and interludes, where easily audible end-rhyme was the chief pattern and earlier stresses in a line could be roughly counted or loosely distributed. But in blank verse, instead of the rhyming click at the end of a line one hears a blank, and the chief rhythmic pattern to be perceived is the meter, which must accordingly be well kept. For a time, therefore, dramatic blank verse, with its tragic subjects and its declamatory delivery, seemed appropriate to a theatrical art of pretentious posturing, not to a drama of recognizable speech and subtle characterization. Blank verse itself must have seemed an odd and empty medium at first, foreign and faulty, lacking in resilience, hardly the verse for a great dramatic literature. It was only when Marlowe began to write plays in this form that some of its wondrous flexibility and force became evident.

Wolfgang Clemen, in his *English Tragedy before Shakespeare,* has carefully analyzed the stages by which Kyd, Marlowe, and others transformed the inert segments of traditional dramatic narrative into passionate poetic speech. *Gorboduc,* the first English play to be written in blank verse, "is a 'Mirror for Magistrates' in dramatic form" (62). The characters all speak in the same stiff, didactic tones, and what any one of them says has no effect on the others (68–73). In later plays written on the same model, characters continue to "'speak past' one another" (69) in argumentative monologues that seem exercises in the public announcement and description of their own predicaments. Whether they speak of their own emotions or of general matters, they use an inflated rhetoric, whose exaggerated mannerisms were probably also reflected in an overemphatic delivery. Contemporary poets and critics use terms like *rant* and *bombast* to describe this style of verse-composition and -recitation. Nashe calls it "the swelling bumbast of bragging blanke verse" and "the spacious volubilitie of a drumming decasillabon" (*Works,* vol. 3, 311–12).

Virtually all speech in such plays is set speech, as Clemen shows, and every speaker of a set speech has an agenda, the items of which must be ticked off in even blocks of long-winded declamation. Such speech is notably unspeechlike: the characters do not address each other as people do in actual life. To be sure, the situations are often highly formal, but the personages are frequently members of the same family and could not always speak to each other so stiffly. Some of this excessive formality persists throughout this period, and many modern readers, accustomed to the looser conversational style of contemporary films, plays, and novels, are still put off by Shakespearean conventions of formal address. But Kyd, Marlowe, and Shakespeare all found ways to connect the patterned verse of drama with a more speechlike language. Eventually, a new style could use some of the old manner's formal features to extend the range, variety, and convincingness of the characters' speech tones, to make characters respond with spirit to each other's words, to distinguish characters by their speeches, and to achieve a grandiloquence beyond the reach of either the earlier inflated verse or ordinary spoken language.

Although other playwrights, notably Kyd with his purposeful development of the dramatic soliloquy (Clemen, 1961, 107–11), helped to make blank verse at home in the theater, it was Marlowe who first loosened the rigidities of dramatic blank verse. In his work, for the first time verse speeches begin to characterize their speakers. As Clemen points out, Tamburlaine is the first notable beneficiary of this technique: the "new passion and drive in Tamburlaine's speeches" disrupts "the static pattern of the old rhetorical structure" (117). The desires of Tamburlaine, Barabbas, and Faustus are made convincing through a dramatic verse of unprecedented power and excitement, and the antagonisms represented on the stage are far more than cardboard conflicts.

Marlowe's achievement in presenting characters whose ambition or lust sounds genuine is partly made possible through long sentences whose dignified segments form strong but separate lines. To take a famous example:

Nature, | that fram'd | us of | four el|ements
Warring | within our breasts for reg|iment,
Doth teach us all to have aspiring minds.
Our souls, whose fa|culties | can com|prehend
The wondrous architec|ture of | the world,
And measure every wand'ring planet's course,
Still climb|ing after knowledge in|finite,
And always mov|ing as | the restless spheres,
Wills us | to wear ourselves and never rest
Until we reach the ripest fruit of all,
That per|fect bliss and sole felic|ity,
The sweet frui|tion of | an earthly crown.

(*Tamburlaine the Great,* Part 1, 2.7.18–29)

As Clemen says: "The scene is built up as a strictly organized dramatic sequence, where the speeches, like massive pillars, both frame and support the statuesque tableau, in which meanwhile only a single slight movement takes place" (126–27). The voice, empowered by passion, never recedes from the high and probably loud level of insistence appropriate to the grandiose claims it is making. But Marlowe's technique represents a significant advance over the frigid uniform procession of five-stressed lines in earlier drama. The mighty Marlovian line is enlivened by skillful threading of a sort of sentence-power through the separate lines and by metrical variations (marked above) that reflect and convey agitation, stress, and violence. Stage speech acquires the surprise of a new dimension as actors do not merely tell us what personages they are supposed to be portraying but impose on us a richer burden of belief. Marlowe's rhetorical verse aggrandizes the ordinary world conjured up by the stage and makes the play's events monumental, hypnotic, enthralling, to a degree never known before on the English stage.[6]

Shakespearean

When Shakespeare's contemporaries read his sonnets from the page, or heard others read them, they must have found it relatively easy to hear the lines as iambic pentameter. In the *Sonnets,* and in the narrative poems as well, all the lines (with perhaps two exceptions in five thousand) are regular—i.e., the variations include only pyrrhics, spondees, trochees, and feminine endings—and most of the lines are endstopped. The plays are very different. It is true that many passages follow the iambic pentameter pattern without making notable departures from it, and an attentive listener can usually hear through most of the plays a steady current of blank verse lines, along with some passages of rhyme. Ophelia can lament Hamlet's apparent loss of sanity in impeccable pentameter verse, as if she were composing a formal dirge:

> Ó, what | a noble mind is here o'erthrown!
> The courtier's, soldier's, scholar's, eye, | tongue, sword,
> The expec|tancy, | and rose | of the | fair state,
> The glass of fash|ion, and | the mold of form,
> The observ'd of all observers, quite | quite down,
> And I of ladies most deject and wretched,
> That suck'd the hon|ey of | his music vows,
> Now see that no|ble and | most sov|ereign reason
> Like sweet | bells jan|gled out of time, and harsh,
> That unmatch'd form, and sta|ture of | blown youth
> Blasted | with ec|stasy, | o woe is me,
> T'have seen what I have seen, | see what | I see!   *(Hamlet, 3.1.150–61)*

Ophelia's grief is conveyed through standard metrical variations that quicken or delay the movement of the line. The lines are all endstopped or syntactically discrete; only the next-to-last is made up of one phrase that completes and a second that begins a thought; each line adds a touch to Hamlet's ideal portrait or to Ophelia's lament for its marring. The euphonious movement of the passage, the lucid imagery (of rose, glass, honey, music, bells), the intensifying spondees, all contribute to the representation of an impassioned yet graceful utterance. The speech is also beautifully formed, the lines one by one building to a rhetorical climax marked by a strong trochee and a culminating half-line phrase:

That unmatch'd form, and stature of blown youth
Blasted | with ecstasy

—after which the part of her sentence concerned with herself resumes ("And I . . . o woe is me") and subsides in heavy self-summary.[7]

Such passages, composed of regular lines, remain central in Shakespeare's metrical drama, and many of his celebrated speeches are written in this style. But many are not. Indeed, in Shakespeare's later plays (from, say, *Troilus and Cressida* to *The Tempest*) we rarely encounter a passage of more than a few lines that does not break the basic pattern in some way. The regular pentameter remains a norm, but a norm from which departures, in certain permissible patterns, are also normal. The art that emerges is unique in the history of iambic pentameter; it is an art initiated in rude form by some of Shakespeare's dramatic predecessors, developed resourcefully by Shakespeare, carried to eccentric extremes by some of his successors—notably, Middleton and Webster—but tempered and finally abandoned by most Jacobean and Caroline dramatists and by every later poet without exception.

The result is an astonishing but rarely noticed paradox—that the greatest of English poets, imitated so slavishly by many writers, is in this respect neglected; much as his successors admire his dramatic verse, they ignore its distinctive metrical features. Poets such as Pope, Wordsworth, Tennyson, and Browning can write many thousands of lines without a single departure from standard iambic pentameter. So could Spenser; so could Shakespeare himself in his nondramatic poems. But the craft of dramatic verse was altogether different, and Shakespeare was one of its earliest practitioners. For short passages in the theater, the ear can tolerate a series of regular verse lines. But, just as in every other aspect of theatrical performance the play must shift from one speed to another, break its tempo, change its characters, its mood, its pace, so the language of the play is required to change its nature from time to time—not only from prose to verse but from standard iambic pentameter to lines of more curious character. No one could have been more aware than Shakespeare, the hardheaded practical man of the theater (see Bentley), of the need for all the elements of his drama, including its metrical language, to be lively, changeable, resistant to obvious and static schematization.

To be sure, the authenticity of Shakespeare's texts is always in doubt.

His apparent indifference to the publication of his plays remains one of the most puzzling facts of English literature. If it tells us anything, however, it is that his primary concern was for how his words and lines sounded in the theater. The texts we have, most of them edited first by Shakespeare's colleagues and then dutifully and sometimes brilliantly by later scholars, provide our only guide to Shakespeare's verse lines and their incorporation in speeches and scenes. Suspicious as we may sometimes be of the texts' authenticity, in most cases they probably show us all we can know of Shakespeare's iambic pentameter. Errors of many kinds may have crept into the texts and may not have been later corrected. But we know far too much to suppose that the texts of any play were once line-perfect or syllable-perfect. The "roughness" of Shakespeare's dramatic verse is a feature of his art—though if we understand its sources and its nature, we may find that it is not roughness at all.

Ophelia's speech, in its metrical context, appears almost excessively constrained, compulsively endstopped, after the fifty lines of agitated prose in which she and Hamlet have been conversing. *Hamlet* is still an early enough play that deviant numbers of syllables or feet do not appear with disquieting frequency, but even here most extended speeches include some departures from pattern. Occasionally a line will seem to lack a single syllable. Extra syllables occur at the midline break (as they never do in the poems); headless lines appear, and even broken-backed lines. Lines that sound iambic but are longer or shorter than pentameter turn up in almost every play, sometimes in large numbers. (See Appendix B.) Short lines often combine to form normal lines, but not always unambiguously. Such split or shared lines often appear at the "hinges" of speeches or scenes, where the speech of one character gives place to the speech of another. Two speeches will share a normal line at such points:

> *Laertes.* It may be death.
> *King.*   Let's further think of this
>
> (*Hamlet*, 4.7.148)

Or there may be an extra syllable before the break:

> *Laertes.* Of my true mo*ther.*
> *King.*   What is the cause, Laertes
>
> (*Hamlet*, 4.5.121)

Frequently, too, a speech will cut off at a short line before the next speech begins with one of normal length:

> King.   Bow stubborn knees; and heart with strings of steel,
>   Be soft as sinews of the new-born babe,
>   All may be well.
> Hamlet. Now might I do it pat, now he is praying.
>
> (Hamlet, 3.3.70–73)

It oftens happens, too, especially in the later plays, that short lines at the hinges will be completed by the next half-line, even as that half-line is itself completed by its own second half. On the stage the phrase just cited, "All may be well" can be heard as waiting for its complementary three-foot segment, which does arrive in the first phrase of Hamlet's speech, though this phrase also initiates another full line. No problem arises here in how to print the lines, even though the conventional printing is unable to call our attention to the pattern just described. But in many cases, as we shall see below (Chapter 8), editors must decide with which of two half-lines, the preceding or the following, to align a middle half-line. With which of the other half-lines, for example, should Claudio's half-line be understood as forming a full verse line?

> Isabella. Or else thou diest to morrow.
> Claudio.   Thou shalt not do't.
> Isabella. O, were it but my life . . .   (Measure for Measure, 3.1.102–3)

The lines before and after these short lines are unmistakably full lines, and an editor who adopts the usual practice of indenting the second half of a split line must decide which two half-lines should be joined in a printed text. But an editorial decision does not resolve the theatrical ambiguity. That is, Shakespeare may have meant us to hear the ambiguity, to hear one line mounted, as it were, on another. Such "squinting lines" are common, but they produce an effect that no manner of printing so far devised can make clear to the reader.

Any account of Shakespeare's iambic pentameter has to cope with the great variety, almost the miscellaneousness, of lines that appear in and around the central verse type. Short lines and alexandrines occur in the midst of speeches, often with expressive force. What sound like iambic lines, both pentameter and short, occur frequently within prose scenes. In Act 4, Scene 3, of *Hamlet,* for example, the King speaks nothing but iambic but not always pentameter lines even when Hamlet is plainly provoking him with his most impertinent prose. In Act 4, Scene 5, both the King and the Queen keep up iambic appearances while mad Ophelia sings and speaks prose in their presence.

But even away from the hinges, in longer speeches where a more regular meter might be expected to prevail, Shakespeare often varies his line-types. When Lear warns Kent to make no further protest against his division of the kingdom,

> The bow is bent and drawn, make from the shaft   *(King Lear,* 1.1.143)

Kent's reply, courteous but fervent, includes several lines that break the usual pattern:

Kent.		Let it fall rather, though the fork invade
145		The region of my heart; be Kent unmannerly
		When Lear is mad. What wouldest thou do, old man?
		Think'st thou that duty shall have dread to speak,
		When power to flattery bows? To plainness honor's bound
		When majesty falls to folly. Reserve thy state,
150		And in thy best consideration check
		This hideous rashness. Answer my life my judgment,
		Thy youngest daughter does not love thee least,
		Nor are those empty-hearted whose low sounds
		Reverb no hollowness.
Lear.		Kent, on thy life, no more.

>   *(King Lear,* 1.1.144–54)

Line 145 has a triple ending; line 148 is hexameter; lines 149 and 151 have extra unstressed syllables before the midline break; line 154 has two such syllables; "wouldest," "flattery," and "majesty" are syncopated to two syllables, "hideous" reduced to two by synaeresis. According to the rather conservative metrical tables compiled by E. K. Chambers (vol. 2, 397–408), the text of *King Lear* includes 191 short lines, 131 lines with extra syllables at the break, and 64 alexandrines (not to mention 580 feminine or triple endings), out of a total of 1,979 blank-verse lines. This means that one line in ten is short, one in fifteen has an extra syllable at the break, and one in thirty-one is an alexandrine, and that in this play these exceptional lines will occur a little less often than once in every five verse lines. If we understand as well that this frequency may be increased by the occasional appearance of other sorts of deviant lines (headless, broken-backed, lines missing a stressed or an unstressed syllable, or lines with double onset or anapests), we come to see that the lines in Shakespeare's later plays diverge from what we think of as regular meter about twenty percent of the time.

Essentially, the verse art of Shakespeare's plays oscillates between the determined and the indeterminate, between "regular iambic pentameter" obedient to rules and an unpredictable mixture of regular and deviant verse lines. Moreover, if iambic pentameter has special dramatic force, it is partly because its own pattern is also as highly indeterminate as a determined poetic meter can be: each line realizes the fixed pattern in highly unpredictable fashion: spondees, pyrrhics, and trochees may or may not appear in one foot or another, and the phrasal breaks and possible enjambments further multiply the variety with which lines may meet the elementary requirements. In a sense, the more deviant patterns (short and long lines, and lines marked by extra or omitted syllables) only extend the degree of indeterminacy inherent in the iambic pentameter line.[8] Furthermore, our frequent uncertainty about the number of syllables in a line (see below, Chapter 10), along with the structurally guaranteed freedom to vary the strength of the stressed syllables and the weakness of the unstressed, contributes to our sense that the metrical principle underlying the art of Shakespeare's dramatic verse is that of great freedom within great order.

The following outline classifies the departures and deviations that appear in Shakespeare's dramatic verse lines. Chapters 7–9 and 11–13 will take them up in order.

I. Departures from iambic pentameter
A. Prose
B. Songs
C. Verse in other meters
II. Deviations from pentameter
A. Short lines (including shared and squinting lines)
B. Long lines
1. Hexameter
2. Heptameter

III. Deviations from iambic
    A. Extra unstressed syllables
        1. At ending
            a. Feminine
            b. Triple
        2. Before midline break
            a. Feminine
            b. Triple
        3. At beginning (double onset)
        4. Elsewhere (anapest)
    B. Omitted syllables
        1. Unstressed
            a. At beginning (headless)
            b. After midline break (broken-backed)
            c. Elsewhere (monosyllabic foot)
        2. Stressed
            a. Fourth syllable omitted
            b. Sixth syllable omitted
            c. Eighth syllable omitted
            d. Tenth syllable omitted
    C. Inverted iamb (trochee)
        1. Ordinary trochees
            a. Initial
            b. Medial
        2. Multiple trochees
            a. Double
            b. Triple
         3. Straddling trochees
        4. Contrary stress (= iambic trochees?)

One effect of these multifarious devices is from time to time to render the meter problematical. Thus, short lines, long lines, and squinting lines momentarily (and sometimes throughout brief passages) *jeopardize our sense of the pentameter*. Lines with extra syllables at midline, or at line-ending, or at line-beginning, or elsewhere, or lines lacking a stressed or unstressed syllable anywhere *jeopardize our sense of the iambic*. They may not come frequently enough to unsettle our perception of the iambic pentameter as the dominant line-pattern, but they are sure to cause us moments of metrical anxiety, moments during which we lose the metrical thread. The hexameter line detains us a shade too long; the short line leaves us wondering if its incompleteness will be attended to by another speaker, or by the same speaker after a pause; the pentameter lines with an extra syllable somewhere or with fewer than we expected may pluck at our metrical attention. None of these is fatal to our sense of the beat; all of them assume that we are experienced listeners and that the actors are performing the play with exquisite concern for the integrity of lines and deviations.

Even in reading a text of a play we may enjoy the experience more if we notice the short lines and try to hear, with our sense of silent timing, which short lines squint, which are completed by the next speaker's first phrase, and which are simply short. But for an acute listener, that metrical uncertainty which is a familiar feature of Shakespeare's later dramatic technique will be most strongly felt in the theater. The principle that verse drama must change its pace and use many deviant line-forms, and often prose and song as well, entails the consequence that it must also run the risk of making listeners uncertain, from time to time, about what they are hearing. Of course, an audience is normally not concerned to analyze; it takes the verse it is given without much reflection, and this is true today of even our most sophisticated audiences, who for the most part ignore the verse to attend to what are thought to be more significant aspects of the play, such as character, theme, imagery, and symbolic design. But if the actors pay only a minimum adherence to the verse form, an audience may not be able, even by the most determined ignorance, to keep from noticing changes in the rhythm of the characters' utterances when they shift from verse to prose, or when the regular five-beat line suddenly gives way to a series of trimeter exchanges. The subtler motions that result from the addition or subtraction of single syllables will be heard only by a few, but they are worth listening for: they may seem, on the whole, to be merely attractive variants to a regular pattern, but they often also serve specific expressive functions, especially that of disturbing the metrical, moral, and psychological peace.

CHAPTER 7

Prose and Other Diversions

Prose

The place of prose in plays mainly written in verse is not as simple as it looks, and it has commanded little attention from Shakespearean critics. For the textual editor, the problem is mainly to decide which word-strings shall be printed as prose and which as verse—no simple task, but surely far easier than that of describing accurately how we experience the unlabeled lines in the theater. There the terms *prose* and *verse* no longer seem quite so clear or so clearly contrary. Normally when we speak of Shakespeare's prose we do not really designate an autonomous form of writing as distinct and well-defined as verse; we mean that other language that Shakespeare writes very well, that part of the Shakespearean drama that is different by not being verse.

As Jonas A. Barish has pointed out (1972), Shakespeare's prose does not change nearly as much as his verse. The later prose is tighter, more serious, less slangy, less involved in word-games, but "the change is largely tonal: the familiar processes of logic, argument, and syntactic patterning have simply been purified of a certain perkiness, and invested with a new solemnity and gravity, while their essential character remains unaltered" (73). The highly figurative patterns of Shakespeare's prose course through the opportunistic forms of the Renaissance English sentence, but they do not need to be adjusted also to the complex system of expectations that metered verse calls into play. Speeches written in verse seem more highly ordered than prose speeches, mainly because we hear in them a discernible metrical pattern along with the rhetorical and grammatical patterns that are audible also in prose. The order of prose may be rich and wonderful to listen to, but we understand it to be, on the whole, a lower order.

As if in approval of this metaphorical description, readers have long thought of prose as used consistently in the "lower plot" of Shakespeare's plays and by lower characters.[1] It is obvious, however, that Shakespeare by no means adheres consistently to this neat division of labor. For a while, he is content to make the distinction between prose and verse mainly on the basis of class or formal occasion, to use prose for low characters, clowns, letters, proclamations, and challenges. But as his interest in patterned prose develops, he becomes more willing to let characters from the upper plot speak it (Rosalind, Henry V, Hamlet, Lear, and others). A highly figured prose provides, on occasion, quite as brilliant a medium for memorable words as blank verse does, and although it remains, by and large, a resource for the most dignified characters to use only at moments of suspended intensity, it plays a part in the orchestration of Shakespeare's themes second only to that of iambic pentameter. For the first fourteen of Shakespeare's plays (see Appendix A below, from Vickers, 1968), prose enjoys a distinctly subordinate role. It is not used at all in *1* and *3 Henry VI*, in *King John*, or in *Richard II*, and those early comedies that do employ it keep it quite strictly in its place—for comic characters or scenes. As the chart shows, however, beginning with *1 Henry IV*, some of the middle plays rely very largely on prose; in five of them prose predominates; and only one, *Julius Caesar*, a play notable for its experiments with short lines (see below, Chapter 8), uses a low proportion of prose.

Nevertheless, all these plays—even *Julius Caesar*—permit prose to perform new functions, and in almost all of them prose is used for noncomic purposes by characters in the upper plot. The mix of prose and verse is especially curious, and nowhere more so than in the first play of the group, *1 Henry IV*. It seems obvious enough for the first few scenes that the court characters should speak verse and the tavern characters prose, but Prince Hal, a court character in the tavern, also speaks verse there (1.2.195–217, 2.2.104–10), and Hotspur turns out to speak excellent prose to his wife and, later, to Glendower, whose regular blank verse he interrupts crudely with "I think there's no man speaks better Welsh. I'll to dinner" (3.1.49–50).

If Hal and Hotspur are comparable in some respects, Hotspur and Falstaff also provide curious contrasts: differently irresponsible, differently wasteful of "time," they discourse differently on honor and on time. As Hotspur "descends" to prose on occasion, even Falstaff sometimes rises to verse, especially when he speaks with zest (however ambiguous) about the glories of the fighting life—in these lines, for example:

> Rare words! brave world! Hostess, my breakfast, come!
> O, I could wish this tavern were my drum! (3.3.205–6)

Again in Act 5, Scene 3, he speaks prose, but when Hal enters and speaks verse to rally him, the passage continues as follows (although editors never print it this way):

40	*Prince.*	What, stands thou idle here? Lend me thy sword.
		Many a nobleman lies stark and stiff
		Under the hoofs of vaunting enemies,
43		Whose deaths are unreveng'd. I prithee lend me
		Thy sword.
	Falstaff.	O Hal, I prithee give me leave
		To breathe a while. Turk Gregory never did
		Such deeds in arms as I have done this day.
47		I have paid Percy, I have made him sure.[2]

Hal's readiness to speak either prose or verse, depending on the occasion and the company, is evident throughout the play.

From a formal point of view, the most notable aspect of Shakespeare's prose is that it is often hard to distinguish from verse. At many junctures prose and verse come together and for a few lines, even with the text before us, we may not be able to say with assurance whether the lines are prose or verse. We can say at a certain point, "Here the text is prose," and a few lines later, "Here the text is verse," but in between we may not be sure; and if we are uncertain when we *see* the text, our uncertainty on *hearing* it is likely to be compounded by our relative inexperience at following lines of blank verse merely with our ears. Shakespeare sometimes modulates back and forth between the forms; one character may continue throughout a scene to speak lines that are at least iambic, if not pentameter, while another character, or several of them, speak prose. But we may be meant to perceive some lines as uncertain, as marking moments when the play is suspended between its prose and verse natures.[3]

One clue to Shakespeare's intentions in some apparently indeterminate passages is the strange metered prose that Pistol speaks. Many editors print Pistol's speeches as verse despite their appearing always as prose in the Folio. But we have no reason to believe that any of his lines are verse, except for their relentlessly iambic character. The point seems to be that Pistol has heard such iambic rant in the theater and has adopted it as his personal style without realizing that for words to be verse they must come not only in iambs but in lines. Pistol's iambic word-strings are often not pentameter or hexameter or anything. So when in conversation he tells the King in *Henry V:* "Tell him I'll knock his leek about his pate upon Saint Davy's day" (4.1.54–55), we should understand that, although this may sound like one line of pentameter and one of trimeter, it is hapless iambic prose (like the sentimental iambic passages in Dickens' early novels). The King's reply parodies Pistol's eccentricity for ten or twelve syllables and then goes pointedly off the metrical track: "Do not you wear your dagger in your cap that day, lest he knock that about yours" (4.1.56–57). Some such mockery, heavy or light, may be the motive behind much of Shakespeare's iambic prose.

Predominantly prose scenes sometimes begin, and later resume, with lines (or at least phrases) that scan as iambic pentameter. For example:

1 Lord.	*You have not given him his mother's letter?*
2 Lord.	*I have delivered it an hour since.* There is something in't that stings his nature; for on the reading it *he chang'd almost into another man.* (*All's Well That Ends Well,* 4.3.1–5)
Oswald.	*Good dawning to thee, friend. Art of this house?*
Kent.	Ay.
Oswald.	Where may we set our horses?
Kent.	I' th' mire. (*King Lear,* 2.2.1–5)

Oswald's polite beginning is refused by Kent in line 2. When, in line 3, Oswald courteously provides a potentially iambic half-line for Kent to complete, Kent's two-syllable reply rudely thwarts this metrical gesture.

Iambic speeches, often pentameter and sometimes headless, can be heard in the midst of passages that are otherwise unmistakably prose:

| Hostess. | *If he swagger, let him come not here.* No, by my faith, I must live among my neighbors; I'll no swaggerers, I am in good name and fame with the very best. *Shut the door, there comes* |

> *no swaggerers here;* I have not liv'd all this while to have
> swaggering now. Shut the door, I pray you.
>
> (2 Henry IV, 2.4.73–78)

> *Autolycus.* My traffic is sheets; when the kite builds, look to lesser linen.
> My father nam'd me Autolycus, who being, as I am, litter'd un-
> der Mercury, was likewise *a snapper-up of unconsider'd trifles.*
> *With die and drab I purchas'd this caparison, and my revenue is*
> *the silly cheat.* Gallows and knock are too powerful on the
> highway. Beating and hanging are terrors to me. For the life
> to come, I sleep out the thought of it.
>
> (The Winter's Tale, 4.3.23–30)

(Shakespeare often uses a word like "caparison" to provide a triple ending [see below, Chapter 11]; and "revenue" is frequently stressed on the second syllable.)

What are we to make of such iambic prose? Does English fall so naturally into iambic pentameter that even a great master cannot keep it from intruding by accident? Or is it part of his wit to let these comic characters fall into it by chance? Some such reason may lie behind most iambic lines found embedded in prose, but we must assume that Shakespeare's audience heard them as iambic and could notice their difference from the prose lines around them. In many places, however, it seems impossible to tell whether a series of short lines is to be heard as verse or prose. Pandarus, in *Troilus and Cressida,* normally speaks prose, but in 4.2.23–24 he may be speaking verse: one line of singsong and another that is both headless and broken-backed (Wyatt's Type 6f):

> How now, how now, how go maidenheads?
> Here | you maid, | where's | my cou|sin Cressid?

In *Twelfth Night* (1.5.150–51), Olivia and Malvolio speak these lines in a passage that is otherwise prose:

> *Olivia.* What kind | o' man | is he?
> *Malvolio.* Why, of | mankind.

Verse or prose? A bit later, Olivia responds to Viola's prose question "Are you the lady of the house?" with

If I do not usurp myself, I am. (1.5.184–86)

These last two examples can (and perhaps should) be performed in such a way as to prevent our mistaking them for verse. For example, "If I do not usurp myself, I am." But, clearly, the division between verse and prose is not so absolute as we are likely to think it. Prose may turn iambic, just as verse, with its manifold variant resources, may take a step in the direction of prose. When either happens, it may not be chance, may even be intended as a jest. The rhythms of prose are, as a rule, freer than those of verse, but, as Vickers shows, they may be almost as highly figured. Hence, to shift from verse to prose is only to move from one kind or degree of patterning to another. It would be excessive to claim that Shakespeare's prose is a deviant form of the iambic pentameter line, but the difference between them is not the difference between metered verse and prose as we normally think of it today: that is, between a highly disciplined metrical language and a flowing discourse that follows no consistent repetitive syllabic or rhetorical principle. Shakespeare's prose is not of that kind; rather, by virtue of its figurative energy and resourcefulness, it typically serves as a worthy alternative mode to Shakespeare's verse, as another register to add to the iambic keyboard, a whole new set of stops, a para-metrical system that works with the metrical system to enable Shakespeare's choices of word, phrase, figure, and rhythm to be not merely various but infinitely graded and toned.

Songs, and Verse in Other Meters

None of Shakespeare's songs is written in iambic pentameter; not one of them includes even a single line in this meter. For Shakespeare, as for English poets generally, the poem that is set to music seems more at home in a briefer line. The songs serve various purposes in the plays: (1) to change the metrical pace, to break up the steady march of ten-syllable lines; (2) to change the dramatic mode, to offer another kind of theatrical entertainment, pleasing in itself; (3) to advance the business of the play by different means: to enable us, for example, to see one of the characters (or actors) in a new role, as singer or musician; or to offer a contrast in mood, usually a moment of lyrical repose set in the midst of the plot's more continuous motion.[4]

Similarly, the brief waves of verse in other meters that occasionally break on our ears serve mainly to change the rhythm or to provide a verse mode more appropriate for certain kinds of characters. The fairies in *A Midsummer Night's Dream*, the witches in *Macbeth*, the caskets in *The Merchant of Venice*, and several speakers of Prologues and Epilogues signal their peculiar status (at least part of the time) through tetrameter couplets. Hamlet, Lear's Fool, Orlando, and others sometimes speak or compose balladlike rhymes. Lovers may utter rhymed couplets, quatrains, or even whole sonnets in such plays as *The Comedy of Errors, Love's Labor's Lost,* and *Romeo and Juliet.* And patterned exchanges in briefer meters sometimes occur, as in this passage from *As You Like It:*

Silvius.	And so am I for Phebe.	
Phebe.	And I for Ganymed.	
Orlando.	And I for Rosalind.	
Rosalind.	And I for no woman.	(5.2.85–88)

This series, repeated twice, the last time with slight variation, gains part of its humor from the way Rosalind's line breaks the meter.

Doggerel couplets, a major verse mode for much pre-Shakespearean drama, including *Gammer Gurton's Needle, Roister Doister,* and *Cambises,* were probably part of the poetic equipment of a young apprentice playwright like Shakespeare. They turn up in considerable numbers in *The Comedy of Errors, The Taming of the Shrew,* and *Love's Labor's Lost.* According to Chambers, there are also eighteen lines of doggerel in *Two Gentlemen of Verona* and a very few others elsewhere. After his early plays, Shakespeare virtually abandoned the four-stress couplet, along with the boisterous comedy or farce it implied. But it may make one remarkable appearance at the end of *King Lear,* where Kent uses it to announce his own imminent death:

> Í have a joúrney sir, shórtly to gŏ,
> My máster cálls me, I mŭst not say nŏ.   (5.3.322–23)

The verse here can be read as iambic pentameter, but only by forcing stresses on "sir," "I," and "not," by denying stress to the important word "must," and by reading a pointless trochee into the fourth foot of the first line (on "shortly"). The doggerel rhythm, which the Folio punctuation supports, is much more expressive here. If it is intrusive, unexpected, disruptive, that is not at all inappropriate. Kent's meter has been rude and disruptive before, as befits his role of anti-courtier, and here he is turning away from the court scene, and from this world. In context, the single tumbling couplet sounds like a criticism, from the perspective of a more elemental reality, of the decorums of kings and courts. Edgar may even recognize the depth from which Kent's response has come, for in his speech that follows, the last in the play, he acknowledges that "we must. . ./ Speak what we feel, not what we ought to say" (5.3.324–25). Iambic pentameter has the last word, but Kent's doggerel lines deepen the concluding moments and suggest, by widening our vision, how much there is for the verse to resolve.[5]

CHAPTER 8

Short and Shared Lines

Go get you home you Fragments.
(Coriolanus, 1.1.222)

Shakespeare's Increasing Interest in Short Lines

Aside from prose, the commonest kind of departure from iambic pentameter in Shakespeare's plays is the short verse line, the line of fewer than five metrical stresses. Although short lines occur in some Renaissance stanzaic poems and later odes, the anomalous short line appearing unexpectedly and unpredictably amid an extended series of longer lines (that is, in "stichic" poems) is rare in English nondramatic poems from Chaucer to Yeats. It occurs frequently, however, in late Elizabethan and early Jacobean plays—probably, to begin with, in imitation of Virgil, who distributes "some sixty" short lines through the *Aeneid,* some with expressive force (Sparrow, 7, 41–45). But Shakespeare carries the practice much further and develops his own short-line craft. Since our views of a correct Shakespearean text may change with each new edition, no precise count of short lines is possible, but the metrical tables developed by E. K. Chambers give us a general idea. According to his figures, about one out of twenty-four unrhymed lines is short.[1] (See Appendix C.)

Associated with the short line is the half-line speech or half-line conclusion of a speech that is completed metrically by another character's words. Shakespeare came to use shared (or divided or split) lines more and more often, "starting about the time of the so-called problem plays," according to Fredson Bowers. "By the last plays [this usage] had doubled in frequency from the problem plays and was close to ten times the frequency of the early comedies" (81). Although shared lines differ from short lines in being heard as metrically complete, they are transparently made up of distinct segments, spoken by different voices, and may consequently be regarded as in some sense *two short lines joined.*

The prominence of short and shared lines distinguishes Shakespeare's verse from almost all pentameter poetry of later periods and especially from later blank verse, where lines shared by separate speeches or paragraphs appear, if at all, only as a faint echo of Shakespeare's technique and without notable expressive function.[2] Nevertheless, most readers of Shakespeare ignore this striking feature of his verse, and scholars and critics rarely comment on it; if they do, they are likely to be chiefly concerned, as Bowers is, with the troublesome editorial problem of how to arrange or join short lines. Although attempts (not always convincing) have been made to justify the shortness of some lines,[3] readers of Shakespeare's dramatic verse have rarely seen short and shared lines as integral elements in his verse technique. But when such lines together make up so large a proportion of Shakespeare's blank verse—more than 20 percent in some of the later plays (Appendix C)—they have to be taken seriously as a major component of his metrical repertoire.

As we saw in Chapter 6, Shakespeare's early dramatic verse, like Marlowe's, took the form of block speeches that were often long and almost always began and ended with full lines of iambic pentameter. A speech was rather like a short poem or stanza spoken from the stage, and, as in most other stanzas of the period, the line-lengths were uniform. Here are the opening speeches of one scene in a very early Shakespeare play. They form three quatrains and a couplet, all unrhymed but resembling a sonnet or other stanzaic poem in having cleanly divided sections and full verse lines:

Queen.   Believe me lords, for flying at the brook,
       I saw not better sport these seven years' day;
       Yet by your leave, the wind was very high,
       And ten to one, old Joan had not gone out.
King.   But what a point, my lord, your falcon made,
       And what a pitch she flew above the rest!
       To see how God in all his creatures works!
       Yea, man and birds are fain of climbing high.
Suffolk. No marvel, and it like your Majesty,

> My Lord Protector's hawks do tow'r so well;
> They know their master loves to be aloft,
> And bears his thoughts above his falcon's pitch.
> *Gloucester.* My lord, 'tis but a base ignoble mind
> That mounts no higher than a bird can soar.
>
> *(2 Henry VI, 2.1.1–14)*

Even in comedy, where we might expect greater looseness in the verse (as we do in the early rhymed doggerel), the iambic pentameter speeches are laid out in measured lines:

> I am not furnish'd with the present money:
> Besides, I have some business in the town.
> Good signior, take the stranger to my house,
> And with you take the chain, and bid my wife
> Disburse the sum, on the receipt thereof.
> Perchance I will be there as soon as you.   *(The Comedy of Errors, 4.1.34–39)*

But sometimes what the characters have to say is only a single phrase that cannot sensibly be drawn out to the length of a full verse line or that serves to introduce a speech or conclude a conversation or a scene:

> We thank you all.   *(2 Henry VI, 1.1.38)*
>
> Away my lord, away!   *(2 Henry VI, 5.2.90)*
>
> How now? what news?   *(3 Henry VI, 2.1.205)*
>
> Here comes Navarre.   *(Love's Labor's Lost, 2.1.89)*

Earlier playwrights had begun to write shared lines—a few appear even in *Gorboduc*—but usually as a mechanical convenience, not as an opportunity to be various, subtle, or stylish. In Shakespeare, too, the technique is often a practical way of linking ordinary brief phrases:

> What is his name?
>   Lucentio, gentle sir.   *(The Taming of the Shrew, 4.5.58)*
> Call Philostrate.
>   Here, mighty Theseus.   *(A Midsummer Night's Dream, 5.1.38)*

But in Shakespeare, even from the first, it often masks some distinctive word-patterning. The verse, which had been long and lumbering, suddenly turns quick and figured:

> Mine was secure.
> And so was mine, my lord.   (*1 Henry VI*, 2.1.66)

> This way fall I to death.
> This way for me.   (*2 Henry VI*, 3.2.412)

> Why call you me love? Call my sister so.
> Thy sister's sister.
> That's my sister.
> No   (*The Comedy of Errors*, 3.2.59–60)

But Shakespeare's practice is extremely various, and a few simply stated formulas cannot do it justice. We do know that he uses short and shared lines more and more, and with increasing dramatic effectiveness. The proportion of short and shared lines to full blank-verse lines increases from about 2 percent in the earliest plays to more than 13.5 percent in every play from *Hamlet* on, and to more than 20 percent in *Macbeth, Antony and Cleopatra, Coriolanus, Timon of Athens,* and *The Tempest* (Appendix C).

These two lines need to be thought of together, partly because they often sound alike. When we hear the first half-line in the theater, even when we recognize that it concludes one speaker's speech, we cannot tell whether it will stand as a short line or be "answered" by a second half-line, or even if something more complicated will happen: the language may shift to prose, or the second half-line may itself be answered by a phrase that completes it metrically. Among these possibilities, what seems certain is that a short-line prosody is at work, embedded from time to time in a long-line prosody. That is, along with the full-line metric that serves Shakespeare and later poets as the continuous (and, for many of them, invariable) current of their verse stream, Shakespeare was also producing an undercurrent of short verse lines, still iambic, some joining to form pentameters, but some curtailed and seeming incomplete. Even when the shared lines form decorous pentameters, we must be more than usually aware that they are composed of two half-lines, because they are spoken by two different voices.

This is not to suggest that within Shakespeare's usual pentameters lurks a memory of the Old and Middle English alliterative line made up of two half-lines, or even that Lydgate's and Wyatt's jointed line is reappearing (see above, Chapter 2). Shakespeare's iambic pentameter, as a rule, is far too smooth and well modulated to bear any resemblance to these earlier, often quite cumbersome forms. Rather, I think, he was induced to develop a prosody that included short lines by his wish to present credible and credibly various language on the stage. One cannot always declaim and complain in pentameters. For a playwright as inventive as Shakespeare, a lively dramatic speech needs to change pace now and then, to break up the uniform procession of pentameter lines. The short line, suggested at first by Virgil, offered opportunities to be terse, curt, swift, ominous, surprising. And as Shakespeare explored the potentialities of short lines, his verse changed its character in some major ways. More and more he ended impressive speeches (eventually, almost any speech) with strong short lines, and his verse-sentences ran increasingly from midline to midline. That the internal punctuation increases sharply in Shakespeare's later plays (see Oras, 46–47) is one sign that more and more half-lines are embedded within the continuous speech. Chapter 14 will follow this development in detail; here we can note that it had its source in Shakespeare's continuing exploration of how short and shared lines could be integrated into a verse in which the heroic line remained central.

Some Types and Functions of Short Lines

The short verse line is not always easy to tell from the short prose line, and at a certain point of brevity or indeterminacy they tend to merge. Short lines of apparent prose may appear between lines of apparent verse:

Hotspur.	Well, I will back him straight. O *Esperance!*
	Bid Butler lead him forth into the park.
Lady H.	But hear you, my lord.
Hotspur.	What say'st thou, my lady?
75 *Lady H.*	What is it carries you away?
Hotspur.	Why, my horse, my love, my horse.
Lady H.	Out, you mad-headed ape!
	A weasel hath not such a deal of spleen.

(1 Henry IV, 2.3.71–78)

This lively prose exchange (lines 73–77) is not without pattern, but we are unlikely to call it verse, and it is certainly not continuously iambic.

In the following example, the generals in *Troilus and Cressida* are pointedly ignoring Achilles in a series of truncated lines. Their short lines (59–69), more or less iambic but not combining to form pentameters, convey the broken connection with Achilles that the Greek leaders are trying to enact:

> *Agamemnon.* What says Achilles? Would he aught with us?
> *Nestor.* Would you, my lord, aught with the general?
> *Achilles.* No.
> 60 *Nestor.* Nothing, my lord.
> *Agamemnon.* The better.
> *Achilles.* Good day, good day.
> *Menelaus.* How do you? how do you?
> *Achilles.* What, does the cuckold scorn me?
> 65 *Ajax.* How now, Patroclus?
> *Achilles.* Good morrow, Ajax.
> *Ajax.* Ha?
> *Achilles.* Good morrow.
> *Ajax.* Ay, and good next day too.
> 70 *Achilles.* What mean these fellows? Know they not Achilles?
>
> (*Troilus and Cressida*, 3.3.57–70)

But the short line that is unambiguously iambic—our main concern here—appears in a variety of metrical situations, which may be classified simply, as follows.

1. *The short line that comes at the end of a verse speech.* In his middle plays sometimes, and in his later plays characteristically, Shakespeare ends speeches in midline and has the next speaker's utterance complete the line. But sometimes he leaves the half-line ending of the speech as it is, perhaps to signal a pause. (See above, Chapter 6, p. 103.) Whether or not such a line is completed metrically, its effect is often highly dramatic. To build to a rhetorical climax through a series of full pentameters and then to complete the period in a line of only four to seven syllables often has a strong impact:

> For Time is like a fashionable host
> That slightly shakes his parting guest by th' hand,

And with his arms outstretch'd as he would fly,
Grasps in the comer.   (*Troilus and Cressida*, 3.3.165–68)

Even without such flamboyant imagery, a tense moment may gain force
and crispness from a decisive closing line that is shorter than the norm:

I can be patient, I can stay with Regan,
I and my hundred knights.   (*King Lear*, 2.4.230–31)

2. *The anomalous short line,* either within a speech or at its begin-
ning, or as a separate spoken line. Such lines may register brief but neces-
sary business (for example, terse replies or pithy exchanges); they may
serve some expressive function; or, in some cases, we may suspect a faulty
text. Many examples will be given in the pages that follow.

3. *The short line that is one of a series.* Sometimes the short line that
ends one character's speech will lead into a series of short lines. We may
hear these simply as short or as combining to form full lines of iambic
pentameter. In the theater, we may not be able to tell which ones are best
combined; we may actually hear, almost simultaneously, alternative possi-
bilities of combination—hear some short lines as isolated and anomalous,
others as ready to combine with short lines preceding or following—or
with both!—to form full metrical lines. The line so formed may itself be
shorter or longer than pentameter. Many of these short-line forms appear
in *Julius Caesar* and suggest that Shakespeare was consciously addressing
the metrical problems they pose.[4]

Short Lines in *Julius Caesar*

Especially when it appears singly in a passage of normal lines, the
short iambic phrase seems a truncated pentameter—like Stephen Dedalus's
pier, a disappointed bridge, a half-line whose other half never materi-
alized.[5] Its different form enables it to set off longer lines and to contrast
suggestively with them. We find short lines even in the midst of what
appear to be carefully constructed rhetorical passages—in *Julius Caesar,*
for example, where from the very first scene Shakespeare engages in such
contrasts. The tribunes Flavius and Murellus use verse to scold the com-

moners, who reply in prose. Murellus then delivers a highly rhetorical oration in verse which is impressive and correct—except that lines 47 and 52 are short. Once, he says, the fickle people used to worship Pompey:

> And when you saw his chariot but appear,
> Have you not made an universal shout,
45 That Tiber trembled underneath her banks
> To hear the replication of your sounds,
> Made in her concave shores?
> And do you now put on your best attire?
> And do you now cull out a holiday?
50 And do you now strew flowers in his way,
> That comes in triumph over Pompey's blood?
> Be gone,
> Run to your houses, fall upon your knees,
> Pray to the gods to intermit the plague
55 That needs must light on this ingratitude.   (*Julius Caesar*, 1.1.43–55)

The second short line presumably makes up in volume what it lacks in length; the first varies the pentameter line and rounds out a rhetorical period.

The next scene begins with a line shared by three speakers:

> *Caesar.*   Calphurnia!
> *Casca.*   Peace ho, Caesar speaks.
> *Caesar.*   Calphurnia!
> *Calphurnia.* Here, my lord.   (1.2.1–2)

Caesar, we note, cannot even speak to his wife without an intermediary; the split line makes that point. All four speeches are brief, but the first three compose an iambic pentameter line. The next does not; it stands alone, as Calphurnia does.

Occasionally, Shakespeare varies the rhythm to provide short-line iambic exchanges:

> *Brutus.*   Not I.
> *Cassius.*   I pray you do.   (1.2.26–27)
>
> *Lepidus.*   What? shall I find you here?
> *Octavius.*   Or here, or at the Capitol.   (4.1.10–11)

Cassius.	I am.	
Brutus.	I say, you are not.	(4.3.33–34)

This last exchange comes in a passage notable for the brevity of all its phrases. Brutus is scolding Cassius for taking bribes:

Brutus.	I had rather be a dog, and bay the moon,	
	Than such a Roman.	
Cassius.	$\qquad\qquad\qquad\qquad$ Brutus, bait not me,	
	I'll not endure it. You forget yourself	
30	To hedge me in. I am a soldier, I,	
	Older in practice, abler than yourself	
	To make conditions.	
Brutus.	$\qquad\qquad\qquad\qquad$ Go to; you are not, Cassius.	
33 *Cassius.*	I am.	
34 *Brutus.*	$\qquad$ I say, you are not.	
Cassius.	Urge me no more, I shall forget myself;	
	Have mind upon your health; tempt me no farther.	
37 *Brutus.*	Away, slight man!	
Cassius.	Is't possible?	
Brutus.	$\qquad\qquad\qquad$ Hear me, for I will speak.	
	Must I give way and room to your rash choler?	

$(4.3.27–39)$

Between the first and last lines of this angry exchange, neither man speaks a full line made up of one continuous phrase. (We can almost call the manner in which they complete each other's metrical lines conspiratorial; when the completion fails, conspiracy is in trouble.) Only lines 33, 34, and 37 are actually short; but the first two combine into a trimeter phrase that echoes the last part of the preceding line:

	Go to; you áre not, Cassius.
I am.	I say, you áre not.

Then the pentameter resumes, but Brutus's insulting characterization of Cassius is conveyed in another short line (37), which Cassius probably receives for a moment in shocked silence before he speaks his next words.[6]

In all the short lines the iambic beat is kept, and without the actors' help any listener would probably have a hard time distinguishing the short lines from segments of normal ones, especially when *all* the full lines (28–38) divide perceptibly in the middle and one of them (32) deepens the music with an epic caesura. Like many others, these short lines may be interpreted as requiring a pause; after line 34 and again after line 37, Cassius might well pause to recover his equanimity. The same is true later in the scene after Brutus speaks with vehemence:

Cassius.	I durst not?	
Brutus.	No.	(4.3.60–61)
Cassius.	I denied you not.	
Brutus.	You did.	(4.3.82–83)

Still later, the quarrel over, Brutus's shocking news evidently stuns Cassius, and the two men leave another line short:

Brutus.	No man bears sorrow better. Portia is dead.	
Cassius.	Ha? Portia?	
Brutus.	She is dead.	(4.3.147–49)

It may be that a large number of short lines can be explained by the presumption that they are to be followed by a pause in the dramatic action. The lines are, in a sense, filled in by the actor's gestures, movements, or notable change in facial expression. But editors are sometimes too quick to imagine such devices, as when they print the following speech by Octavius thus:

> Come, come, the cause. If arguing make us sweat,
> The proof of it will turn to redder drops.
> 50 Look,
> I draw a sword against conspirators:
> When think you that the sword goes up again? (5.1.48–52)

But the Folio joins lines 50 and 51 in a single line, which can be understood as headless with a triple ending (see below, Chapters 11 and 12). Thus:

$$\text{Lo\u043ek, | \u012d dr\u0101w | \u0103 sw\u00f3rd | \u0103g\u00e1inst | c\u014fnsp\u00edr\u0103t\u014frs}$$

Similarly, after Richard II has dramatically halted the joust between Bolingbroke and Mowbray by throwing his warder down, a trumpet gives a "long flourish," and Richard says portentously, in the lineation given by most modern editors:

> Draw near,
> And list what with our council we have done.   (1.3.123–24)

The Quarto and Folio versions seem more convincing, though they divide the sentence into two short lines, one slow and deliberate, the second swift and authoritative:

> Draw near and list
> What with our council we have done.

Readers of modern editions may have noticed other eloquent short lines. Juliet, for example, with a strong short line wedged between two normal ones, fixes her own attention and that of her audience on the sleeping draught she is about to quaff:

> My dismal scene I needs must act alone.
> Come, vial.
> What if this mixture do not work at all?   (4.3.19–21)

Similarly, Portia, at one climax of the judgment scene in *The Merchant of Venice,* by means of a portentous monosyllabic line keeps Bassanio from paying Shylock and letting him go free:

> Soft,
> The Jew shall have all justice. Soft, no haste   (4.1.320–21)

One final example: When Hamlet proposes that Horatio and Marcellus swear an oath to keep what they have seen to themselves, the Ghost three times *"cries under the Stage"* in short lines. The second time the text reads:

> *Hamlet.*   Swear by my sword.
> *Ghost.*   Swear.   (1.5.154–55)

126

So mighty a directive abrogates the merely metrical requirement.

Or so it seems. But the short lines of Juliet and Portia prove only that modern editors take this view of them. In both cases the Folio does not print the short line separately but incorporates the short phrase in the line that follows it here. The Ghost's command in *Hamlet,* however, does end an expressive short line.

In *Julius Caesar,* at least twenty-three speeches end with short lines, and a great many more end in half-lines completed by the next speaker. Shakespeare is beginning here that long and gradual development toward a versification in which the speeches often, even characteristically, travel from midline to midline (see Chapter 14). *Julius Caesar* is notable for its interest in rhetoric and oratory, but its large number of short lines shows another side of that interest: lines and speeches, after all, are composed of phrases. The playwright seems to be studying his line and its component phrases, with a view to possible ways of restructuring it—not abandoning the combinations he has already mastered (the continuous line, the occasional enjambment), but inspecting new ways of arranging half-lines. He has been studying this all along, of course, but to inspect the technique in *Julius Caesar* is to isolate a particularly crucial stage in the development of Shakespeare's craft.[7]

When the Soothsayer catches Caesar's attention, his famous message is properly iambic, and its six syllables are completed by four of Caesar's:

Soothsayer. Beware the ides of March.
Caesar.   What man is that?   (1.2.18)

It is as if Caesar's speech, by finishing the line, has neutralized the ominousness of the warning. When the soothsayer speaks again, however, his message occupies a whole short line:

Soothsayer. Beware the ides of March.   (1.2.23)

The short line here implies a pause before Caesar, recovering his poise *in the verse,* decides:

Caesar.   He is a dreamer, let us leave him. Pass.   (1.2.24)

Later, when Caesar returns to the Capitol, the following exchange takes place:

> *Caesar.* The ides of March are come.
> *Soothsayer.* Ay, Caesar, but not gone. (3.1.1–2)

Hexameter, or trimeter exchange? However we classify the sound, we are certainly meant to hear the devastating metrical echo. But perhaps the most theatrical use of short lines in this play comes at the moment of Caesar's death. He has been pontificating in full iambic lines, then is interrupted as the conspirators press around him:

> *Cinna.* O Caesar—
> *Caesar.* Hence! wilt thou lift up Olympus?
> *Decius Brutus.* Great Caesar—
> *Caesar.* Doth not Brutus bootless kneel?
> *Casca.* Speak hands for me.
> [*They stab Caesar*]
> *Caesar.* *Et tu Brute?*—Then fall Caesar. (3.1.74–77)

The short-line speeches of Cinna, Caesar, Decius Brutus, and again Caesar, though they combine to form full lines, serve as a first scarring of the smooth verse. Casca's speech is still iambic (spondee and pyrrhic), but short. Is it verse or prose? For a moment then the stabbing arms and daggers efface the need for spoken language. What follow are the famous Latin words, whose rhythm is echoed by Caesar's final English phrase: ˘ ´ ´ ˘ | ˘ ´ ´ ˘. The moment of assassination has burst free of the iambic framework. Immediately thereafter the words of the triumphant conspirators reconstruct it—in their own image, as it were—out of short phrases similar to those we have been hearing all along:

> Liberty! Freedom! Tyranny is dead!
> Run hence, proclaim, cry it about the streets. (3.1.78–79)

Meditative or conspiratorial speeches in *Julius Caesar* often use full lines and lengthy sentences. But the play is rich in utterances that end in midline, either to be completed by the next speaker or left dangling. Occasionally, as we saw in Chapter 6, the second of three half-lines, at a point

where the speakers change, may seem both to finish the previous metrical
line and to begin the following one:

Portia.	Hark, boy, what noise is that?
Lucius.	I hear none, madam.
Portia.	Prithee listen well.

(2.4.16–17)

Brutus.	After my speech is ended.
Antony.	Be it so;
	I do desire no more. (3.1.251–52)

Following the tradition of printing that dates only from the eighteenth
century, Antony's last clause becomes in modern texts a separate short line.
But it ought to be evident to our ears that "Be it so" can complete the
previous line or begin another (headless) one that the next clause will
complete. Differently printed, but similar in design, is the following
exchange:

Cassius.	Then, if we lose this battle,
	You are contented to be led in triumph
	Thorough the streets of Rome?
Brutus.	No, Cassius, no. Think not, thou noble Roman

(5.1.107–10)

Clearly, "No, Cassius, no" completes the previous metrical line even as it
begins another.

Such squinting constructions appear from time to time in every play
from *Julius Caesar* on and in some earlier ones as well, and they make it
virtually impossible at times for a listener to detect the beginnings and
ends of pentameter lines. Hearing a four-syllable phrase that fits with a
six-syllable phrase before and after, we may easily lose track of where in
the line we are. And when we come across so long a stream of short phrases
as we do in the following exchange from *Hamlet* (in *The Riverside Shake-
speare*'s lineation), all we can really maintain is a sense of iambic rhythm;
the pentameter must be momentarily lost. Or, rather, unless the actors give
us clear auditory signals, it will be forged and reforged in a series of com-
pounding segments. (Lines 128, 130, and 138 are short.)

King.   Tell me, Laertes,
         Why thou art thus incens'd. Let him go, Gertrude.
         Speak, man.
Laertes.   Where is my father?
King.   Dead.
Queen.   But not by him.
130 King.   Let him demand his fill.
Laertes.   How came he dead? I'll not be juggled with.
         To hell, allegiance! vows, to the blackest devil!
         Conscience and grace, to the profoundest pit!
         I dare damnation. To this point I stand,
135   That both the worlds I give to negligence,
         Let come what comes, only I'll be reveng'd
         Most throughly for my father.
King.   Who shall stay you?
Laertes.   My will, not all the world's:
         And for my means, I'll husband them so well,
         They shall go far with little.
140 King.   Good Laertes

                                        (*Hamlet*, 4.5.126–140)

Any reader alert to what I have called squinting lines will see at once
that in the theater these lines can be divided differently and still be heard as
pentameter:

King.   Tell me, Laertes, why thou art thus incens'd.
         Let him go, Gertrude. Speak, man.
Laertes.   Where's my father? *
King.   Dead.   [*Pause*]
Queen.   But not by him.
King.   Let him demand his fill.

Or, from that point on, they could be heard this way:

King.   Let him demand his fill.
Laertes.   How came he dead?
         I'll not be juggled with. To hell, allegiance!
         Vows, to the blackest devil! Conscience and grace,

* "Where's" is the Folio reading.

> To the profoundest pit! I dare damnation.
> To this point I stand, that both the worlds
> I give to negligence, let come what comes,
> Only I'll be reveng'd most throughly for my father.

King.   Who shall stay you?

Laertes.   My will, not all the world's:

And so on. This lineation requires only that we admit one hexameter and one headless line, and these, as we shall see, are not unusual in Shakespeare. I do not suggest that this is as satisfactory a line-arrangement as the one supported by the Second Quarto and the Folio and approved by most editors, only that when the lines are fluently spoken on stage, hardly any skillful listener to iambic pentameter can be sure where the pentameter begins and ends. In contrast, a competent listener to rhymed couplets by Dryden or Pope never loses track of the pentameter form. In Shakespeare all we can be sure of at such moments is the iambic rhythm. What we mostly hear are half-line iambic phrases fitted variously together. At such moments our very competence in hearing iambic pentameter is enabling us to deconstruct it, helping to render it problematical.[8]

Another notable technique Shakespeare uses is the series of short lines spoken by two or several characters, often between longer, more flowing lines of iambic pentameter. Such short lines often serve to convey excitement or hurry between more deliberate, considered, and controlled thought and action. We have already seen one example from *1 Henry IV* and another from *Troilus and Cressida* (pp. 120–21). *Julius Caesar* also can illustrate this point. When Antony addresses the people, they at first respond to his careful iambics as they have responded to the speech of Brutus—in well-behaved iambic verse of their own:

> *1 Plebeian.* Methinks there is much reason in his sayings.
> *2 Plebeian.* If thou consider rightly of the matter,
> Caesar has had great wrong.
> *3 Plebeian.*   Has he, masters?
> I fear there will a worse come in his place.

(Julius Caesar, 3.2.108–11)

But by the time Antony has roused them fully, their brutalization has proceeded so far as to be signaled even in their verse:

All.	Come down.
2 Plebeian.	Descend.
3 Plebeian.	You shall have leave.
4 Plebeian.	A ring, stand round.
1 Plebeian.	Stand from the hearse, stand from the body.
2 Plebeian.	Room for Antony, most noble Antony.
Antony.	Nay, press not so upon me, stand far off.
All.	Stand back; room, bear back!
Antony.	If you have tears, prepare to shed them now. (3.2.161–68)

Only one or two later lines of the crowd could be construed as iambic pentameter, and we are probably meant to hear a striking contrast between the cool, controlled, sometimes inflated periods of Antony's address and the plain, blunt, broken lines of his primitive audience. Indeed, the situation in the play echoes the one in the theater: the grace and elegance of Antony's verse, like Shakespeare's, has its profound effect on groundlings who cannot tell verse from prose.

The exchange between plebeians and Cinna the Poet in Act 3, Scene 3, is similar in character, the short lines suggesting a kind of agitation, a madness, a childishness, an anarchy, that metrical verse can hardly convey (though Shakespeare later attempted it in some speeches he gave to Lear, Othello, and Macbeth; see below, Chapter 15):

Cinna.	I dreamt to-night that I did feast with Caesar,
	And things unluckily charge my fantasy.
	I have no will to wander forth of doors,
	Yet something leads me forth.
1 Plebeian.	What is your name?
2 Plebeian.	Whither are you going?
3 Plebeian.	Where do you dwell?
4 Plebeian.	Are you a married man or a bachelor?
2 Plebeian.	Answer every man directly.
1 Plebeian.	Ay, and briefly.
4 Plebeian.	Ay, and wisely.
3 Plebeian.	Ay, and truly, you were best. (3.3.1–12)

The first speech of the first Plebeian both finishes Cinna's line and begins a new tune, a new line of questioning, in which there is more method than at first appears, as Cinna's orderly (but prose) answer confirms. The short lines capture the curtness and menace that prove fatal first to his undistinguished blank verse—and then to him.

Troilus and Cressida

By the time Shakespeare came to write *Troilus and Cressida,* his management of prose and verse, short lines and normal lines, those basic instruments in his metrical ensemble, had become exceedingly adroit.[9] Nowhere is this more evident than in Act 5, Scene 2, in which Troilus and Ulysses observe the dallying of Cressida and Diomed and are observed in their observing by Thersites. Up to this point, Shakespeare has used great numbers of deviant lines—most notably, the line with an extra syllable at the midline break (104 of these in this play, according to E. K. Chambers; see below, Chapter 11), and the short line, which serves many of the purposes we have been observing in *Julius Caesar.* Now the presence of three separate groups on the stage permits Shakespeare to mount a complex music reminiscent, for modern readers, of Verdian opera. We can identify four registers, indicated here as follows: *prose* (unmarked), *iambic pentameter* (preceded by a circle), *split lines* (by a triangle), *short iambic lines* (by a square). But all four registers are composed mainly of short phrases, which either do or do not combine into longer units—either verse lines or prose sentences.

		Enter Diomed.
	Diomed.	What are you up here, ho? Speak!
	Calchas.	Who calls?
	Diomed.	Diomed. Calchas, I think. Where's your daughter?
□	*Calchas.*	She comes to you.
		Enter Troilus and Ulysses.
5 ○	*Ulysses.*	Stand where the torch may not discover us.
		Enter Cressid.
△	*Troilus.*	Cressid comes forth to him.
	Diomed.	How now, my charge?
○	*Cressid.*	Now, my sweet guardian, hark, a word with you.
□	*Troilus.*	Yea, so familiar?
	Ulysses.	She will sing any man at first sight.
10	*Thersites.*	And any man may sing her, if he can take her clef; she's noted.

133

□	*Diomed.*	Will you remember?
□	*Cressid.*	Remember? yes.
□	*Diomed.*	Nay, but do then,
15 ○		And let your mind be coupled with your words.
	Troilus.	What shall she remember?
	Ulysses.	List!
○	*Cressid.*	Sweet honey Greek, tempt me no more to folly.
	Thersites.	Roguery!
20 □	*Diomed.*	Nay then—
□	*Cressid.*	I'll tell you what—
○	*Diomed.*	Fo, fo, come, tell a pin. You are forsworn.
○	*Cressid.*	In faith, I cannot. What would you have me do?
	Thersites.	A juggling trick—to be secretly open.
25 ○	*Diomed.*	What did you swear you would bestow on me?
○	*Cressid.*	I prithee do not hold me to mine oath,
○		Bid me do anything but that, sweet Greek.
△	*Diomed.*	Good night.
	Troilus.	Hold, patience.
30	*Ulysses.*	How now, Troyan?
	Cressid.	Diomed—
○	*Diomed.*	No, no, good night, I'll be your fool no more.
△	*Troilus.*	Thy better must.
	Cressid.	Hark a word in your ear.
35 □	*Troilus.*	O plague and madness!*
○	*Ulysses.*	You are moved, Prince, let us depart, I pray,
○		Lest your displeasure should enlarge itself
○		To wrathful terms. This place is dangerous,
○		The time right deadly. I beseech you go.
△	*Troilus.*	Behold, I pray you.
40	*Ulysses.*	Now, good my lord, go off;
○		You flow to great distraction. Come, my lord.
△	*Troilus.*	I prithee stay.
	Ulysses.	You have not patience, come.
○	*Troilus.*	I pray you stay. By hell and all hell's torments,
△		I will not speak a word.
	Diomed.	And so good night.
△	*Cressid.*	Nay, but you part in anger.

*The three half-lines that end in line 35 and those that end in line 48 may be heard as squinting lines.

134

45		*Troilus.*	Doth that grieve thee?
	△		O withered truth!
		Ulysses.	How now, my lord?
		Troilus.	By Jove
	△		I will be patient.
		Cressid.	Guardian! Why, Greek!
	□	*Diomed.*	Fo, fo, adieu, you palter.
	○	*Cressid.*	In faith, I do not. Come hither once again.
50	○	*Ulysses.*	You shake, my lord, at something; will you go?
	△		You will break out.
		Troilus.	She strokes his cheek.
		Ulysses.	Come, come.
	○	*Troilus.*	Nay stay, by Jove I will not speak a word.
	○		There is between my will and all offenses
	○		A guard of patience. Stay a little while.
55		*Thersites.*	How the devil Luxury, with his fat rump and potato finger,
			tickles these together! Fry, lechery, fry! (5.2.1–57)

Throughout the scene, Thersites speaks prose. The other characters all speak verse most of the time, but often their lines are short, and many of them cannot be easily classified as verse or prose. In fact, for the first thirty-five lines, the basic speech-unit is the short phrase, sometimes iambic, a background against which some lines of clear iambic pentameter (5–7, 18, 22, 23, 25–27, 32) stand out in relief. Some of the shorter lines combine to form good blank verse (6 and 28–31). Neither pair of characters establishes a preeminent right to speak full iambic lines; rather, their words form half-lines or full lines as best they can. A further irony shows in the way Troilus and Cressida sometimes share lines without sharing a conversation.

The rest of the scene is mainly in verse, and only for a few lines do we find the same intertwining of speeches. At some points, however, Cressida's lines seem assemblages of short speech-fragments:

He lov'd me—O false wench—Give't me again. (70)

Ay, come—O Jove!—do, come.—I shall be plagued. (105)

Gradually, the verse speeches lengthen into Troilus's elaborate reflections on Cressida's falseness, before Aeneas enters and, with Ulysses, ends the scene with a brief short-line exchange—except for a final blast of Thersites' prose.

As we have come to expect of Shakespeare's art, the arrangement here is not at all schematic. The playwright does not follow any systematic division (prose for one group, verse for another), except that Thersites speaks only prose. The rest of the speeches look improvised, arranged on the spot, the characters speaking verse or prose, long lines or short, split or discrete (or squinting), according to the playwright's sense of what the dramatic moment requires. This means that although the basic metrical norm in all but a few plays is iambic pentameter, a form that the writer finds perfectly congenial, he feels a freedom *at any point*—in midspeech, between speeches, at the hinges—to vary the meter, shorten or lengthen the line, introduce hypermetrical syllables, place lines in ambiguous metrical relation to each other, or break the meter altogether for a prolonged excursion into prose or just for a momentary disruption of the verse. With such an art, especially when the text is as often suspect as Shakespeare's is, there can be no question of finding an expressive or decorous reason for every decision to vary or dislodge the meter. But it seems clear that, along with the general principle that the verse should never continue too long in any uniform mode, Shakespeare also kept in mind the Elizabethan ideal of decorum and suited the verse style of each passage to the characters and action that it treats.

Some Further Implications

But the broader question remains largely unanswered: why did Shakespeare use so many short lines in a drama whose verse norm is iambic pentameter? Certainly one can point to many passages where the shorter line is more expressive than the longer one would have been, and the preparation of plays for production rather than for publication might have encouraged a playwright to be less scrupulous about perfecting (that is, carrying out to its decorous pentameter length) every line of his dramatic text. At least until Ben Jonson appeared, the commercial deviser of plays was not held (and did not hold himself) to the same standard of correctness as the sonneteer. But Jonson's example did not lead Shakespeare to reduce the number of short lines in his plays. As we have seen, his later plays use more short, shared, and squinting lines than ever. Whether or not his model was Virgil (see above, p. 116), this kind of line became important to Shakespeare's dramatic verse, both for its expressive potentialities and for its structural implications.

In the first place, the frequent use of short lines makes Shakespeare's dialogue sound more convincing. People do not speak for long in pentameter phrases; much of their ordinary talk comes in shorter spurts—brief replies, orders, greetings, farewells, asides, remarks, not long-breathed exposition and declamation. Even eloquent speech can sometimes be terse and curt; it does not always work itself up to five-foot oratorical passions. In his sonnets, Shakespeare had presented with becoming grace and subtlety the quiet voice of passionate feeling, a voice he would use to good effect on the stage. But the major business of drama is dialogue, people talking to each other, and Shakespeare apparently learned quite early the different role that a poetic line plays in the exchange of dialogue on the stage. Although iambic pentameter is a powerful combiner of speech tones and metrical insistence, Shakespeare evidently wanted wider options for his stage speakers, an array of phrasal maneuvers that ranges from the anomalous phrase through the shared line to the regular pentameter.

We noted earlier how effectively a short line could cap a rhetorical passage. In later plays Shakespeare also develops a contrary technique, that of concluding a speech or a scene with a kind of throwaway half-line. Whereas early characters may formally announce where they are ("I am come to survey the Tower this day," *I Henry VI,* 1.3.1; "These are the city gates, the gates of Rouen," *I Henry VI,* 3.2.1), his later work often presents only the busy middle of a scene. In *Antony and Cleopatra,* for example, many scenes break off abruptly in midconversation. Concluding short lines often look and sound as if something more might follow:

> Doubt not, sir,
> I knew it for my bond. (1.4.83–84)

> With news the time's with labor, and throes forth
> Each minute some. (3.7.80–81)

> Our fortune lies
> Upon this jump. (3.8.5–6)

It is easy to imagine that Shakespeare has been listening to the shape of conversation, noticing that its significant moments sometimes come in short bursts and trail off again into what the stage treats as inaudible, like scraps of talk heard in London streets.

A similar change from early to late plays is evident in Shakespeare's handling of angry or intense speech. In *1 Henry VI,* even great anger usually speaks in full lines:

> *Pucelle.* A plaguing mischief light on Charles and thee!
> And may ye both be suddenly surpris'd
> By bloody hands, in sleeping on your beds!
> *York.* Fell banning hag, enchantress, hold thy tongue!
>
> (*1 Henry VI*, 5.3.39–42)

In effect, the spoken phrase of whatever pitch of passion is regulated by the iambic pentameter line. But Lear's fury is curter:

> Degenerate bastard, I'll not trouble thee;
> Yet have I left a daughter. (*King Lear*, 1.4.254–55)

Such a speech makes it seem as if strong feeling has spilled over the line in the form of the leftover phrase. The short, pithy line has the urgency and bite of ordinary fervent talk, and Shakespeare deliberately combines it with normal pentameters to achieve the effect of impassioned speech bursting out of its social (that is, its metrical) constraints.

But this is not the whole story. As we have seen, the half-lines that bring such speeches to an end are often completed metrically by the next speaker's first words. When the first half-line has been notably passionate, the effect is sometimes to tone it down again, to recall the outburst to its metrical connections and, by implication, to its social and affectional ties. The phrase that concludes is linked to the phrase that begins, and this linkage binds more tightly together the successive human speeches that compose a drama. That speakers should share not only the general metrical form but individual lines as well mirrors the special relation of speech to drama. For drama presents human beings bound to each other by speech, not merely declaiming but defining themselves through words they speak to and receive from one another. Speech breeds speech, requires it, goads it, desires it—in life as in drama—and the shared line only realizes more intently that condition of being bound together in a common action that the play as a whole affirms.

Thus the shared line can be a means first of permitting speech to burst out of its usual constraints and then of reaffirming its metrical ties. A notable example is the exchange between the lovers Lorenzo and Jessica in *The Merchant of Venice*:

 Lorenzo. The moon shines bright. In such a night as this,
     When the sweet wind did gently kiss the trees,
     And they did make no noise, in such a night
     Troilus methinks mounted the Troyan walls,
5   And sigh'd his soul toward the Grecian tents,
     Where Cressid lay that night.
 Jessica.   In such a night
     Did Thisby fearfully o'ertrip the dew,
     And saw the lion's shadow ere himself,
     And ran dismayed away.
 Lorenzo.   In such a night
10   Stood Dido with a willow in her hand
     Upon the wild sea-banks, and waft her love
     To come again to Carthage.
 Jessica.   In such a night
     Medea gathered the enchanted herbs
     That did renew old Aeson.
 Lorenzo.   In such a night
15   Did Jessica steal from the wealthy Jew,
     And with an unthrift love did run from Venice,
     As far as Belmont.
 Jessica.   In such a night
     Did young Lorenzo swear he lov'd her well,
     Stealing her soul with many vows of faith,
     And ne'er a true one.
20 *Lorenzo.*   In such a night
     Did pretty Jessica (like a little shrew)
     Slander her love, and he forgave it her. (5.1.1–22)

Only two years or so earlier, Shakespeare had signaled the immediate intimacy of feeling between Romeo and Juliet by casting their first words to each other in the form of a sonnet whose *rhymes* are at first independent, then linked and shared. But here Shakespeare attempts something subtler—to signal through the technique of shared *lines* the union of Lorenzo and Jessica. Bowers points out that even the kinds of linked lines here proceed in pairs: lines 6 and 9 compose normal pentameters, lines 12 and 14 have an epic caesura, lines 17 and 20 omit a central stressed syllable; in each case it is Jessica who first defines the shared line-structure, and Lorenzo who follows her lead, although in a way he compels these innovative steps on her part by setting the formulaic phrase ("In such a night") at the beginning and by then facing her with an extra syllable in line 12 and an insufficient number of syllables in line 17. She returns these favors in lines 14 and 20. As in the passage from *Romeo and Juliet,* the succession of linked speeches forms a graceful dancelike motion, in which each step compels a further step.[10]

In later plays, shared lines often link speeches in such a way as to suggest the casualness of natural conversation, in which syntactical units are not all five feet long. Enobarbus is speaking of Antony:

> And for his ordinary pays his heart
> For what his eyes eat only.
>
> *Agrippa.*   Royal wench!
> She made great Caesar lay his sword to bed;
> He ploughed her, and she cropp'd.
>
> *Enobarbus.*   I saw her once
> Hop forty paces through the public street;
> And having lost her breath, she spoke, and panted,
> That she did make defect perfection,
> And breathless, power breathe forth.
>
> *Maecenas.*   Now Antony
> Must leave her utterly.
>
> *Enobarbus.*   Never, he will not   (2.2.225–33)

Shared lines can even present with dramatic intensity the contrasting moods of two conversations taking place contrapuntally:

> *Macbeth.*   . . . that function
> Is smother'd in surmise, and nothing is
> But what is not.

Banquo.	Look how our partner's rapt.
Macbeth.	If chance will have me king, why, chance may crown me
	Without my stir.
Banquo.	New honors come upon him,
	Like our strange garments, cleave not to their mould
	But with the aid of use.
Macbeth.	Come what come may,
	Time and the hour runs through the roughest day.

(Macbeth, 1.3.140–47)

What emerges here is the schizophrenic character of this state, its two opposed elements unaware of the pattern they form.

More generally, the habit of linkage impels the speeches forward. Although long pauses do occur (see Chapter 13, note 12), their tendency is to obscure the meter, so normally the characters must keep completing each other's lines without undue delay. Likewise, their own sentences, incomplete at line's end, must reach the next line without breaking the tempo. Each speech and each line draws the next after it, compels it into being. To take but one further example, too long to quote but worth citing: all thirty-eight speeches in *The Winter's Tale,* Act 5, Scene 3—or all but one?—are metrically linked either to the preceding or to the following speech; twenty-three are linked to both.

For Shakespeare, then, the shared line that links two speeches usually has the effect of tightening the dramatic relationships between people in addition to giving the characters a further metrical framework (the short line) in which to cast some part of their utterances. So long as the half-line is completed, the decorum of verse drama is kept. But the uncompleted short line, even at the end of an orderly speech, suggests a momentary breakdown of the system, a paring of the normal two-phrase line to a single phrase. When several such lines occur in a passage, the effect can be almost that of a runaway language, still iambic but alarmingly unstrung. The immediate result is not chaos; short lines themselves, as we have seen with the crowd in *Julius Caesar,* can develop their own counter-order or can modulate into prose. By keeping the proportion of short lines to normal verse lines quite low (no higher than about one in five), Shakespeare sustains the verse order. But as we survey the rest of Shakespeare's deviant lines (Chapters 11–13) and follow his handling of the relation between phrase and line (Chapter 14), we shall continue to see how these verse techniques gradually turn the reliable Elizabethan pentameter into a verse fit to present a Jacobean, even a Mannerist, world threatened at every point by reduction to its elements. The line does not dissolve; it holds up; but it does so only by exposing its essential and fatal dependence on the spoken phrase.

CHAPTER 9

Long Lines

If short lines come in many varieties and may sometimes be read as either separate or shared, long lines present problems of their own. It is difficult even to say how often they occur. Some scholars think them extremely rare: "A proper alexandrine with six accents . . . is seldom found in Shakespeare" (Abbott, 397). Concerned to regularize Shakespeare's lines, such scholars find ways (many plausible, some not) of reducing Shakespeare's apparent hexameters to pentameters. More tolerant editors view the hexameter line as a legitimate feature of Shakespeare's dramatic verse; according to E. K. Chambers, it occurs once in every sixty-nine blank-verse lines. After short lines and lines with extra syllables at a mid-line break, hexameters make up the largest number of metrically deviant lines in Shakespeare's plays. They appear only occasionally in the early plays (though *Richard II* eccentrically contains fifty-four of them), but much more often in the portentous plays from *Hamlet* through *The Winter's Tale* (see Appendix B).

Shakespeare seems to have been willing to use hexameters whenever they seemed apt to his purposes. For most such lines, that probably means whenever some possible pattern of antiphonal balance between echoing three-foot line-segments can achieve a momentary special effect. For the chief difference between pentameter and hexameter lines is not that the latter has two more syllables or one more foot but that it has a strong tendency to divide into two equal segments, which the iambic pentameter line *cannot* do (see above, Chapter 1, pp. 4–5). But this readiness to divide into two halves makes a reader or listener uncertain as to whether some verse is best described as hexameter or trimeter. Hexameters often *sound like* double trimeters.

So it is when Richard III (at this point still Duke of Gloucester) courts Anne:

192	*Anne.*	I would I knew thy heart.
	Gloucester.	'Tis figur'd in my tongue.
	Anne.	I fear me both are false.
	Gloucester.	Then never was man true.
196	*Anne.*	Well, well, put up your sword.
	Gloucester.	Say then my peace is made.
	Anne.	That shalt thou know hereafter.
	Gloucester.	But shall I live in hope?
200	*Anne.*	All men, I hope, live so.
	Gloucester.	Vouchsafe to wear this ring.
	Anne.	To take is not to give.

(*Richard III*, 1.2.192–202)

Such antiphonal passages occur with some frequency in Shakespeare's plays. But this one is different from most in its resistance to a strict hexameter reading. For the first four lines, Anne's speech begins and Gloucester's completes an apparent hexameter. But then, as a metrical echo to what has been happening in the scene, lines 196–98 modulate to a reverse order, in which Gloucester's trimeter leads and Anne's follows (lines 199–202). The sense of hexameter is as strong at the end as it was at the beginning, but it has been arrived at through a metrical *bouleversement* which may be unique.[1]

The occasional sudden appearance of such symmetrical exchanges provides a pleasurable metrical variation from the usual unbalanced pentameter. We hear this pattern frequently in what appear to be shared hexameters:

Petruchio. I say it is the moon.
Katharina.   I know it is the moon.

(*The Taming of the Shrew*, 4.5.16)

Queen. To whom do you speak this?
Hamlet.   Do you see nothing there?

. . . .

Hamlet. Nor did you nothing hear?
Queen.   No, nothing but ourselves.

(*Hamlet*, 3.4.131, 133)

144

Lear.	So young, and so untender?	
Cordelia.		So young, my lord, and true.

(King Lear, 1.1.106–7)

This high degree of pattern may also be realized in the continued speech of one character:

To have what we would have, we speak not what we mean.

(Measure for Measure, 2.4.118)

None that I know will be, much that I fear may chance

(Julius Caesar, 2.4.32)

But all hexameter lines are not so highly patterned. Especially in the middle and later plays, where Shakespeare's sentences characteristically run from midline to midline, we frequently meet a line whose first half ends one segment of thought and whose second half begins another:

Hath this extent, no more. Rude am I in my speech   (*Othello*, 1.3.81)

I leave him to your hand. What muffled fellow's that?

(Measure for Measure, 5.1.486)

In such a line, the thought may be quite continuous, but divided rhetorically or grammatically in the middle:

Most of our city did; only myself stood out   (*Twelfth Night*, 3.3.35)

That father lost, lost his, and the survivor bound   (*Hamlet*, 1.2.90)

There may be even more divisions within the line. Here is Olivia, smitten with Cesario's charms, which (she says)

Do give thee five-fold blazon: not too fast: soft, soft

(Twelfth Night, 1.5.293)

Five-fold blazon in a six-foot line. Here is Macbeth answering Lennox's question, and then, with an accuracy only the audience will pick up, correcting himself:

> Goes the King hence to-day?
>
> > He does; he did appoint so.
>
> > > *(Macbeth, 2.3.53)*

When alexandrines occur in shared speeches, as they often do, the second speaker may respond to the first:

> *Westmoreland.*   O that we now had here
> > But one ten thousand of those men in England
> > That do no work to-day!
>
> *King.*   What's he that wishes so?
>
> > > *(Henry V, 4.3.16–18)*

Or the second speaker may introduce an ostensibly new subject. In this example, we are free to think, or the actor to suggest, that it is not a new subject at all:

> *Goneril.*   My fool usurps my body.
> *Oswald.*   Madam, here *comes* my lord.
>
> > > *(King Lear, 4.2.28; emphasis added)*

Sometimes an alexandrine will be made up of three or more speeches:

> *Cassius.*   I do not think it good.
> *Brutus.*   Your reason?
> *Cassius.*   This it is:
>
> > > *(Julius Caesar, 4.3.198)*

> *Fairies.*   Ready; and I, and I, and I. Where shall we go?
>
> > > *(A Midsummer Night's Dream, 3.1.163)*

Hexameters may also be used for special occasions, such as the emblematic verses prepared for the caskets in *The Merchant of Venice* (2.7.5, 7, 9):

> "Who chooseth me, shall gain what many men desire"
>
> "Who chooseth me, shall get as much as he deserves"
>
> "Who chooseth me, must give and hazard all he hath"

Some hexameters do not break into component phrases but simply require twelve syllables to say what they have to say:

How dares thy harsh rude tongue sound this unpleasing news?

(Richard II, 3.4.74)

Fleeter than arrows, bullets, wind, thought, swifter things

(Love's Labor's Lost, 5.2.261)

Hexameter lines, then, appearing occasionally in pentameter verse, may vary the pace of the line, heighten its patterning, or provide some more particular effect: a filling out; a deliberate resumption of the rhetoric after a deliberate pause; grandeur; portentousness; a smooth and rhythmic transition to the next speaker. But we need not hunt down specific expressive functions for every alexandrine we find in Shakespeare. Some, no doubt, are the result of later authorial revision (cuts or insertions); some arise from mislineation by compositors or editors; and some are probably fictional hexameters invented by our own misreading. Many lines apparently twelve syllables long dissolve into pentameter when we understand the syllabic conventions Shakespeare is using (see below, Chapters 10 and 11).[2]

The hexameter line may stand out momentarily from others when they are spoken together in the theater; along with other variant and deviant forms, it provides some variety and temporary relief from strict iambic pentameter. But it still carries forward the iambic pattern, still rides that iambic current. If anything, patterned hexameters are likely to be more insistently iambic than pentameters. The alexandrine often functions as a resting line, more roomy than most, but offering refuge only for a moment from the tenser, harder-working, less symmetrical pentameter.

Many long lines in Shakespeare (and other playwrights) apparently are produced by the addition of a "vocative or other phrase of direct address, or occasionally by an exclamatory adverb" such as "Ay" or "No" (Brooke, 194–95). Such lines often look as if the extra element had been inserted or a name changed, perhaps during production, to secure emphatic identification of the person to whom a speech is addressed, to make a character's position clearer, or to dramatize some essential rhetorical point. Some examples, with the "extra" element in brackets:

[Ay,] much is the force of heaven-bred poesy.

(Two Gentlemen of Verona, 3.2.71)

[Sirrah,] get thee to Plashy, to my sister Gloucester   (Richard II, 2.2.90)

Now [Ulysses] I begin to relish thy advice   (Troilus and Cressida, 1.3.386)

At some late point in the production of a play, Shakespeare may have cared less about breaking the meter than about increasing dramatic immediacy and strength. Other lines, too, may have arrived at a longer-than-usual form through revision during production, either for reasons of staging or because the author had a happy second thought. In the previously quoted line from *Love's Labor's Lost* (5.2.261), "Fleeter than arrows, bullets, wind, thought, swifter things," we may imagine (without any authority) that "arrows" or "bullets" was a later addition and a sufficiently felicitous one to justify breaking the pentameter.

A handful of heptameter lines appear in Shakespeare's plays:

Rouse up revenge from ebon den with fell Alecto's snake

(2 Henry IV, 5.5.37)

By the way we met my wife, her sister, and a rabble more

(The Comedy of Errors, 5.1.235–36)

Lock'd in her monument. She had a prophesying fear

(Antony and Cleopatra, 4.14.120)

I cannot tremble at it. Were it Toad, or Adder, Spider

(Cymbeline, 4.2.90)

The first line helps to characterize Pistol's bizarre English; as I have suggested above (Chapter 7), it may be merely iambic prose. The second line looks as if two lines have been somehow truncated and made into one. The third and fourth may be the result of revision (the addition of "prophesying" and "Toad, or Adder").

Such lines represent extremes in Shakespeare's practice; the pentameter line is always central. But, as the next three chapters will show, before we can follow the five-foot line with confidence, we need to understand the conventions that govern the counting, the frequent crowding, and the occasional omission of Shakespeare's syllables.

148

CHAPTER 10

Shakespeare's Syllabic Ambiguity: More Than Meets the Ear

Shakespeare's English was different from ours. Whatever modern dialect we speak, Shakespeare and his contemporaries certainly pronounced many words—even words that are still essentially *our* words— quite differently. Because of differences in *intonation,* our own speaking of lines written by Shakespeare may, even at its most expressive, have a somewhat different tune, though Shakespeare's words still lend themselves splendidly to witty and vehement speech. Shakespeare's *syntax,* too, may at times take forms that we find unfamiliar, but, by and large, the structure of most of his sentences, even when obscure, is quickly recognizable as that of our own English. A more substantial difference is that which divides Shakespeare's *vowels* from our own. Although scholars have disagreed on this matter, the view that now appears dominant (see Cercignani and Dobson) is that Shakespeare and his contemporaries gave to the vowels of great numbers of English words different values from those that are now understood as Received Pronunciation, and these in turn are often different from the vowel-values active in the speech of many communities of speakers— Americans, for example, whose regional dialects are also numerous.

No one now, however, believes that Shakespeare's plays should regularly be performed in their original London or Warwickshire dialect. Although the effectiveness of rhyme, puns, assonance, and other sound devices is altered by historical changes in vowel-values, modern audiences must be content to receive the sound of Shakespeare's melodious English on the new terms that four hundred years' evolution of the language has imposed on our ears. We are still not foreign to Shakespeare's English, but the formidable systems of sound that his plays present to our linguistic and poetic sensibilities have always to be transformed into a different current—our own as we read, and that of our actors when we hear the plays spoken in the theater.

The difficulties of this transformative enterprise are not the chief subject here, but some aspects of it are relevant. For the purposes of metrical study, we can usually ignore the differences in intonation, syntax, and vowel pronunciation. But we cannot ignore those features of Shakespeare's English that make for syllabic ambiguity in the verse of his plays. This is much less true for the poems. There, like other poets from Surrey on, Shakespeare consistently aimed to make his lines unambiguously decasyllabic, except for some feminine endings (see Ramsey, Appendix 1, 191–208). But in the language he prepared for the stage, probably to make it sound more like ordinary English speech, the evidence seems overwhelming that Shakespeare increasingly cultivated both metrical and syllabic conventions aimed at making the verbal texture less obviously iambic. The later plays use devices of syllabic compression and expansion that readers, actors, and audiences must recognize if they are to hear Shakespeare's lines as metrically coherent.

Seymour Chatman tells us in *A Theory of Meter:*

> Although there are differences of opinion about the constitution of the syllable, the problem does not seem serious from the point of view of metrics. Metrics is concerned mostly with the number of syllables-as-events; syllables are easily recognized, and the problem of identifying their boundaries rarely matters. . . . The only important question for metrics is "How many syllables are there?" (39)

For almost all of English iambic pentameter verse after Wyatt, including most of Shakespeare, what Chatman says is true: readers have little difficulty in deciding how many syllables there are. When they appear on the page, anyone who has a pretty good idea of what a syllable is can count them. The questions of where to assign stress and how much stress to assign are often more debatable. But many lines and passages in Shakespeare raise perplexing questions about the number of syllables we are meant to hear, or about the number Shakespeare and his contemporaries apparently did hear. Contractions, elisions, and syncopations render many of Shakespeare's lines metrically problematical, and an even more troublesome question is whether these adjustments are made to the meter or to the spoken sound or to both.

Paul Ramsey, in *The Fickle Glass,* distinguishes three positions taken by scholars on whether "apparent extra syllables" occur in the *Sonnets:* (1) they occur and should be "sounded and counted metrically"; (2) they are "semisyllables, lightly sounded and not counted metrically"; (3) "they do not exist" (191). Ramsey sensibly "supports the third position for the sonnets, and strictly only for them, even though a good deal of the evidence goes beyond" (191). Ramsey is probably right about the *Sonnets,* where a strict syllabism seems appropriate to well-made courtly poems; but the flowing dialogue spoken from the stage can benefit greatly from a more relaxed treatment of syllables, and the evidence seems strong that in his plays, along with other techniques for representing speech convincingly (less rhyme, more enjambment, more various line-forms), Shakespeare also made increasing use of syllabic ambiguity. It is true, as Ramsey observes, that Elizabethans actually reduced some forms further than we are likely to think possible (199), but the middle to late plays of Shakespeare put us so often to the test that we may wonder whether all metrical reduction resulted in a perfectly clipped syllabism.[1]

In any case, everyone who wants to hear or speak the verse of Shakespeare's plays should understand sixteenth-century conventions of syllable and stress. The subject is notoriously treacherous, but the following concise list summarizes the chief syllabic conventions of compression and expansion that Shakespeare uses in his plays. (Here and elsewhere, unless the text makes entirely clear the need to fuse syllables, elision or syncopation of syllables will be indicated by a slur mark: for example, *hideous, general.*)

Compression

1. Contiguous vowels may be elided, either within a word or at word-margins: *I am, you are, he is, to us, th'effect, superfluous, happier, Aufidius, hideous, mutual.*

Silent or almost silent *h* presents no barrier to this elision, and phrases like the following may be monosyllabic: *I have, thou hast, he had, th'hour.*

Elision may also occur when a glide intervenes between the two vowels: *I would, merry as, my invention, borrower.*

In obedience to this convention, words that we may think of as disyllabic are often treated as monosyllabic in Shakespeare's meter: *being, seeing, knowing, power, flower, hour, fire, prayer.*

2. Common disyllables that show an intervocalic *th, v,* or *r* will often be treated as monosyllables: *either, neither, whether, whither, even, heaven, seven, never, given, having, over, ever, spirit, marry* (as interjection), *Sirrah, warrant.* Presumably, poets heard such intervocalic consonants as less than fully formed.

3. Especially in his later plays, Shakespeare frequently reduces the syllabic value of prepositional phrases that include *the: in the* may become *i' th'; of the* may become *o' th',* and so on. Apostrophes, however, may well have been supplied by the compositor and are not always to be relied on. For example, in

Th'ex|pedition of my violent love   (*Macbeth,* 2.3.110)

the apostrophe is unnecessary and, if heeded, would result in a headless line.

4. Sixteenth-century poets commonly syncopate (compress) polysyllabic words; in particular, they often treat words stressed on the antepenult as if their last two syllables were reduced to one; the penultimate vowel disappears. Thus, *natural* becomes *nat'ral, general* becomes *gen'ral, Majesty* becomes *Ma'sty,* and so on. From this period forward, such syncopation was conventional when the consonant following the vowel being lost was a liquid or nasal (as in *general* or *cardinal*), but Shakespeare's syncopation may extend to words like *vagabond* (*vag'bond*), *eloquence* (*el'quence*), *impediment* (*imped'ment*), *innocent* (*in'cent*), and *Imogen* (*Im'gen*)[2]— indeed, in his later plays, to almost any polysyllable: *importun'cy, count'feit, rem'died, marr'ges, rec'mend, lib'tine, enm'ties,* and *carc'sses.*[3]

Reading Shakespeare's verse, one needs to employ these techniques of compression and sometimes to make choices between them. For example, when Hamlet responds to the King's question about his cloudy mood,

Not so my lord, I am too much i' th' sun,   (*Hamlet,* 1.2.67)

we can read the verse two ways—either by taking the apostrophes seriously:

Not so, my lord, | Ĭ ám | tŏo múch | ĭ̄ th' sún,

or by eliding "I am":

Not so, my lord, | Ĭ̄ am tŏo | much ĭ' | th' sún.

Expansion

The devices for compressing syllables are merely optional, and words or phrases reduced in some lines may in others receive full syllabic value. Diphthongs, triphthongs, and contiguous vowels either in the same or in separate words may be treated metrically either as monosyllabic or as disyllabic. But on the same principle, some words that are reduced in contemporary English may be expanded.

5. Some contiguous vowels that we always pronounce as one may be disyllabic. The most notable example is the *-tion* suffix which Shakespeare treats variously as monosyllabic or disyllabic (*ti-on* or *si-on*), according to his metrical convenience. This usage may have been somewhat archaic even in Shakespeare's day, as the pronunciation of final *-e* was in Chaucer's, but other poets use it as he does, and it apparently was a plausible way of treating this suffix, even though to our ears the disyllabic pronunciation, unless it is limited to the merest hint, always makes the verse stumble. By a similar process, the adjectival ending *-ious* or *-uous* may be treated as disyllabic, and such words as *ocean, patient, marriage, soldier,* and *sergeant* as trisyllabic.

6. Some words that many contemporary speakers regard as monosyllabic may occasionally be treated as disyllabic in Shakespeare's verse if their vowels are (or can be construed as) diphthongs, especially when the vowel is followed by an *r*. All the following words are evidently treated at least once as disyllabic: *weird, more, fair, poor, bear, boar, hair, yours, door, tears, fierce, fourth,* and perhaps *whore* and *score; nine, slain, thyme, right,* and *sweet*. By the same process, the disyllable *bounty* is expanded to a trisyllable (*Richard II,* 2.3.67); so is *frailty* (*Othello,* 4.3.101).

7. Some words may appear to insert an extra vowel, usually before

one of the "semi-vowels" *r* or *l* when it occurs medially and after the word's principal accent: *angry, Henry, monstrous, children, remembrance, fiddler, dazzled, wrastler, changeling, unmingled,* and even perhaps *country* (*Twelfth Night*, 1.2.21; *Coriolanus*, 1.9.17) and *England* (*Hamlet*, 4.3.46). Probably the most famous example appears in these lines of Lady Macbeth's:

> The raven himself is hoarse
> That croaks the fatal en|trance | of Duncan
> Under my battlements.   (*Macbeth*, 1.5.38–40)

This figure is known as anaptyxis to English rhetoricians and is familiar to us in some modern speakers' pronunciation of *el-m, fil-m,* and *ath-lete.*

8. Like other contemporary poets and playwrights, Shakespeare also uses the *-ed* suffix of verbs and participial adjectives as an extra syllable when the meter requires it, even where Elizabethan speakers of English had apparently long since dropped it from their pronunciation. In some early plays, he also occasionally voices the silent *-es* ending: e.g., *dayes* and *whale's.*[4]

Scholars and editors aware of these syllabic conventions have not always appreciated their full import for Shakespeare's verse. They have often proceeded on such assumptions as the following: that the lines of Shakespeare's texts are either metrically "correct" or metrically deviant; that the syllabic conventions function essentially as a means by which we can regularize (or "resolve") thousands of lines; and that for Shakespeare, his actors, and his audience, the pronunciation cleared up the problem and resolved the metrical ambiguity one way or the other. Behind such assumptions lie the further ones that regular verse is best and that the aim of the critic of Shakespeare is to explain away all apparent metrical irregularities. For most sensible scholars, the difficulty in doing this has been the serious implausibility of some of the more extreme elisions and syncopations (*he was, vag'bond*), especially when the words and phrases in question appear elsewhere unelided and unsyncopated. The example of Chaucer's ambiguous *-e* is relevant, but Shakespeare's practice is far more complex, involving not just a single phoneme but a wide range of uncertainly sounded syllabic elements. Iambic pentameter is in large part a syllabic meter, but its count of syllables, at least in its dramatic (Shakespearean) form, is both strict and uncertain.

It is evidently meant to be so. In many passages, and in the late plays often, Shakespeare apparently preferred the number of syllables to be problematical. As readers, our most appropriate response is not to decide whether a given cluster of phonemes is one or two syllables, but to recognize and savor—recognize in order to savor—their problematical condition.

Consider, for example, the following words spoken by Iago in the course of his deception of Othello:

What

If I had said I had seen him do you wrong?</div>   (*Othello*, 4.1.23–24)

Knowing how Shakespeare often reduced syllables, and how readily English speakers do so, and responding to the metrical current of the line, we can see at once that the second "I had" can be reduced to "I'd." (Shakespeare was unlikely to write "I'd" because that contraction in his work always means "I would.") But how far is it reduced? All the way to "I'd" (one syllable), or only to "I(u)d" (a bit more than one syllable)? As the line stands, we are likely to give the second "had" almost as much syllabic value as the first, just as we give to the second, unstressed "I" almost as much speech-stress as to the first, metrically stressed one. To reduce the second "I had" to a monosyllabic "I'd" diminishes the rhythmic interest of the line. The second "I had" needs to retain some shadow of its disyllabic origin, so that we hear it as an only faintly diminished echo of the first. To my ear the two phrases sound very similar, the second "had" only slightly reduced from what it was earlier.

Why is it reduced at all? The speech reason is that "seen" is the focal syllable of the whole line and the "I had" that precedes it will probably be reduced to prepare for the added emphasis on "seen." Perfectly in harmony with the phrasal patterns of speech, the meter here treats the two instances of the phrase very differently:

155

Ĭf Ĭ | hăd sáid | Ĭ hăd séen | him do you wrong?

The point is that in Shakespeare such slur marks as we may place over "I had" may not entirely reduce two syllables to one. There is a residue of syllabic value that makes us realize how blurred the margin is between a nonsyllable and a syllable[5] (as between information and insinuation).

Another passage that may show how differently Shakespeare sometimes treated diphthongs or triphthongs according to his metrical convenience is the one that precedes John of Gaunt's famous celebration of England. Words with similar or comparable contiguous vowels have been italicized:

> Methinks I am a prophet new *inspir'd*,
> And thus *expiring* do foretell of him:
> His rash fierce blaze of *riot* cannot last,
> For *violent fires* soon burn out themselves;
> Small *show'rs* last long, but sudden storms are short;
> He *tires* betimes that spurs too fast betimes;
> With eager feeding food doth choke the feeder;
> Light vanity, *insatiate* cormorant,
> Consuming means, soon preys upon itself.   (*Richard II*, 2.1.31–39)

We cannot tell whether the first line's ending is masculine or feminine, but in five other words the same stressed triphthong is twice metrically disyllabic (in *riot* and *fires*) and thrice metrically monosyllabic (in *expiring, violent,* and *tires*). (In two other words, *show'rs* and *insatiate,* contiguous vowels are also monosyllabic.) Yet the actual sound of several of the five is virtually identical—in *fires* and *tires,* for example. Shakespeare usually treats both these words as monosyllabic, but the variability of his practice is evident in this line from *Julius Caesar* (3.1.171):

Ăs fĭ|re drĭves | oŭt fíre, | so pity pity

Shakespeare's meter determines that the first *fire* must be disyllabic; it does not guarantee that the second one will be pronounced in a way that is unambiguously monosyllabic. In most lines, certainly, Shakespeare aims to write a "regular" iambic line, and Dorothy Sipe has meticulously shown that in using variant forms of a word (for example, *bide* or *abide, kindled* or *enkindled, twixt* or *betwixt*) his principal consideration must have been metrical. He usually avoids anapests and the more bizarre metrical anomalies. Still, close study suggests that he makes deliberate and increasing use of syllabic ambiguity to give his lines more texture. In later plays especially, more syllables than the meter requires seem present in many lines:

1. Not to | knit my | soul to an | appro|ved wanton

    (*Much Ado about Nothing*, 4.1.44)

2. She was false as water.

    Thou art rash as fire to say   (*Othello*, 5.2.134)

3. Given to | capti|vity me | and my ut|most hopes   (*Othello*, 4.2.51)

4. I drink | to th' ge|neral joy |o' th' | whole table   (*Macbeth*, 3.4.88)

5. Than car|ry it but | by the suit | of the gen|try to him

    (*Coriolanus*, 2.1.238)

6. The life | o' th' need: | having found | the back | door open

    (*Cymbeline*, 5.3.45)

7. *Lafew.*   Then here's | a man | stands that | has brought | his pardon.
    I would | you had kneel'd, | my lord, | to ask | me mercy,
65   And that at | my bid|ding you | could so stand up.
King.   I would I had, so I had broke thy pate,
    And ask'd thee mercy for't.   (*All's Well That Ends Well*, 2.1.63–67)

It will be evident from these examples how casually Shakespeare contracts when he needs to and declines to contract when he doesn't. But even some contractions must be of different dimensions. Was "to an" (1) or "Given" (3) or "for't" (7, line 67) as convincingly monosyllabic as "here's" (7, line 63)? Did "captivity" (3) wholly lose its third syllable? Do we not hear some small coda to the metrical single syllable in "She was" and "Thou art" (2) and "you had" (7, line 64)? How complete is the elision in "my ut-" (3) and "carry it" (5)? And is what we hear in these contracted phrases significantly less than what we hear in the uncontracted "me and" (3), "that has" (7, line 63), "to ask" (7, line 64), or the second "I had" in example 7, line 66? Finally, it is worth noting that the second set of contracted words in example 4 turns out not to need abbreviating: abbreviation has become a compositor's habit. It may, to be sure, serve as an accurate guide to pronunciation (more or less), but not to th' meter, all of which suggests that any phonetic distinction made on or off the stage between th' abbreviated and the unabbreviated forms was slight. Even when we can trust th' apostrophes, it may be that many o' th' elisions they request us to make, and the sync'pations required by the meter, are metrical only, not phonetic, that they signal a direction, not an achieved pronunciation, that we may *pronounce* one way and *measure* another. Or at least it is possible, even likely, that Shakespeare's ear could tolerate in such lines, and enjoy, the extra little tail, the enclitic half-syllable, that makes the line sound fuller than usual, crammed with more phonemes than it technically has room for.

That Shakespeare in many lines deliberately cultivates this metrical ambiguity seems clear when we recall how clean and definite the lines of most of his lyrical and dramatic predecessors were. Surrey, Gascoigne, Googe, Turbervile, Sidney, and Shakespeare, too, in his nondramatic poetry, avoid writing lines in which the number of syllables is problematical. Marlowe's metrical irregularities are different in character: mainly regular, he prefers outright anapests to questionable elisions and syncopations. Spenser elides some contiguous vowels but is otherwise much more restrained in his treatment of syllabic value. Only a few of Shakespeare's younger fellow playwrights imitated the master's syllabic freedom; most of them followed Jonson's lead toward the regularities of Augustan verse. Probably Shakespeare, in eliding vowels and compressing syllables as freely as he does, is emulating writers of Latin and Italian poetry, though he varies his practice at will, whereas they (like Jonson)[6] follow strict rules. Like Wyatt, he may have realized that a line could gain in richness of sound and sense if its meter trips hurriedly over some syllables, as if the thought or feeling of the speaking character were fuller than its words could quite articulate. To write ten-syllable lines that have, in a sense, eleven or twelve syllables (or eleven and a half) is to crowd the air with meanings only half-spoken, partly concealed. The hypermetrical half-syllables imply that, just as the line contains more in the way of syllables than the meter promises, so too in the meanings conveyed by the words there is more than meets the ear.

Shakespeare's syllabic freedom combines with his metrical variety (the subject of Chapters 11 to 13) and his remarkable inventiveness in adjusting English phrases and sentences to the metrical line (Chapter 14) to produce an iambic pentameter verse which, for all its powerful influence on later poets, is unique in the English tradition. The verse of Shakespeare's later plays is different in its structure and manner from any earlier English poetry. After his time it was often censured for "incorrectness," but its syllabic, metrical, and phrasal freedoms have rarely been understood as working together to create Shakespeare's singular verse art.[7]

CHAPTER 11

Lines with Extra Syllables

As we noted earlier, although the lines of Shakespeare's poems are almost always perfectly regular, in the plays many lines diverge from the standard form. Some divergences we accept as normal: feminine endings, for example, or trochaic variations. But some are unfamiliar to later ears, though most of them occur in such earlier poets as Lydgate, Wyatt, and Chaucer. These optional forms of the iambic pentameter line help to make Shakespeare's rhythmic language abundantly various and offer opportunities for richly expressive metrical effects. This chapter will describe how Shakespeare's pentameter lines can remain pentameter and yet include more syllables than the usual ten.

Feminine Endings

For more than a century, scholars interested in feminine endings have mainly wanted to count them. It was observed that playwrights in the 1590s and after resorted to them more frequently than before, that Shakespeare and some of his contemporaries varied in the extent to which they used them, that Shakespeare himself wrote more of them as he grew older, and that counts of feminine endings could therefore provide evidence for the dating or attribution of plays or parts of plays. Since normally authors do not themselves count such stylistic features and may not deliberately increase or decrease their numbers from one work to the next, this method of analysis has to be employed with some care.[1] Still, it is certain that Shakespeare's feminine endings became more numerous over the years; Tarlinskaja estimates that their percentage in successive periods of Shakespeare's work rises from 10.8 percent to 18.4 to 26.9 to 32.9.[2] So sharp an increase subtly affects the structure of the poetic line and the way we hear it in the theater.

For most readers of English poetry, a line with a so-called feminine ending (one unstressed syllable following the last stressed syllable) is familiar enough. At first sight, or sound, it seems a modest and inoffensive, even attractive, variation, a decorative endline flourish which does not substantially change the character of the iambic pentameter line. Such early Tudor writers as Surrey and Gascoigne rarely use the feminine ending, apparently sensing that the extra syllable blurs the iambic purity of the line. Although such endings occur sometimes in songs and seem at home in the more lyrical poetic forms, Sidney's sonnets in *Astrophil and Stella* deploy not a single feminine ending. Gradually, however, writers appear to have become more tolerant of this variation. Puttenham suggests that a strong accent on the preceding syllable makes a final unaccented one seem hardly to be there at all: "the sharpe accent falles upon the *penultima* or last save one sillable of the verse, which doth so drowne the last, as he seemeth to passe away in maner unpronounced, and so make the verse seeme even" (59). Shakespeare and Spenser use feminine endings freely in their sonnets and other poems, often to secure a distinctly lyrical effect, even in poems written entirely or largely in iambic pentameter. In a rhymed poem, after all, one feminine ending requires another; the effect is, consequently, less casual than in blank verse. In English, where feminine rhymes often (and triple rhymes always) run the risk of seeming comic, they may impart a playful spirit to the lines. Thus, Sonnet 87:

> Farewell, thou art too dear for my possessing,
> And like enough thou know'st thy estimate.
> The charter of thy worth gives thee releasing;
> My bonds in thee are all determinate.
> For how do I hold thee but by thy granting,
> And for that riches where is my deserving?
> The cause of this fair gift in me is wanting,
> And so my patent back again is swerving.
> Thyself thou gav'st, thy own worth then not knowing,
> Or me, to whom thou gav'st it, else mistaking;
> So thy great gift, upon misprision growing,

Comes home again, on better judgement making.
Thus have I had thee as a dream doth flatter:
In sleep a king, but waking no such matter.

In such a poem, the extra identical unstressed syllable becomes a norm, which heightens the degree of correspondence at line's end; the final foot is regularly an amphibrach ($\smile\smile\smile$)—only lines 2 and 4 depart from this pattern—and the poem's sound takes on a distinctive character. We soon begin to listen for the extra syllable, especially since every line is endstopped and the rhyme scheme tells us what to expect at the end of each quatrain's later lines. The little twirl at the end, a more extended echo than the single rhyming syllable, contributes to the light mockery which the speaker apparently directs at the young man, at himself, at his own argument, at his own predicament.

In a different spirit, when Tarquin, in *The Rape of Lucrece,* gives free rein to "his veins," their anarchic release is described in a stanza distinguished by its feminine endings, which have the effect of increasing the wildness of the turmoil:

And they like straggling slaves for pillage fighting,
Obdurate vassals fell exploits effecting,
In bloody death and ravishment delighting,
Nor children's tears nor mothers' groans respecting,
Swell in their pride, the onset still expecting.
   Anon his beating heart, alarum striking,
   Gives the hot charge, and bids them do their liking.   (428-34)

The intent here, of course, is not mockery; the extra syllables convey crowdedness, excess, lack of restraint.

If feminine rhymes enhance our sense of pattern, a series of feminine endings makes blank verse seem more speechlike, *less* patterned, exactly because, as in phrases of ordinary speech, rhyme is absent and the final unstressed syllables fail to match:

To be, or not to be, that is the question:
Whether 'tis nobler in the mind to suffer
The slings and arrows of outrageous fortune,

Or to take arms against a sea of troubles,
And by opposing, end them.[3]   (*Hamlet*, 3.1.55–59)

Shakespeare's later plays, in fact, show four related style changes: feminine endings appear much more frequently; the verse in which they appear is usually blank; the phrasing breaks more often after the sixth syllable (or later) rather than after the fourth or fifth (see Oras); and most of the lines are enjambed. These four developments make the line-ending seem less of a boundary than it is in earlier sixteenth-century verse; the phrase that begins late in the line will more often run over its ending, and if the ending is feminine, the extra syllable will occur in mid-phrase. Here are two examples from the same scene in *The Winter's Tale:*

Or hand of man hath done. Therefore | I keep it
Lonely, | apart   (5.3.17–18)

Hermione was not so much wrin|kled, nothing
So a|ged as | this seems.   (5.3.28–29)

The last foot of each first line above is an amphibrach, which introduces another variant into the iambic pattern. In the first example, the amphibrach modulates into the trochee that begins the next line, and the repeated motif—the falling rhythm ending one line, beginning the next—emphasizes the melancholy shading on "lonely." In the second line, whose rhythm has been trochaic throughout, the extra syllable enforces a slight hesitation at the end of the line, a hesitation which the enjambment had appeared to deny. (If Shakespeare had written "not" instead of "nothing," for example, we would probably feel less inclined to hesitate at the line-ending.)

One variation employed with restraint by Shakespeare but developed vigorously by some younger Jacobean playwrights is the "heavy" feminine ending, in which the metrically unstressed final syllable actually receives a secondary speech stress.[4] Here, for example, is Deflores speaking in Middleton's *The Changeling:*

O, this act
Has put me into spirit; I was as greedy on't

As the parch'd earth of moisture, when the clouds weep.

109   Did you not mark, I wrought myself into't,
      Nay, sued and kneel'd for't: Why was all that pains took?
      You see I have thrown contempt upon your gold,
      Not that I want it not, for I do piteously:
      In order I will come unto't, and make use on't,
      But 'twas not held so precious to begin with;

115   For I place wealth after the heels of pleasure;
      And were not I resolv'd in my belief
      That thy virginity were perfect in thee,
      I should but take my recompense with grudging,
      As if I had but half my hopes I agreed for.   (3.4.106–19)

Only three of the lines do not have feminine endings, and one effect of the frequent heavy ending is to make even the normal feminine endings—in lines 115 and 118, for example—sound heavier. After a while we expect the heavy ending and are likely to hear it in the normal eleven-syllable line.

Here and in many contemporary passages, the additional syllable at the end seems a major element in the line's structure. Since the final foot is the variant one, we listen for it, and if the verse is endstopped, the device is almost as effective as rhyme in drawing our attention to the line-ending, where something turbulent or pathetic is about to happen, some structural disturbance of the basic iambic pattern. But whereas rhyme makes for pattern and resolution, the usual blank-verse feminine ending often makes the line seem either to trail off—to be swallowed up, as Puttenham suggests—or, when it is enjambed, to scurry over two unstressed syllables. Or if the final syllable receives partial stress, it can perceptibly reinforce a sinister or sentimental, mournful or caressing tone.

Whether the choice of *feminine* as a term to describe this ending was accidental or fitted contemporary notions of gender, iambic verse that regularly ends with an unstressed syllable takes on a quality which, in different lines, may variously be described as soft, haunting, yearning, pliant, seductive. In verse that is enjambed, it helps to threaten our sense of the line as a line, as pentameter; in endstopped verse, it subtly undermines the line's iambic (or masculine) character.

Epic Caesuras

That Shakespeare's plays include more than sixteen hundred lines with an extra syllable before a midline pause may surprise many readers; but this kind of line, with its epic or lyric or feminine caesura, was a standard feature of fifteenth-century verse (see Chapter 2). Although after Wyatt it disappears from courtly poetry, which follows a stricter syllabic tradition, it survives in the drama of Shakespeare and his contemporaries. Shakespeare himself uses it in every play, especially from *The Merchant of Venice* on (see Appendix B).[5] Over his whole career it turns up once in every thirty-eight lines of blank verse; from *Twelfth Night* on, once in every twenty-one lines. It never appears in the poems.

The epic caesura, as its name suggests, harks back to a time when the iambic pentameter line was more consciously stitched together out of two half-lines. The extra syllable is almost always followed by punctuation, and the resumption after the implied pause seems like a new beginning, often restrained, hesitant, or deliberate. Some famous examples appear below with the extra syllable italicized:

His acts being se|ven *ages.* | At first the infant   (*As You Like It*, 2.7.143)

Must I | remem*ber:* | why, she would hang on him   (*Hamlet*, 1.2.143)

Lag of | a bro*ther?* | Why bastard? Wherefore base?   (*King Lear*, 1.2.6)

That my | youth suf*fer'd.* | My story being done   (*Othello*, 1.3.158)

Wake Duncan with | thy knock*ing!* | I would thou couldst!

(*Macbeth*, 2.2.71)

The pattern usually requires that a strong speech juncture separate the unstressed syllable before the break from the one after it. Even when the foot following the break is inverted, a speech juncture or a pause seems obligatory:

The fair | Ophe*lia.* | Nymph, in | thy orisons   (*Hamlet*, 3.1.88)

You heavens, give me | that pa*tience,* | patience | I need!

(*King Lear*, 2.4.271)

The pattern is especially common in shared lines:

Richard. Meantime, | hăve pátĭence. |
Clarence.   I must perforce. Farewell.

(*Richard III*, 1.1.116)

In all such lines, the extra syllable either allows the line's first segment to draw to an offbeat finish or insures a longer-than-usual pause at midline, or both. Sometimes, as in Edmund's and Lear's lines quoted above, the extra syllable may seem to provoke as well as to express increased agitation. In all cases, the line with such an extra syllable changes the procedures a little, ruffles the current, modifies the pattern.

As critics have often observed, the epic or feminine caesura has the same amphibrachic effect as a feminine ending, but at midline. This suggests that even as late as Shakespeare's time, when poets and audience had long become accustomed to writing and hearing some lines in which no pause is discernible, the midline seam is still potentially there. It may momentarily remind us of older line-patterns with fixed caesuras, but here it does not persist: the next line's phrasal break, if it occurs at all, will probably come in a different place. And, in concert with lines that do not so audibly break, the occasional line with an epic caesura encourages a more continuous sentence flow from a strong midline beginning to a midline feminine ending:

In the affliction of these terrible dreams
That shake us night*ly*. Better be with the dead,
Whom we, to gain our peace, have sent to peace,
Than on the torture of the mind to lie
In restless ecs*tasy*. Duncan is in his grave   (*Macbeth*, 3.2.18–22)

Later in the history of English iambic pentameter, the midline amphibrach virtually disappeared. Later still, the midline anapest became common, but this is an entirely different phenomenon. In Shakespeare's plays anapests occur (see below), but extra midline syllables most frequently follow the epic caesura pattern. That is, the key unstressed syllable belongs to the same word or phrase as the preceding stressed syllable, clinging to it as an "outride," to borrow Hopkins' term for similar effects in his system of sprung rhythm.

The extra syllable before a midline break sometimes occurs in hexameter lines:

Hyperion to a sat*yr:* so loving to my mother   *(Hamlet,* 1.2.140)

For ending thee no soon*er.* Thou hast nor youth nor age

(Measure for Measure, 3.1.32)

Sometimes the pattern appears earlier or later in the pentameter line than we expect for a "midline" break:

Early

Prevent *it,* | resist it, let it not be so   *(Richard II,* 4.1.148)

I have lov'd *thee—* |

      Make that thy question, and go rot!

(The Winter's Tale, 1.2.324)

Late

The under-hangman of | his king*dom,* | and hated   *(Cymbeline,* 2.3.130)

So dear the love my peo|ple bore *me;* | nor set   *(The Tempest,* 1.2.141)

I do not understand.

      | He's mar*ried.* |

           To who?   *(Othello,* 1.2.52)

It may even appear twice in the same line:

This Cas*ca;* | this Cin*na;* | and this, Metellus Cimber

(Julius Caesar, 2.1.96)

The increasing use of epic caesuras helps Shakespeare's later dramatic verse secure special effects of variety and tension and an extraordinarily dense poetic texture.

Triple Endings

Given the extreme flexibility of Elizabethan pronunciation, the extra syllable at line-ending or midline may be or appear to be two syllables. When two such unstressed syllables conclude a line already long enough to be heard as iambic pentameter, the line is probably meant to be heard not as hexameter with a final pyrrhic foot but as pentameter with a triple ending:

And tediousness the limbs and out|wărd floŭrĭshēs   *(Hamlet, 2.2.91)*

What's Hecuba to him, or he | tŏ Hĕcŭbă   *(Hamlet, 2.2.559)*

My thought, whose murther yet is but | fántăstĭcăl   *(Macbeth, 1.3.139)*

Shakespeare may well have been aware of the comparable Italian verse line known as *sdrucciolo* (see Giamatti, 150).

Triple endings occur frequently in Shakespeare's plays, especially the later ones, and many words that conclude this kind of line are used for the purpose again and again. Among the most common are names: Antony, Charmian, Lepidus, Octavia, Aufidius, Valeria, Cassio, Angelo, Isabel, Benedick, Diomed, Lancaster, Ireland, and Padua. Other favorite words that incorporate triple endings include *majesty, gentlemen, messenger, Capitol, followers, honesty, impossible.* Dozens of other words receive this treatment at least once. We cannot tell how far the two final syllables may have been reduced to one in performance, but it hardly matters. Whatever the practice, the impression given at the end of the line is of extra syllables (that is, somewhere between one and two).

Occasionally, not single words but phrases function in the same way as "heavy" feminine endings: "lovest me," "pardon me," "warrant thee," "slaughter thee," "follow me," "follow her," "swallow 'em," "able 'em," "pray you, sir," and even "what's her name" (*Antony and Cleopatra,* 3.13.98). The effect, once again, is to make the iambic pentameter more like speech. If English often ends phrases and sentences on strong monosyllables, its very tendency to move the primary stress of words forward to the initial syllable leads to final elements going unstressed. Shakespeare's triple ending, like his line-final pyrrhic foot—a usage rare in Milton, among others—shows his interest in having his verse reflect the casual speech patterns of ordinary talk.[6]

Two Extra Syllables at Midline

As we might expect, if the extra syllable at line-ending is occasionally expanded to two syllables, over which the tongue races trippingly, the same pattern is sometimes found at midline. Before the midline pause signaled by punctuation we may find two unstressed syllables instead of one:

> Than is | your Májestў. | There's not, I think, a subject
>
> (Henry V, 2.2.26)
>
> Orsi|no's enémỹ. | A witchcraft drew me hither   (Twelfth Night, 5.1.76)
>
> Unto | that élemẽnt. | But long it could not be   (Hamlet, 4.7.180)

In saying such lines, the actor presumably compresses the two extra syllables into what sounds like one to his ear. The effect is of one phrase coming to an end on a speechlike complex of unstressed sounds; then, after a pause, a new phrase reestablishes the iambic current.

Much more rare is the line with two extra syllables *both* at the midline break and at line's end:

> He were | much good*liĕr*. | Is't not a hand|some géntlemãn?
>
> (All's Well That Ends Well, 3.5.80)
>
> In base | appliắncẽs. | This outward-saint|ed depútỹ
>
> (Measure for Measure, 3.1.88)
>
> Here comes | the Émperŏr.
>   Is it not strange, | Caní*diŭs*
>
> (Antony and Cleopatra, 3.7.20)

In such exotic variations the extra, only half-hidden syllables all but overflow the line's metrical bounds.

Double Onset

Shakespeare apparently also wrote lines that include an extra unstressed syllable at the beginning. This too is a traditional variation; we have met it before in Wyatt and earlier poets. Like the feminine ending, the extra syllable at the beginning has an effect that may be perceived as external to the basic structure of the iambic pentameter line: it falls outside the ten-syllable core. To put it differently, both devices interpose an extra unstressed syllable between the last stressed syllable of one line and the first of the next. A line with a hypermetrical onset will rarely follow one with a hypermetrical ending, or at least not without a full phrasal break, for that would result in an awkward cluster of unstressed syllables.[7]

The line with a double onset is not always distinguishable from normal lines that begin with two easily elidable syllables:

> *I have yield*ed to. Fresh embassies and suits   *(Coriolanus, 5.3.17)*
>
> *If't be* the affliction of his love or no   *(Hamlet, 3.1.35)*

Shakespeare begins many lines with syllables that are probably meant to be elided or syncopated, but some combinations are easier to compress than others. Such an initial phrase as "Thou wilt," "You were," "You shall," "Do you," "I was," "She was," or "They were" is immediately followed by a strongly stressed syllable. Other lines begin with what is probably a monosyllabic word such as "Over," "After," "Having," or "Father." These cases suggest that other apparent instances of trisyllabic openings in Shakespeare are meant to show a hurried pronunciation of several syllables, even to the point of slurring. Most often the first two syllables lead up to a very important third one:

> *Or we'll burst* them open, if that you come not quickly
>
>   *(1 Henry VI, 1.3.28)*
>
> *And so riv*eted with faith unto your flesh   *(The Merchant of Venice, 5.1.169)*
>
> *Let's be sac*rificers, but not butchers, Caius   *(Julius Caesar, 2.1.166)*
>
> *Not a word,* a word, we stand upon our manners
>
>   *(The Winter's Tale, 4.4.164)*

Shakespeare uses this form sparingly. When it appears, it evidently signals quick, strong speech, not the lightness or languor typically conveyed by nineteenth-century anapests.

Anapests

Since at least the middle of the eighteenth century, poets and readers have known that an extra unstressed syllable might appear anywhere within the iambic pentameter line. Augustan poets and critics frowned on this practice and thought it a sign of incompetence, carelessness, or even moral corruption (see Fussell, 1954). Conformity to the metrical paradigm was a proof of moral integrity, its violation a breach of decorum and a likely sign of revolutionary proclivities. Clearly, the iambic pentameter line had a semiotic function by this time: a social institution itself, it could represent the whole social order. A more experimental Romantic aesthetic admitted occasional anapests, and many Victorian poems mix iambs and anapests freely, especially in stanzas that are moving steadily closer to accentual rhythms. For the Augustans were right: the extra midline syllable would eventually subvert the traditional iambic line from within. The extra unstressed syllable, if it appears often, has the effect of making the iambic beats more isochronous and more level, more equal in time and in force, and so of turning the speechlike, uneven iambic-pentameter discourse into a more chantlike or drumlike procession.

But in sixteenth-century iambic pentameter, anapests are still fairly rare. When extra unstressed syllables occur, they usually form the patterns we have already noticed: the feminine ending, the epic caesura, and the double onset, none of which is a genuine midline anapest. As we saw in Chapter 10, anapests that do not vanish through the trapdoors of elision, syncope, and synaeresis may not occur at all in the *Sonnets*. The extent to which they appear in the plays is something of a puzzle.

By now we have seen enough of Shakespeare's syllabic practices to understand that devices of syllable reduction were essential to his metrical art and that lines like the following are not in his system hypermetrical:

Our grandam earth, | having this | distemperature   (*1 Henry IV*, 3.1.33)

I am a gen|tleman of | Verona, sir   (*The Taming of the Shrew*, 2.1.47)

It is really not possible to count the anapests in Shakespeare's plays, because we cannot be sure how far two apparently unstressed syllables preceding a third, stressed one were reduced in value. Such reduction has two limits: at one extreme it is complete and results in total compression of two syllables into one (as in contemporary "I'll" or "can't"); at the other, it does not succeed at all in merging or compressing the two syllables. But there are many uncertain stages in between. In a metric which involves the very frequent reduction of two syllables to one, it is likely that an author who pushes the practice to its limits will sometimes go further than we can follow him. Shakespeare not only pursues elision and syncopation as far as he can, but he evidently means us to slur phrases, drop (or almost drop) unstressed final syllables of words or phrases, or say several syllables so quickly that they sound like fewer than they are.

You made | *ĭn ă dăy,* | my lord, whole towns to fly (*2 Henry VI*, 2.1.160)

Be execu|*tĕd bў nĭne* | tomorrow morning (*Measure for Measure*, 2.1.34)

Sometimes a strongly stressed trochaic word invites us to all but drop its second syllable:

A poor physician's daugh|*tĕr mў wĭfe!* | Disdain
(*All's Well That Ends Well*, 2.3.115)

She'll hamper thee, and dan|*dlĕ thĕe lĭke* | a baby (*2 Henry VI*, 1.3.145)

The same technique of stressing one syllable strongly and scanting one or two others can often be heard when an apparent anapest straddles two phrases; the effect is to knit the phrases more closely together:

Could have persua|*dĕd mĕ; nŏw* | I dare not say
(*Two Gentlemen of Verona*, 5.4.65)

How goes | *ĭt nŏw? Hĕ* | looks gentler than he did. (*Othello*, 4.3.11)

But do not speak | *tŏ mĕ. Lĕad* | me to my chamber.
(*Antony and Cleopatra*, 2.5.119)

Hotspur's high-stepping pentameter takes the same form:

Let me not understand | *yŏu thĕn; spĕak ĭt* | in Welsh
(*1 Henry IV*, 3.1.117–18)

These are all very different from nineteenth-century anapests, which, except in Browning, rarely straddle phrases.

No proposed techniques for eliminating, reducing, or discounting syllables can quite restore such lines to the Augustan model of regular decasyllabic iambic pentameter. However such lines were heard by Shakespeare and his contemporaries, they apparently violate the usual tensyllable form. But anapests of this kind probably signal a quickened speech. One or the other or both of the unstressed syllables that are thrown together are almost always meant to be shortened or slurred. Anapests form one part of the swelling syllabic movement of this verse which is so full of marginal half-syllables, and when we meet them we should understand that they normally invite the raciest delivery we can give them. Some examples:

> And kiss me, Kate, we will be mar|riĕd ă' Sūndăy
>
> (The Taming of the Shrew, 2.1.324)
>
> If that be true, | Ĭ shăll sēe | my boy again   (King John, 3.4.78)
>
> All sects, all ages smack | ŏf thĭs vĭce|—and he   (Measure for Measure, 2.2.5)

It is in the nature of Shakespeare's system of versification, especially as it developed in the later plays, that it should be constantly on the verge of producing hypermetrical syllables. The full anapestic variation, along with all the conventions that work to deny its presence—the casual elision, the nonsyllabic th', the implausible syncopation—and like the epic (and dactylic) caesura, the feminine and triple ending, and the double onset, introduces an extra syllable or half-syllable into lines that are otherwise iambic. The effect of all these devices is almost always of intense and hurried speech.[8]

CHAPTER 12

Lines with Omitted Syllables

Are they not lamely writ?
No, boy, but as well as I can do them.
(*Two Gentlemen of Verona,* 2.1.91–92)

If the extra syllable works with techniques of syllabic compression
to produce a verse that seems overloaded with information-bearing syl-
lables, the occasional *loss* of an expected syllable, unstressed or stressed,
will have a different effect. The line with an omitted syllable, however,
does not work *against* the overcrowded texture of the verse, largely because
such lines are relatively rare. Chambers' tables do not include figures for
headless and broken-backed lines or for other lines with monosyllabic feet,
and lines that appear to be missing a single stressed syllable are quite
uncommon, averaging fewer than four appearances in each play and about
six in the later plays. But one result of their rarity is that lines with missing
syllables have a good chance to be noticed as such. They are apt to appear
suddenly, starkly, rising out of the densely textured procession of fuller
lines. They often occur at moments of tension and typically produce an
effect of abruptness, anger, or astonishment. The absence of one syllable
usually throws special, even thunderous, emphasis on another—but only
if we hear the absence. As with all variations from accentual-syllabic verse,
the difference of any line from the expected pattern can be registered only
if it is *heard* as a difference.

For the convenience of the reader throughout this chapter, a caret
will show where, in a normal line, we might have expected another
syllable.

Headless Lines

The headless line—that is, a line with a missing unstressed syllable before the first stressed one—appears infrequently but at least once in every play that Shakespeare had a hand in. Sometimes he uses this kind of line to convey a speaker's impatient or peremptory tone:

    ∧Where the devil should this Romeo be?   *(Romeo and Juliet,* 2.4.1)

    ∧Jailer, take him to thy custody.   *(The Comedy of Errors,* 1.1.155)

A tired Richard III growls at the servant who brings him wine on the night before his fateful battle:

    ∧Set it down. Is ink and paper ready?   *(Richard III,* 5.3.75)

And after 117 lines of regular iambic pentameter in *Richard II,* just as Bolingbroke and Mowbray are about to begin their joust and the charge has sounded, the Lord Marshal interrupts with

    ∧Stay, the King hath thrown his warder down.   *(Richard II,* 1.3.118)

Other examples, each contributing to some tone of simplicity, freshness, abruptness, or energy:

    ∧Alexander Iden, that's my name   *(2 Henry VI,* 5.1.74)

    ∧Witty, courteous, liberal, full of spirit   *(3 Henry VI,* 1.2.43)

    ∧Bootless home and weather-beaten back   *(1 Henry IV,* 3.1.66)

Especially when the headless line has a feminine ending, some readers will prefer to read it as a trochaic line, different from other lines with trochaic inversions in that it remains trochaic all the way through. But the opening of such lines is headless, and they lack the little rhythmical fillip that lines with trochaic feet in an iambic context always show when the meter returns to iambic. (See Chapter 13 below, p. 196.)

175

Broken-backed Lines

The broken-backed line, it will be remembered, lacks an unstressed syllable after a midline pause. Here, as in the headless line, the iambic current in the rest of the line is usually strong. When either the line or the second half-line begins with a stressed syllable, the effect is often temporarily trochaic. The omission of an unstressed syllable at the beginning (headless) may give the line a racy, tripping air; the omission of one at the break (broken-backed) may secure an effect of energetic resumption after a pause. The speaker of such a line often shifts from one kind of syntax to another (question to command, statement to exclamation, and so on):

> Yea, look'st thou pale? ∧Let me see the writing.   *(Richard II, 5.2.57)*
>
> Struck Caesar on the neck. ∧O you flatterers!   *(Julius Caesar, 5.1.44)*
>
> Come hither, Count, ∧do you know these women?
>   *(All's Well That Ends Well, 5.3.165)*
>
> Horrible sight! ∧Now I see 'tis true   *(Macbeth, 4.1.122)*

The tonal effects signaled by the omission of an unstressed syllable at the break can be very various. In *Richard II,* the unctuous Northumberland responds this way when the Duke of York rebukes him for referring to King Richard simply as Richard:

> Your Grace mistakes: ∧only to be brief
> Left I his title out.   *(Richard II, 3.3.10–11)*

Hotspur, somewhat calmed down after a long tantrum, urges Worcester to carry on:

> Good uncle, tell your tale; ∧I have done   *(1 Henry IV, 1.3.256)*

Hamlet is horrified to hear his mother suggesting that the Ghost he has just seen is a figment of his ecstasy (that is, his madness):

This bodiless creation ecstasy
Is very cunning in.
          ∧Ecstasy?

(Hamlet, 3.4.138–39)

Othello's fury over the loss of Desdemona's handkerchief gives her little syllabic room to answer his questions:

Is't lost? Is't gone? ∧Speak, is't out o' th' way?   (Othello, 3.4.80)

A more laconic Claudio lets an almost imperceptible beat go by before he thanks his sister for her willingness to give up her *life* to save him, an offer that, under the circumstances, he finds rather empty:

Isabella.   O were it but my life,
          I'd throw it down for your deliverance
          As frankly as a pin.
Claudio.   ∧Thanks, | dear Ĭsăbel.

(Measure for Measure, 3.1.103–5)

Especially in later plays, Shakespeare's broken-backed lines, like his late headless ones, are likely to serve a more condensed style and strong effects of sharpness or gravity:

The curtain'd sleep; ∧witchcraft celebrates   (Macbeth, 2.1.51)

On those that are, revenge: ∧crimes, like lands   (Timon of Athens, 5.4.37)

Break open shops, ∧nothing can you steal   (Timon of Athens, 4.3.447)

Other Lines with Monosyllabic Feet

Occasional lines appear to be missing an unstressed syllable in some other position than at line-beginning or after a midline break. Anomalous lines of this kind appear in some early plays, sometimes (as in the work of Shakespeare's predecessors) without notable expressive effect. But as Shakespeare develops the technique in his middle and later plays, it becomes a deliberate device for conveying emotional excitement. All of the following lines appear to involve a foot-long monosyllable intended to be spoken with great force or weight:

ᴧNurse, ᴧwife, what ho? what Nurse I say? *(Romeo and Juliet, 4.4.23)*

ᴧStay: ᴧspeak; ᴧspeak: I charge thee, speak *(Hamlet, 1.1.51)*

ᴧSaw? ᴧWho?
　　　　　　My lord, the King your father. *(Hamlet, 1.2.190–91)*

I humbly thank you: well, ᴧwell, ᴧwell. *(Hamlet, 3.1.91)*

Several striking examples occur in *King Lear:*

ᴧHear | ᴧNa|ture, hear | dear god|dess, hear ¹ *(1.4.275)*

Blow winds, and crack your cheeks; ᴧRage, ᴧblow *(3.2.1)*

Nay, send in time.
　　　　　ᴧRun, ᴧrun, O run *(5.3.248)*

Lines of this kind that appear in later plays sometimes show an extraordinary expressive force and even appear to have gone beyond iambic pentameter to become accentual five-stress lines. To find comparable lines in works written in a basic iambic pentameter, we would have to look to the twentieth-century verse of Wallace Stevens and Robert Lowell.

ᴧYouth, ᴧbeauty, wisdom, courage, all *(All's Well That Ends Well, 2.1.181)*

ᴧAy.
　　　ᴧHark, who lies i' th' second chamber? *(Macbeth, 2.2.17)*

ᴧGold? ᴧYellow, glittering, precious gold? *(Timon of Athens, 4.3.26)*

But not approach'd.
　　　　　ᴧAll is well ᴧyet. *(Cymbeline, 2.4.39)*

Is goads, ᴧthorns, ᴧnettles, tails of wasps *(The Winter's Tale, 1.2.329)*

Sometimes the "monosyllabic" foot is not really monosyllabic but includes a feminine ending, either at midline or at line-ending. When this happens in the final foot, the result may be as close as Shakespeare ever comes to composing a fifth-foot trochee (see p. 197 below):

ᴧDie, | ᴧperish! | Might but | my bending down
　　　　　　　　　(Measure for Measure, 3.1.143)

∧How? | ∧Traitor? |

     Nay, tem|perately: your promise.

              (Coriolanus, 3.3.67)

My husband say she was false?

        ∧He, | ∧woman   *(Othello, 5.2.152)*

They have travell'd all the night? ∧Mere | ∧fetches *(King Lear, 2.4.89)*

Hark, do you hear the sea?

        ∧No, | ∧truly   *(King Lear, 4.6.4)*

The con|sul Cori|ola|nus.

        He | ∧consul!   *(Coriolanus, 3.1.278)*

∧Kill, ∧kill, ∧kill, ∧kill, | ∧kill him!   *(Coriolanus, 5.6.130)*

Here as elsewhere, the aim in citing so many examples is not to overwhelm the reader but to show the pattern convincingly. Although some shared speeches might be arranged differently, the lineation given above is that usually preferred by modern editors.

Lines Missing a Stressed Syllable

A monosyllabic foot results from a missing unstressed syllable. Very occasionally an expected *stressed* syllable will be missing from a line. A cursory count turned up the following figures, which are certainly incomplete:

Lines missing the fourth syllable 10
Lines missing the sixth syllable 58
Lines missing the eighth syllable 14
Lines missing the tenth syllable 33

I have found no lines in which a stressed *second* syllable is missing, probably because such a line, if it followed the pattern of the others in this group, would have to begin with a single unstressed syllable followed by a pause, an unlikely arrangement. The poet could achieve the same effect for the ear by giving one line a feminine ending and the next line only four feet.[2]

Here are some examples of lines that appear to be missing stressed syllables. One curious note: when the missing stressed syllable is the fourth or eighth of the line, the pattern is most often found in split or shared lines.

Missing the fourth syllable

> *Othello.*   'Tis a good hand,
>   A frank one.
> *Desdemona.*   ∧You may, indeed, say so   (*Othello*, 3.4.43–44)

> *Exeter.*   Like music.
> *Canterbury.*   ∧Therefore doth heaven divide
>   (*Henry V*, 1.2.183)

> *King*
>   *Richard.*   What says he? ∧
> *Northumberland.*   Nay, no|thing, all is said.
>   (*Richard II*, 2.1.148)

Missing the sixth syllable

> That you are welcome? ∧
>   That you are worthless.
>   (*Two Gentlemen of Verona*, 2.4.115)

> A brother's murder. ∧ |Pray can | I not   (*Hamlet*, 3.3.38)

> *Desdemona.*   A man that all his time
>   Hath founded his good fortunes on your love,
>   Shar'd dangers with you—∧
> *Othello.*   The handerkerchief!
>   (*Othello*, 3.4.93–96)

> *Lucentio.*   Pardon, sweet father. ∧
> *Vincentio.*   Lives my sweet son?
>   (*The Taming of the Shrew*, 5.1.112)

Missing the eighth syllable

> *Othello.*   I'ld not have sold her for it. ∧
> *Emilia.*   My husband?
>   (*Othello*, 5.2.146)

> *Desdemona.* And bid me to dismiss you. ∧
> *Emilia.*   Dismiss me?
>   (*Othello*, 4.3.14)

Worcester. And that same greatness too which our own hands
Have holp to make so portly. ∧
Northumberland. My lord—

(1 Henry IV, 1.3.12–14)

There is usually good reason for the speaker of the final phrase to miss a beat: the court's astonishment at Worcester's impertinence, Emilia's double takes, Vincentio's dim-witted recognition of his son. But it is easier to account for such lines than to say exactly how we hear them. Do we hear only the words, or do we hear also a kind of soundless thump where the pause is, a thump that registers the missing beat? Or is the beat marked by a speechless gasp or a decisive gesture, some aural or even visual business that takes up a metrical moment of the line? When, in an echo of the defective Worcester-Northumberland line quoted above, Henry IV late in the play picks up Worcester's pious assurance that "I have not sought the day of this dislike," and testily asks,

You have not sought it: ∧how comes it then? (1 Henry IV, 5.1.26–27)

the momentary beat-filling pause is almost audible. We can imagine Henry sniffing, snorting, even stamping, or turning dramatically toward Worcester. Iago's answer to Othello's question about Cassio perceptibly delays till an unsounded beat has lapsed:

Is he not honest? ∧
Honest, my lord? (Othello, 3.3.103)

At the end of the play (which is rich in such lines), Othello, intent on murder, waits in silence (or groans?) through a wordless beat before he answers his wife with a heavy pun (Ay/I):

Who's there? Othello? ∧
Ay, Desdemona (5.2.23)

A missing fourth or eighth syllable may be equally dramatic. Hamlet, as he talks with Horatio and Marcellus, astonishes them by drifting into a visionary trance:

My father— ∧methinks I see my father (Hamlet, 1.2.184)

The strong dash marks an almost audible, perhaps kinesthetic beat. Later, as he comes to the end of one long speech of furious rebuke to his mother, she or the air or the soon-to-materialize Ghost seems to breathe in the space, in the beat, between their speeches:

> *Hamlet.* And put it in his pocket. ∧
>
> *Queen.*   No more.   (3.4.101)

Finally, Cressida, in giving Troilus's pledge to Diomedes, betrays her former lover so gratuitously that the line misses a beat—during which, perhaps, Troilus, who is watching, and we, who are watching the doubled scene (tripled, since Thersites is there, too) have space to gasp before Diomedes' all-too-pertinent question:

> *Cressid.* But now you have it, take it. ∧
>
> *Diomed.* | Whŏse wãs ĭt?
>
>   (*Troilus and Cressida*, 5.2.90)

Missing the tenth syllable

Lines in which the tenth syllable is missing are not marked by a strong break and appear as random, perhaps mistaken, violations of the norm:

> Farewell, commend me to thy mistress. ∧   (*Romeo and Juliet*, 2.4.193)
>
> My nobler friends, I crave their pardons ∧   (*Coriolanus*, 3.1.65)

Possibly, explanation can be found even for these, as it can for others. Some break off inconclusively, plausibly marked by dashes in modern editions:

> But yet they could have wished—they know not—∧
>
>   (*Timon of Athens*, 2.2.207)
>
> Than music from the spheres.
>
>   Dear lady—∧   (*Twelfth Night*, 3.1.110)
>
> He writes me here, that inward sickness—∧   (*1 Henry IV*, 4.1.31)

Some show agitation:

> Damn her, lewd minx! O damn her, damn her! ∧   (*Othello*, 3.3.476)

I am dying, Egypt, dying; only ∧   *(Antony and Cleopatra, 4.15.18)*

(Antony's line, however, could be a headless one, and the text of Othello's is uncertain.) Some lines sound as if they are missing an interior foot (has the poet miscounted? Has a foot been deleted in production?

To wreak the love I bore my cousin ∧   *(Romeo and Juliet, 3.5.101)*

Look how he makes to Caesar; mark him ∧   *(Julius Caesar, 3.1.18)*

Only readers who are listening can hear such effects; for a theater audience, the actors must make them audible. Similarly, a metrical analysis that registers each ictus but does not hear it embodied in a pulsing beat will be deaf to touches like these. Merely to note analytically which syllabic positions are unoccupied by actual syllables (or are occupied by more than one) is too dry a procedure to permit us to hear the surprise in the particular lines. The artistry with which Shakespeare manipulates his rhythmic speeches within the framework of acceptably variant lines must be heard to be believed; it is no mere matter of statistical departures from norms but of the dramatic and audible reinforcement of sense by metrical pattern or by the breaking of metrical pattern.

Why is it that Shakespeare, in his plays but not in his formal poems, felt free to use the old line-types we have met already in Wyatt and Lydgate? He is not, of course, using them on the same terms. They do not function as equally acceptable paradigmatic lines but as variant forms to be employed occasionally and with restraint, often for specific purposes but sometimes to serve more general aims of variety and grace. On the whole, the conventions that permit *extra* syllables contribute to the effect of crowdedness and the impression that a character, or the characters as a group, have a great deal to say, more than can be accommodated in the usual frameworks. The conventions for *omitting* syllables usually contribute to an effect of impatience or breathlessness and an impression that a character is speaking with an urgency too imperious to permit the orderly procession of a just number of syllables. Both vary the meter in the direction of natural (especially of agitated) speech, as do the simpler and more standard ways of increasing or decreasing the expected stress on syllables anywhere in the line.

Clearly, such lines were useful to Shakespeare, and he appropriated them for his plays. Where did he find them? Certainly not in his contemporaries' nondramatic poetry, where they had scarcely appeared since the time of Wyatt. Conceivably, he had noticed them in Lydgate or in other older poets; they may have survived in the memories of old teachers he knew; he could have heard them from touring players. Perhaps he heard or thought he heard them in the work of contemporary playwrights. Marlowe occasionally uses such lines deliberately and with expressive force,[3] though the printed texts of his plays look too rough, and may be too late, to have made, in this respect, a strong impression on Shakespeare beyond assuring him (if he needed any assurance) that dramatic verse could take advantage of licenses not acceptable in more formal poetry. We cannot tell, however, whether Shakespeare derived his knowledge of deviant verse lines from reading printed texts, or from listening to theatrical performances,[4] or from his own experience as an actor in learning aberrant lines of verse along with "correct" ones. Exigencies of production may often have deformed lines of scrupulously composed iambic pentameter. We do know that Shakespeare could pick up stylistic hints from any source and work them into major techniques. Whatever his models, then, Shakespeare experimented with many kinds of variant and deviant lines in his early plays, and in the later ones developed a style (or styles) in which all these resources, used without prejudice, could produce a spoken verse of unprecedented resilience, flexibility, variety, and force.

CHAPTER 13

Trochees

Trochaic Theory

Trochees are among the most puzzling of metrical units. Unlike spondees and pyrrhics, those pairs of almost equally stressed (or un-stressed) syllables which appear only as variant forms in meters that are basically something else, trochees often define meters of their own: the difference in stress between the two syllables is great enough, as in the iamb, to induce in readers a sense of an alternating rhythm. On the face of it, trochaic ought to be as popular an English meter as iambic, but in practice poets find it not nearly so resilient. In English its only successful form is tetrameter—especially with catalexis, a truncated last foot, as in "Tĕll mĕ | whĕre ĭs | fáncy̆ | brĕd" (*The Merchant of Venice*, 3.2.63)—and neither its tetrameter nor its pentameter form (for example, in Browning's "There they are, my fifty men and women / Naming me the fifty poems finished!" ["One Word More," lines 1–2]) admits rhythmic variations so easily or so accommodatingly as iambic meter does. Why this should be so is difficult to say, but English poets affirm its truth by their overwhelming preference for writing iambic verse.

Trochees are different. And when they occur in iambic verse, as a variation from the dominant rhythm, they *sound* different.

1. *Wishing* me like to one more rich in hope   (Sonnet 29:5)

2. The eye *wink at* the hand; yet let that be   (*Macbeth*, 1.4.52)

3. To give them seals, *never* my soul consent   (*Hamlet*, 3.2.399)

4. And play the mother's part, *kiss me*, be kind   (Sonnet 143:12)

5. But let the famish'd flesh *slide from* the bone   *(Timon of Athens,* 4.3.528)

6. The capon burns, the pig *falls from* the spit   *(The Comedy of Errors,* 1.2.44)

7. It is because *no one* should sway but he   *(1 Henry VI,* 3.1.37)

8. *Speak with* me, pity me, *open* the door   *(Richard II,* 5.3.77)

Through much of English metrical history, poets and theorists alike have usually been content to read the italicized words as constituting trochaic variations within a basically iambic line: the first syllable of a pair is stressed, the second unstressed, and then the line returns to the normal pattern. The jog in the meter is heard as a displacement, as a temporary disruption, galling to Augustans, but familiar enough to most earlier and later readers; and habitual listeners to iambic pentameter have long been accustomed to the trochaic "inversion" as a normal deviation of the iambic current, especially when it occurs at the beginning of a line or after a midline break. A trochaic foot, with its early stress and its subsequent unstressed syllable which often unites with the following one to form a little rhythmic fillip, confers variety, grace, or energy on a line, "relieving us," as even the metrically regular Dr. Johnson admitted, "from the continual tyranny of the same sound."[1]

The status of the trochaic inversion has nevertheless seemed to many modern metrists highly questionable. Doubts proceed essentially from two sources. First, from the linguistic analysis of meter, which is little interested in dramatically appropriate or graceful reversals of stress pattern (such aesthetic evaluations are sometimes said to lie outside its purview and competence) but much concerned with the extent to which stressed syllables occupy, or fail to occupy, the metrically prominent positions of a line. For such analysts, all the old Latin terms are misleading, and *iambic pentameter* is tolerated only because its wide currency has made it indispensable. But *trochee* is suspect; what occurs is a "stress displacement": the ictus falls on an unstressed syllable, the stress on a syllable that is metrically weak. When this happens, we can perceive it as establishing a counterpoint against the standard metrical pattern. In some versions of the theory, we need only become intellectually aware of this counterpoint without hearing it. In others, we actually hear the stress pattern (´˘) and the ictic pattern (˘´ or ˘ —) at the same time: néver simultaneously with an abstract and silent ˘´ that beats in our own minds. That is, we hear ˘́ ˘̋ together.

But *does* anyone hear such patterns together? The claim appears to depend on the premise that our perception of such counterpointing in verse is analogous to our perception of a musical beat even through pauses or syncopated phrases in a musical piece. But this parallel is equally dubious. Insofar as the line is like music and the foot like a musical measure (an analogy that cannot be pressed very far without encountering grave theoretical problems), the beat in a trochaic foot shifts to the stressed syllable. Not

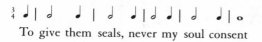

To give them seals, never my soul consent

but

To give them seals,   never my soul consent;

not

Wishing me like to one more rich in hope

but

Wishing me like to one more rich in hope

As I make it out, either there is a pause before the stressed syllable of a trochaic foot, or else the voice lingers on the preceding syllable (if the trochee is medial) while enough time passes to let the next syllable be positioned to accept the beat. If the trochee followed the previous syllable quickly, it would seem awkwardly rushed, as the reader will hear by trying to say "never" very quickly after "seals" while still stressing both contiguous syllables. The effect is nervous, dissonant, and disagreeably constrained, quite different from the sweeping, free, and vigorous effect that most experienced readers recognize as usual in a trochaic variation. Despite its great vogue through much of the twentieth century, the counterpoint theory is inaccurate. When metrical variations occur, we do not hear the actual line against a model line that is constantly ticking away in our heads. We hear only the actual line, and in it we hear the familiar pattern embodied in a particular passing form.[2]

A different analogy may help. When we see a dog on the street, we do not see it against a model figure, Dog, of which we form a distinct image. Even to observe that this creature is large or small, shaggy or shorthaired, does not require that we form a mental image of a dog average in size and hair. Rather, having encountered many dogs, we have noticed that they come in different sizes and styles. On the whole, we take lines of verse in the same way, not measuring them against an abstract model but aware nevertheless that, however individual their bulges make them, they still are specimens of the genus iambic pentameter or trochaic tetrameter or whatever. More detailed observation of either a dog or a line of verse may lead to further useful information, but we will not be helped by a precision that misjudges in a fundamental way the nature of what we are looking at. Cissie Sleary knew what a horse was, better than the pedant M'Choakumchild.

The second source of doubt about trochees proceeds from the analysis of literary metrists, who listen to such lines as those on pages 185–86 and notice that we usually do not, in fact, apprehend the italicized syllables as trochaic feet. They make this claim in part because they sense accurately that when we hear such lines we do not hear them at all as a succession of feet of any kind—iambic, trochaic, spondaic, or anything. That is, we do not hear the syllables two by two. Rather, the phrasing of different lines is differently segmented. We do normally hear a succession of relatively lightly and relatively strongly stressed syllables, but to divide that stream into pairs of syllables is to distort our experience of the line. It is worth remembering, though, that analysis always distorts experience; to analyze is to distort, and to reveal.

It is to the credit of these literary metrists that they continue to use the way we hear verse lines as the basis of their analysis. Listening to trochees, they notice that at least sometimes we do not really hear them as trochees. We may hear paired syllables in examples 3 and 4 above, where the punctuation and syntax isolate them. But in 5 and 6 many readers will hear "slide | from the bone" and "falls | from the spit" rather than "slide from | the bone" and "falls from | the spit." In effect, they note (correctly) that in such a combination the ictus moves to the stressed word and the next three syllables frequently behave like an anapest. What happens in the usual "trochee" is that a stress that occurs one syllable earlier than we expect is compensated for by our finding an additional unstressed syllable later on—usually immediately.

But the anapestic feel of the syllables that follow the stressed syllable in "falls | from the spit" results from the performer's decision not only to stress "falls" but to linger on it. The longer we take to say "falls," the greater the likelihood that the next three syllables will be perceived as a rhythmic unit. But we do not need to linger on "falls"; stress, sharp stress, is enough to accent the word. In fact, insofar as our voices do linger on such words (stressed words in weak positions), we transform iambic pentameter into accentual five-stress verse, which is not at all the same meter. In doing so, we disregard the intimate connection that exists between successive pairs of syllables in this meter and that, in such phrases, draws "slide" and "from," "falls" and "from," closer together than they would have to be in prose, in free verse, or in accentual poetry. Just as Shakespeare's shared verse-line draws a second speech after a first (Chapter 8), so the stressed syllable of a trochaic variation must be followed fairly quickly by its unstressed companion. The same symbiotic relationship characterizes the two syllables of spondaic and even pyrrhic feet. As we saw in Chapter 1, we do not say,

When | to the sessions | of sweet | silent | thought

but

When to | the ses|sions of | sweet si|lent thought,

a verse line of considerably greater syllabic continuity, distinction among its stresses, and consequently subtler substance. Scholars have sometimes wondered how Shakespeare's long plays could possibly have been performed in two hours, as lines from *Romeo and Juliet* and *Henry VIII* suggest was the case. One partial answer is that the metrical lines, exercising a continual obligation on the syllables of feet to follow each other closely even when a new phrase begins in midfoot, had to be spoken with some urgency, and without the metrically slack long pauses and preparations that distinguish most modern productions.

This is an important principle, and a stricter observance of it could guard a reader of verse (and an actor of plays) from two related misreadings of Shakespeare's lines, both of which obscure the role trochees play in them. The first misreading obscures it by changing iambic pentameter into accentual five-stress verse in the way I have suggested, by separating the stressed syllable of a trochee too far from the unstressed syllable that follows. This result is likely to follow from an overdramatic reading of the text: "*slides* | from the *bone!*" Such a reading carries the trochaic figure so far that it ceases to be trochaic (and those theorists who read trochees this way are at least consistent in denying their existence).[3] The other kind of misreading obscures the nature of trochees by finding many more of them than Shakespeare and his contemporaries probably did. But this point will become clearer after we have glanced at a related subject: the stressing of minor words in Shakespeare's verse.

False Trochees and True

In analyzing Renaissance meter, linguistic and literary scholars have learned to pay some attention to the way English phrases are stressed, but they have frequently gone about this work with rather rigid and faulty assumptions. The common misconception, for example, that words of major grammatical categories almost always receive greater stress than minor words (prepositions, conjunctions, and particles) has resulted in some preposterous scansions of Shakespeare's verse and has only begun to be corrected by the formulation of elaborate rules and counter-rules (and sometimes even by common sense). On the whole, metrists have tended to find far more examples of stress displacement (trochees) than it is likely Shakespeare and his audience heard. Every noun, verb, and adjective that finds itself in the same foot with a preposition or a conjunction does not instinctively seize the metrical stress. On the contrary, minor words can sustain fairly strong stress when they appear in stressed (ictic) position under such conditions as the following:

1. When the minor word bears unusual dramatic emphasis:

On *him,* on *him:* look you how pale he glares   (*Hamlet,* 3.4.125)

O, yes, my lord, he wore his beaver *up.*   (*Hamlet,* 1.2.230)

O, *to* him, *to* him wench: he will relent   (*Measure for Measure,* 2.2.124)

Sicinius.   It is a mind
            That shall remain a poison where it is;
            Not poison any further.
Coriolanus.   *Shall* remain?
            Hear you this Triton of the minnows? Mark you
            His absolute "*shall*"?
Cominius.   'Twas from the canon.
Coriolanus.   "*Shall*"?

(Coriolanus, 3.1.86–90)

2. When rhetorical stress falls with at least moderate force on a minor word or syllable:

Aye, marry, sweeting, *if* we *could* do *that*   (*1 Henry VI*, 3.3.21)

And *with* them words of so sweet breath compos'd   (*Hamlet*, 3.1.97)

Why then the world, and all that's *in't,* is nothing

(The Winter's Tale, 1.2.293)

What case stand *I* in? *I* must be the poisoner   (*The Winter's Tale*, 1.2.352)

3. When a usually minor word, such as a preposition or auxiliary, receives phrasal stress because of some clear semantic contrast, explicit or implicit:

The King had cut off *my* head with my brother's   (*Richard II*, 2.2.102)

Your cares set up do not pluck *my* cares down   (*Richard II*, 4.1.195)

Your part in her, you could not keep from death,
But heaven keeps *his* part in eternal life   (*Romeo and Juliet*, 4.5.69–70)

This *was* your husband. Look you now what follows.
Here *is* your husband, like a mildew'd ear   (*Hamlet*, 3.4.63–64)

4. When a preposition falls in final stressed position between two other unstressed syllables, a very common pattern in Shakespeare's verse. (See Suhamy, 243–46. The frequency of such contractions as *to't, in't,* and *for't* implies that the stress in these phrases was typically on the preposition.)

At such a time I'll loose my daughter *to* him   (*Hamlet*, 2.2.162)

That has no relish of salvation *in't*   (*Hamlet*, 3.3.92)

Bade me come smiling and cross-garter'd *to* you   (*Twelfth Night*, 5.1.337)

And be a thwart disnatur'd torment *to* her.   (*King Lear*, 1.4.283)

Sometime like apes, that mow and chatter *at* me   (*The Tempest*, 2.2.9)

As these examples show, a preposition or other minor word is more likely to be stressed if the final syllable of the preceding word is unstressed. Compare "bárk a̯t me̯" with "chátter a̯t me̯." (But see *Richard III*, 1.1.23.) An iambic setting invites the reader to lean a little more strongly on every other syllable, whether or not it is minor.

5. When a word that usually functions as a preposition appears in stressed position as the second element of a phrasal verb and may command at least as much stress as, and perhaps more than, the verb it follows.[4] In some cases the verb may not be exactly phrasal, but the preposition is still somehow capable of receiving strong stress, and the meter is badly disrupted if we insist deafly on stressing the verb. Some examples, in which the verb and the following preposition are italicized:

The stairs as he | *treads on* | them kiss his feet   (*Love's Labor's Lost*, 5.2.330)

As he | *takes from* | you, I engraft you new   (Sonnet 15:14)

O, I will to him, and | *pluck out* | his eyes!   (*Measure for Measure*, 4.3.119)

Take to | you, as your predecessors have   (*Coriolanus*, 2.2.143)

For he was likely, had he been | *put on*   (*Hamlet*, 5.2.397)

Will't please your highness walk?
                          You must | *bear with* me
                                              (*King Lear*, 4.7.82)

                    All the charms
Of Sycorax, toads, beetles, bats, | *light on* you   (*The Tempest*, 1.2.339–40)

The phrasal verb may even consist of three words:

To *make* | *room for* | him in my husband's bed   (*King John*, 1.1.255)

6. When the elements of a phrasal verb are separated and the second element falls in a stressed position:

Your cares set up do not | plŭck mȳ | càres dówn   *(Richard II, 4.1.195)*

                                     tăke
No stricter ren|dĕr óf| me, than my all   *(Cymbeline, 5.4.16–17)*

Táke the | bòy tó | you; he so troubles me   *(The Winter's Tale, 2.1.1)*

7. When syntactical inversion requires some unusual stress on a minor word to make the syntax clear:

Ănd tó | him in his barge with fervor hies.   *(Pericles, 5.Prologue.20)*

Thy grandame loves thee, and thy uncle will
As dear | bĕ tó | thee, as thy father was.   *(King John, 3.3.3–4)*

8. When successive stressed positions (and the adjacent unstressed positions) are occupied by minor words or syllables and stress on one of the words in a stressed position (or even on both) does not seem to violate natural phrasing:

Didst thou deli|vĕr tó | mĕ òn | the mart.   *(The Comedy of Errors, 2.2.164)*

Well guess'd, believe | mĕ, fòr | that wás | my meaning.
                                                    (3 Henry VI, 4.5.22)

Which puts | sòme óf| ùs ín | distemper, but   *(The Winter's Tale, 1.2.385)*

9. When a normally unstressed syllable precedes a spondaic foot— for example, a phrasal verb. Such a syllable need not receive strong stress, but it retains enough to justify its ictic position:

That would I, had I king|dòms tó | gìve wíth her   *(As You Like It, 5.4.8)*

We'll teach | yŏu tó | drìnk deép, | ere you depart   *(Hamlet, 1.2.175)*

I seek | nŏt tó | wàx greát | by others' waning   *(2 Henry VI, 4.10.20)*

The italicized words in these examples do not deserve to be given great thumping stresses. Small notice ought to be enough to insure them the place in the line to which their appearing in a stressed position entitles them, but some moderate stress on them is essential in every case if the word that occurs two syllables later is to receive the full stress it deserves. The point is that speakers of English often stress minor words, especially when their speech has some urgency to it, and dramatic speech often does. Although we have been schooled to think that trochaic variations usually confer energy on a line, the tension in the voice achieved by resisting the trochaic variation is often just as effective and more in accord with the metrical sense of a line. In many cases, though, stressing the minor word keeps the line from falling into unnecessary combinations of anapests and monosyllabic feet, or even into more bizarre four-stress patterns, either of which can result from misreading, as of this line from *King John* (4.3.38):

1.   Doth láy it ópen to úrge ón revénge

2.   Doth láy it ópen to úrge on revénge

More coherent and sensible is this reading:

Dŏth láy | ĭt o|pĕn *tŏ* | úrge ŏn | rĕvénge

What makes this view of meter more persuasive is that Shakespeare and other poets often place minor words in stressed positions *in order to* emphasize their importance and to make some rhetorical point more clear. This metrical underlining is a favorite technique of Donne's (see Chapter 17), but Shakespeare's use of it is also impressive:

> I'll say as *they* say, and persever so   (*The Comedy of Errors*, 2.2.215)

> Call up my brother: O would *you* had had her   (*Othello*, 1.1.175)

> How *can* it? O how *can* love's eye be true   (Sonnet 148:9)

10. When a minor word not usually stressed appears in stressed position after a monosyllabic adjective and a monosyllabic noun (a so-called enclitic phrase).[5] If the noun is a generic term like *man* or *love* or *day,* the preceding adjective usually receives the chief phrasal stress and the generic term may attract no more stress than the minor word that follows it. Sometimes previous lines in a passage have made the noun so familiar (emptied it, in effect) that it requires no emphasis.

> And one | dáy ĭn | a week to touch no food   (*Love's Labor's Lost*, 1.1.39)

> Ay, my good lord, and no | mán ĭn | the presence   (*Richard III*, 2.1.85)

It is the bright | day, *that* | brings forth the adder   (*Julius Caesar*, 2.1.14)

The italicized words here do not receive strong stress, but they receive as much as the usually more important but here unemphatic word they follow.

In all the lines quoted in these last few pages, the iambic pattern is not displaced; we can still hear the metrical beat on the even-numbered syllables. But in an authentic trochee the beat *is* displaced; it moves to the stressed syllable of a trochaic foot. To make this clearer, we need to understand three related but often confused terms: *stress, beat,* and *ictus*. Linguistic and other metrists hold that the ictus does not move, that it always marks the second, fourth, sixth, eighth, and tenth syllabic positions in an iambic pentameter line.[6] What we hear, they say, has no bearing on the ictus, which is simply an aspect of the intellectual analysis of sequences of syllables in verse.[7] Stress, in contrast, is a function of the spoken language, regardless of the meter; all the syllables in a line receive varying degrees of stress. *Linguists* interest themselves only in the relations between stress and ictus, in the extent of the congruence or divergence of what these two terms denote: the marked syllables of the meter, and the stressed syllables of the line. But for *poetic* analysis, *beat* is a necessary third term to describe what we actually hear in verse lines. In most feet of most lines the beat and the ictus fall on the same syllables. We hear a light beat sometimes on unstressed syllables (in pyrrhic feet); and sometimes we fail to hear it on stressed syllables (as on the first syllable of a spondee). But in a trochaic foot, or a so-called inversion or displacement of stress, we hear the beat on the first syllable, not the second. The ictus still falls on the second syllable of the pair even though this syllable has lost its strength. But the beat has parted company with the ictus:

1. Spur them | to ruthful work, | rein them | from ruth

                                                (*Troilus and Cressida*, 5.3.48)

2. For brave Macbeth | (*well he* | deserves that name)   (*Macbeth*, 1.2.16)

3. Why then I think | *Cassio* 's | an honest man   (*Othello*, 3.3.129)

4. I may be negligent, | *foolish,* | and fearful   (*The Winter's Tale*, 1.2.250)

5. Which at the first are scarce | *found to* | distaste   (*Othello*, 3.3.327)

Every such line we hear as a five-beat line, and we hear the beats on the even-numbered syllables except when the stress-displacement occurs. Then we hear the beat on the first syllable of the pair, not the second. What happens is that a speech juncture always intervenes before the trochaic foot; a slight phrasal pause precedes the stressed syllable. In Shakespeare's work (as in English poetry generally), by far the greatest number of trochees occur either at the beginning of a line (after an endstopped line or a line that ends with a completed phrase) or in midline after punctuation (as in 1, 2, and 4 above). But even where no punctuation precedes the trochaic foot (as in 3 and 5 above), the voice can easily produce enough deliberate hesitation there to achieve the same effect and keep (as it must) the sense of a five-beat line.[8]

In sum, a trochee always involves three features: a speech juncture before the foot; an immediately following stressed syllable which displaces the beat from the unstressed one that follows; and an extra little fillip as the line gets back on track. The fillip, of course, comes in the form of the two unstressed syllables that are thrown together, either immediately or later, as a result of the trochaic variation. We may view this fillip, this apparently extra unstressed syllable, as a way of compensating for the unstressed syllable that did not appear before the stressed one. But in any case the trochee tends to produce an effect of the line drawing in momentarily (at the speech juncture), releasing its pent-up energy (in the stressed syllable), and hurrying over an apparently extra syllable before it recovers the iambic pattern.[9]

In this movement the resumption is a necessary feature. Trochaic disruption without iambic restoration nullifies the metrical figure. This is why in an iambic passage a line that continues unswervingly trochaic to the end is best thought of as a headless line with a feminine ending (see above, p. 175):

∧Witty, courteous, liberal, full of spirit. *(3 Henry VI, 1.2.43)*

∧Then, the whining school-boy with his satchel *(As You Like It, 2.7.145)*

∧Kill them, cut their throats, possess their houses

(Sir Thomas More, Addition II, 120)

∧Save him, save him!

This is practice, Gloucester. *(King Lear, 5.3.152)*

∧Never, never, never, never, never. *(King Lear, 5.3.309)*

For the same reason, fifth-foot trochees are rare in English poetry. They omit the third essential feature of the trochaic variation: the return to normalcy. Without this return, a fifth-foot trochee seems pointless, its variant pattern incomplete. Only a few lines in Shakespeare appear to use final trochees, and all of them are suspect. (But see above, pp. 178–79.)

That married with Othello. You, *mistress*   (*Othello*, 4.2.90)

Put strength enough to't.

     Wherefore, bold *peasant*   (*King Lear*, 4.6.231)

And I will kill thee if thou dost deny
Thou'st made me cuckold.

     I'll deny *nothing*.   (*Cymbeline*, 2.4.145–146)

That wants the means to lead it.

     News, *madam*   (*King Lear*, 4.4.20)

'Tis but the boldness of his hand *haply*   (*All's Well That Ends Well*, 3.2.77)

Most of these examples are questionable. The last is prose in the Folio. The first four may all be read differently, as examples of lines in which a stressed syllable is missing at the midline phrasal break. Although this is odd, the fifth-foot displacement of stress is odder. In the iambic poetry of many English poets a line may end in a final pyrrhic foot, but the final trochee is felt as an extremely wrenching variation, likely to be heard not as expressive of significant emotion but as displacing attention from the matter to the metrical anomaly.

Double Trochees

If the single trochee causes a noticeable stir in a line, the double trochee ought to seem even more disruptive, but in practice the result is usually mixed. In the following examples, the trochees certainly make for a lively rhythm:

Villains, | answer | you so the Lord Protector?   (*1 Henry VI*, 1.3.8)

Brothers, | help to | convey her hence away   (*Titus Andronicus*, 1.1.287)

He and | Lepi|dus are at Caesar's house   (*Julius Caesar*, 3.2.264)

Léd hĭm, | bégg'd fŏr | him, sav'd him from despair   (*King Lear*, 5.3.192)

Hónŏr, | héalth, ănd | compassion to the Senate.   (*Timon of Athens*, 3.5.5)

But the additional trochee, though it may help to convey anger, scorn, or some other intense emotion, does not decisively increase the dramatic quality of the lines. For it is an oddity of the pattern that when there are two successive trochees, there need be only one preceding speech juncture (although there is one for each trochee in each example above except the third), and there can be only one return to normal iambic meter (though this may be quite expressive, as in the fourth example above). As a consequence, the double trochee is not notably more useful than the single trochee and is much more rare.[10]

When two successive trochees are followed by a strong phrasal break, this pattern may conceivably be interpreted as a headless line complicated by an epic caesura (cf. Wyatt's type-7 line):

Marriage Uncle? | Alas my years are young   (*1 Henry VI*, 5.1.21)

Therefore merchant, | I'll limit thee this day   (*The Comedy of Errors*, 1.1.150)

Give me, give me, | O tell not me of fear!   (*Romeo and Juliet*, 4.1.121)

O my follies! | then Edgar was abus'd   (*King Lear*, 3.7.91)

'Save your honor. |
From thee: even from thy virtue
                    (*Measure for Measure*, 2.2.161)

If in such lines the break is strong enough, then we do not hear the quick little "extra" syllable that normally marks the return to iambic meter. Rather, we hear a trochaic or feminine first half-line, then a pause, and an iambic second half-line. It is not surprising that some examples of this kind of line are shared by two speakers (as in the fifth example above), for the effect is always of two half-lines uneasily linked together, betraying sometimes deeply different views or emotional states.

Very rarely, too, triple trochees appear:

One word more, good lady. |
                    What shall I do?   (*Hamlet*, 3.4.180)

O, 'tis treason! |

         Madam, I trust not so.   *(Antony and Cleopatra, 1.5.7)*

Seize him, aediles! |

         Down with him, down with him

                  (Coriolanus, 3.1.183)

Why me, *Timon?* |

         That by killing of villains   *(Timon of Athens, 4.3.106)*

Some of these, too, may be read as headless lines with epic caesuras, and in some the midline break may keep us from perceiving a continuous series of trochees. The same may be true of the following line, which is otherwise a quadruple trochee.

Oh, my fear interprets. What is he dead?   *(Othello, 5.2.73)*

Straddling Trochees

We consider finally two maverick varieties of trochee, both of which involve phrasing that seems trochaic but may not be. The first is the apparent trochee that straddles two phrases. Earlier we noticed that a minor word in stressed position may receive stress when it begins a new phrase and follows an enclitic phrase if the enclitic phrase ends on a word of "broad" or "empty" meaning. But even when the enclitic phrase ends on a more fully significant word, trochaic inversion or displacement may not occur. In each of the lines below, the italicized words appear to justify a trochaic reading, but an alternative level-stress reading is possible and perhaps preferable:

And lards the lean | *earth as* | he walks along   *(1 Henry IV, 2.2.109)*

So shines a good | *deed in* | a naughty world.

                (The Merchant of Venice, 5.1.91)

But are not some | *whole that* | we must make sick?   *(Julius Caesar, 2.1.328)*

In these examples the three key syllables occur on some SWS (Strong-Weak-Strong) positions in the line; the first phrase of each ends with two strong monosyllables on SW, and the following S falls on a preposition or other minor word that begins the next phrase. The question is how the meaning of such phrases compels us to speak them. If the important word on W is a word of broad or empty meaning, we have (as we saw earlier, p. 194) no difficulty in keeping the stress on that syllable down to the level of the minor word that follows:

S   W   S
And one *day in* a week to touch no food   (*Love's Labor's Lost*, 1.1.39)

It would seem unidiomatic to say "day" deliberately, with strong stress and a following pause. In such situations we can easily withhold strong stress from the word on W and give the following syllable just enough strength to retain the beat. The key to the saying of such lines is, first, to stress the first S rather strongly and, second, to refuse to pause either between the S and the W or between the W and the S.

In short, the principle that should guide our reading of such lines is that which ought to govern our reading of Shakespeare's lines generally— Kemble's rule, as formulated by Herbert Howarth: "All unnecessary emphasis must be bad emphasis. . . . Kemble's first preference, in the study of a Shakespearean passage, was to conserve the regular iambic rhythm . . . [and] to allow any extra variation of the iambic pattern only where trial convinced him that he would otherwise miss the point" (211–12).[11] In other words, if a trochee is not obligatory, it is not a trochee. This excellent principle can be applied to the following lines, which at first sight appear to be genuine trochees.

1. Aye, like a black *dog, as* the saying is.   (*Titus Andronicus*, 5.1.122)

2. That warns my old *age to* a sepulchre.   (*Romeo and Juliet*, 5.3.207)

3. I was a poor *groom of* thy stable, King   (*Richard II*, 5.5.72)

4. And now this pale *swan in* her wat'ry nest

5. Begins the sad *dirge of* her certain ending   (*The Rape of Lucrece*, 1611–12)

6. Taming my wild *heart to* thy loving hand.
          (*Much Ado about Nothing*, 3.1.112)

7. That shows his hoar *leaves in* the glassy stream   (*Hamlet*, 4.7.167)

8. And 'twixt the green *sea, and* the azur'd vault   (*The Tempest*, 5.1.43)

Sometimes the close syntactical connection between the words in SW positions is that of a noun and an adjective, a noun and a verb, or some other combination:

9.   More are men's ends *mark'd, than* their lives before   *(Richard II, 2.1.11)*

10. And now my sight *fails, and* my brain is giddy   *(2 Henry IV, 4.4.110)*

11. 'Tis not so sweet *now, as* it was before.   *(Twelfth Night, 1.1.8)*

In all such pseudo-trochaic patterns, the linking foot draws the line's component phrases together; too long a pause after the first phrase would violate the line's integrity. Here again, as with the line shared between speakers, Shakespeare uses prosodic means to bring together discrete speech elements. From one point of view, the central foot in the straddling trochee is stretched, and we sense that the first and second syllables can hardly continue to be felt as a unit. But from another point of view, the two half-lines are spanned, bridged, connected, by the unusual foot. The first syllable belongs by phrase to the first half-line, the second to the second. But insofar as the foot holds together at all, is still sensed as a metrical unit, it joins the two half-lines, the two phrases, in a uniquely intimate connection. It suggests as well that the comma (or any punctuation) in Shakespeare does not necessarily signal a pause or caesura. If to some degree such a foot renders the line problematical, that may explain why Shakespeare chose to cast Hotspur's contemptuous definition of metrical verse in this kind of line:

12. 'Tis like the forc'd *gait of* a shuffling nag.   *(1 Henry IV 3.1.133)*

Many readers will not find it easy to deny major stress to the word in odd-syllable position in all of the examples offered above. My own barely suppressible instinct is to give some syllables a greater prominence than I am arguing for. But close study of Shakespeare's line supports the account given above. Hamlet's objection to the players' disposition to "mouth" syllables rather than to speak them "trippingly" (2.2.1–4) may spring from an impatience with some actors' treatment of just such combinations as these, in which excessive attention to the odd-syllable word will destroy the bond between the syllables in the foot and the bond between the phrases in the line. Iambic pentameter is a closely woven meter; if the strands are separated too far, the fabric will unravel.[12]

Looked at another way, the straddling (or pseudo-) trochee, and perhaps even the normal trochee, may well be heard to combine the two other deviations from the iambic discussed in the last two chapters: the omitted syllable (monosyllabic foot) and the additional syllable (anapest). When we read a trochee, aloud or silently, we do not, after all, pause after the trochaic foot; we do not mark it off mentally from the foot that follows; there is no time to do so. Only when a distinct pause follows the trochee ("And play the mother's part, *kiss me,* be kind"—Sonnet 143:12) does the inverted foot sound like one; normally, it is caught up in the rhythm of a phrase that is longer than the foot. The peculiarity of the straddling trochee, if it is given a trochaic reading, is that it belongs to two such phrases, from the first of which an unstressed syllable may appear to be missing and to the second an unstressed syllable added. But the Elizabethans probably did not think this way about a trochee; their training in writing and scanning Latin poetry must have given them confidence in the idea that a foot was indeed a foot and a trochee really a trochee.

Still, if straddling trochees are to be read as I suggest, the poet who writes them can expect them to be misread. Once medial trochees have become fairly common, to write "fails, and" (10) in the fifth and sixth positions of a line is to invite a trochaic reading that will be more showy and less subtle. A poet as perceptive as Shakespeare may have heard the theoretical trouble inherent in the straddling trochee. And the practical trouble as well—he may not have trusted all his actors to refrain from mouthing such lines. For whatever reason, his later plays make only sparing use of lines with this interesting structure. I have found thirteen examples in the *Sonnets,* eleven in *Richard II,* thirty-one in *King John,* eighteen in *Julius Caesar,* but only five each in *Hamlet, Othello,* and *Troilus and Cressida,* six in *Cymbeline* and *The Winter's Tale,* three in *Coriolanus,* two in *The Tempest,* and one in *All's Well That Ends Well* and *Measure for Measure.* I have found no more than six in any play written as late as 1600. Poets after Shakespeare usually avoid this straddling construction, perhaps out of some such suspicion of its metrical ambiguity as I have been raising, or from some obscure principle of decorum that regards a trochee as sufficiently disruptive of a line's iambic integrity without its stretching across the gap between distinct syntactical units of speech.[13]

Contrary Stress

As a rule, trochees can be decisive: "*Coral* is far more red than her lips' red" (Sonnet 130:2); dramatic: "The eye *wink at* the hand; yet let that be" (*Macbeth*, 1.4.52); grandiose: "On horror's head, *horrors* accumulate" (*Othello*, 3.3.370); or mild and marginal: "Play with his locks; *then would* Adonis weep" (*Venus and Adonis*, 1090).

One apparently trochaic pattern, however, is strikingly different from the rest, so different as to raise a question as to whether it is trochaic at all. In this pattern the second syllable is strong—usually a word or syllable syntactically important enough to sustain the chief stress in its phrase; but the syllable that precedes it receives special emphasis for rhetorical purposes. That first syllable is almost always a word that belongs to a minor grammatical category (usually a pronoun):

Unless (perchance) *you* come to me again   *(Twelfth Night,* 1.5.281)

Your servant's servant is *your* servant, madam   *(Twelfth Night,* 3.1.102)

For if *she* be not honest, chaste, and true,
There's no man happy.   *(Othello,* 4.2.17–18)

If, rather than to marry County Paris,
Thou hast the strength of will to slay thyself,
Then is it likely thou wilt undertake
A thing *like* death to chide away this shame   *(Romeo and Juliet,* 4.1.71–74)

In such lines, the most likely way to emphasize the italicized words is by an abrupt rise in pitch that lasts only for the single syllable. Furthermore, there is no obligatory speech juncture before that syllable, the beat in such a phrase is not displaced, and no subsequent fillip occurs to signal a return to iambic. These three essential signs of a trochee are absent, even though the first syllable is spoken louder or more sharply than the second. Other examples:

Then if | *he* thrive | and I be cast away   (Sonnet 80:13)

They had not skill enough | *your* worth | to sing   (Sonnet 106:12)

Upon my life, | *she* finds, | (although | *I* cannot)   *(Richard III,* 1.2.253)

              whereof a little
More than a little is by much | *too* much   (*1 Henry IV*, 3.2.72–73)

I would it were | *my* fault | to sleep so soundly.   (*Julius Caesar*, 2.1.4)

If I quench thee, thou flaming minister,
I can again thy former light restore,
Should I repent me. But once put out | *thy* light   (*Othello*, 5.2.8–10)

To make | *them* kings, | the seeds of Banquo kings.   (*Macbeth*, 3.1.69)

            You have brought
A trembling upon Rome, such as was never
S' incapable of help.
         Say not | *we* brought it.   (*Coriolanus*, 4.6.118–20)

Hath given me some worthy cause to wish
Things done, | *un*done: | but if he be at hand   (*Julius Caesar*, 4.2.9)

Shakespeare's subtle poetry includes many such lines, in which the stress arrangement is the reverse of what we should expect from the iambic pattern and the two words in question, considered abstractly as likely candidates for stress. The semantic context requires this contrary stress pattern. There are also a great many lines that will be felt by some readers to invite such reversal of stress, marginal cases which other readers will prefer to read as normal iambs.

But such lines present a metrical anomaly. The solidity of the foot's second syllable (and its syntactical importance) is so palpable that, despite the previous syllable's greater volume or higher pitch, despite its higher standing in the scale of linguistic stresses (primary over secondary, for example), the beat remains on the second syllable. As we have seen above, the normal trochee works differently. The contrary stress pattern that I have described follows perfectly the linguists' notion of inversion, in which the ictus is not displaced even though the degree of stress is greater for the syllable in weak position. But the difference in sound is important. As a way of differentiating this pattern from that of the normal trochee, we might call this one a *trochaic iamb,* a term which would acknowledge its paradoxical nature. For purposes of scanning, some such method as the following might do:

Upon my life, | she finds, | (although | I cannot)

That is, a parenthetical double stress might indicate both the strong speech stress (and rise in pitch) and the retained iambic strength of the second syllable.

The pattern occurs also in tetrameter:

As you from crimes would pardon'd be,
Let your indulgence set *me* free.   (*The Tempest*, Epilogue.19–20)

It occurs also in later poets and is occasionally an important source of emphatic interest:

Nor is she more at ease on some *still* night
                                (Wordsworth, "Descriptive Sketches," line 186, his italics)

Others because *you* did not keep
That deep-sworn vow have been friends of mine;
Yet always when I look death in the face,
When I clamber to the heights of sleep,
Or when I grow excited with wine,
Suddenly I meet *your* face.   (Yeats, "A Deep-Sworn Vow," 154)

In Donne's highly argumentative verse, this pattern often serves to heighten some rhetorical contrast:

And, having little now, have then *no* sense   (191:16)

For, if above all these, *my* sins abound   (296:10)

As the trees sap doth seeke the root below
In winter, in *my* winter now *I* goe   (322:13–14)

And even these teares, which should *wash* sin, *are* sin   (255:11)

                    nor are we growne
In stature to *be* men, till we *are* none   (212:145–46)

Milton uses the technique occasionally, again in passages of subtle reasoning:

And me *with* thee hath ruined, for with thee   (*Paradise Lost*, IX.906)

In this line the device lets Milton (and us) enjoy the metrical pleasure of hearing the same phrase treated differently in two appearances. Others:

So may some gentle Muse
With lucky words favor *my* destined urn   ("Lycidas," 19–20)

       whether our angry Foe
Can give it, or will ever? How he can   (*Paradise Lost,* II.152–53)

That such an apparently counter-metrical pattern should be available to poets and that it can be used freely without disturbing the iambic structure of a line only shows how extraordinarily versatile iambic pentameter is and how far it can accommodate speech rhythms that normally would seem anything but iambic. As far as I know, this kind of line has not been treated before as a distinctive metrical pattern.[14] It seems, in fact, an auditory illusion: by all the methods of analysis commonly used by metrists and linguists, the pattern ought to be a trochee, but it is audibly different from all the usual varieties discussed above in not displacing strong stress and a sense of the beat from the second syllable. Shakespeare and most other poets use this metrical figure with some restraint, but one mark of the meter's readiness to reflect English speech is that it can adapt such a pattern to its own purposes.[15]

CHAPTER 14

The Play of Phrase and Line

The tunes that he writes to, the whole great art of his
music-making, we can master.
(HARLEY GRANVILLE-BARKER, I.14)

From Uniformity to Variety

We saw earlier (Chapters 3 and 4) that Tudor poetry treated the iambic pentameter line as the sum of two phrases, the first of four syllables, the second of six. To meet this structural requirement, poets from Surrey to Sidney understood that they needed to find English phrases that filled the measurements: phrases exact in length and sounding an iambic pattern. For such an art, the phrase is clearly subordinate to the line. Among all the English phrases that occur to the poet as suitable to his other-than-metrical purposes, the poet must search for those that fit not only the iambic mold but the four-six pattern as well. Even today, amateur poets who try their hand at iambic pentameter will start in much the same way—by fishing among the phrases that carry the right content for the ones that also have the right form.

This way of writing verse imposes a grim authority on the metrical line and a rigid subservience on English phrases. It leaves the poet unable to select freely from the immense range of possible English phrases. In time a practicing poet—Gascoigne, for example—learns to cope cheerfully with this system of limited choices. But its implacable metrical requirements inevitably hamper his freedom of movement. The verse becomes an arrangement of phrases-that-meet-the-requirement, not a form that makes full use of the rhythmic resources of the English language. It is only after the rigid structure of the line has been modified that iambic pentameter verse becomes capable of accommodating a full spectrum of English phrases. By the end of Shakespeare's career, partly through the work of his predecessors and contemporaries, and partly through his own tireless experimentation, the English dramatic blank-verse line has become hospitable to virtually any phrases the poet wants to use. The clumsy and formulaic Tudor pentameter is gradually transformed into the flexible, sinuous line of Shakespeare's later plays.

This change comes about as the result of several related changes in the perception of the iambic pentameter line. We have noted them earlier, but they are worth reviewing. First, the poets become aware that, unlike the stress of Latin poetry, English verse stress may be of different degrees. The five stressed syllables in a line need not be equal in stress; neither must the unstressed syllables. All that is required to keep the meter is a sense of alternating stresses, and this can be maintained by a line that permits different levels of stress in the correspondingly placed syllables of successive feet. The line thus implicitly recognizes that in English speech the syllables that serve as successive peaks of intensity do not all possess the same degree or kind of prominence, and the same is true of successive minor syllables.

The poets also become aware that they can make the iambic pattern more deliberate and grave through spondees, more rapid through pyrrhics, or more urgent through trochees.[1] To admit these possible patterns into iambic pentameter verse with some frequency is to admit a great number of potential English phrases, phrases that show not only a pattern of

    Thĕ níght ĭs dárk

and

    Thĕ níght ĭs dárk ănd stíll,

but also

    Dárk ĭs thĕ níght,
    Ĭn thĕ dárk níght,

The dark, still night,

Now the dark night,

and so on, patterns that appear frequently in Sidney's *Astrophil and Stella*.

In addition, the poets come to see that the line need not pause after the fourth syllable; it may pause instead after the sixth, or after the fifth or seventh, or later, or earlier, or not at all. So long a line must frequently break somewhere; most phrases in English are not ten syllables long, and although phrases can often be combined into larger word-groups that require no pause, readers and actors are likely in most lines to hear or enact a pause somewhere. But the increased freedom in placing the line break means that poets may now write phrases of three, five, or seven syllables as readily as phrases of four or six syllables. Obviously, tens of thousands of potential phrases will now be available to the poet which would not earlier have fitted the meter easily, and in time lines may divide after any syllable, or not at all:

Love? His affections do not that way tend   (*Hamlet*, 3.1.162)

My thought, whose murther yet is but fantastical   (*Macbeth*, 1.3.139)

Then trip him, that his heels may kick at heaven   (*Hamlet*, 3.3.93)

If you have tears, prepare to shed them now   (*Julius Caesar*, 3.2.169)

Her father lov'd me, oft invited me   (*Othello*, 1.3.127)

Love looks not with the eyes, but with the mind

     (*A Midsummer Night's Dream*, 1.1.234)

I come to bury Caesar, not to praise him   (*Julius Caesar*, 3.2.74)

If music be the food of love, play on   (*Twelfth Night*, 1.1.1)

Why speaks my father so ungently? This   (*The Tempest*, 1.2.445)

This supernatural soliciting   (*Macbeth*, 1.3.130)

Finally, the poets come to see that even the end-line stop is not sacred, that if the sense of a phrase may run over the midline pause, the sense of a line may run over the line-ending. At first, the freedom to extend the phrase over the line is used with considerable restraint; later, Shakespeare and others enjamb their lines frequently and even use the line-ending to separate words that belong to the same phrase.

Clearly, if the phrase can run over the line, and if the midline break can come anywhere or nowhere, the poet is under virtually no restriction in choosing his English phrases and sentences. They may be long or short, compressed or expanded; all that is required is that they be iambic. But even this requirement is much easier to meet when pronunciation is as flexible as Shakespeare's was, when trochaic, pyrrhic, and spondaic variation is frequent, when phrasal rhythms are more deeply attended to, and when the line may have extra syllables at the midline break or at the line-ending, may omit syllables at the beginning or at the middle of a line, or, if it is important, may admit or omit syllables anywhere. When we consider further that the mature Shakespeare feels free to write short lines and long ones, we can see that, unlike the earlier strict Tudor verse, Shakespearean iambic pentameter in its fully developed form alters the meter in a dozen ways to accommodate the variety of English phrasing. Under Shakespeare's direction, the phrase becomes liberated from the severe stewardship of an autocratic meter; indeed, by the end of his career the phrase sometimes appears to have taken the line into its own hands.

The Odd-Syllable Phrasal Break

Ants Oras's extensive survey of pauses marked by punctuation in the verse of Shakespeare and other poets and playwrights showed with great clarity the readiness with which late Elizabethan writers learned to let their lines pause after other syllables than the fourth.[2] Oras called particular attention to two developments in Shakespeare's pausing practice: an increase in odd-syllable pauses, and an increase in late-line pauses. Both these changes have momentous consequences for Shakespeare's iambic pentameter and for that of later poets and playwrights.

As we noticed earlier (see Chapters 3 and 4, above), Spenser's readiness to break the line frequently after the fifth (or another odd) syllable accounts in part for the easy, melodious movement of his verse, its occasional trochaic current, and its rhythmical variety. This change immediately transformed iambic pentameter; it broke the iambic lock on the verse phrase. Whereas Gascoigne and poets of his generation wrote a verse that sounded essentially the same in every line—a four-syllable phrase followed by a six-syllable phrase—the perception that a line could as conveniently break after an odd syllable as after an even one made it possible for poets to achieve great variety: to break the ten-syllable line early or late; after a stress or an unstress; decisively, faintly, or not at all. Like Spenser, Shakespeare learned to write successive lines with very different rhythmical contours that nevertheless remained metrically iambic:

> Why rather, Sleep, liest thou in smoky cribs,
> Upon uneasy pallets stretching thee,
> And hush'd with buzzing night-flies to thy slumber
>
> (2 Henry IV, 3.1.9–11)

The second and third lines follow a mainly trochaic inner rhythm, in contrast to the stronger iambic cast of the first, though "rather" and "smoky" foreshadow what will in the next lines become the dominant trochaic pattern. Shakespeare and his most capable contemporaries knew how various a passage can sound when, with or without punctuation, the phrasing in one line breaks after the fourth or sixth syllable and the phrasing in the next one breaks after the fifth syllable (or vice versa)—in effect, when the phrasing of one line is iambic and that of the next (or last) is trochaic:

> Nor Mars his sword nor war's quick fire shall burn
> The living record of your memory.   (Sonnet 55:7–8)
>
> Thus was I, sleeping, by a brother's hand
> Of life, of crown, of queen, at once dispatch'd   (Hamlet, 1.5.74–75)

The perception that an iambic line does not have to be composed entirely or even largely of iambic segments but may comprise as many as four trochaic words and phrases must have been liberating to the poets:

> Like strengthless hinges, buckle under life   (2 Henry IV 1.1.141)
>
> And never trouble Peter for the matter   (Romeo and Juliet, 4.4.19)
>
> Malice domestic, foreign levy, nothing   (Macbeth, 3.2.25)

Most mighty sovereign, on the western coast
Rideth a puissant navy; to our shores
Throng many doubtful hollow-hearted friends   *(Richard III,* 4.4.433–35)

From this point on, all competent writers of iambic pentameter verse will take it for granted that the inner rhythm of the line may—indeed, must—be varied, that iambic lines will assimilate trochaic (or amphibrachic, or sometimes even dactylic) phrases. Henceforth, the better poets will recognize that variety is the key to energy, and they will use feet as various as those that appear in the opening line of Sonnet 30:

When tŏ | the ses|siŏns ŏf | swēet sĭ|lent thought

Such a line would probably have disconcerted Gascoigne. Its two trochaic words are painlessly absorbed into the iambic meter. A break in phrasing occurs after the fifth syllable, and the line uses a pyrrhic, a spondaic, and a trochaic foot. Only one *foot* is trochaic here, but it is not one that involves either of the trochaic *words.* Shakespeare's iambic pentameter characteristically creates such complex and contradictory relations between iambic and trochaic feet, iambic and trochaic phrasing. In doing so, it shows that the art of iambic pentameter consists very largely in keeping such relations various, interesting, and, in some sense, natural.

The fifth- (or seventh-) syllable break also makes it possible to write lines in which the stress and the beat hold to the even syllables while the phrase and some major words do not:

His eyes saw *her* eyes *as* they had not seen them   *(Venus and Adonis,* 357)

As he takes *from* you, I engraft you new   (Sonnet 15:14)

On this side *my* hand, *and* on *that* side *yours*   *(Richard II,* 4.1.183)

In these lines the even (iambic) *beat* is kept, the major stresses falling on alternate syllables; but the even-syllable phrasing and the expectation that stress will fall on words that belong to the major grammatical categories are *not* kept; and still the phrasing sounds natural. In Gascoigne's metric, all these variables had to fall together: beat, ictus, stress, phrase, major words. This much more subtle metric permits some of them on occasion to run counter to others, as they do in actual English speech, and results in a richer, more engaging line. The variety and vitality of Shakespeare's verse and that of many of his contemporaries depend substantially on the readiness with which they embed trochaic phrases, with or without punctuation or pauses, in the iambic line.

To sum up: the odd-syllable pause enables the poet to make use of differently shaped metrical segments, deploy a trochaic inner rhythm, and yet still adhere to an iambic meter, the iambic nature of a line becoming its deep structure, though not necessarily its surface form. Feet, as feet, become less audible. We can still locate them by analysis, but since, in the feminine line, the phrases run over the foot-margins, the way such lines conform to the meter will be less obvious. In time, scholars and poets may even come to doubt whether such lines, or *any* lines, are really composed of feet. That is, they will come to think of feet as intrusive markers and not merely as any set of syllables that constitutes one of the recurrent and constituent rhythmic units in a line; and they will therefore think the analysis of lines by feet a tedious, academic, and insensitive business (as it certainly can be when it is done in a tedious, academic, and insensitive way). But it is also possible to see the development of the odd-syllable pause as leading, in conjunction with many of the other refinements we have been tracing, to a subtle metric that conceals its artifice, in which the phrasing veils the structure. The iambic body runs on, foot by foot, but its bones show less and less: its segments varied in length, its iambs varied in strength, its feet hidden in the phrase.

Counterpoint of Line and Sentence

The other notable shift in Shakespeare's line is from a strong reliance on pauses after the fourth (or fifth) syllable to a preference for pauses after the sixth (or seventh), or even later. As Oras demonstrates (15–16), the late break makes enjambment more likely.[3] The frequent extra-metrical syllables and feminine (or even triple) endings contribute further to our impression, strong for the later plays, that Shakespeare is saying more than even the most elliptical lines convey.[4] But once enjambment becomes the rule rather than the exception, once the phrase typically ends in midline and the line in midphrase, we can see that there are two different orders at work in this verse: the metrical order, which obliges us to sustain, by voice or ear, the approximate regularities and lengths of a rhythmic pattern; and the grammatical order, which obliges us to follow the emerging structural relationships among the elements of our common speech and to apprehend these passing structures as meaningful aggregates, formally coherent, semantically significant, and rhetorically compelling. Both these orders we may, as listeners, occasionally lose track of; but they run a dual course, and if we fail to hear how they carry and shed one another, we miss a significant dimension of the play.

In Shakespeare's poems and earlier plays the two orders usually work together, without tension, in highly patterned single and double lines:

> Queen
>   Elizabeth. What stay had I but Edward? and he's gone.
> Children.   What stay had we but Clarence? and he's gone.
> Duchess.   What stays had I but they? and they are gone.
> Queen
>   Elizabeth. Was never widow had so dear a loss.
> Children.   Were never orphans had so dear a loss.
> Duchess.   Was never mother had so dear a loss.   (Richard III, 2.2.74–79)

> For wisdom's sake, a word that all men love,
> Or for love's sake, a word that loves all men,
> Or for men's sake, the authors of these women,
> Or women's sake, by whom we men are men,
> Let us once lose our oaths to find ourselves,
> Or else we lose ourselves to keep our oaths.
> It is religion to be thus forsworn:
> For charity itself fulfills the law,
> And who can sever love from charity?   (Love's Labor's Lost, 4.3.354–62)

Impressive longer periods can be built out of such smaller units:

> This royal throne of kings, this sceptred isle,
> This earth of majesty, this seat of Mars,
> This other Eden, demi-paradise,
> This fortress built by Nature for herself
> Against infection and the hand of war,
> This happy breed of men, this little world,

This precious stone set in the silver sea,
Which serves it in the office of a wall,
Or as a moat defensive to a house,
Against the envy of less happier lands;
This blessed plot, this earth, this realm, this England,
This nurse, this teeming womb of royal kings,
Fear'd by their breed, and famous by their birth,
Renowned for their deeds as far from home,
For Christian service and true chivalry,
As is the sepulchre in stubborn Jewry
Of the world's ransom, blessed Mary's Son;
This land of such dear souls, this dear dear land,
Dear for her reputation through the world,
Is now leas'd out—I die pronouncing it—
Like to a tenement or pelting farm   (*Richard II*, 2.1.40–60)

But the syntax gradually becomes more flexible and sinuous, and sentences flow through less line-bound rhetorical units. As we saw earlier, Lorenzo and Jessica share each other's lines in love, Brutus and Cassius in quarrel. Boundaries of line and phrase are less often congruent. In *As You Like It*, Jaques's speech on the seven ages begins in midline, and so does his evocation of all ages but the second. For twenty lines, line and sentence never end together until the last line arrives at the completeness of death:

Sans teeth, sans eyes, sans taste, sans every thing.   (2.7.166)

Most speeches of this period still include many sentences or clauses that match the lines in length, but Shakespeare is increasingly willing to break the pattern of congruence by free enjambment and sentences that end in midline. By the end of *Hamlet,* a new speech can be heard, at least briefly:

Hamlet.   Sir, in my heart there was a kind of fighting
5   That would not let me sleep. Methought I lay
              Worse than the mutines in the bilboes. Rashly—
              And prais'd be rashness for it—let us know
              Our indiscretion sometimes serves us well
              When our deep plots do pall, and that should learn us
10   There's a divinity that shapes our ends,
              Rough-hew them how we will—

Horatio.   That is most certain.

Hamlet.   Up from my cabin,
                 My sea-gown scarf'd about me, in the dark
                 Grop'd I to find out them, had my desire,
15   Finger'd their packet, and in fine withdrew
                 To mine own room again, making so bold,
                 My fears forgetting manners, to unseal
                 Their grand commission; where I found, Horatio—
                 Ah, royal knavery!—an exact command,
20   Larded with many several sorts of reasons,
                 Importing Denmark's health and England's too,
                 With, ho, such bugs and goblins in my life,
                 That, on the supervise, no leisure bated,
                 No, not to stay the grinding of the axe,
25   My head should be struck off.   (5.2.4–25)

The passage still includes lines that read as complete sense-units from beginning to end (8, 10, 20–22, 24). But the special authority of Hamlet's voice, which many readers have interpreted as signaling a new maturity, derives from the assurance with which these sentences negotiate the metrical boundaries. Hamlet's excitement ("That would not let me sleep") is conveyed by the enjambment of "lay / Worse" in lines 5–6, by the break after the ninth syllable in line 6, and by the extended self-interruption that follows. Strong punctuation divides these lines (5–7) into segments of very different lengths and into phrases severely disconnected from one another. This segmentation continues in Hamlet's next speech, whose first seven-and-a-half lines are entirely composed of short phrases.

This kind of arrangement, especially when it begins with a short line, jeopardizes the listener's sense of the meter. We are given every opportunity to go astray as we try to fit the phrasal segments together to form lines that satisfy the ear's demand for metrical completeness. We may even think, for a couple of lines, that Hamlet, like so many Shakespearean speakers, has slipped once more into prose. Even if we do not go wrong, even if the printed page or the audible iambic current keeps us on track, we may experience the lines in this passage as composed of oddly fitted segments and as very different in character from the lines that follow (20–24), masterly in their way but eccentric, perfectly suited to Hamlet the impresario but needing, like him, to be watched.

From at least this point on in Shakespeare's career, line and sentence appear to have achieved a comparable eminence, the sentence acknowledging the metrical authority of the line on its own ground but extending the flow of words beyond the single or double line, and doing so primarily by means of more frequent midline beginnings and endings. These now take three distinct forms, depending on whether they begin or end in midline.

Some run from midline to midline (*a*):

> No! to be once in doubt
> Is once to be resolv'd
>
> (*Othello*, 3.3.179–80)

> O brave new world
> That has such people in't!
>
> (*The Tempest*, 5.1.183–84)

Others run from midline to full line (*b*):

> What beast was't then
> That made you break this enterprise to me?
>
> (*Macbeth*, 1.7.47–48)

> Look with what courteous action
> It waves you to a more removed ground.
>
> (*Hamlet*, 1.4.60–61)[5]

Still others run from full line to midline (*c*):

> It was the lark, the herald of the morn,
> No nightingale.
>
> (*Romeo and Juliet*, 3.5.6–7)

> The dark and vicious place where thee he got
> Cost him his eyes.
>
> (*King Lear*, 5.3.173–74)

Any of these forms may be amplified by means of additional lines between the first and the last. (Subscripts after the letter indicate the number of intervening lines.)

(a_1)
> You seem to understand me,
> By each at once her choppy finger laying
> Upon her skinny lips.
>
> (*Macbeth*, 1.3.43–45)

(*b*₁)   If she must teem,
       Create her child of spleen, that it may live
       And be a thwart disnatur'd torment to her.   (*King Lear,* 1.4.281–83)

(*c*₂)   If thou didst ever hold me in thy heart,
       Absent thee from felicity a while,
       And in this harsh world draw thy breath in pain
       To tell my story.   (*Hamlet,* 5.2.346–49)

       In the later plays of Shakespeare, these are the principal components of the characters' metrical speeches, which combine them into a smooth and various union of line and sentence. The two rhythmical powers, metrical and syntactical, are clearly distinct, with neither subservient to the other; both are impressive, formidable, even majestic structures, but they remain separate, held by the now commanding poet not in resolution but in poise.

       We can see this system actively at work in the great speech Shakespeare provides for Macbeth to debate the murder of Duncan. The whole speech alternates from one to another of the three modes outlined above, *a*, *b*, or *c*, and we can chart them easily in the speech, noting as well the way subordinate cola *within* the sentences and within each other also vary from one of these line-arrangements to another. (See Figure 1.)

       The only departures from these three basic line-movements come in one or two short phrases, shorter than their lines, which, though caught up in the measured flow, still stand in some sense on their own: certainly "He's here in double trust" (12), and conceivably "which o'erleaps itself" (27). Such short phrases, and phrases shorter still, will appear much more frequently in later plays and break up what is here, in spite of everything, the graceful forward movement of the passage. Here the midline pauses momentarily halt that flow, but the ubiquitous enjambment starts it going again, and the principal impression of the verse, on anyone who can maintain a steady sense of the counterpoint between line and phrase, line and sentence, is of a sequence of lines more disposed to interior than to final pauses. Insofar as we register the ends of the lines at all, they resemble those hesitations that occur in speech not at the expected junctures, or not there only, but within phrases and before important words. Halted in the middle, hurried or hesitant at the end, the lines nevertheless continue to

If it were done, when 'tis done, then 'twere well
It were done quickly. If th' assassination
Could trammel up the consequence, and catch
With his surcease, success; that but this blow
5 Might be the be-all and the end-all—here,
But here, upon this bank and shoal of time,
We'ld jump the life to come. But in these cases
We still have judgment here, that we but teach
Bloody instructions, which, being taught, return
10 To plague th' inventor. This even-handed justice
Commends th' ingredience of our poison'd chalice
To our own lips. He's here in double trust:
First, as I am his kinsman and his subject,
Strong both against the deed; then, as his host,
15 Who should against his murtherer shut the door,
Not bear the knife myself. Besides, this Duncan
Hath borne his faculties so meek, hath been
So clear in his great office, that his virtues
Will plead like angels, trumpet-tongu'd, against
20 The deep damnation of his taking-off;
And pity, like a naked new-born babe,
Striding the blast, or heaven's cherubin, hors'd
Upon the sightless couriers of the air,
Shall blow the horrid deed in every eye,
25 That tears shall drown the wind. I have no spur
To prick the sides of my intent, but only
Vaulting ambition, which o'erleaps itself,
And falls on th' other—

Figure 1. *Macbeth*, 1.7.1–28. Subscripts indicate the number of interior lines included in larger cola or sentences.

sound like iambic pentameter, but they seem cracked and weathered—like Hermione, showing their wrinkles, their lines of stress.

The Segmented Line

This counterpoint style is far removed from that of the early plays, with their long, continuous lines and line-by-line accumulation of rhetorical segments. But Shakespeare was to go further still. In *Antony and Cleopatra, Coriolanus, Timon of Athens, Cymbeline,* and the first half of *The Winter's Tale,* he develops a yet more radical and jagged technique for posing antagonistic lengths of line and phrase against each other. Most of the previous plays, from *Richard II* to *Macbeth,* include numerous passages notable for their mellifluous phrasing and gracefully extended arguments. But, except for a few famous measures in *Antony and Cleopatra,* this later group of plays contains almost no set speeches likely to tempt the inveterate memorizer. Speech here tends to be abrupt and agitated, the rift between phrase and line a constant feature of the verse. Shakespeare seems to have noticed that although sentences of English speech are often longer than a line, phrases are usually shorter, and that often a short phrase will constitute a short sentence. This perception results in a notable increase in short phrases that constitute whole sentences or cola, a tactic which sharply increases the number of breaks in some lines. Instead of the long, magisterially controlled sentences that stride through the flowing lines of the middle plays, Shakespeare now allows his characters to speak in short bursts much of the time. The phrases, syntactically disconnected, are at least as metrically regular as the verse of that earlier period (if anything, we find in these plays fewer medial trochees and proportionally fewer short lines and alexandrines). But the line is now capable of bearing almost any kind of phrasal freight; it can be broken into several segments, shaped and combined in a great variety of ways. In turn, it can break up the phrase into bits and pieces of any description. The strangeness of this verse increases with each play in the series, at least up to *Cymbeline* and the first half of *The Winter's Tale:*

> So, so; come give me that: this way—well said.
> Fare thee well, dame, what e'er becomes of me.
> This is a soldier's kiss; rebukable
> And worthy shameful check it were, to stand
> On more mechanic compliment. I'll leave thee
> Now like a man of steel. You that will fight,
> Follow me close, I'll bring you to't. Adieu.   (*Antony and Cleopatra,* 4.4.28–34)

> Your voices? For your voices I have fought;
> Watch'd for your voices; for your voices bear
> Of wounds two dozen odd; battles thrice six

I have seen, and heard of; for your voices have
Done many things, some less, some more. Your voices?
Indeed I would be consul.   *(Coriolanus, 2.3.126–31)*

              O Jove, I think
Foundations fly the wretched: such, I mean,
Where they should be reliev'd. Two beggars told me
I could not miss my way. Will poor folks lie,
That have afflictions on them, knowing 'tis
A punishment or trial? Yes; no wonder,
When rich ones scarce tell true. To lapse in fullness
Is sorer than to lie for need; and falsehood
Is worse in kings than beggars. My dear lord,
Thou art one o' th' false ones. Now I think on thee,
My hunger's gone; but even before, I was
At point to sink for food.   *(Cymbeline, 3.6.6–17)*

As we can see from these passages, Shakespeare's later dramatic verse alters the classical line technique by adding other possibilities of line arrangement. These appear in earlier verse as well, but infrequently. Now they become characteristic.

1. The segmented line may be divided more than once:

How, dare not? do not? do you know, and dare not?
     (The Winter's Tale, 1.2.377)

The laws, your curb and whip, in their rough power
Has uncheck'd theft. Love not yourselves, away,
Rob one another, there's more gold, cut throats
     (Timon of Athens, 4.3.443–45)

           Music; awake her: strike:
'Tis time: descend: be stone no more: approach
     (The Winter's Tale, 5.3.98–99)

2. It may be divided into notably unequal segments:

Hath borne his faculties so meek, hath been   *(Macbeth, 1.7.17)*

Why speaks my father so ungently? This   *(The Tempest, 1.2.445)*

Such, and such pictures: there the window, such   *(Cymbeline, 2.2.25)*

3. The sense runs over much more often into the next line, a tendency facilitated by Shakespeare's radically increased usage of weak and light line-endings. That is, Shakespeare ends many lines in his late plays with words we usually expect to *begin* phrases, word-groups, or clauses: *and, but; I, you, we,* and other nominative pronouns; *to, for, from, with, at, by,* and other prepositions; *which, that, who, whom, where, when, as if;* auxiliary verbs followed immediately by the main verb: *have / Done, would / Have, might / Be;* and *such / As, as / If, O,* and other introductory particles. Such endings lead us without pause over the line-ending. Along with Shakespeare's frequent fifth-foot pyrrhics, the weak or light ending (which is also pyrrhic) continues that diminution of emphasis with which Shakespeare frequently treats the line's last foot. That foot has already, in blank verse, lost its rhyme; now it loses its position as the foot most certain to receive strong stress and becomes, at least occasionally, as weak and transient as any other foot.

As we read or listen to this verse, as we are carried on the current of its sound, the end of the line is no longer our unambiguous destination. The phrase carves up the line, runs over the edges, comes to a stop where it pleases. Such at least is the impression it gives of having its own order to impose on the pliant line (which, as we have noted, is often remarkably regular). We have come a long way in a few years: from the line in which the component phrases followed to the end without demur the correct syllabic outline, to one in which a free and flexible sentence keeps the beat in its own highly individual way, the breaks coming anywhere—or, as one sometimes feels, anywhere but at the end of the line.

Such verse requires us to be equally attentive to the claims of the line and the claims of the sentence. We take for granted the syllable-and-stress requirements of the line, which are met here very complacently, but this verse has made us aware as well of the different kind of order to be found in the sentence, a grammatical order not easily described but known to every competent speaker of English. In Shakespeare's earlier verse, and in the verse of his older contemporaries, the order of the sentence is never so deeply insisted on. The usual problem for the poet, as we have seen, is to tame the phrase to the line, to look for phrasal combinations acquiescent enough in their rhythms not to rock the pentameter canoe. No doubt public conditions favorable to poets encouraged them to move quickly beyond this relatively primitive situation, and the enthusiastic response of

a theater audience led a few poets to venture boldly toward grander con-
ceptions of the relations between line and phrase. But it is Shakespeare,
more even than Spenser or Donne or Jonson, who develops a style (or
styles) capable of revealing in the most profound ways what the two orders
mean, what different powers they stand for, and how both can be embod-
ied at once, but differently, in identical sequences of words.

In the later plays especially, Shakespeare develops a tense verse art to
which, in the English tradition, only those of Donne and Hopkins are
comparable. Powerful prose passages compete with the verse for some of
the sublimest material. The line is more and more cast into structural
doubt by the techniques we have noticed: late-line pauses and free enjamb-
ment; a sentence that flows freely over the metrical margins; rashes of
short-line exchanges that hover between verse and prose; brief and abrupt
bursts of staccato phrases that in their jagged discourse seem almost, at
times, to mock both line and phrase.

The style of these late plays (from *Antony and Cleopatra* to *Cym-
beline*) bespeaks a distrust of sententious rhetoric, of the deceitful uses and
users of language such as they all touch and turn on. Shakespeare is clearly
rethinking the whole relationship of line and phrase. Both are in some
sense treated as shams, as cheats, whatever their glories—like the gran-
diosities of Antony and Cleopatra, the honors of Coriolanus and the favors
of the Roman people, the claims of friendship and patriotism in *Timon*, the
flattery and empty vows of *Cymbeline*. *The Winter's Tale* and *The Tempest*
quite obviously deal with the problem of extracting a gifted speaker from
such disillusion. The enchanted worlds of the last full play and a half
partake of that harmonious grace, that significant deliberateness, that Jane
Donawerth has shown proceeds from Shakespeare's high command of the
language theory of his time (see her chapter 2).

Equilibrium

The hallmark of the new verse is the autonomy of the phrase, no
longer obedient to the line or the line-segment but with its own authority
well established. In *The Winter's Tale*, the lines are still heavily punctuated;
pauses are invited everywhere. But now, in the redemptive second half of
the play, the tone has utterly changed, and techniques once used to halt the

flow of speech serve only to divert it into the most graceful pools and eddies. (The punctuation, except for some apostrophes and hyphens, is that of the Folio.)

Perdita.		Now (my fair'st friend),
		I would I had some flowers o'th' spring, that might
		Become your time of day: and yours, and yours,
115		That wear upon your virgin-branches yet
		Your maidenheads growing: O Proserpina,
		For the flowers now, that (frighted) thou let'st fall
		From Dis's wagon: daffodils,
		That come before the swallow dares, and take
120		The winds of March with beauty: violets (dim,
		But sweeter than the lids of Juno's eyes,
		Or Cytherea's breath) pale primroses,
		That die unmarried, ere they can behold
		Bright Phoebus in his strength (a malady
125		Most incident to maids:) bold oxlips, and
		The crown imperial: lilies of all kinds,
		(The flower-de-luce being one.) O, these I lack,
		To make you garlands of) and my sweet friend,
		To strew him o'er, and o'er.
Florizel.		What? like a corse?
130 *Perdita.*		No, like a bank, for love to lie, and play on:
		Not like a corse: or if: not to be buried,
		But quick, and in mine arms. Come, take your flowers,
		Methinks I play as I have seen them do
		In Whitsun pastorals: Sure this robe of mine
		Does change my disposition:
135 *Florizel.*		What you do,
		Still betters what is done. When you speak (sweet)
		I'ld have you do it ever: when you sing,
		I'ld have you buy, and sell so: so give alms,
		Pray so: and for the ord'ring your affairs,
140		To sing them too. When you do dance, I wish you
		A wave o'th' sea, that you might ever do
		Nothing but that: move still, still so:
		And own no other function. Each your doing,
		(So singular, in each particular)
145		Crowns what you are doing, in the present deeds,
		That all your acts, are queens. (4.4.112–46)

Now and then the periods open up for stretches as long as a line and a half (lines 113–14, 115–16, 119–20, 133–34), but never for longer than that, unless the last four lines are heard as providing a more ample climax to the rhetoric of flower and sea. Most of the phrases are closely guarded by commas or stronger punctuation. The marking is largely internal: twenty-two of the full lines have final punctuation, thirty interior; of these thirty, thirteen have more than one interior mark of punctuation. The strongest punctuation (periods, colons, question marks) is almost always interior (twenty-one to three); when it is not, it concludes very brief phrases (lines 129, 130, 142). But, despite the multitude of brief phrases, which constantly carve the line into short segments, the tone of the passage is unfailingly lyrical. Shakespeare has succeeded in adapting the staccato style to a legato technique; the mellifluous phrasing—marked by varied vowels, un-clustered and largely liquid and nasal consonants, and graceful patterns of alliteration and assonance—gives to the passage (a survey of whose punctuation alone might lead us to expect it to be jagged and harsh) a smooth, unruffled flow. The almost entirely regular iambic character of that flow is disguised by the highly varied segmentation, which lends itself to pauses of different lengths and frequent minor shifts in tone. Indeed, this is justly one of the most admired lyrical passages in all of Shakespeare. But it achieves this eminence not through the swelling period and the resonant phrase. Each item in Perdita's cornucopia, or in Florizel's recitation of Perdita's graces, is struck off fresh, not weighted with grandiose phrasing. Even the classical references are to simple matters perfectly in harmony with the pastoral imagery—a far cry from the way Lear, Othello, and even Isabella grandly invoke nature and supernature to reinforce much more theatrically their much more melodramatic emotions:

> And O you mortal engines, whose rude throats
> Th'immortal Jove's dread clamors counterfeit,
> Farewell! Othello's occupation's gone. (*Othello*, 3.3.355–57)

> Blow winds, and crack your cheeks; rage, blow
> You cataracts, and hurricanoes spout,
> Till you have drench'd our steeples, drown'd the cocks. (*King Lear*, 3.2.1–3)

> Could great men thunder
> As Jove himself does, Jove would never be quiet,

For every pelting, petty officer
Would use his heaven for thunder,
Nothing but thunder!   *(Measure for Measure, 2.2.110–14)*

The emotions are different, the people are different, the genres are different. But it is also the style that has changed, and characters in the last two plays are not so ready to invest in swollen rhetoric.

When Prospero then, in the highest-reaching speech of *The Tempest,* bids farewell to the magical powers he has grown old in exercising, his speech has a different relation to grandness from those we have been accustomed to hear from the commanding male protagonists of earlier plays. In many respects, the passage appears to return to the classical midline-to-midline arrangement of the great middle plays, from *As You Like It* to *Macbeth.* But the rhetoric is now more restrained than it has usually been. The references to supernatural forces are literal: Prospero, after all, has performed the acts he refers to, and specifically with the help of the powers he here invokes. To record this invocation, Shakespeare employs an iambic pentameter whose major variations come in the form of phrasal variety (the sense distributes emphasis to form pyrrhics, spondees, and trochees of different strengths, and even one straddling trochee), along with an unusually flexible management of the sentence-flow from midline to midline over line-endings that themselves may bear any degree of emphasis from slight to strong. Verse line and phrasal or clausal unit are rarely congruent. The sentences and the sentence parts run over the margins constantly and require different numbers of syllables in the succeeding lines to complete their sense. This passage perhaps most perfectly illustrates the concluding stage of Shakespeare's metrical artistry and exhibits the highest achievement of his art, attained precisely in the act of renouncing it:

Ye elves of hills, brooks, standing lakes, and groves,
And ye that on the sands with printless foot
35   Do chase the ebbing Neptune, and do fly him
When he comes back; you demi-puppets that
By moonshine do the green sour ringlets make,
Whereof the ewe not bites; and you whose pastime
Is to make midnight mushrumps, that rejoice
40   To hear the solemn curfew: by whose aid
(Weak masters though ye be) I have bedimm'd

226

> The noontide sun, call'd forth the mutinous winds,
> And 'twixt the green sea and the azur'd vault
> Set roaring war; to the dread rattling thunder
> 45 Have I given fire, and rifted Jove's stout oak
> With his own bolt; the strong-bas'd promontory
> Have I made shake, and by the spurs pluck'd up
> The pine and cedar. Graves at my command
> Have wak'd their sleepers, op'd, and let 'em forth
> 50 By my so potent art. But this rough magic
> I here abjure; and when I have requir'd
> Some heavenly music (which even now I do)
> To work mine end upon their senses that
> This airy charm is for, I'll break my staff,
> 55 Bury it certain fathoms in the earth,
> And deeper than did ever plummet sound
> I'll drown my book.[6]   (5.1.33–57)

The rhetorical impulse to divide a subject into parts, and its parts into parts, an impulse often thwarted by the short-burst technique of the plays from *Antony and Cleopatra* through *Cymbeline,* recovers its energy here. Essentially, the passage says: (1) You minor natural and supernatural agents, (2) by whose aid I have exercised command over natural elements and processes, (3) I am now about to resign these powers. But each of these three cola is divided or developed differently, and with an impressive ease and force. Listening to the passage (even if we only read it from the page), we must attend at once to the strong rhythms of each individual line (the metrical measure) and to the imperious, complex sentences (the syntactical measure). But the measure counterpointed with the meter is more than syntactical: it is rhetorical as well. We find in such a speech not simply a succession of sentences but a rounded structure of assertions. The series of four invocations (lines 33–40); the recitation of Prospero's powers in four distinct cola, the first and fourth divided into three parts, the second and third into two ("given" and "rifted," "made shake" and "pluck'd up"); and, after the formal abjuration, the detailing of Prospero's three intended actions of renunciation: all these measure out stages in the procedure of imperial resignation. We follow, that is, all at once the metrical lines, the winding sentences, the tally of significant series, and the emotional curve of the entire rhetorical design.

It is this polyphony, this fourfold rhythm—of line, sentence, argumentative detail embodied in imagery, and accumulating rhetorical impact—that underlies most of Shakespeare's impressive dramatic poetry and is audibly present in this speech. The four are, of course, different in function and operation: the last two are carried forward on the first two—semantic content and emotional design ride on the meter and the syntax. But any account of the way a speech like Prospero's works must notice how all four proceed in time to achieve their collective design, which is complete only with the final word.

At the heart of this design is the meter, which has enabled the whole complex artifice to work so effectively. The midline-to-midline arrangement makes the metrical pattern less obtrusive, less evident, but it is still present to the ear and, in some sense, more deeply emphatic for its being less insistent. It helps the sentences and clauses to take their natural courses through the lines; it allows the rhetorical itemizing that goes on so prominently here; and, aided by euphonious sound devices (alliteration, assonance, and so on) and by metrical variations and segmentation that have emotional significance, it permits the passage to build and to resolve its syntactical and argumentative tension. Unhurried, magisterial, integral, this verse confirms the pact between phrase and line, phrase and sentence, at least as completely as any verse Shakespeare had previously written—evidence that his staff was not yet broken and buried, his book not yet drowned.

CHAPTER 15

Shakespeare's Metrical Technique
in Dramatic Passages

Actually, I see no reason to deny that the constants of
music, which begin with rhythm and meter and go on
to cover all the possible combinations within any har-
monic series, are not only structural elements for aid-
ing memory but expressive vocabularies as well. Not
dictionaries of emotion, not at all, but repertories of
devices for provoking feelings without defining them.
(VIRGIL THOMSON, 49)

The sound must seem an echo to the sense.
(ALEXANDER POPE)

Natural and Dramatic

One major aim of rhetorical technique from ancient times to Shake-speare's was the affecting representation of passionate feeling, and modern scholars have frequently pointed out that Elizabethan actors had, in effect, a codified set of gestures, a "vocabulary of the passions" (Marker, 90), from which they could select the most appropriate ones to convey the emotions of characters and to underscore the meanings in their words. Insofar as such gestures were codified and instantly recognizable by an audience as conveying specific emotions, the acting was stylized, but the most admired actors were evidently those whose gestures and vocal techniques went beyond the mere mechanical procedures and achieved a more subtle expressive power (Marker, 104) without violating the decorous smoothness and continuity of the play's dramatic flow.

229

Something of the sort is probably true also of the verse. We have little direct evidence about how actors spoke the lines, but if the aim of the gestural language was to accompany dramatic action and speech and to mark them with appropriately human movements of hand or body, the speaking of the lines must have followed a similar path. Its aim, as Marker says of the Elizabethan acting style generally, was "not to reduplicate behaviouristic 'naturalness' in the sense in which that term is understood today, but to create a structural through-line cleansed of all distracting accidentals, disfiguring blemishes, indecorous declamation, or unsuitable gestures" (100). This suggests that in speaking the lines, actors would be concerned to keep but not to exaggerate the meter, to avoid extravagant and showy readings of metrical variations, and to suit the phrase to the meter with as much ease as the text required (but no more). Shakespeare's text is full of small variations and departures that can be heard with pleasure if the pulse is kept but will be lost if it is either suppressed or distorted. The expressiveness of the verse can emerge only if that "through-line" of which Marker speaks is kept audible as a base from which the dramatic effects can rise to attention.

"Naturalness" is certainly one of the qualities we admire in Elizabethan verse, but it is a naturalness embedded in a highly figured medium. The fresh-sounding single line that carries the energy of a human voice is one discovery in which poets of the period, as we saw earlier, often reveled: in Donne's "For Godsake hold your tongue, and let me love" ("The Canonization"); in Drayton's "Since ther's no helpe, come, let us kisse and part" (*Idea*, 31 : 1); or in many engaging regular lines of Shakespeare that range in tone from Richard III's sulky "I am not in the giving vein to-day" (*Richard III*, 4.2.116) to Romeo's enchanted "It is my lady, O it is my love" (*Romeo and Juliet*, 2.2.10). Shakespeare is capable even of conveying deeply felt human responses in very brief metrical phrases, from Leontes' sneer at those who do not perceive evil all around him: "You're liars all" (*The Winter's Tale*, 2.3.146); or his wonder as he touches the sculptured Hermione: "O, she's warm!" (5.3.109); to Cordelia's tearful assurance that she has no reason to hate her father: "No cause, no cause" (*King Lear*, 4.7.74); or Othello's unconvincing denial that he is disturbed by Iago's insinuations: "Not a jot, not a jot" (*Othello*, 3.3.215).

But the speeches of Shakespeare's characters are usually more complex in syntax, diction, and metaphorical range. If we still find them in some degree natural, it is largely because the tones of natural speech have uncannily been kept even when the language has been elevated and intensified by syntactical or figurative designs. Shakespeare manages with unparalleled flexibility and resourcefulness to suit the syntax and meter of almost any important passage to its occasion—to the character, the emotion, the dramatic situation. Here, for example, are two contrasting passages that work with the same metrical keyboard to underscore very different kinds of feeling.

The first is Orsino's speech that opens *Twelfth Night*. (The punctuation is that of the First Folio; I have modernized the spelling.)

```
    If music be the food of love, | play on,
2   Give me | excess | of it: | that surfeiting,
    The appetite may sicklen, and | so die.
    That strain again, it had a dying fall:
5   O, it | came o'er | my ear, | like the | sweet sound
    That breathes | upon | a bank of violets;
    Stealing, | and givling odor. | Enough, no more,
8   'Tis not so sweet | now, as | it was before.      (Twelfth Night, 1.1.1–8)
```

Shakespeare conveys the impetuous languor of the Duke in a style as mellifluous as the music the Duke commands. The liquids and sibilants, the absence of complex consonant clusters, the varied length of the phrases and the different segmentation of the lines, assonance, alliteration, and the final rhyme—all these contribute to our impression of an unusually melodious passage.

Several kinds of metrical variation, too, help to give us this sense of smoothness and grace. Initial trochees make for a more than usually energetic onset in lines 2, 5, and 7. At least six pyrrhic feet appear in at least four of the eight lines and help to give them an appropriately softer, smoother, and swifter-moving sound. The final spondee of line 1 gives force to the phrasal verb "Play on"; that of line 5 intensifies "sweet sound"; and the mild medial trochee in the last line (a straddling trochee) perhaps registers, more quickly than we might expect from a Duke who a moment before has been calling for musical "excess," an impatience which we will soon come to see is appropriate to the thinness of his feelings. Along with the extra syllable before the midline break in line 7 (where the pause is evidently to be held while the music plays), these slight metrical variations help both to establish the mood and to give a sense of the Duke's faint character. Spondees and trochees can confer energy and intensity; the pyrrhic foot can make the line sound delicate and soft. With apparently slight rhythmic resources, Shakespeare—using, of course, such other poetic means as a remarkably tactful and various choice of words, phrases, and sentence forms—can make his lines memorable in themselves and richly apposite to their place in the play.

The second passage appears at a highly dramatic moment in *Macbeth,* a moment of great tension and suspense. It is part of the plan concocted by Macbeth and his wife that the "sleepy grooms" should appear to have murdered Duncan. (Why, after doing so, presumably at the instigation of some more powerful party, they should have remained on the scene, is a riddle never satisfactorily explained.) When, on entering Duncan's chamber with Lennox, Macbeth kills the grooms, his action appears to the group of horrified nobles by no means natural and inevitable. Macduff immediately asks, in effect, "Why in the world did you do *that,* when we might have learned so much by questioning them?" Macbeth's answer, which has to be convincing, is a model of metrical expressiveness. (I have marked only the notably variant feet and the apparently fused syllables.)

Macbeth.	O, yet do I repent me of my fury,	
	That I did kill them.	
Macduff.		Wherefore did you so?
Macbeth.	Who can | be wise, amaz'd, | temp'rate, | and furious,	
	Loyal, and neu|tral, in | a mo|ment? No man.	
110	Th'ex|pedi|tion of | my violent love	
	Outrun the pauser, reason. Here | lay Duncan,	
	His silver skin | lac'd with | his golden blood,	
	And his | gash'd stabs | look'd like | a breach in nature	
	For ruin's wasteful entrance; there, the murderers,	
115	Steep'd in | the col|ors of| their trade, their daggers	
	Unmannerly breech'd with gore. | Who could | refrain,	
	That had a heart to love, and in that heart	
	Courage | to make's | love known?	(2.3.106–18)

The turbulence of Macbeth's state of mind is strongly conveyed by this whirlwind of metrical variations. Initial trochees, by themselves no sure sign of remarkable energy, here combine with other kinds of variation to exhibit a soul in extreme agitation. Two trochees in line 108 begin this tempestuous speech, and they are abetted by the extra syllables at the end of the line ("furious"), by the initial trochee in the next, and by the medial pyrrhic, which allows us to race through the line only to pull up before the end at the question mark. How is "No man" to be said? Firmly, decisively: Macbeth must convince his hearers that what he has done is no more than a man must do, and his own manhood has already been repeatedly questioned. The meter directs stress to "No," but one can imagine many actors in the role preferring a different reading: "No *man!*"[1] After this momentary stop, the next (possibly headless) line's medial pyrrhic picks up the pace again, underlining the "expedition" (haste) of which Macbeth speaks. At the mention of "the pauser, reason," the line, in midline, pauses, and now Macbeth begins to paint the scene for his enchanted audience, a scene which, like the rhetoric of his speech, is almost perfectly symmetrical: in the speech, the opening and closing questions ("Who . . . ?") effectively frame the symmetrical syntax of the scenic description ("Here . . . Duncan . . . there, the murderers"); in the conjured tableau, Macbeth pictures a stage, just offstage, divided in visual interest between two bloody groups. The lines in which the details are presented run essentially from midline to midline; extra syllables appear at the end of four out of five lines here, which gives them an amphibrachic cast ("lay Dŭncăn," "ĭn nătŭre," "thĕ mŭrderĕrs," "thĕir dăggers"; and the smooth flow of the regular blank verse is diverted by further metrical variations: strong medial trochees in lines 112 and 113, garnished with a pyrrhic-spondee combination in line 113; an initial trochee in line 115, followed shortly by a line-hurrying pyrrhic. The breaks after odd syllables in lines 111 and 114, combined with all these divergent metrical motions, contribute to the hurtling rhetoric. The final sentence begins with another medial trochee (116) and swiftly reaches its concluding short line, which starts with a trochee, requires a somewhat unaccustomed elision ("make's"), and drives to a resonant spondee. Throughout the passage, strong monosyllabic words receive many of the major stresses and reinforce our sense of the speaker as, despite all contrary indications (odd-syllable breaks, feminine and triple endings, syllabic ambiguity), a decisive and forceful man. Macbeth's extraordinary agitation is audible in these headlong lines. Lady Macbeth's pretended swoon, which follows immediately, and the flight of Duncan's sons evidently distract everyone but Banquo from suspecting that Macbeth's killing of the grooms has been motivated by something other than "violent love."

In both these passages the same principle is at work: like other devices of euphony and syllabic ambiguity, the meter reinforces feeling that is already suggested by the words. It does so largely through the three standard variations in iambic rhythm: the intensified unstressed syllable (spondee); the reduction in stress of a stressed syllable (pyrrhic); and both of these together (trochee). But it also makes the most of variations in phrasal length that result in different segmentation patterns for lines in succession or series; and of a continuing counterpoint between the line and the sentence. The line's length, usually determinate, is rippled by surface variations; the sentence, normally determinate only in the sense that we expect it to have some kind of recognizable grammatical structure, curls its successive coils through the lines like a designing Spenserian dragon. To achieve different effects, the poet need only vary his syllabic, metrical, and syntactical means; more pyrrhics for speed, softness, lightness; medial trochees for violence, anger, abruptness, shock; spondees for intensification and emphasis; liquid, nasal, fricative, and sibilant sounds for the gentler feelings; plosives and consonant clusters ("*gash'd stabs look'd*") for brutality and mayhem; dark vowels ("m*u*sic . . . f*oo*d . . . *o'*er . . . *ea*r . . . br*ea*thes") for melancholy; vowels quickly shifting between open and closed, back and front, dark and light, assonating and contrasting ("w*i*se, am*a*z'd, temp'rate . . . f*u*rious"; "s*i*lver sk*i*n lac'd"; "g*a*sh'd st*a*bs look'd . . . br*ea*ch"; "d*a*ggers / Unm*a*nnerly br*ee*ch'd . . . g*o*re") to signal emotional agitation; in a rushing style, feminine endings to add to the bedlam; graceful periods for serenity; brief bursts, sometimes contrasting with longer syntactical dartings, for anxiety; an eventual congruity of line and sentence, for effects of harmony, ease, and emotional resolution; but, along the way, a frequent failure of line and sentence to begin and end together, to suggest deeper disjunction within the character or between the character and the world.[2]

This catalogue does not exhaust the metrical and syntactical resources of Shakespeare's verse. It should be taken only as partial, suggestive, as indicating the kinds of devices he uses, and the kinds of purposes they serve; but some of these devices may be used for other purposes as well as for those listed above. The possible combinations are too numerous for any catalogue to exhaust, and individual passages are too subtle for the devices to work in easily predictable ways. Gutturals and plosives cannot be entirely banned from serene passages ("*Give . . . appetite . . . sicken*") or may take on a more soothing character in them ("*Breathes upon a bank*"). But in any stretch of verse in which we feel a significant correspondence between the meanings and the sounds, some such devices as those listed above are probably at play and can, if we like, be singled out as contributing to the whole sound and sense of the passage.[3]

What successful metrical variations do, in company with all effective devices of syntactical arrangement, figurative language, and other devices of style, is to intensify and heighten the passages in which they occur. Within three lines, even in a single line, Orsino, superficial character that he is, appearing out of nowhere and speaking words that begin the play, immediately enters upon language that is elevated not by its high diction but by other kinds of richness: imagistic, metrical, figurative. At once an audience is given to understand that it is to hear neither bombastic rhetoric nor flat speech but a language already heightened by poetic devices and one that, as we soon learn, will continue to arrange long series of successive rises and falls in intensity, tunes and turns of feeling, achieved and secured by the deftest management of meter, syntax, image, and figure.

Inflected

Change is the nursery
Of musicke, joy, life, and eternity.
(DONNE, "Elegie: Change")

We saw in Chapter 14 how Shakespeare built up his rhetorical speeches differently from Marlowe and other earlier poets, who composed their series of blockish lines in such a way that each made its equal contribution to the sturdy structure. Shakespeare's method, we noted, is to vary the line-by-line accumulation of rhetorical building-blocks, to break the congruence of line and rhetorical segment, and to permit, at first occasionally, later typically, the pieces of argument to run from midline to midline rather than from line-beginning to line-ending. But the effect of this procedure is not only to change the relation of line and sentence, of line and phrase; it is also to alter the principle of line-equality. According to this principle, which underlies virtually all pre-Shakespearean iambic pentameter in English, every line carries about the same emotional weight, the only exception being the line whose key position in a stanza or speech (usually at the end) allows it to speak with special authority, crispness, or elegance.

This way of arranging a succession of endstopped lines is bound to recommend itself to the journeyman writer whose job is to put together a string of enough blocklike speeches to make a play. But theatergoers do not remember a play as a succession of similar verse blocks; they remember moments and characters of special urgency, force, and grace: Hieronymo, Tamburlaine, and lines that stand out from the rest, like

> Was this the face that launch'd a thousand ships,
> And burnt the topless towers of Ilium?
> Sweet Helen, make me immortal with a kiss
>
> (Marlowe, *Doctor Faustus*, 5.1.99–101)

As a man of the theater, Shakespeare appears to have realized quite early the value of change, which works at different levels. His plays are remarkably different from one another; within the play, scenes are constructed and developed in the most various ways; and within the scene, Shakespeare usually follows the poetic principle that from a series of metrically equal verse lines some should stand out more than others, should be remembered and repeated as distinctive, as carrying a greater radiance of style or image than the surrounding lines in which, one by one or group by group, they are embedded.

In the following section of Mark Antony's speech to the Roman crowd, for example, the lines, mostly endstopped, pause at various places within the line. The short sentences and clauses at the beginning (lines 169–75) give way to a longer sequence (176–80), which is followed, first, by another series of short sentences (181–83) and then by two consecutive longer sentences (184–86, 186–89). The longer periods, in fact, are begun (176) or preceded (183) by full sentences that set out in the same vein and structure as the preceding lines but suddenly are treated to unexpected amplification. The simple statements are direct and factual (although they report as facts what Antony could not know—whose stabs made which rents in Caesar's mantle), but not only are the passages of amplification syntactically more complex, but they introduce the elements of mythification and miracle which have such a profound effect on Antony's audience. In effect, the lines are no longer equal, as they usually are in Marlowe or early Shakespeare; instead, different lines or groups of lines are weighted with different emotional force. As we read or listen to the passage, our emotion is likely to rise and fall as these lines or groups direct it.

> If you have tears, prepare to shed them now.
> 170 You all do know this mantle. I remember
> The first time ever Caesar put it on;
> 'Twas on a summer's evening, in his tent,
> That day he overcame the Nervii.
> Look, in this place ran Cassius' dagger through;
> 175 See what a rent the envious Casca made;
> Through this the well-beloved Brutus stabb'd,
> And as he pluck'd his cursed steel away,
> Mark how the blood of Caesar followed it,
> As rushing out of doors to be resolv'd
> 180 If Brutus so unkindly knock'd or no;
> For Brutus, as you know, was Caesar's angel.
> Judge, O you gods, how dearly Caesar lov'd him!
> This was the most unkindest cut of all;
> For when the noble Caesar saw him stab,
> 185 Ingratitude, more strong than traitors' arms,
> Quite vanquish'd him. Then burst his mighty heart,
> And in his mantle muffling up his face,
> Even at the base of Pompey's statue
> (Which all the while ran blood) great Caesar fell.
> 190 O, what a fall was there, my countrymen!
> Then I, and you, and all of us fell down,
> Whilst bloody *treason* flourish'd over us.
> O now you weep, and I perceive you feel
> The dint of pity. These are gracious drops.
> 195 Kind souls, what weep you when you but behold
> Our Caesar's vesture wounded? Look you here,
> Here is himself, marr'd as you see with *traitors*.   (3.2.169–97)

The mere succession of mighty lines in Marlowe usually has none of this rise and fall; Spenser's smooth stanzas are designed to mute any sudden rushes of feeling (though Keats was to use them very differently). But in Shakespeare, elsewhere as here, the onset of emotion is sudden and overwhelming. The ordinary sentences in such a passage as Antony's, and even the syntactical structures, serve as a kind of base or background against which the highly emotive lines, with their metaphorical suggestion that the natural universe is itself aroused and participating in the event, define an intenser register. Lines 177–80 swiftly charge the situation with feeling; then, on a higher level, lines 184–89 perform the same intensification, so that when the short sentences return, they do so at a higher pitch of passion. In the closing lines, Antony withdraws twice to a nonfigurative discourse, but only *pour mieux sauter* toward the words "treason" and "traitors" (italicized above). The earlier appearance of "traitors" in line 185 seems more casual, quieter, as if to test the waters. The lines throughout direct changes in intensity. As his speech, or this part of it, nears its conclusion, Antony controls the intensity for a moment ("These are gracious drops"), having engineered the basic change in feeling on which he will presently capitalize. Then immediately, with a long, enjambed question that rises in pitch to its last key words ("vesture wounded") and the final, revealing gesture of tearing the mantle from the disfigured body, he leads his simpleminded audience to the climactic utterance, "traitors."

Meter, syntax, imagery, and mythic suggestion all play a part in this imaginative manipulation of the audience, to which we are just as susceptible as the Roman crowd. The metrical variations are actually quite modest here—initial trochees (no medial ones till the last line); only a few expressive spondees, mainly in the passages of amplification: "him stab," "more strong," "Quite van-," "Then burst," "ran blood," "great Cae-," "Kind souls," and "what weep"; on the whole, the iambic beat is maintained firmly. But the line is often filled up with trochaic words or phrases, which seem part of a counter-rhythm (for example, in lines 172, 187, 192, and 196) and sometimes work with feminine endings to give a distinctly trochaic cast to a line (as in lines 170, 181, 182). Other lines are torn between iambic and trochaic phrases. Some lines contain whole sentences or seem otherwise syntactically complete. But four sentences end in midline, three others include two bits of midline punctuation, and the phrasal structure of the component phrases of these regular lines is remarkably various. To any alert reader, Antony's rhetorical tricks are apparent, even obvious: the identification of wounds, the tracing of the blood from Brutus's dagger, the re-creation of Caesar's last, heartbroken moment of recognition. A brilliant casual detail is that of the statue running blood, tossed off cynically in a parenthetical clause, as much as to say, "Well, why not?—I can make them believe anything." But the mastery of sentence and phrase, as they interplay with the meter, is an achievement beyond the reach of most other poets, even of most other great poets, in English. And this is a relatively simple Shakespearean passage.

Is it new, this way of suddenly enlarging and elevating the discourse? Not exactly. All able poets know that some of their lines and passages are more eloquent than others, that try as they may they cannot load every rift with ore. But no poet since Chaucer had had a highly developed sense of how to prepare for and then realize passages of special dramatic force. Under Shakespeare's guidance, the lines of iambic pentameter begin to come free from the routine pattern and to take their different, their graded, places in a rhetoric and a metric that call for a high degree of differentiation among the elements that compose the basic pattern. Again this is hardly new: every teacher of rhetoric from the Greeks and Romans down to contemporary Englishmen was accustomed to showing potential speakers and writers how to manage the successive phases of their discourse in the most effective ways, and Shakespeare's metrical, syntactical, and figurative devices are best understood as rhetorical means appropriate to his purposes. But although much has been written on the subject of Shakespeare's rhetoric, most of it has not much illuminated this aspect of his art, addressed the central issues, or helped explain Shakespeare's incomparable command of words.

The principle that Shakespeare mainly follows in his dramatic verse (and it holds for his poems, too) is that virtually every moment must be marked by some significant change in form, emotional temperature, point of view, or other stylistic or dramatic feature. The feet in a line must be varied; the lines themselves must differ from one another in syntactical structure, in force, in metrical patterning, in rhetorical character; scenes and parts of scenes must develop in different ways. As a consequence of this requirement, the emotional or imaginative heat of a passage or a scene is constantly changing. Characters in earlier plays, from *Gorboduc* to Marlowe, often carry on their blank verse discourse in an emotional monotone; their intensity may not vary a degree in five minutes; and all the characters onstage are likely to be equally hot or cold, though only one of them is talking. But Shakespeare, from the beginning of his career, relishes that root situation of drama—two persons in dispute—and uses it, not, as his predecessors did, to present long wooden debates between persons in official contention, but to dramatize the deep and sometimes sudden anger and animosity that harrow political and domestic life.[4] Much of the the-atrical interest of the first Henriad comes from the hot-tempered quarrel-ing of the characters and how little it can be restrained by rules of courtesy or the authority of the King, to the point where Suffolk and Warwick, entering the King's presence with swords drawn (2 *Henry VI,* 3.2), are subject only to a mild rebuke instead of the traditional penalty of instant death (*1 Henry VI,* 3.4.38–39). The plays, in fact, aim mainly at showing how personal quarrels and selfish interests can ruin a kingdom, and Shakespeare presents the quarrels with great spirit.

The way such quarrels can suddenly flare up is evident at the very beginning of *1 Henry VI.* The opening scene, funereal and stately, in which the surviving leaders mourn Henry V, suddenly boils over in heated dispute:

> *Winchester.* The battles of the Lord of hosts he fought;
> The Church's prayers made him so prosperous.
> *Gloucester.* The Church? where is it? Had not churchmen pray'd,
> His thread of life had not so soon decay'd.
> None do you like but an effeminate prince,
> Whom like a schoolboy you may overawe.
>
> (*1 Henry VI,* 1.1.31–36)

This abrupt shift from stately official ceremony to personal spite is not unusual in the early plays. In the second play of the series, for example, York's polite but pointed reply to Winchester excites this testy response from Suffolk:

> *York.* I will, my lord, so please his Majesty.
> *Suffolk.* Why, *our* authority is his consent,
> And what *we* do establish *he* confirms
>
> (*2 Henry VI,* 3.1.315–17; italics added)

In scene after scene—from the railing of English and French commanders to the noble debate between Talbot and his son over which of them should run and save himself for England's sake (*1 Henry VI*, 4.5–6)—the characters dispute with one another, and much of the verve that Elizabethan audiences evidently found in these plays is owing to the energy of the language they use to quarrel:

> Talbot (*to La Pucelle*).
> Devil, or devil's dam, I'll conjure thee:
> Blood will I draw on thee, thou art a witch
>
> (*1 Henry VI*, 1.5.5–6)
>
> Foul fiend of France, and hag of all despite,
> Encompass'd with thy lustful paramours
>
> (*1 Henry VI*, 3.2.52–53)

Threats, curses, calling of names—all have a place in this showpiece of vituperative energy.

> Pucelle. Then lead me hence; with whom I leave my curse:
> May never glorious sun reflex his beams
> Upon the country where you make abode;
> But darkness and the gloomy shade of death
> Environ you, till mischief and despair
> Drive you to break your necks or hang yourselves!

To this curse of bad weather and mental depression, York, after she has been led off, guarded, can only respond:

> Break thou in pieces and consume to ashes,
> Thou foul accursed minister of hell! (*1 Henry VI*, 5.4.86–93)

That the good strong curse can be exhilarating Shakespeare never forgot, but he learned in time to form his characters' best invective more skillfully—Lear's, for example—and not to let it go on too long. The sudden flare-up of feeling, however, is a favorite resource of Shakespeare's, and some of the most memorable moments in his plays involve characters in sudden rages or recognitions:

O thou dissembling cub: what wilt thou be
When time hath sow'd a grizzle on thy case?   *(Twelfth Night,* 5.1.164–65)

Why, *yet* he doth deny his prisoners
(*1 Henry IV,* 1.3.77; italics added here and below)

What gives some such speeches, especially later ones, their notably furious sound is that much of the anger seems concentrated in single words. This is an important Shakespearean metrical technique: one extremely forceful syllable (or sometimes two) may come to dominate a whole line and destroy any appearance of stress-equality among its strong syllables:

Love? His affections do not *that* way tend   *(Hamlet,* 3.1.162)

What *beast* was't then
That made you *break* this enterprise to me?   *(Macbeth,* 1.7.47–48)

Sometimes the strongly stressed syllables rise out of a long series of fairly strongly stressed ones, like suddenly dramatic peaks in a range of mountains:

Villain, be sure thou *prove* my love a whore;
Be sure of it. Give me the *oc*ular proof,
Or by the worth of mine eternal soul,
Thou had'st been better have been born a *dog*
Than answer my wak'd wrath!   *(Othello,* 3.3.359–63)

Bloody, bawdy *villain!*
Remorseless, treacherous, lecherous, kindless *villain!*
(*Hamlet,* 2.2.580–81)

The suddenness of Richard III's anger at Lord Hastings is a classic case:

Hastings.   If they have done this deed, my noble lord—
Gloucester.   *If?* thou protector of this damned strumpet,
                Talk'st thou to me of *Ifs?* thou art a *traitor,*
                Off with his *head*[5]   *(Richard III,* 3.4.73–76)

Lear's style is to heat up more slowly, through a series of controlled and probing questions:

Nothing?

.   .   .   .

Nothing will come of nothing, speak again.

.   .   .   .

How, how Cordelia? Mend your speech a little,
Lest you may mar your fortunes.

.   .   .   .

But goes thy heart with this?

.   .   .   .

So young, and so untender?

.   .   .   .

Let it be so, thy *truth* then be thy *dower*   (*King Lear*, 1.1.88–108)[6]

The skill with which Shakespeare allows such focal words to shape
the utterance shows how aware he is that in speech we single out, particu-
larly at moments of emotion, the words and syllables that seem specially
empowered to carry the force of our feeling, and that such singling out
often gives a stretch of words its distinctive character. Even in longer
speeches, where Shakespeare had learned to let the rhetorical rise and fall
follow a clear emotional curve, as in some of Lear's majestic cries or curses,
a crowning emphasis may fall on a single word. If Goneril cannot be
sterile, at least her child may cause her such pain

> that *she* may feel
> How sharper than a serpent's tooth it is
> To have a thankless child   (1.4.287–89)

And the storm may do its worst against the genuinely wicked, but

> *I* am a man
> More sinn'd against than sinning.   (3.2.59–60)

Rage is not the only emotion that heats up the verse; fear, love, re-
morse, revenge, anguish, relief, or joy may have the same effect. Any emo-
tion, discovery, perception, any change in understanding, may find voice in
a quickened language. Certain characters—Hotspur, Capulet, Shylock,
and Coriolanus, among others—are distinguished by their readiness to
passion, by the rapidity with which they rouse when crossed. Certain

plays—especially *Romeo and Juliet, Coriolanus,* and *King Lear*—are constructed in series of flare-ups. Indeed, Shakespeare's plays, in comparison with others of the period, are notable for the way they usually follow carefully managed arousals and diminutions of dramatic intensity. Passion is the sea on which these plays must navigate, and its successive waves rise and fall as unevenly, as unpredictably, as the "unpath'd waters" of the actual ocean. Shakespeare's profound insights into time include an understanding of perpetual momentary change as providing the central dynamic principle of his verse as well as the spring of its dramatic action.[7]

In one way or another, characters throughout Shakespeare's plays become excited or inflamed; we see it happening to them, we register differences in intensity between the characters, and we understand the action of the plays as negotiating the differences of time and person. This negotiation may take different forms—murder, pact, learning, dying—but through it the Shakespearean character rides up and down the scale of intensity. That is, at any one moment there may be characters on the stage who are feeling the events differently and with different intensities; and any one character may undergo changes in understanding or sensibility that reduce or raise the intensity with which that character responds and acts. These differences and changes can normally be spotted in the expressive metrical artistry of Shakespeare's verse line.

The ways speech and meter intensify each other can be seen in a line like the following:

Áfter | lĭfe's fĭt|fŭl fĕ|vĕr, hé | sleēps wéll   *(Macbeth,* 3.2.23)

The unstressed third and ninth syllables are strengthened, and the stress pattern in the first foot is reversed; these are the *metrical* shifts from regular pattern. From the point of view of syntax, we find comparable shifts: "life's" and "sleeps," though important words, appear in unstressed positions; "he," normally not a recipient of major stress, requires it here for rhetorical contrast; unlike *us,* whose sleep is interrupted by bad dreams, *he* sleeps well. The result is a line in which almost every syllable has a distinctive relation to the metrical line and to the rhetoric of the sentence. Along with the meter, the multitudinous fricatives (six in the first four words), the four *l*'s, and the strong assonance (in *fe-, he, sleeps*) reinforce the dominant feeling of the line.

Indeed, throughout the whole speech we can hear similar exchanges of prominence between syllables: major words reduced in stress, minor ones advanced; stressed positions reduced in stress, unstressed ones advanced. The meter enforces the first reduction and advancement; rhetoric enforces the second. The two frameworks, like warring powers, compel changes in each other's contours; on the microcosmic stage of the verse line, too, the wheel of fortune turns. And we arrive at a judicious saying of a line only when we have quickly consulted both these powers and negotiated the differences between them. If the line above were prose, there are other ways in which it might be spoken, such as:

After life's fitful fever, he sleeps well

But when it appears as verse, we cannot give it such a reading; we must be guided by the meter, too, to find a reading that is faithful to both meter and rhetoric. This may (and, at its most interesting, does) involve some subtle adjudication among claims of syllables to rhetorical or metrical stress; usually, every line in a well-wrought passage will have a different profile of prominences, as we can see if we extend our analysis to the longer speech from which Macbeth's line is taken. (I have marked only the variant feet and the fused syllables.)

We have scorch'd the snake, not kill'd it:
She'll close, and be herself, whilest our | poor malice
15 Remains in dan|ger of | her former tooth.
But let the frame of things disjoint, | both the | worlds suffer,
Ere we will eat our meal in fear, and sleep
In the | afflic|tion of | these terrible dreams,
That shake | us nightly: | Better | be with | the dead,
20 Whom we, to gain our peace, have sent to peace,
Than on | the tor|ture of | the mind to lie
In rest|less ecstasy. | Duncan | is in | his grave;
After | life's fit|ful fever, he | sleeps well,
Treason | has done | his worst: | nor steel, | nor poison,

25 Málice | domestic, foreign le|vy, nóthing,
    (ž)
    Can touch | him fúrther.   *(Macbeth,* 3.2.13–26)

The late iambic pentameter style of Shakespeare, with its cola that persistently stretch from midline to midline, is audible even through the linear deformations (the short line 13; the possible long lines that editors usually make out of 16 and 22, though each is printed as two lines in the Folio; and the extra syllable at midline in 19 and in 22, where the slurred ending of "ecstasy" is hypermetrical). Rhetorical *and* metrical stress falls emphatically on many key words, often on monosyllables; trochees initial in the line (23, 24, 25) or initial in a clause that begins in midline (19, 22) contribute to the energy and decisiveness of Macbeth's world-shattering envy. But the structural contrast between "we" and "Duncan" is what gives special tension not only to the whole argument but also to the metrical condition of many syllables, which hover between stress-values. We are likely to feel this especially in the pronouns: in "our" (14—unstress or secondary stress?), "our" (20), "his" (24—that is, Duncan's: the worst that can happen to him), and "him" (26). The same rhetorical contrast insists on strong stress for "he" (23) and "Duncan" (22); and the sense of some argumentative contrast adds force to such other words or combinations as "scorch'd . . . kill'd"; "former," "Both," "sent"; and "domestic, foreign . . . nothing."[8]

Almost every line, then, makes some move, as it were, against the iambic pentameter. Line 13 is short; line 14, strongly iambic, is carved into three segments, the last of which is intensified by the uncertain stress of "our" and "poor"; line 15 is hurried by the medial pyrrhic; line 16 is odd, whether we take it as a single line, either hypermetrical or eccentric in its syncopation and elision ("But lét | the fráme | óf thíngs dís|joint, bóth | the worlds súffer"), or as two short lines; line 17 is doggedly regular, except that the defiant assertion combined with the extraordinary assonance (the five stressed vowels in *e* are almost identical) invites a sneering delivery, and the last two syllables run the sense over into the following line. Line 18's two pyrrhics and syncopated "terrible" make it race to a strong stress on the monosyllabic "dreams" and, in line 19, on "shake" and "nightly." Here the midline extra syllable ends one sentence; a trochee begins another clause that initiates the contrast between themselves and their fortunate victim. Line 20 aligns two parallel phrases in the last four feet, with strong ironic implications for the pronunciation of "our" and perhaps the final "peace." Line 21's two pyrrhics again follow a regular line with one that races headlong toward the last two assonating mono-syllabic stressed syllables; these lead, in line 22, to two more and a cascade of sibilant sounds that compress and almost collapse at the end of the sentence. At midline another sentence begins with a trochee followed by a pyrrhic. Line 23, as we have seen, has several problematical syllables, line 24 at least one, plus a trochee; its ending, however, is more deliberate as Macbeth begins his catalogue, which in line 25 uses the strong contrast between "domestic" and "foreign" and follows it by the "nothing" which contrasts even more strongly with both. The final line includes one more syllable, "him," that is given additional weight by rhetorical contrast.

Something happening everywhere, some change induced by the action of meter on phrase or by phrase on meter—this is the principle that governs Shakespeare's expressive iambic pentameter. The current is steadily iambic, but there is much in the water to divert it. At the same time, it is not feasible to claim that any single diversion is crucial, or that these variations can be guaranteed in other situations to express exactly these emotions, only that a passage so disturbed as this is appropriate speech for a dramatic character imaginatively sounding his predicament. In Shakespeare's art, syllabic compression, metrical variety (contrast) in successive lines, counterpoint between the sentence and the line, and the necessary negotiation for stress between rhetorical sense and metrical pattern (resulting, frequently, in certain syllables enjoying an almost imponderable—and hence tension-generating—degree of stress) all play a role in making us feel that a group of lines is expressive, that it is carrying the character's passion.

In most performances of Shakespeare's plays, when the rhetorical structure and the metrical pattern diverge slightly, the actor lets the meter go slack and responds only to the phrase; or, on occasion, he obeys the meter and makes hash of the words. But the tension one rarely hears in professional performances of the lines is the tension that is generated by just such uneasy divergences of meter and prose sense. "We go wrong, we go wrong," says Agamemnon in *Troilus and Cressida* (5.1.67), but the actor who says both phrases in the same way (e.g., Wĕ gó wrŏng, wĕ gó wrŏng") goes even more wrong. In the first phrase, the major stress is on "go," in the second on "wrong": "Wĕ gó | wrŏng, wĕ | gó wróng." The differences to the ear are slight, but the poetry is in such differences. The actor who makes the phrases identical misses the anxiety, the peevishness, in Agamemnon—and in his words.⁹

One final point is essential. Speech crafted for the stage can achieve great force only if it is responsive to more than the usual linguistic constraints and opportunities. Prose speech can do much, but verse speech, that contradiction in terms, can heighten the usual forcefulness of the spoken language by making its linguistic measures (phrase and sentence) struggle against the bonds of a strong meter, a meter that gives but does not let go, that reminds the characters' language of hidden responsibilities to an invisible order, and that fixes their speech and their action in the grip of a benevolent but unforgiving time.

CHAPTER 16

What Else Shakespeare's Meter Reveals

Meter as Clue

The analysis of speeches in Chapter 15 suggests how tellingly meter can display a dramatic character's emotional agitation, distraction, urbanity, reserve, or other states of mind and can signal shifts from one emotional state to another. But this is not quite the same as revealing character, and the question naturally arises: to what extent is a speaker's metrical style a clue to his or her character? To the extent that character is revealed by states of mind, meter is obviously an important guide: someone who shows anger on the stage is capable of anger. But the claim that different characters in the same play have sharply distinctive metrical styles is one that needs to be closely questioned.

This is not to deny that for certain characters Shakespeare devised unmistakably individual speaking voices. Richard III, Capulet, the Nurse, Mercutio, Shylock, Hotspur, Pistol, Constance, and the Bastard of Faulconbridge develop highly idiosyncratic verse styles marked by speech mannerisms that are almost Dickensian: repetitions, self-interruptions, and personal habits of rant, drift, mockery, self-dramatization, and word-play (see Hibbard). The prose styles of Bottom, Falstaff, Shallow, and others are equally distinctive (see Vickers). In later plays, many readers will discern what sounds like a personal verse style in at least some of the speeches of Hamlet, Polonius, Claudius, and the Ghost; of Iago and Othello; of Lear, Goneril, and Coriolanus; and of both Macbeths. In these middle and later plays, however, and in later ones still—it is probably true for most of the characters in most of the plays—the people on stage usually borrow their metrical habits from a repertoire that is standard for the whole play, and critics who find deep psychological significance in a char-

acter's "choice" of imagery or syntax should not read it in metrical varia-
tions of the most ordinary sort.[1]

The point is one that bears repeating. Certainly in the speeches of
many of Shakespeare's antic characters we find their personalities deeply
inscribed: Polonius's love of ornamental figurative pattern and of rhetori-
cal forms for their own sake; the younger Mercutio's equal zest for word-
play and greater taste for puns and sexual innuendoes; Shylock's short-
phrased reversals and repetitions; the Nurse's wandering discourse, barely
on track and now and then losing the meter; Pistol's bombastic treatment
of the most ordinary matters, in a verse or an iambic prose that all too soon
runs ragged. Even though some of the same techniques convey related
habits of mind in very different characters (wordplay for Polonius and
Mercutio, drifting from one thought to another in Shylock and the Nurse,
energy in all of them), the versification and syntax work with the mean-
ings of the words to give us, in every such case, a sense of the speaker's
distinctive personality.[2]

Even to present his less antic characters, Shakespeare uses a variety of
contrastive techniques. He shows us how characters may shift in tone and
feeling, either within a single speech (as Hamlet does in his "O what a
rogue" soliloquy) or in the course of a single scene (Isabella's increasing
confidence in her first scene with Angelo; Othello's psychological deteriora-
tion at the hands of Iago). Furthermore, many of Shakespeare's people—
Richard III, Iago, Lady Macbeth, Lear's elder daughters—talk one way
for public consumption and differently to themselves or their closest col-
leagues. Characters who assume disguises—Kent, Edgar, Viola, Portia,
Helena, Imogen—may adopt more than one verse style. When the same
character is seen in different moods during the course of a play—Richard II,
Hamlet, Lear, Othello, Macbeth—the effect is often of a various and hence
deeper sensibility. Finally, differences between characters are often empha-
sized by contrasting personal verse styles, especially between elevation,
elaborateness, and pompousness on the one hand, and plainness, simplic-
ity, and directness on the other—Osric-Hamlet, Oswald-Kent, Goneril-
Cordelia, Glendower-Hotspur.[3]

In studying certain metrical features of Shakespearean characters'
utterances, Tarlinskaja (1987, chapter 4) finds further kinds of metrical
patterning. On the whole, Shakespeare provides a more regular verse for
heroes than for villains, for women than for men, and for a "wiser, more

sophisticated personage" than for "an impulsive, whimsical" one. Further research may succeed in describing more exactly the specific metrical styles of individual characters. But the differences discerned by Tarlinskaja and other critics are often exceedingly small, and we probably do well to recognize that by far the greatest number of people in Shakespeare's plays speak a standard verse speech, the standard changing slightly with each play but radically over his career. Critical analysis of a character's verse style in a given passage may therefore show only the agitation of a moment, not a genuinely individual set of stylistic features. Even Macbeth's turbulent speeches can best be read as expressing a moment's emotion through metrical-syntactical features available in Shakespeare's current standard style, not as showing a distinctive Macbethian idiom.

The issue here is whether a speech may convey strong feeling on the part of a character without showing much of that character's character. Take, for example, the rhapsody on the horrors of death that Claudio speaks to Isabella in *Measure for Measure* (3.1.117–31):

> Ay, but | to die, and go we know not where;
> To lie in cold obstruc|tion, and | to rot;
> This sen|sible | warm mo|tion to | become
> 120 A kneaded clod; | and the | delighted spirit
> To bathe in fiery floods, | or to | reside
> In thrilling re|gion of | thick-rib|bed ice;
> To be | impri|son'd in | the viewless winds
> And blown with restless violence round about
> 125 The pendant world; | or to | be worse than worst
> Of those that law|less and | incertain thought
> Imagine howling—'tis | too hor|rible!
> The wea|riest and | most loath|ed worldly life
> That age, | ache, pe|nury, and | impri|sonment
> 130 Can lay on na|ture is | a pa|radise
> To what we fear of death.

The passage is distinguished by its rich sound effects, by its parallel phrasing, and by its crescendo of feeling rising in pitch and intensity to a peak in line 127, then subsiding gradually in the last three lines. As we might expect of a play written in this period of Shakespeare's career, the lines are segmented variously, and the cola take up different lengths of line and half-line. The metrical variations, mainly pyrrhic and spondaic (the trochee in the first foot of the first line is the only one in the passage), contribute to the quickening and slowing of the pace, in tune with the erratic pulse of Claudio's imaginative perturbation. It seems that every image, every inch of his terror, is graphically conveyed by some technique of repetition or variation, and the whole speech is a showpiece for the rhetorical interweaving of sound and sense. In particular, the *i*'s and *o*'s of lines 117–18 (the *i*'s continue in lines 120, 121, 122, and 124); the ubiquitous *l*'s; the repeated *th, r* (probably trilled), and *ĭ* of line 122; the three *wor-*'s of line 125; the aspirates of "*h*owling" and "*h*orrible"; the *w*'s from line 125 picked up in lines 128 and 131; the *a*'s of "age, ache . . . lay . . . nature"; and the *p*'s of "imprison'd . . . pendant . . . penury . . . imprisonment . . . paradise"; these and other sounds help to reinforce Claudio's horror of death. His state of mind is by these instruments vividly conveyed, on the principle that such patterns of textural repetition reinforce whatever feeling is being expressed in the words.

But, brilliant as the speech is, it does not tell us much about Claudio, who soon disappears from view (after this scene he has only one further speech, of two-and-a-half lines) and whose earlier speeches are not especially consistent with this one. Shakespeare's highly developed sense of dramatic conflict needs Claudio and his emotionally heightened speech to make sufficiently vivid the strain, the pressure, on *Isabella*. Her decision to refuse Angelo's offer has to be seen from another side, from the side of the brother for whom the ghastliness of death seems a lot more important than his sister's virginity. A more sentimental playwright (or a Gothic novelist) might have the brother immediately recoil in horror from Angelo's villainy, embrace his sister, and approve her rectitude. Shakespeare's version is more plausible, more in keeping with anyone's observation of human (or at least Western) nature. But the speech is instrumental to the development not of Claudio's character but of Isabella's, and to the presentation of her moral dilemma, which becomes more problematic now not only for her but for us. Even when Claudio, recovering his poise moments later, takes back his plea (seeing that it has done no good), neither Isabella nor we are likely to forget the power of his speech, which has appropriately reminded us that not only death but to resign anyone else to death "is a fearful thing." The speech has the dramatic effect of making Isabella seem partly responsible for Claudio's coming execution. Her purity becomes, at least temporarily, an ambiguous virtue, though this verdict, too, is subject to later revision, for subsequent events prove her view effectively practical if not morally right: agreeing to Angelo's scheme would not have saved Claudio's life.

Thus, the main dramatic function of Claudio's expressive speech is not to express his character, which from other indications is not cowardly, obsessed with death, highly imaginative, or credulous; it expresses not so much his own emotion as one that is general, even universal. Rather than say that his speech characterizes Claudio, we might more accurately say that what we have so far learned about him—his youthful, manly directness and courage: his character—is essential as a background to this speech. This is no monstrous brother pleading for his life, but a normal young man; it is Isabella's awareness of her brother's fundamental worthiness that permits Claudio's speech to distress her so much. It tells us no more about his character than that he is human like everyone else.

What is true here is true elsewhere: a speech is, first of all, instrumental to the exposition of a dramatic situation or action. To a certain extent, the revelation of a situation requires that the playwright establish the characters of his personages; this is one of the essential tasks that the playwright cannot evade. But it does not mean that he holds any realistic notion about the consistency of characters. Character itself is usually instrumental to some further range of Shakespearean purposes. In every scene characters respond to an immediate situation before them and establish their personalities through what they do and say. But everything they do and say does not necessarily establish their characters. As Wylie Sypher puts it: "a consuming emotion may *play through* a character at a certain instant but may not seem to *belong* personally to that character" (150) (see also Kennedy, 62, and N. Brooke).[4]

In our eagerness to understand Shakespeare's characters as coherent personalities, we may easily fail to recognize that there is frequently a certain disjunctiveness between their appearances. What is true of Hamlet or of the Duke in *Measure for Measure* is true of most major characters, that they are not entirely consistent, not because human nature is inconsistent but because the various scenes of the play require them to perform different functions: the play *needs them differently* in their successive appearances. Or perhaps that *is* one basis of human inconsistency, at least as a Renaissance playwright could see it (without our anachronistic partiality to Gothic innerness): that life needs us differently from moment to moment, changes our situations, assigns us numerous roles that require contrasting responses; and when we respond differently, we *are* different. The Duke in *Measure for Measure* is needed by his several functions (Renaissance grandee, medieval priest, stage director or playwright, biblical lawgiver and Christlike judge, eligible bachelor) and our notion that all these roles compose his "character" is sure to mislead us. What Shakespeare does with the Duke is give him only so much character as an audience needs to accept him in all of these roles—for the sake of the play.

Meter as Figure

In an otherwise useful, often perceptive study, one student of Shakespeare's treatment of character in *Measure for Measure* assumes "that each character speaks the way he does because he is the kind of person he is" (Brashear, xxviii) and regularly not only sees metrical styles as significant for the study of each person's character in the play but considers the characters as in some degree in charge of their metrical destinies. We are told that Angelo "speaks prose with reluctance" (98), and of Claudio's "refusal to speak prose" (227).[5] Some such assumptions underlie the writings of other scholars as well, although they rarely admit to them in print. But the question is a crucial one for the study not only of Shakespeare's but of all dramatic verse (and of much nondramatic verse as well): on what terms do we understand the peculiar circumstance that the characters speak verse? How conscious can they become of their own metrical or other sound patterns?

The answers seem fairly obvious. Normally, the characters make no reference to the verse (or the prose) they speak except at moments when, like Hamlet (as reported by Polonius) or the lovers of *Love's Labor's Lost,* their versifying is part of the action. The rare harmonies of Romeo and Juliet or of Lorenzo and Jessica (see Chapter 8) seem clearly a means of showing us the blessedness they feel in each other's presence. If Angelo and Lucio betray no astonishment at Isabella's brilliance in argument, they also show no surprise that she is speaking in verse; naturally enough, when they are doing the same. We might be tempted to understand that this is a world in which it is natural for characters to speak verse and that, consequently, there is no more reason for them to remark on that fact than there is for people in actual life to show surprise at each other's speaking at all.

But to read it this way is probably to misread it. Verse may be the normal speaking medium for most of Shakespeare's characters, but that does not mean they are usually aware of it in themselves or others. Rather, the characters' iambic pentameter should be taken as a kind of figure for natural speech. Verse works to achieve intensity, compactness, and elevation in the language of dramatic characters. But the mode in which a character speaks—verse or prose—and the style adopted for any particular conversation are usually to be understood as having been chosen by the poet, not by the character, and the choice is made on the basis of Elizabethan principles of decorum. Shifts in style (from verse to prose, for example) are normally a signal of some shift in the stance or feeling of a character or in the pace or mood of a scene, and such signals can be sent subtly and surely through a patterned system that uses an extensive array of structured oppositions and graded variations.[6]

It may be objected that some characters *do* notice the verse that they or others speak. The most notorious examples are those of Jaques and Posthumus:

Orlando.	Good day, and happiness, dear Rosalind!
Jaques.	Nay then God buy you, *and you talk in blank verse.*

(As You Like It, 4.1.30–32)

Posthumus.	Nay, do not wonder at it; you are made
	Rather to wonder at the things you hear
	Than to work any. Will you rhyme upon't,
	And vent it for a mock'ry? Here is one:
	"Two boys, an old man (twice a boy), a lane,
	Preserv'd the Britains, was the Romans' bane."
Lord.	Nay, be not angry, sir.
Posthumus.	'Lack, to what end?
	Who dares not stand his foe, I'll be his friend;
	For if he'll do as he is made to do,
	I know he'll quickly fly my friendship too.
	You have put me into rhyme. (*Cymbeline,* 5.3.53–63)

But these observations by characters within the play only reflect the familiar situation in life when we notice that someone else has spoken a line that sounds like verse, or that we ourselves have done so. In fact, part of the joke is that Jaques himself, though he appears unaware of it, has already spoken memorable verse in this play, and that Posthumus, catching himself in an inadvertent rhyme after attempting a deliberate one, doesn't realize that most of his words to this point have been in meter. The convention that the characters are normally unconscious of their verse is essential to the joke.

Although characters frequently comment on the styles of other speakers, their comments normally address only general characteristics of style, such as brevity, pompousness, inarticulateness, and speech mannerisms. The basic elements of Shakespeare's verse style—its dense metaphorical texture, its metrical variety and inventiveness, the very fact that it *is* verse—must all be taken as composing a verse speech that is itself the dramatic equivalent of human talk and discourse, just as actors (men and boys in costume) are the stage representations of kings, women, nobles, Greeks, and Romans. If the actors ever come out of their roles to show an awareness of their condition as actors—as they do, for example, in epilogues—their doing so constitutes a joke and does not affect the basic understanding that in their roles they must normally seem unaware that they are acting on a stage, making leaps in time and space, and speaking English verse even when playing French, Greek, Italian, or Roman characters.

The hardest case is probably that of *Love's Labor's Lost,* where the characters self-consciously finish each other's lines and rhymes and compete in fashioning linguistic patterns of the most elaborate kind. Jane Donawerth has shown (chapter 4) how complex and significant these games of language are and how relevant to Shakespeare's presentation of young people falling in love. As she rightly shows, the court characters are well aware of the patterns they are making, which include metrical imitation as well as rhyme. Like Posthumus or Iago (*Othello,* 2.1) or Cyrano de Bergerac, they can make up rhymes on the spot, a talent that (except in black "rap") has vanished in the modern world for want of practice and point. But even here the principle I have proposed governs their *other* speeches, and it can still be claimed (for the Shakespearean characters as well as for Cyrano) that their rhymed speeches represent a heightening of the normal human capacity for improvisational patterning, a heightening that carries it beyond the reach of even the most brilliant living speaker.

Meter as Symbol

Verse is the major mode of the plays—appropriately so, for it realizes in its own form, especially in the unusually accommodating version of iambic pentameter preferred by Shakespeare, the range of oppositions and linkages inherent in drama itself. Compared with his predecessors on the English stage, or even with nondramatic English poets, Shakespeare evidently had a more highly tuned sense of differences, of oppositions between classes, worlds, manners, and personalities. He must have felt more variously and profoundly the elemental dramatic situation: that two significantly different forces meet and contend on the stage, that the contending forces are not just disembodied voices or interests or titles (King, Queen, First Lord, Second Lord, and so on) but distinctive personalities with different views of the world. Shakespeare's scenes almost always (perhaps always) involve some sharp contrast between positions, genders, ages, or interests, and what Shakespeare is recognizing as he thrusts them on the stage is that life unfailingly pits opposites against each other, perpetually places us in relations of contrast (male-female, elder-junior, master-servant) with virtually all the other persons we meet (English against French, sons against fathers, friends against friends), and that we are always working out such relationships. Shakespeare carries these oppositions further and deeper than any other playwright, but he develops them with a feeling for nuances and subtleties that no mere dialectician could contrive. Most of his predecessors are simple and childlike in comparison; it is Shakespeare whose psychological penetration and layered plotting give a dense lifelikeness to the bare dramatic principle of opposition.

Something similar goes on within the iambic pentameter line. And here again it is Shakespeare's feeling for variety and contrast that helps to make his lines smoother and more melodious than most others—and much more dramatic. First, the line can appear in many more forms than earlier, with almost infinite internal variation, and unpredictably enjambed or endstopped. The sentence and the line, like human personalities, may meet in inexhaustible combinations, never immediately repeating exactly the same rhythms or the same larger units. The line becomes a miniature of the infinitely various and variously polarized larger world. In meter, even the syllables compete, cannot avoid doing so, as two people in the world cannot avoid the necessity that requires them to parry and thrust, to be and act differently toward one another, even in love. No relation is static, without rivalry or differently based understanding. For all of this the relations of meter are emblematic, for well-made iambic pentameter lines satisfy our appetite for perpetual adjustment, that need of ours to dwell more on some stressed syllables than on others, more on some unstressed syllables than on others, just as in speech we single out, especially at moments of emotion, the words and syllables that seem in a stretch of words to carry the heart of our feeling, but do so only in patterned conjunction with the rest.

In effect, meter looks at least two ways: toward the sentence, which it both reflects and rivals, and toward the larger world of character and character, whose relations it mirrors—ultimately, to that world's structure of authority and resistance, and of inner selves and outer layers of reality (other person, family, party, state, cosmos). Of course, iambic pentameter is used also in nondramatic poetry, but it has a special relevance to drama which Shakespeare seems instinctively to have exploited.

The structure of oppositions that we find in meter is also a structure of linkages. The meter of Shakespeare's dramatic verse, though it looks looser than the iambic pentameter of traditional later poets, is only carrying further than they do the principle of linkage that is inherent in iambic (or, more broadly, in metrical) poetry, and it does so largely as an appropriate means of recognizing the linkages inherent in drama. If earlier Tudor poets had a sharpened sense of the foot as linking two syllables and of a line as linking five feet (see Chapter 3), Shakespeare's dramatic verse keeps stressing the way other elements of line, speech, scene, and play are shared. The straddling trochee links two phrases, the shared line links two voices speaking two phrases, syllables share feet, phrases share lines. On a larger scale, speeches share scenes, characters share the stage, audience and actors share the theater, play and reality share the world.[7] The plays often make the point that power and love, splendid in themselves, result in disaster when they are too narrowly and selfishly pursued. An aesthetic and an ethic of mutual dependence and obligation are deeply inscribed in Shakespeare's drama. More intently than in most nondramatic verse, we hear the elements of Shakespeare's language exercising a force on each other, one element compelling another to respond. Actor and audience, text and reader, require each other. Syllable, foot, phrase, line, speech, scene, even play invites or challenges its companion, its cohort, its rival, its reader to supply its needed complement. Not that there is usually any obvious principle of pairing that one can follow through the verse. In this respect, as in others, Shakespeare's art eludes excessively symmetrical arrangement.

This disguised but insistent compelling of one entity by another serves finally as a mirror of Shakespeare's (and our) world. Both in speech and action we make and meet demands; complex sequences are composed of small patterned units; heartbeats, elementary physical movements, images, phonemes combine to form words, languages, actions, lives. In Shakespeare more than in other English poets, the intense connections, the fierceness of the linkages, are conveyed through every feature of the verse, through the departures from the norm even more than through the norm, because departures constantly question the norm and require it to reassert itself, something which is never asked of prose and which is asked more politely of the comparatively "correct" pentameter written by later English poets. Most later iambic pentameter is, as a consequence, relatively inert. Unlike Shakespeare's dramatic verse, it never comes close to prose and usually avoids all those questionable forms which for Shakespeare enlarge and extend the challenges and the domain of verse: short, long, and deviant lines, straddling trochees, highly segmented lines, and midline-to-midline arrangement of sentences and paragraphs. Later iambic pentameter, too, is not so intimately and fully connected to the human voice, to people actually talking to each other on a stage. Nondramatic verse in this form, whether lyric, meditative, or narrative, never again (or only perhaps in a comparatively few poems by such poets as Donne, Hopkins, and Yeats) enjoys the same wealth of speech-tones that the plays of Shakespeare luxuriate in. And neither the rhymed plays of Dryden nor the closet drama of nineteenth-century poets (drama not written for speaking voices at all) shows anything like the range or exuberance that we find in the dramatic speech written by Shakespeare, Jonson, and some of their contemporaries.

In short, the iambic pentameter used by Shakespeare in his plays is *charged* with implications. The intensity of its system of internal obligations mirrors the intensity of relations within and between people and between people and the divine order, between the aspirations of flawed individuals and the principle of universal mortality. Not only the normal iambic pentameter line but all its departures and deviations help to imply a world-view of continuing reciprocal engagement and mutual responsibility. No syllable, no foot, no phrase, no line, no sentence, no speech, no scene is an island entire to itself. Shakespeare's verse, far from being looser than that of other writers of iambic pentameter, incorporates that principle of exploration and return which the drunken Stephen Dedalus enacts and discovers in almost the same moment (in that novel which itself serves better than most commentary to reflect and annotate Shakespeare's achievement): "the greatest possible interval which . . . Is the greatest possible ellipse. Consistent with. The ultimate return" (504).

If Shakespeare's verse system stands generally but persistently for the principles of opposition and linkage which are felt everywhere in his work, it may also reflect and affirm more particularly the world order that underlies Shakespeare's writing. We have already noted (in Chapter 11) that eighteenth-century prosodists came to identify strict observance of metrical propriety with moral probity; in effect, they saw iambic pentameter as a social institution in the contemporary social order. In Renaissance iambic pentameter, something of the same force is felt: meter appears to be identified, however, with cosmic rather than social order, and departures from it (Macbeth's extreme agitation is a useful example) represent efforts of energetic human individuality to burst out of the confining framework ("But let the frame of things disjoint"). In the plays, in the sonnets, in the metrical line, we can trace a powerful continuing struggle between authority and rebellion, between law and impulse, between divine order and the beauty of particular evasions of it. When, in the last of his first group of sonnets, Shakespeare presents beauty's prolonged tenure in the fair young man as a caprice of Nature, who will ultimately be compelled to surrender her prize, he uses two highly dramatic metrical variations to make his point emphatic:

> Her audit (though delay'd) | ánswer'd | mŭst bé,
> And her quietus is to render thee. (Sonnet 126:11–12)

The middle phrase in the penultimate line performs the delay it discusses, and the dramatic trochee and spondee, even in asserting the necessity of Nature to conform at last to Time, seem to make a final metrical protest against it, before the concluding line returns to a regular measuring out of the iambic pulse. It is not hard to find in such practice a view of individual aspiration and of its limits in mortality that the sonnets and plays keep testing and confirming in more direct ways as well.[8]

Shakespeare's later dramatic verse uses different tactics—especially the late pause, the run-on line, and the line broken into several segments—to achieve equally profound effects. Not that it abandons the graphic possibilities of trochaic and spondaic intensification; but its experiments with the deepest relations of line and phrase count finally as resonant structural inquiries. Meter stands (but not simply) for some such principle as order, truth, certainty, completeness—doom; deviation is energy, mischief, trouble—and beauty. Even when the character's perception of truth is clouded, the calmness of the perceiving perhaps steadies the beat. But in the later plays at least, from *Hamlet* on, hardly anyone is perfectly steady. As the characters are flawed, so is the meter, which betrays them, either by its genuine metrical deviations or by the continual divergence of line and phrase. As Tarlinskaja observes (1987, chapter 4), heroic characters, or those who are trying to appear so, are likely to speak in a more regular line. The broken line testifies to anxiety, either immediate, in the present situation (Othello, Macbeth, Leontes), or ingrained in the character (Iago, Coriolanus, the Queen in *Cymbeline*) or universal, in the nature of intense human experience (Isabella, Lear, Prospero), or some strong combination of these. Not all segmented lines express anxiety or distress, but the pervasive use of them (in Shakespeare's manner) seems to, and the return to the full line at the end of a final scene (like the return of the full court) marks the resumption of order. As Auden puts it in the commentary on *The Tempest* which he assigns a scrubbed-up Caliban to deliver: "the sounded note is the restored relation" (340).

Compared with Shakespeare's, most later iambic pentameters are much less inclusive. The return to correctness amounts to an abandonment of those deviant forms and features which helped Shakespeare's verse establish its illusion of mimesis—that the language, though formal, is that of actual people talking to each other in a world governed by mutual and structural obligations. In later verse, some of the elements in this equation are relaxed or withdrawn, and iambic pentameter comes to carry a different set of implications. In Augustan verse only the rhymed form survives, and other deviations are cut to the bone. Within this narrower, tidier range, the structural forms of foot and rhyming line are held taut, small variations count for a great deal, and the art at its best is one of great intensity. But as verse in the nineteenth century drifts toward accentualism, the principles of linkage, mimesis, and meaningful variation grow more diffuse. The wide range of voices and tones that animated Shakespeare's plays had been sustained in less various form by Milton's supple manipulations of a highly figured but advancing sentence and by Dryden's and Pope's rhetorical assumption of an observant and animated speaker addressing an informed audience. But in most nineteenth-century verse the variety of voices has dwindled, and we hear iambic pentameter no longer as, literally, a figure of speech (and *for* speech) but as the language's Sunday preacher, with a satchel of familiar tones: admonition, elevation, indignation, and wonder. Even the exceptional poets who try to recover the meter's connections with living speech—notably, Browning and Hopkins—are working with a form that has been largely automatized (to use the language of Russian and Czech Formalism), and the best they can do is to foreground some patches of it. The full force of the verse, its carrying power, is spent.

We cannot here approach this later verse, except to suggest in the sketchiest manner how the different concerns of Romantic and post-Romantic poetry put it in different relation to iambic pentameter. For the Renaissance, the central problem to be coped with in verse is mortality— of the person, of beauty, of power, of fortune. For later centuries, it is the transitoriness of the moment. And these two ways of formulating the problem, though related, are not the same. The first is centered in the divine order, the second in personal experience. "How to keep . . ." is the modern complaint; "Stay, thou art so fair." The Renaissance epic or dramatic poet looks on this struggle mainly as an awed spectator; the nineteenth-century lyric poet presents it from the point of view of an involved protagonist. For Shakespeare, mortality is a condition; for Pater, evanescence is an experience. To be sure, Shakespeare and others let us see people and speakers (of sonnets) experiencing change and loss, but the emphasis, especially and unmistakably in the plays, is on experience as an instructive spectacle. As Stephen Dedalus observes ([1916], 204), we sympathize either with the sufferer or with the secret cause; but the difference is chronological as well as generic.

To put it all too blatantly: iambic pentameter in the Renaissance symbolizes a cosmic order that limits human aspiration; human experience can be heard in the counter-rhythm; together, the two compose a system of creative departures from metrical authority. That is, in any verse the ground-rhythm is likely to represent whatever human experience is tested by—in Renaissance verse the divine order, in eighteenth-century verse the social order. But in nineteenth-century verse, as conceptions of human existence begin to change, the old orders seem shaky, and what now appears as the ground of reality—either the natural world, in which we participate, or our perceptions and experiences of it—can no longer be appropriately expressed by a traditional line whose measure is neither one thing nor the other—looser than the beat, tighter than the phrase.

As a consequence, Romantic poetry begins to move in the two contrary directions indicated by its separating components—toward the wholly accentual and toward the wholly phrasal. The beat of the former easily becomes identified with the physical rhythms of Nature—the sea, the moon's phases, the pulse—against which no intelligible countercurrent can contend. In free verse, on the other hand, the phrase achieves the apotheosis toward which the whole metrical development of Renaissance poetry had been carrying it. At first subservient to the line, then in late Shakespeare and late Milton becoming a powerful rival authority to the verse line, then dammed for a century at the line-ending by the couplet of Dryden and Pope, the phrase at last breaks free to *become* the line. The liberation is an exuberant one, but the price it pays is formidable: loss of tension, loss of inflection, loss of the power to represent symbolically in the verse itself the defining oppositions and linkages of life in English.

Yet even this is not the end of the story. Iambic pentameter survives in twentieth-century verse in a dwindling remnant of superb practitioners, most notably Yeats, Stevens, Eliot, Berryman, Lowell, Larkin, Wilbur, Merrill, Hecht, and Hollander, for some of whom, as for the poets of the Renaissance, the regular meter once again seems a figure for normal life, departure from it a trope for individual eccentricity, manner, or mania. Rarely, however, does "normal life" mean anything so grand as "the cosmic order"; and departures from it usually have the effect, at best, of elegant pathos rather than high tragedy. The world has changed, and iambic pentameter, whose deepest connections must always be to contemporaneous world-views, has had to change with it. Verse at present, which always somewhat blindly chooses its forms, has made other arrangements for mirroring the world, and iambic pentameter is no longer conspicuous on the program.

CHAPTER 17

Some Metrically Expressive Features
in Donne and Milton

The iambic pentameter verse Shakespeare devised for his plays was clearly a distinctive and even an eccentric form of the standard meter. Most of his contemporaries preferred a smoother verse, and Spenserian elegance and Jonsonian plainness soon converged on the main path that the English heroic line would henceforth take, a path plotted and smoothed by such seventeenth-century craftsmen as Waller, Denham, and Dryden. Shakespeare has remained for centuries an extraordinarily influential poet, and many of his metrical maneuvers are among the most impressive in literature. But his metrical devices were never adopted as a system by any formidable later poet. (In this sense, Lydgate had more imitators than Shakespeare.) While Shakespeare's younger contemporaries and successors, including most of the playwrights, were consolidating a standard line, two poets, Donne and Milton, continued to write in some respects against the current, in an effort, comparable to Shakespeare's, to fashion an expressive poetic speech. An account of Shakespeare's experiments seems incomplete without a brief glance at theirs.

Donne

Donne's lines are notoriously so difficult as to provide a test case for any theory of iambic pentameter. Readers who have learned to feel comfortable with other poets' use of the national meter will find Donne seeming to force stress onto wrong syllables, and the marriage of speech and verse often sounds harsh, even ugly. Theorists sometimes respond to this

situation by accusing Donne either of metrical deafness or of antic extrava-
gance. Everything appears to depend on the reader's ability to tolerate
divergences from the standard pattern, and readers will vary in their will-
ingness to do this. But despite the capacity this poetry has of making all its
readers at moments metrically ill at ease, Donne is working from quite
consistent metrical principles to compose a verse that is, within its nar-
rower limits, as expressive as Shakespeare's.[1]

Unlike Shakespeare, Donne avoids the deviant lines of the Lydgate
tradition and most of the other metrical anomalies that play so large a role in
Shakespeare's versification.[2] Neither does he syncopate words as radically as
Shakespeare, but he goes much further in eliding. Donne's elision regularly
not only fuses contiguous weak vowels in adjoining words but compresses
strong vowels and weak into a single syllable, works across *h*'s and glides,
and is not deterred by commas or even stronger punctuation. We find
such combinations as "no one," "now outwore," "idle, as," "deeply hath,"
"my humility," "nature hath," "tremblingly aske," "by one," and "sh'was."[3]

To most modern readers, these practices seem extreme, but that is
partly because later iambic pentameter is more formal and less colloquial.
Donne's elision is based on the recognition that in ordinary English speech
many syllables are slurred or swallowed, that rapid speakers often do resort
to such concisions as "nature'th" or "nat'r'th," and that poetry can take
advantage of this articulatory freedom either to slur or to give full value to
such combinations. Shakespeare and Jonson work on the same principle;
Donne just carries it further. The effect is of animated speech, hurrying
from one syllable to another, from one phrase to another, racing past punc-
tuation to merge separate phrases in a single breath:

> Yet deare|ly I love | you, and would | be lov|ed faine . . .
> Divorce | mee, untie, | or breake that knot againe
>
> (Holy Sonnet XIV:9, 11)

The pauses that the commas here invite are retracted by the elision, and
the effect is of impassioned speech, too urgent to honor the usual breaks
that separate phrase and phrase. The voice goes hurtling on over the
barriers.

A second source of difficulty in Donne's lines is that, more than any
other English poet writing later than Wyatt, Donne arranges his phrasing

so that frequently the syllables we might normally expect to stress do not fall in the stress positions. We find in his lines a constant, a chronic, competition for stress among the syllables. It is not merely that pyrrhics, spondees, and trochees appear often; there are many poems in which no medial trochees appear at all, or only after long intervals. It is, rather, that Donne is altering somewhat the system of expectations that governs our usual reception of the ten-syllable line. He appears to have perceived that this line can be used in two opposing yet complementary ways. First, the line's stress-positions can be used to direct stress to syllables that command rhetorical stress but which, if the lines appeared as prose, might not receive it:

Nor so write *my* name in thy loving bookes (Elegie VI:4)

That we may open *our* eares, Lord lock thine. ("The Litanie," 234)

And death shall be no more; death, *thou* shalt die (Holy Sonnet X:14)

In such lines the italicized words (often pronouns) receive strong stress not just because they happen to be in stress-positions; rather, their being in such positions helps the intelligent reader to see that stressing them strongly is a key to the rhetorical plot of the sentence.

Reason is our Soules *left* hand, Faith her right
("To the Countesse of Bedford," 1)

And *if* things *like* these, have been said by mee
("To the Countesse of Salisbury," 37)

Though you be *much* lov'd in the Princes hall (Elegie IV:63)

Such lines spoken with a tentative stress on the italicized word would seem metrically unstable or problematical but become metrically secure once that word is strongly stressed. Donne was keenly aware that the spoken language distributes stresses variously, in obedience to rhetorical requirements of contrast and emphasis. His metrical stresses usually give us the clues we need to make the most sense of his sentences.[4]

But if the *meter* can direct stress to unlikely (because minor) syllables, the *phrasing* can insist on stress being placed on some syllables that appear in *un*stressed positions. The normal trochaic variation is the commonest instance, and Donne uses it abundantly, sometimes several times in a line: "*Living, barrells* of beefe, *flaggons* of wine" (Satyre IIII:236). But the trochees that cause difficulty in Donne are those that appear without a preceding speech juncture, unless we manufacture one because we are so used to finding one before a medial trochee:

Wee see in Authors, too | *stiffe to* recant   ("The Second Anniversary," 281)

She gave protections; the | *thoughts of* | her brest

                                       ("The Second Anniversary," 371)

A pyrrhic followed by a trochee is an awkward sequence for iambic pentameter; most poets avoid it altogether. If lines containing this sequence are to continue to be perceived as iambic pentameter, the pyrrhic must not be hurried but must be accorded its due (if submissive) share of the advancing line.

Guyanaes har|vest is | nip'd in | the spring

                     ("To Mr. R.W.: If, as mine is . . . ," 18)

Sweetnesse and wit, | they are but | *Mummy,* | possest

                           ("Loves Alchymie," 24)

So, if one knowl|edge were | *made of* | all those

                 ("Obsequies to the Lord Harrington," 57)

Like Shakespeare, Donne frequently allows trochees to straddle two phrases; in some such phrases the trochaic effect is still quite strong, in others mild or muted. Different readers will hear such lines variously, depending on the kind of stress and duration they choose to give the first of the two italicized syllables and the syllable that precedes it. Usually a strong stress on the preceding syllable, along with a refusal to linger on the first syllable of the "trochee," will result in a series of more or less level stresses rather than in a trochee, a tendency perfectly in keeping with Donne's racy, speechlike verse (see above, Chapter 13).

I must not laugh, nor weepe | *sinnes, and* | be wise   (Satyre III:3)

So doth, so is Religion; and this blind-
nesse too | much light | *breeds; but* | unmov|ed thou   (Satyre III:68–69)

For most of his poems Donne provides a strong base of vigorous and regular iambic pentameter lines, but against this background he frequently arranges such an encounter of phrasing and meter as will make the assignment of stress anything but clear-cut. In particular, he gives us many sequences of syllables only minimally differentiated in stress. This practice suggests that especially when we are passionately pleading, praising, or arguing we speak phrases composed of syllables that are only slightly distinguished from one another in force or strength.

We căn | nŏr lŏst | friĕnds, nŏr | sŏught fŏes | rĕcŏver   ("The Calme," 21)

Ŏft frŏm | nĕw prŏofes, | ănd nĕw | phrăse, nĕw | dŏubts grŏw
                                    ("To the Countesse of Bedford: You have refin'd mee . . . ," 65)

Griĕfe brŏught | to numbers cannot be so fierce,
Fŏr, hĕ | tămes ĭt, | that fetters it in verse.   ("The Triple Foole," 10–11)

This last example is especially instructive because it enacts what it says. Donne's "Griefe" is the pain of love. What goes on in the second foot of the final line is a miniature taming: the verb, out of stress position, threatens to break the alternating pattern, but the word that follows is strong enough to retain the metrical stress. In the previous foot, "he" needs some slight stress because it has to serve as antecedent for the delayed relative clause; and "tames it" is followed by a momentary pause before that clause begins. Both of these features help to make the suggested scansion more plausible. Even if we give a stronger secondary stress (^) to "tames," the combination "tames it," though mildly trochaic, still seems a taming when we compare it to the normal stress pattern that we would find in most prose appearances of the phrase: tămes ĭt.

In such a system, terms like *pyrrhic, spondee,* and *trochee* hardly do justice to the great variety of relationships that may exist between any odd syllable in the line and the one that follows it. The principle is deeper. In fact, the peculiarity of Donne's verse enables us to see more clearly that the feet by which verse lines are usually defined are only an analytical convenience. What is essential is the alternation between lesser and greater stress. Occasional minor disturbances of the system, such as the dropping of the line's first syllable or the addition of an unstressed one at the end, hardly count as disturbances at all. More serious is the failure to achieve five alternations in a line (rare in Donne), or exceeding five (also rare), or omitting syllables or adding extra ones anywhere between the beginning and the end (also rare), or in some way compromising the principle of alternation (exceedingly common in Donne).

There are several ways of tampering with the principle of alternate weak and strong syllables. One way is to alter the expected order in any set of two syllables, especially by reversing a weak-strong pair into a strong-weak pair. But although such trochaic feet disturb the meter they do not imperil it: a compensation principle keeps the lines on an even keel so long as the line returns finally (and soon) to an iambic pattern. But the pyrrhic and spondaic patterns, though common enough in the work of other contemporary poets, become in Donne dangerously subversive of the iambic principle of alternating stresses, to the point where some scholars see Donne as writing a different sort of verse altogether, a "transitional" verse between syllabic and accentual (Tarlinskaja, 1976, 187–98) or one based on the rhythms of prose (Woods, 249–58).

Since one basic principle of the meter is alternation of strength throughout the sequence of syllables, *any perceived equality of stress in adjacent syllables tends to obscure the alternating pattern.* If we perceive one set of adjacent syllables as carrying about the same degree of stress, that will not seriously jeopardize our sense of alternation; on the contrary, the second syllable will still be heard as slightly stronger than the first. But if it happens twice or more often in a line, we may well lose temporarily our sense of the meter. To avoid having that happen, our sense of the meter may do whatever it can to restore itself. In practice, this means that we do not follow deafly the "prose reading" of the words if to do so leads us into metrical incoherence. We make some minimal adjustments. Some of these adjustments every experienced reader nowadays is likely to make as a concession to reading the verse as verse: eliding syllables according to the poet's evident practice; reversing the stress pattern where trochaic words or phrases require us to do so; intensifying the first syllable of a "spondee" or relaxing the second syllable of a "pyrrhic," in order to avoid impossibly singsong phrasing. The problem arises in what appear to be the more extreme adjustments required by Donne's verse, and especially in those lines that involve the distribution of stress among syllables whose claims are nearly equal. In "Loves Deitie," for example:

Love might make me leave loving, or might trie
A deeper plague, to make her love me too   ("Loves Deitie," 24–25)

The reader who believes we must read such lines with a prose rhythm and then let our ears distinguish that rhythm from a normal line that we also hear (see above, Chapter 1, on Counterpointers, p. 11) will have a hard time with this passage. Such a reader may very well come up with a scansion like this:

Lóve mĭght máke mĕ leăve lŏvíng, ŏr mĭght trĭe
Ă deĕpĕr plágue, tŏ măke hĕr lŏve mĕ tŏo

This would be, I think, at least one plausible way to say the line if it were prose, and theorists who think they never make any concession to the meter when they read verse but always adopt the prose rhythms as a counterpoint to the iambic pentameter norm will presumably have to allow such a reading. But it is hard to imagine any such counterpoint going on between two rhythmic units so entirely disparate. Hearing the lines so scanned, we probably *could* not continue to hear a regular iambic pentameter line against it in our heads. No, the only way to read such lines is by trying to find a phrasing that is at once natural (which is to say, rhythmically and rhetorically plausible) and closer to the metrical pattern of alternating stresses. The alternation cannot be perfectly regular without distorting English speech patterns; words like "Love," "make," and "leave" cannot go completely unstressed. But as we read the lines closely and respond where we can to the meter's apparent interest in syllables that often in English seem less important than "Love" and "make," we can find such a reading as this:

Lŏve míght | măke mé | leăve lóv|ĭng, ŏr | mĭght tríe
Ă deĕp|ĕr plágue, | tŏ máke | hĕr lóve | mĕ tóo

This reading preserves both the iambic (alternating) character of the lines (only in the third foot of the first line is the first syllable stronger than the second—an example of contrary stress) and the naturalness of the reading. The tension between meter and phrasing is very strong, and the reading that, despite strains, is faithful to both derives greater intensity from the conflict. The grid reading, on the other hand (iambic pentameter placed like a grid over the prose rhythm) carries no strain, no tension, no intensity, in the words, but only, like quantitative verse, in the mind. We may perceive the contrast intellectually, but it is embodied in no sensuous aesthetic medium.

Donne's verse is full of such difficult, problematical lines, which require the reader to choose shrewdly among stress-levels in order to find readings that are both natural and metrical. Some examples:

There is | not now | that man|kinde, which | was then

("The First Anniversary," 112)

All whom | the flood | did, and | fire shall | o'erthrow

(Holy Sonnet VII : 5)

Labour | to admit | you, but | Oh, to | no end

(Holy Sonnet XIV : 6)

One of the most disputed lines in Donne is line 3 of Elegie X. Thirty years ago it came up for discussion in a celebrated *Kenyon Review* symposium involving notable critics and linguists (see A. Stein, 1951; Chatman; and Ransom).

> Image of her whom I love, more then she,
> > Whose faire impression in my faithfull heart,
> Makes mee her *Medall,* and makes her love mee,
> > As Kings do coynes . . .   (Elegie X : 1–3)

Clearly, the third line is of the type we have been considering. The linguist or critic who believes in the counterpoint theory will probably prefer a "prose reading":

Makes mee her *Medall,* and makes her love mee

But this is to miss Donne's play of emphasis among the last four syllables. Emphasis needs to be placed on the second "her," because it appears in contrast to the first "mee;" and the second "mee" needs emphasis in order to set up the contrasting parallel phrase in the next line: "makes *her* love *mee* / As *Kings* do *coynes*." So we can read the line thus:

Mákes mée | hĕr *Mĕ|dăll,* ănd | mákes hĕr | lŏve mée

Donne's metrical variations orchestrate the rhetorical turns of his sentences; by doing so, they charge his style with tension. Although he can and does write lines that flow easily and smoothly, especially in the *Songs and Sonets,* he is tolerant of a degree of metrical disruption that Shakespeare and others rarely resort to; either the meter and the syntax seem at odds, or else the meter is forcibly directing stress to minor words in the neighborhood of major ones in a fashion that is rhetorically plausible but full of articulatory tension ("All whom the flood did, and fire shall o'erthrow").

In sum, Donne admits certain species of variation that Shakespeare and later poets avoided and that not even Donne's contemporary admirers learned or labored to admit. If they had done so, English iambic pentameter might have developed differently. But they all drew back, in favor of a more Jonsonian smoothness and detachment. Although Donne surely never saw his own verse in such an historical light, we can in retrospect see that the choice made by his successors was essentially a choice to marry speech and meter on more decorous terms—that is, not to make bold metrical sacrifices for the sake of reproducing a natural speech emphasis but to seek a more melodious compact between them.

Even though no one followed Donne through all the perversions of his idiosyncratic metric, he and Shakespeare succeeded in permanently ridding English poetry of the superannuated notion that stress in English poems is a function only of a syllable's standing in two hierarchical orders: phonological (within a word, which syllable gets the stress?) and grammatical (within a phrase, which monosyllabic word belongs to one of the major categories: noun, verb, adjective, adverb?). They saw, and lavishly illustrated in their practice, that stress is also and chiefly a function of a syllable's importance in the rhetorical phrase, regardless of its theoretical standing in some abstract dictionary of significant syllables. That is, the importance of a syllable in English verse is not, as in Latin verse, *pre-assigned;* it depends on what work it is given to do *in this sentence.* Although later poets usually made this point less aggressively, it has remained an unstated principle of iambic verse to the present day. It is only some modern linguistic metrists who have turned back the clock and adopted Gascoigne's mistaken belief that the stress of a word in a poem is predetermined by its earlier history. By 1600 the poets had long known better.

After Donne and Shakespeare

It seems unlikely that Shakespeare and Donne ever thought of themselves as leading a movement to write a more complex and problematical iambic pentameter line. Yet in retrospect their work has that in common, and their success in fashioning such a line for their different sorts of poetry is almost without precedent or comparison. Few later poets have tried to push the form to its limits, to exercise lavishly some of the options that obscure its status as a meter and emphasize its nearness to speech: the occasional extra or omitted syllable, syllabic ambiguity, level stress, a high degree of enjambment and segmentation, and so on. Profoundly as Shakespeare and Donne influenced their successors, seventeenth-century versification followed a different line. If iambic pentameter, after all, was to remain a standard resource of poets, it probably had to do so in a more genial form. Just as Wyatt's interesting but difficult sonnets had to give way to a more usable version of the meter, so the arts of Donne and of the later dramatic Shakespeare could only survive as eccentric versions of a meter whose ordinary forms were familiar to their readers. This is true even within their own work, where the odder lines and passages are perceived against a background of lines that have a more readily identifiable pattern.

The development of a standard iambic pentameter from Ben Jonson to the Augustans is a familiar story. It employs such diversions as initial trochees, is sparing in its use of pyrrhic and spondaic feet, makes sharp and easily recognized distinctions between stressed and unstressed syllables, avoids syllabic ambiguity and problematical lines, and aims at tight syntactical conveyance of ideas and a conjunction of line and phrase. Eventually, its favored figure is the antithesis, its intuitive form the rhymed couplet. As a prosodic vehicle, iambic pentameter becomes more firmly fixed in its habits; observing a familiar set of metrical proprieties, it functions as a social institution; and departures from it are regarded not merely as lapses of taste but as signs of moral degeneracy.

Before it could reach such a canonized state, the metrical licenses of

Donne and Shakespeare had to be stigmatized as not merely peculiar (as contemporary readers or rival poets may well have thought them) but as perverse or artless. The high art of the Augustan couplet had presumably left all earlier English poets far behind, whatever their untutored genius. (Milton, of course, was a highly tutored counterexample.) But signs of this patronizing attitude toward the more eccentric practitioners of iambic pentameter are evident already in remarks by Ben Jonson: that Shakespeare wrote lots of bad lines ("Would he had blotted a thousand!" 969), and that Donne deserved to be hanged "for not keeping of accent" (990).

Both Shakespeare and Donne had their immediate imitators. By 1596 or 1597 Shakespeare was easily the dominant playwright on the Elizabethan stage—remarkably successful, remarkably prolific. Such rivals as Marlowe, Kyd, Greene, and Peele were all dead by 1597, and younger rivals like Jonson had not yet risen to challenge him.[5] (Spenser, a poet of another sort, was off in Ireland, writing a literally interminable courtly poem.) But when they appeared, most of them learned much from Shakespeare, a few even from his versification. The story of such influence is too complex to be treated here, but it seems clear that, among these playwrights, only Middleton and Webster tried deliberately to imitate the broken, agitated style of Shakespeare's later plays. In some respects, the verse of *The Duchess of Malfi* is more bizarre than Shakespeare's ever is. But other playwrights picked up isolated features of Shakespeare's verse without absorbing the whole system. So the extravagant use of feminine endings by Fletcher seems (like some of Shakespeare's own early decorative verse) the borrowing of a mannerism rather than the working out of an essential feature in an integrated design. In any case, the influence of Shakespeare's eccentric late verse is no match for that of Jonsonian or even of Shakespearean smoothness. Long before the theaters closed in 1642, dramatic blank verse had found a sturdy, regular, and unoffending norm in the plays of Ford and Shirley.

Donne's metaphysical followers learned much from his conceits, but their versification is smoother than his by far and closer to the emerging standard. Like Donne, some of them invented stanza forms with lines of varying lengths, but in the arrangement of these they follow Herbert rather than Donne, and in Herbert's stanzas the pentameter lines are divested of the special role they play in Donne's.[6] Indeed, it is the short line that often, in Herbert's verse, concludes an extended statement with the same direct and sudden force we have noticed in Shakespeare's middle and later verse (Chapter 14). Compare:

> The dark and vicious place where thee he got
> Cost him his eyes.   *(King Lear,* 5.3.173–74)

> If goodnesse leade him not, yet wearinesse
> May tosse him to my breast.   ("The Pulley," 19–20)

Herbert can also arrange his lines in the opposite pattern, equally familiar in Shakespeare, in which a short first line (or phrase) opens out to a longer second line:

> nothing that's plain,
> But may be wittie, if thou hast the vein.   ("The Church-porch," 239–40)

Cf. Shakespeare's

> Ever till now
> When men were fond, I smiled, and wondered how.
>   *(Measure for Measure,* 2.2.185–86)

The ingenuity and devotion of seventeenth-century poets insured the survival of stanzaic verse as an important medium for later poets, but the poetry of rhymed couplets gradually began to dominate English poetry. This development does not notably reduce the production of stanzaic verse, but it virtually obliterates the blank verse, which does not reappear until the 1740s as a major verse form. The great exception is Milton, whose work in all the relevant forms—including stanzas, sonnets, prose, couplets, blank verse—is crucial to later literary history. His management of the verse line, and his treatment of the opposition between line and phrase, not only were extraordinary in themselves but had far-reaching consequences.

Milton

Milton's verse has been minutely examined by some able critics, notably Bridges, Sprott, Prince, and Weismiller, all of whom have helped us to see its metrical and syntactical principles. Bridges and Sprott essentially describe in detail the metrical structure of Milton's lines: the number of syllables and stresses, the practices of elision, enjambment, and line-break. Prince disputes many points with Bridges, claiming that the chief influence on Milton's blank verse is not classical foot-prosody but sixteenth-century Italian *versi sciolti*. Weismiller, in a series of perceptive essays, has sensitively and with a kind of Miltonic strength described the movement of Milton's lines and their intimate relations with syntax and syntactical patterning.

In addition, Wylie Sypher, comparing achievements in different arts with a freedom not always approved by aesthetic critics but with a perspicacity and an eloquence worthy of his heroic subject, has placed Milton's blank verse style with the architectural and artistic monuments of the high Baroque and has pointed out in particular its apparent debts to the Baroque churches Milton visited in Rome. Sypher connects the Baroque with Galileo's introduction into physics of "concepts of dynamic force, of inertia, of weight, mass, and motion," and the idea "that matter is endowed with power, that bodies do not need to be kept moving by Aristotle's Unmoved Mover, but that once set in motion they behave according to certain laws of force" (201). So it is with Milton's verse, which arranges its masses, its lines of force, in accordance with a principle of "motion compounded" (201); "high-baroque art tends to expand by ample movements bursting into jubilant rhetoric" (203). The "resolution of mass into motion is performed in his sustained verse paragraphs with their wasteful reduplication of phrase, their accumulation of grandiloquent names into strong cadences that break open the metrical closures into a 'total' rhythm" (205). Sypher is probably right in connecting the movement of phrase, line, sentence, and verse paragraph with other large elements in Milton's work—the epic manner, the cosmic oppositions, the grandiose iconography: "if baroque means release and expressive energy, as indeed it does, it also means august equilibrium, restabilized masses, idealized forms, and grand simplified planes—an academic co-ordination on an impressive scale" (222).

Sypher's constant reference to particular material forms, either of architecture or of verse lines, enables these broad, dense general terms to carry conviction. His metaphors of space and motion are not fanciful inventions but reminders that the fundamental character of art is illusion. Just as we learn to see people in paints and to speak of movement in monumental stone, so the unpredictability and indeterminacy of verse lines within a basically determined metrical framework fosters the illusion that the verse has a life of its own, that within it is something living that directs its own development and works out its own form. This is partly the illusion that most great art gives that there is intention in the work itself, that the painting directs our response to it, that the actors on the stage will the events in the lives of the characters they portray, that there is a voice *in* the sonnet. But illusions vary. Shakespeare's later verse is preeminently a verse of the theater, and its sound emerges from different actual voices, which we hear elaborating their sensory imagery from within a visual field of scenes and actions. Milton's verse, in contrast, is nothing but silent sound and potential image. As, in his blindness, he composed his lines, he may have visualized them on a page; we, as we read the lines from the page, may imagine or try to reproduce their sound—its solemn, segmented motions and its blazing intensity.

Milton's strong, regular lines, his extensive phonemic, lexical, and phrasal repetitions (for example, "But hard be hardened, blind be blinded more," *Paradise Lost,* III.200), his syntactical complexity, and his powerful enjambments are well-known features of his verse and need not be amply illustrated here. Like Shakespeare's late verse, Milton's keeps distributing the segments of sentences over the edges of lines. If we read the lines from the page, we have no difficulty in telling where each line begins and ends, as we do when we listen to Shakespeare's drama. But the wayward Miltonic sentence puts severe strains on the steady verse line. Like Shakespeare, Milton may use his pentameter line to link phrases unlinked by syntax. But the various compulsions inherent in English *sentences* establish their own systems of linkage. They set up expectations which usually must be fulfilled, postponed, or surprised. Ordinary syntax leads us to expect that certain phrases or words will be followed by others—nouns by verbs, verbs by objects, and so on. To postpone the fulfillment of these expectations, or to invert what we think of as normal English word order, is to increase the tension: embedded phrases and appositives, or backward-working grammatical constructions, keep heightening our sense of still unachieved resolution. As we feel our way through the ambiguous constructions, we hope to realize at last some satisfactory whole sentence. Milton uses all the syntactical and rhetorical techniques he can devise (and can adapt from the visual dynamics of Baroque Roman ecclesiastical architecture) to delay, divert, and mask the development of sentences whose segments, in retrospect, perhaps like divinely ordained history, fall into place in a large lucid design. But in the process the phrasal relationships grip the single metrical lines more tightly than is usual for English poets; and, on the other hand, the syntactical thread that pulls the segments of the sentence together through several successive lines is likely to exert a stronger force. The order of the line and the order of the sentence are both formidable, the tension between them at any point vibrant, and it is only because all these elements are so strong that the formal relationship between the basic ones, line and phrase, is felt to be finally harmonious.

To take one exemplary passage:

So say|ing, her | rash hand | in e|vil hour
Forth reach|ing to | the fruit, | she plucked, | she eat.   (IX.780–81)

Like the Chaucerian passage we examined long ago (Chapter 2), this pair of lines incorporates several different elements: here, two participial introductory phrases (though they have different structures) and two simple noun-verb phrases. The pairs are not, however, distributed evenly through the two lines. Instead, the first participial phrase is short, like the two verb-phrases; but the second participial phrase runs over the line-ending and occupies thirteen of the twenty syllables. The sentence, as it were, opens up into the more generous and explicit description of the second phrase before it reaches the compressed disaster of the final four words. Although the pause after "saying" is negligible and need not be observed, the commas in the second line are highly dramatic. The first is prepared for by the gathering participial phrases; the second is the most telling pause in English poetry. For eight-and-a-half books we have been approaching this moment, which has determined all subsequent human history. Milton registers its monumental character with the simplest of phrases but with an intensity that the preceding phrases have done much to build. The temperature of Milton's poetry often rises with astonishing quickness, and the tremendous import of Eve's action can be powerfully conveyed by the end of only the second line.

But if the pauses and the simple iambic phrases ("she plucked, she eat") are impressive, so are the participial phrases that open the sentence. As in other Miltonic passages Stanley Fish has studied for us, these phrases build up intensity partly because we may, as we read, misinterpret them, may even hold to our misreadings all the way through. The first phrase, simple enough, prepares us to expect a subject, an agent of some action to come, and we seem at first to be offered one in "her rash hand." If so, we may think the first phrase a daring dangling modifier (how can a hand "say"?). As we read on, however, expecting a verb in the second line, we find instead another participle, and now we are likely to understand the long second element in the sentence as an absolute phrase ("her rash hand . . . Forth reaching"). But when we arrive at the sentence's subject ("she"), even as we are taking in the magnitude of this appalling moment, we must revise once again our understanding of the syntax. It is Eve, not her hand, who has been "saying," and it is Eve who reaches forth her hand: "hand" is object, not subject, of the participle. We have moved through this series of misreadings from a view that the action described is performed by the hand (Eve is not responsible) to the simple, direct view of a moral action performed by an erring person ("she plucked, she eat"). One evidence of the way responsibility is at first apparently transferred is the transferred epithet "rash." But it is Eve who is rash, not her hand.

The metrical variations at this moment of human crisis are more numerous than usual in Milton, but even here the strong iambic force of the Miltonic line is not crossed by a trochaic variation. The spondees emphasize the gravity of the occasion, as the pauses score the fall. (After four feet of the second line, the fall has not occurred; one foot later, it has.) In such a passage, Milton's powers of expressive arrangement are unsurpassed. The repeated elements (alliteration and assonance, participial and verbal structures, "she"), the metrical line, the syntactical complexity even in such short compass, the different heft of the successive phrases, the dramatic pauses, the lapsarian iambs, amount to an economy of means and effect that is matched only in Shakespeare.

If we find in Donne, in Shakespeare's later plays, and in *Paradise Lost* the most intense versions of English iambic pentameter, that is largely because these poets show an extraordinary sensitivity to the rhythmic subtleties of the phrase and the sentence. For all of them the play between phrase or sentence and verse line serves as a figurative embodiment of the strongest oppositions they perceived in the world they lived in. Milton's profound paradoxical commitment to rebellion and to authority is deeply inscribed in his verse, like Donne's allegiance to (and distrust of) advance-

279

ment in love or fortune, or like Shakespeare's celebration of heroic passion and its limits in human fallibility and mortality. The condition of all three prosodies is the final submission of the phrase (no matter how cantankerous) to the formal authority of the line. In the work of these poets, nevertheless, we can see how obstreperous the phrase might be if it ever got loose—What would it stand for? Who could control it?—questions that must be put to the different verse of our own time.

CHAPTER 18

Conclusion: Verse as Speech, Theater, Text, Tradition, Illusion

The metrical system Shakespeare developed for his plays diverges from the contemporary practice of iambic pentameter in several respects. Aiming always at variety, grace, energy, elevation, verisimilitude (the speechlikeness of the line generally), and dramatic expressiveness (of the specific line or passage), Shakespeare learned to deploy strategically his different kinds of lines, his metrical variations, and his two orders of meter and phrase. The verse that results never loses its connections with the rhythms of spoken English. It is formed, determined, by its constant obligation to maintain a creative equilibrium between two poles of linguistic force: the continually recurring metrical pattern and the rhythmic phrase.

This equilibrium is inherent in iambic pentameter and is the source of its fascination for English poets. But from Surrey on, nondramatic poets have hardly made any use at all of the most radical syllabic and metrical deviations: headless and broken-backed lines, epic caesuras, and monosyllabic feet; short, shared, or squinting lines; triple endings, anapests (till the nineteenth century), and straddling trochees; indeterminate passages and the company of prose. For Shakespeare and some of his contemporaries (writers of plays, not of lyrical or narrative verse), it was important to make the verse spoken by characters—that is, by living actors on a stage—sound like speech as well as like verse. The speech may be elevated, grand in its diction, noble in its periods, but its tones and rhythms must not stray too far from the familiar ones of everyday experience. Only natural English phrases can convey these tones and rhythms, though they may be provided elaborate syntactical gowns for some occasions. But the deadliness of that earlier English verse in which the metrical requirements of every foot are

281

painstakingly met, Shakespeare deliberately avoids in favor of a verse whose departures from pattern can better convey the unpredictable vitality of human beings talking to one another in English.[1]

In effect, two forces contend in Shakespeare's verse: the force of life and the force of pattern. From one point of view, pattern *is* life; order and design are fulfilling, satisfying, even redemptive, while human passion is clumsy, destructive, and blind. But pattern may also be neat and trivial, merely pretty, merely decorative; and from it the vigorous and insistent human force rebels and flinches, asserts its powerful individuality in exceptional action and verse. Departure is character. Yet within the superficial neatness of showy pattern ("the forc'd gait of a shuffling nag") a stronger order inheres: that order of divine design, of cosmic perfection, to which all the departures from pattern and moral action are ultimately accountable, the order at last of mortality and completeness. The drama of Shakespeare is played out not only through a dialogue of characters but also through a dialogue of differently formed and framed verse lines, which speak to each other and to us of the variety, grace, and plenitude of human speech and trouble.

But the combination in Shakespeare's late verse of all its unusual features produces a verse rhetoric that is hard to hear and appraise. It is hard even to say what "we hear" in this verse: what we hear in the theater or what we imagine we hear as we read the texts in silence. Deprived, in the theater, of those favorite clues—rhymes, endstopped lines, and foursquare speeches—which Shakespeare had used earlier to locate his listeners in the verse, how is the spectator to keep a sense of this elusive late meter? Or should we assume that the author is unconcerned, that he does not think of the verse as something that an audience must follow consciously? Shakespeare's dramatic art, after all, as we know from centuries of the most elaborate study, is an art whose linguistic, imagistic, thematic, and ethical patterns are far too complex for any listener to fathom from any single performance. Shakespeare appears, within a few years, to have made the verse, too, as problematical as these other elements—not to be grasped at once but heard or only half-heard from one passage to another.

How far this effect is intended is difficult to say. Shakespeare himself, throughout his career, is unmistakably examining new possibilities of arrangement in which short lines, extra syllables, heavy syncopation of medial syllables, prose, lines that pause in several places, or sentences that run from midline past the endline barrier are given key roles in the development of a new verse art. But even Shakespeare cannot always have been conscious of the effects he produced, and he can hardly have fully appreciated what no one has yet much noticed: the way an audience takes in lines of verse, hearing imperfectly, hearing perhaps an iambic current rather than full lines of verse, usually uncertain of the stresses and almost always uncaring, willing to let some lines of the play go by without measure, as some speeches go by without being understood, hardly knowing whether lengthy passages are prose or verse and not even wondering about it, and yet absorbing, in ways we still have scarcely an inkling of, the deep rhythmical currents of the verse that measure out the characters' utterances line by line.

Is that what we hear in the theater—a current, not a line? Though we can pick up the pentameter in Shakespeare's early plays, do we mainly have to be content in the later ones with iambic? If so, we are in the same situation as Pistol, who knows what he hears is iambic but cannot hear it ordered in lines (see Chapter 7, above). As we listen to Shakespeare's late plays, our sense of the meter may be confirmed and reinforced by longer speeches, which tend to be more regular than shorter ones (see Tarlinskaja, 1987, chapter 4). But we are likely to follow the metrical frame for only a few lines at a time. Then it is lost again, recovered, forgotten, noticed again and again let slip, an audible pattern of which we remain intermittently aware, a perpetual clouded presence, gone in the prose scenes except for iambic lines embedded even there, then reappearing fully or partly, fully and partly, as haunting and elusive as a glimpse of divine order (for which it may serve as a figure). Whereas at a concert many members of the audience, and presumably all the performers, will be continuously aware of the beat and will follow the tempo measure by measure, probably no one listening to any of Shakespeare's last ten plays will be able to follow the verse lineation by ear.

Of course, the reason is partly that unlike most musical scores, the Quarto and Folio texts of Shakespeare's plays present many problems of lineation. Shared lines are not represented as such; prose is sometimes printed as verse, and verse as prose. Typesetting errors abound and are not always easy to put right. In addition, discrepancies between different contemporary versions of the "same" play, even of the same line, may offer perplexing choices. But whether the complexities that make Shakespeare's lines so uncertain are complexities of printing or of production is hardly possible to say, because both are parts of a continuous process the segments of which are not clearly separable and distinct. The production of plays in the theater of Shakespeare's time, or perhaps of any time, is a dynamic process, in which each play is constantly undergoing changes. Lines are always being added or discarded, improved or cut short. There must be a hundred valid dramatic reasons for deforming the verse here and there: to make sure a character's name is given or repeated and the audience knows it, to cut short an overlong scene, to extend a moving one, to direct or control stage movement, to give voice to an afterthought, an additional image, a just-now-thought-of forcible way of making a point, even if such last-minute changes disfigure the iambic pentameter. In such a theater, meter is merely a means, an instrument. If it is audible most of the time, that will be enough to assure elevation, dignity, and grace, but it also may have to give way before any exigent demands of production. A particular version of a dramatic text can therefore be only tentative; it represents the latest hypostasis of a perpetually changing entity, and even the way it represents that entity falsifies to some extent the nature of dramatic production. It pretends that this version of the play is *the* version, is *the* play, when in fact we all know that every future production of the text will change some word, some line, some scene, that every representation will *mis*represent "the text" in some way.

For the text, as we all must know in this age of proliferating editions, is only *a* text, one version. To Shakespeare himself (it seems as good an explanation as any for his apparent indifference to the publication of his plays), a play-text was not at all like a poem-text, not an artifact valuable in and for itself, but the most recent or relevant version of a script used to guide performance of a play. At least some of Shakespeare's plays were performed on different occasions for different audiences and in different versions; if so, each text we have gives us a play arrested in one form. In this sense, plays are like people, and "Which King Lear?" is a question that might apply equally to the character, the production, or the text.

All this implies that reading a play-text is a very partial and incomplete experience and not one that was valued highly or thought of as central by Shakespeare (though he certainly learned from reading the plays of others). A text can be misleading if it encourages us to think that a play of Shakespeare's has an intended final form comparable to that of a sonnet or that any of the plays ever reached such a form. Reading a play from a text also obscures essential differences between nondramatic and dramatic verse, especially that the former is usually not written specifically for voices talking to each other and declaiming on a stage. The orientation toward performance distinguishes dramatic verse from other kinds, which are only *capable* of being recited but are often written to be read from the page by a mind that takes in even their potential sound effects silently. Shakespeare uses expressive metrical effects in his poems as well as in his drama, but the wider range of line-forms and the more complex system of prosodic relationships in the plays, along with the assurance that the sounds he devises will literally be heard by an audience, afford the play-wright grander and more extensive opportunities for expressive effects than any nondramatic English poet but Milton has ever tried to seize.

But for whom are these effects intended? Who is to hear them? Actor? Theater audience? Or reader? It appears that Shakespeare's verse (like his prose) is designed as a medium through which the characters' utterances can be formed. Knowing the direction and tone a speech or scene is to take, the playwright evidently chose to cast it in verse or prose, and in verse or prose of a particular description, because that kind of language was needed to bring out the special intentions he had for this point in the play. Once started, the verse (or prose) might lead the author to effects and felicities beyond those he first imagined, but his principal aim is to provide a fit language, whether verse or prose, for the characters to utter. Shakespeare knew well the inherent capabilities of his verse line, what heights of passion it could reach, what depths of anguish it could sound, what harmonies of dramatic action and resolution it could help the characters achieve. To compose a speech in verse is to signal actor and reader that the character's language now has available to it (and will incorporate as "natural") a fuller range of feeling, thought, imagery, and metaphor than are normally available to speakers of English outside the theater. To compose a speech in prose is to signal actor and reader that the character's language has available to it not a poorer but a different range of feeling, thought, imagery, and metaphor not only from that of verse but also from that which we normally make use of in our own less highly figured speech. By speaking the lines with a due sense of their metrical patterning as well as of their expressive departures from strict pattern, the actor can make the theater audience aware of the kind of language that is now being spoken.

They may not consciously formulate their knowledge that a speech is in verse, but if the actor's metrical work is done well, the audience will sense on every level (including the metrical) that the language of the play has taken a turn toward higher passion, more resonant feeling, or profounder resolution than it was reaching only moments ago: that it is verse, that it is poetry. With such effects possible in the theater, why should the poet care whether his play appeared in print?

Oddly enough, Shakespeare's play-by-play metrical development has never really been charted. Prosodic scholars have counted his feminine endings and other metrical idiosyncrasies, but the stages by which he worked out his complex system of verse design have not been carefully distinguished, and his late verse textures have not often been sensitively described in detail.[2] It seems clear that in *Julius Caesar* and *Troilus and Cressida* Shakespeare is experimenting with short lines; that in *Much Ado about Nothing, 1 Henry IV,* and *Hamlet* (among others) he is extending his knowledge of how prose can function in a play; and that in *Othello* he is working deliberately to achieve smooth verse textures even through a lavish assortment of deviant verse lines. But the whole story is much more involved than this, and it may take generations to sort it out.

The question of how we can "recover" Shakespeare's verse lines is a tricky one. Since we do not really wish to recover his pronunciation—at least in the sense that we want our productions performed in Shakespeare's or a contemporary London dialect—we cannot recover his language. Nor can we be sure that the intonation systems we bring to Shakespeare's plays are quite identical to Shakespeare's own. Was emphasis given to words and phrases by exactly the same means we use today? But the question answers itself, for different actors even now use different methods of speaking and stressing phrases, and the differences between, say, American and British actors are sometimes very great. But this situation only brings out one more oddity in our relation to Shakespeare. We cannot recover his accent or his actors' style of emphasis, and yet we do not doubt for a moment that the words and syntax still give their clues to any actor with a sense of sentence structure and dramatic opportunity. The same is probably true of the meter. The metrical system Shakespeare is using, particularly in his later plays, has never been satisfactorily described; its expressive habits and patterns have resisted even the minimum codification that would help our actors see how it works. We can hope, at least, that, given a few basic principles, actors might make a more heroic effort to let audiences hear the rhythms, the prose and the verse, the short lines and the long, the lines of peculiar metrical structure, and the expressive metrical variations, all of which are Shakespeare's means of letting us know more deeply what is going forward onstage.

A generation ago, many actors grew tired of the pounding rhythms of Shakespearean declamation they had grown up with; they learned to hate the tedious old style of Shakespearean production. But, "properly" performed, the rhythms of Shakespeare's dramatic verse are not pounding and dull but subtle and full of meaning. A new generation of actors has been discovering that Shakespearean characters find their meter and language *as they speak* (see Barton). This is the spirit one hopes will guide most productions in coming years. For, far from restricting expression, the texts of Shakespeare's plays offer an incomparably flexible score, with a wide range of discretionary variations, enough to satisfy the appetite for expressive departures of even the hungriest actor.

The effort on the part of contemporary scholars to recover some sense of how a Shakespearean text may have evolved: how it originated in the playwright's imagination from suggestions in earlier writing, in the contemporary scene, in his private life, in his knowledge of books, people, and other plays; how it took form as a play; how the script emerged from the author's possession to that of the company, from foul papers to promptbook and thence to a published text, with or, usually, without the revision or connivance of the author—all this directly parallels our effort to understand how the verse of Shakespeare's plays might have been heard in the theater and is subject to the same uncertainties, the same speculative dangers, the same regret over the paucity of facts. Little by little we acquire a more adequate notion of the physical theater for which Shakespeare wrote, of the companies and their business, of the audience who attended the plays, but the voices that spoke the lines remain silent. We cannot quite recover their accents, timbre, speed of phrase, their attention to beat and line, the technique of pause or rhetorical climax, the manner of treating elision, syncopation, enjambment, or changes in measure. What hints we have are few and inconclusive: inferences by modern scholars who study Elizabethan pronunciation and acting techniques; debates over meter by such poets as Gascoigne, Campion, and Daniel; remarks by rhetoricians like Puttenham, poets like Jonson, or characters like Hamlet. Otherwise, and principally, our knowledge of how the verse is to be spoken must emerge from a sensitive reading of its lines. The best score is the page of verse, if we have the skill to read it. But that skill requires an understanding, instinctive or studied, of the structural subtleties and expressive powers we have been tracing here.

In my view, the history of iambic pentameter is best understood, not as a sequence of changes in the use of one metrical position or another, but as a succession of insights, realized in practice, into the capabilities of this sort of verse: Chaucer's perception that iambic pentameter can be used for swift and melodious narrative; Lydgate's, that many kinds of modified line structures can carry his English; Wyatt's, that those structural kinds can be augmented by expressive variations to secure effects that are exceedingly subtle (though perhaps, for most readers, inaccessible); Surrey's, that English blank verse can transmit some of the complex grandeur of ancient epic; the insight of Sackville and Norton, that a blank verse play can convey to a theater audience something of the tragic dignity of classical drama; Sidney's insight into the power of regular iambic pentameter to carry passionate amorous speech; the insight of numerous poets, that the usual pause after the fourth syllable could be set after the sixth for variety, and Spenser's, that if it is set after the fifth it may produce an iambic line with a pleasing quasi-trochaic rhythm; Marlowe's insight into the power of blank verse to present such feelings as ambition, desire, frustration, and remorse; Shakespeare's numerous insights into the multitudinous ways in which a varied verse line and a heightened (or suddenly plain) poetic language can combine to present complex psychological states of mind and elevate the opposite sides of personal and public quarrels into profound philosophical issues; Jonson's insight, that even street language can be framed in iambic pentameter; Donne's perception, that an antic iambic pentameter line, or a line countered by lines of other lengths, can faithfully present the wavering between seriousness and gaiety, between assurance and doubt, that may inhere in all strong postures; and similar insights by other resourceful poets who have written in iambic pentameter.

Taken in this way, a verse form is indeed a tradition, something handed down from one poet or generation to another, accruing and combining potentialities as it passes from skilled hand to skilled hand. In time, too, it may lose some force or strength, be weakened or narrowed by the turns it takes in the work of certain poets (Lydgate certainly, and perhaps Jonson or Dryden). But if the way a poet uses meter can be understood as constituting a unified system, we can make at least a beginning toward describing this elusive and illusive material.

The illusion presented by iambic verse resembles the theatrical illusion—that spoken language falls naturally into alternating stressed and unstressed syllables, and that it comes from our mouths in lines. In late Shakespeare and the Jacobean playwrights, the line becomes more jagged, suggesting that an iambic rhythm rides the language or that passion drives speech. Speech lends itself to the illusions that it is iambic, that life might actually be lived in lines, and that lines can both contain and resolve the disorder of life.

The illusion of the iambic verse theater was that we speak by the foot and by the line; the illusion of the free verse theater is that we speak without preparation, without plan, phrase by phrase, as if there were no past or future but only an eternal present of short-breathed speech. The foot and line implied an ordered universe, a final order we could trust, a beginning and an ending, toward which the whole creation moved. The master illusion of free verse—of William Carlos Williams as of Gertrude Stein—is that we are always beginning again in every moment, and this has the same truth and the same falsity as the Renaissance illusions that normal speech has a regular rhythm or that passion must yield to order.

This book has been much about joinings: of syllables, feet, half-lines, and lines; of phrase and line; and of meter and meaning. As the terms grow larger, the disparities between them grow also, to the point where we separate them in our minds and regard meter and meaning as subjects for separate inquiry. But what is true of music and architecture is true also of metrical verse: its strongest meanings are rooted in numbers. Metrical lines are mathematical, musical, architectural constructs, and iambic pentameter is a numerical syllabic and accentual form charged by the technical achievements mainly of sixteenth-century poets to address and embody the largest human issues. The key to its impressive powers (like those of organic life) has always been its essential simplicity—its economy of means and their capacity for complex organization. All that a metrical critic can hope to do is to describe those means and those powers in terms that make them accessible to interested readers.

APPENDIX A

Percentage Distribution of Prose in Shakespeare's Plays

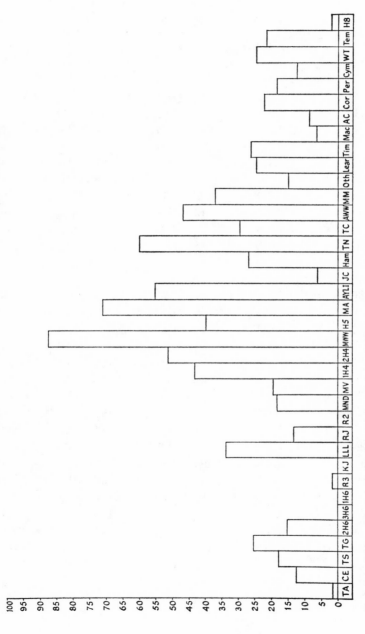

From Brian Vickers, *The Artistry of Shakespeare's Prose* (London: Methuen, 1968), p. 433. Reprinted by permission.

Main Types of Deviant Lines in Shakespeare's Plays

Play	Blank Verse Lines	Epic Caesuras		Short Lines		Hexameters	
TA	2,299	12	(192)[a]	36	(64)[a]	17	(135)[a]
1H6	2,328	3	(776)	21	(111)	8	(291)
CE	1,130	2	(565)	17	(66)	8	(141)
2H6	2,448	13	(188)	52	(47)	15	(163)
3H6	2,727	9	(303)	37	(74)	9	(303)
TS	1,773	20	(89)	67	(26)	31	(57)
R3	3,274	11	(298)	100	(33)	10	(327)
TG	1,430	5	(286)	74	(19)	6	(238)
LLL	562	1	(562)	18	(31)	4	(141)
MND	741	2	(370)	5	(148)	0	—
RJ	2,045	12	(170)	47	(44)	9	(227)
R2	2,100	17	(124)	74	(28)	54	(39)
KJ	2,418	13	(186)	15	(161)	5	(484)
MV	1,820	32	(57)	49	(37)	14	(130)
1H4	1,534	19	(81)	65	(24)	8	(192)
2H4	1,381	21	(66)	31	(45)	8	(173)
MWW	204	8	(26)	7	(29)	3	(68)
MA	611	11	(56)	26	(24)	7	(87)
H5	1,458	25	(58)	33	(44)	13	(112)
JC	2,140	35	(61)	108	(20)	21	(102)
AYLI	877	22	(40)	41	(21)	8	(110)
TN	698	28	(25)	55	(13)	9	(78)
Ham	2,247	78	(29)	154	(15)	43	(52)
TC	1,876	104	(18)	147	(13)	42	(45)
MM	1,395	98	(14)	117	(12)	65	(21)
Oth	2,289	208	(11)	166	(14)	73	(31)
AWW	1,117	66	(17)	68	(16)	18	(62)
Tim	1,285	50	(26)	171	(8)	57	(23)
Lear	1,979	131	(15)	191	(10)	64	(31)
Mac	1,560	78	(20)	97	(16)	35	(45)
AC	2,542	120	(21)	143	(18)	47	(54)
Cor	2,370	120	(20)	136	(17)	43	(55)
Per[b]	640	28	(23)	133	(5)	8	(80)
Cym	2,494	90	(28)	70	(36)	43	(58)

Play	Blank Verse Lines	Epic Caesuras		Short Lines		Hexameters	
WT	1,986	60	(33)	58	(34)	63	(32)
Tem	1,359	33	(41)	67	(20)	19	(72)
H8 [b]	1,105	34	(33)	25	(44)	24	(46)
TNK [b]	1,007	30	(34)	41	(25)	2	(504)
TMore [b]	114	6	(19)	10?	(11)	0	—
Total	63,363	1,655	(38)	2,772	(23)	913	(69)

These figures are derived mainly from E. K. Chambers' tables, in *William Shakespeare: A Study of Facts and Problems,* 2 vols. (Oxford: Clarendon, 1930), vol. 2, pp. 400–405, with some corrections. The chronology is essentially that of Wentersdorf, as reported in Tarlinskaja, *Shakespeare's Verse* (New York: Peter Lang, 1987). Note that Tarlinskaja's figures for total lines are somewhat different.

[a] Parenthetical figures show how frequently each sort of deviant line appears: once in every ( ) lines.
[b] Figures are for those parts attributed to Shakespeare.

Short and Shared Lines

Play	Blank	+	Hex.	+	Short	=	Total	Shared	% Short & Shared
TA	2,299		17		36		2,352	17	2.25
1H6	2,328		8		21		2,357	17	1.61
CE	1,130		8		17		1,155	8	2.16
2H6	2,448		15		52		2,515	13	2.59
3H6	2,727		9		37		2,773	8	1.62
TS	1,773		31		67		1,871	37	5.56
R3	3,274		10		100		3,384	66	4.91
TG	1,430		6		74		1,510	43	7.75
LLL	562		4		18		584	11	4.97
MND	741		0		5		746	28	4.42
RJ	2,045		9		47		2,101	71	5.62
R2	2,100		54		74		2,228	34	4.85
KJ	2,418		5		15		2,438	64	3.24
MV	1,820		14		49		1,883	79	6.80
1H4	1,534		8		65		1,607	43	6.72
2H4	1,381		8		31		1,420	43	5.21
MWW	204		3		7		214	9	7.48
MA	611		7		26		644	35	7.92
H5	1,458		13		33		1,504	31	4.26
JC	2,140		21		108		2,269	129	10.45
AYLI	877		8		41		926	34	8.10
TN	698		9		55		762	44	12.99
Ham	2,247		43		154		2,444	194	14.24
TC	1,876		42		147		2,065	133	13.56
MM	1,395		65		117		1,577	148	16.80
Oth	2,289		73		166		2,528	268	17.17
AWW	1,117		18		68		1,203	138	17.12
Tim	1,285		57		171		1,513	145	20.89
Lear	1,979		64		191		2,234	243	19.43
Mac	1,560		35		97		1,692	246	20.27
AC	2,542		47		143		2,732	470	22.43
Cor	2,370		43		136		2,549	394	20.79
Per[a]	640		8		133		781	84	27.78
Cym	2,494		43		70		2,607	393	17.76

Appendix C

Play	Blank	+	Hex.	+	Short	=	Total	Shared	% Short & Shared
WT	1,986		63		58		2,107	330	18.41
Tem	1,359		19		67		1,445	227	20.35
H8[a]	1,105		24		25		1,154	179	17.68
TNK[a]	1,007		2		41		1,050	124	15.71
Total	63,249		913		2,762		66,924	4,475	10.81

These figures are derived mainly from E. K. Chambers' tables, in *William Shakespeare: A Study of Facts and Problems,* 2 vols. (Oxford: Clarendon, 1930), vol. 2, pp. 400–405.

[a] Figures are for those parts attributed to Shakespeare.

Notes

CHAPTER 1

1. Martin Halpern's explanation is by far the best: "Iambic verse rides *with* the more softly contrasted rising rhythm of monosyllables, and *softens* the sharp contrast in trochaic disyllables by setting against their natural movement a contrary metrical movement; the accented syllable thus becomes the major syllable in *one* foot, while the unaccented syllable becomes the minor syllable not in the same, but in the *next* foot" (184).

Bayfield tries to show that all of Shakespeare's lines are essentially trochaic and that the initial unstressed syllable that appears in most of them is an upbeat. Gerard Manley Hopkins's sprung rhythm is based on the same idea. On the other hand, Tarlinskaja makes out a good but not conclusive case for regarding English as a predominantly iambic language (1987, chapter 9). Cf. Thompson's view (1961, 1970) that iambic pentameter imitates the structure of the English language.

2. Cf. the frequently expressed contrary view, that poetic language is different from ordinary language. My point here is simply that most features of poetic language, however stylized and exaggerated in verse, have their source in spoken language. We rhyme in verse, for example, because we have heard ourselves rhyming in speech.

3. Cf. Jespersen: "we have to do with *relative degrees of force only:* a sequence of syllables, a verse line may produce exactly the same metrical impression whether I pronounce it so softly that it can scarcely be heard at two feet's distance, or shout it so loudly that it can be distinctly perceived by everyone in a large theatre; but the strongest syllables in the former case may have been weaker than the very weakest ones in the latter case" (255).

4. See Attridge (1982), who claims (123) that all such lines have essentially the same four-beat rhythm, which is filled out with silent pauses if necessary. This claim seems to me excessive, because verse time is not usually as strict as musical time. (Cf. Wimsatt and Beardsley, 589–90.)

5. See, for example, Chatman (1965), Bolinger (1965), Crystal, and Halle and Keyser (1971) for studies of stress and intonation.

6. Among the influential holders of this view are Thompson, McAuley, Chatman (see esp. 1968), and authors of many poetry textbooks. This was the standard explanation of metrical variation in the 1960s and 1970s, but it appears as early as 1930 in Hamer.

7. Chief among those who hear a four-stress meter under iambic pentameter is Northrop Frye, whose discussion of meter in *Anatomy of Criticism* (251–262, 270ff.) charac-

teristically relies much more heavily on precocious generalization (Roman Jakobson's phrase) than on evidence. The principal evidence for believing in the four-stress theory is that in many iambic pentameter lines one of the five stresses falls on a minor word or syllable. If this were to happen regularly, we would begin to hear a four-stress meter emerging and we would hear the meter as less speechlike and more songlike, because four-stress meters are likely to be more accentual and isochronous than normal iambic pentameter. But in iambic pentameter, that meter in which the poles of speech and song are drawn together, the effect of an occasional weakness in a strong syllable is to make the meter more speechlike, not more songlike. If all five strong syllables were equally strong, the meter would grow tiresome, so in many lines poets weaken one or two of them (or even three), not in order to set up a more accentual meter, but in order to make this meter sound *less* accentual.

Critics, including Frye, who cite passages in which several successive lines exhibit weak syllables in strong positions do not succeed in showing that an alternative rhythm has replaced the pentameter. On the contrary, they only show how peculiarly they must read the lines. Here is Frye's scansion (252) of the opening lines of *Paradise Lost:*

> Of man's first disobedience, and the fruit
> Of that forbidden tree, whose mortal taste
> Brought death into the world and all our woe,
> With loss of Eden, till one greater Man
> Restore us, and regain the blissful seat

Does Frye really stress only the syllables he has marked? To make Hamlet's most famous soliloquy fit his theory, he misquotes it (251).

If poets regularly weakened the *same* strong position in an iambic pentameter line, as sometimes Pope does, dividing them down the middle to emphasize antithetical contrasts, we might indeed come to hear in them a four-stress rhythm:

> Be stopp'd in vi|als, or | transfix'd with pins,
> Or plunged in lakes of bitter washes lie,
> Or wedg'd whole a|ges in | a bodkin's eye;
> Gums and poma|tums shall | his flight restrain . . .
> Or alum styp|tics with | contracting power
> Shrink his thin es|sence like | a rivell'd flower . . .
> The giddy mo|tion of | the whirling mill   (*The Rape of the Lock,* II.126–29, 131–32, 134)

But even Pope does not go on like this very long (I have omitted two lines to make the case appear stronger), and most writers of iambic pentameter, though they may indeed frequently weaken one of the strong syllables, usually weaken a different one in successive lines, or weaken two of them or none at all, as Milton does in the passage Frye so mischievously misreads:

> Of man's | first dis|obe|dience, and | the fruit
> Of that forbidden tree, whose mortal taste
> Brought death | into | the world and all our woe,
> With loss of E|den, till | one great|er Man
> Restore | us, and | regain the blissful seat

In line 1, the fourth foot is weak; in line 2, all are strong; in line 3, the second foot is weak; in line 4, perhaps the third foot; in line 5, the second foot. Only a compulsive insistence on theory could fail to appreciate that a word like *that,* though minor, is naturally stressed in the second line, or could lose the rich gradations of stress that the iambic pentameter affords—for example, in "first dis-," in "Brought death," and in the variety of pyrrhic feet dispersed about these lines but in Frye's transcription "all, all lost, quite lost" (*The Tempest,* 4.1.190).

Malof's article, too, has been influential in persuading scholars that the "native" strong-stress meters are occasionally challenged by "foreign elements." But because stress-verse is "natural" and syllabic verse "artificial," "in time the native element reasserts itself and renaturalizes the line, transforming the foreign element into something new as it does so" (591). Malof's terms prejudice the case to begin with, but he also seems to ignore the dominance of iambic pentameter in English poetry for at least three hundred years. How much longer a tenure would make it "native"? Halpern's account of the relation between iambic and other English meters seems much more accurate, partly because it does not rely on dubious genetic metaphors.

8. Among those I classify as Phrasalists are Southworth, Robinson, Harding, Southall, and Bertram. (To locate discussions of their views, see the Index.)

I have not here attempted or adopted any technical analysis of *phrase* or *sentence,* fearing to complicate unduly my account of the way metrical and syntactical segments and wholes either converge or diverge in verse. Although phonological studies suggest that speakers may break their utterances at various points not always marked by syntactical completeness, it may be argued that the grammar and phonology of Renaissance poetry, even of drama, and certainly of Shakespeare's sophisticated dramatic verse are characteristic of a literate culture and that this verse, even when rendered with appropriate feeling, was in some degree formally recited. The shape of a developing complex sentence or the force of a rhetorical contrast could only be conveyed through an elocutionary style that normally marked the syntactical segments with appropriate breaks and pauses.

For readers who would prefer greater technical precision in defining phrase, stress, intensity, and similar terms, I can only emphasize that my main interest is in describing and clarifying the expressive uses of meter, and that for such purposes too much precision may be as fatal as too little. As Aristotle said wisely long ago:

> Our discussion will be adequate if it has as much clearness as the subject-matter admits of, for precision is not to be sought for alike in all discussions. . . . We must be content, then, in speaking of such subjects [as fine and just actions] and with such premises to indicate the truth roughly and in outline, and in speaking about things which are only for the most part true and with premises of the same kind to reach conclusions that are no better . . . for it is the mark of an educated man to look for precision in each class of things just so far as the nature of the subject admits. (1.3.1094b)

9. Mukarovsky (1977) has noticed the frequent tension between "the intonational schemes of the sentence and the rhythm" (123). "Thus the intonation of verse is always carried by a dual, virtual intonational scheme" (125). But, unlike those linguists who hear a counterpoint between the actual and the theoretical pattern of a line (see above, p. 11), Mukarovsky does not claim that we *hear* both lines at once. On the contrary, "the duality of the intonational scheme in verse and the tension within this dual scheme exist indepen-

dently of empirical sound" (126). But where can the tension exist if not in the sound? In establishing that verse lines are spoken differently from prose, Mukarovsky does not succeed in establishing that when we say the words as verse we simultaneously hear the prose intonation in them. In my own view, to say the words as verse blocks out our hearing them as prose.

Cf. E. H. Gombrich's important point that we cannot see an ambiguous drawing simultaneously as a rabbit and a duck: "we cannot experience alternative readings at the same time" (5). The point tells equally strongly against Northrop Frye's claim that much iambic pentameter veils a four-stress rhythm (see note 7, above) and against the Counterpointers cited above on p. 11 and in note 6.

10. Some of these stages have been traced in detail, notably by Thompson (1961), Tarlinskaja (1976, 1987), Woods, and Fussell (1954), whose helpful and in some respects definitive studies will be referred to frequently in later chapters. On the present point, see esp. Tarlinskaja's statistical studies (1976, 1987) of stylistic differences between eras, between poets, and between periods of a poet's work.

11. Since *iambic pentameter* was not used widely until the nineteenth century to describe English verse, scholars sometimes prefer the term *decasyllabic,* which emphasizes the connection of the English line of ten syllables to its Continental counterparts in French and Italian verse. This term, too, suggests that the syllabic count rather than the count of stresses or accents is what matters for English poets from Chaucer to Surrey. See Woods, Chapter Two. Although this view seems reasonable enough, it has the disadvantage of implying that a poet like Chaucer was unaware that his stresses were commonly falling on alternate syllables, and it ignores the fact that many "decasyllabic" lines have more or fewer than ten syllables. It is true that fifteenth-century poets often lost the iambic beat while keeping the syllable count, but it also makes sense to recognize that the ten-syllable line Chaucer achieved works on essentially the same principles as the iambic pentameter line of Shakespeare, Pope, and Tennyson. Each of these poets develops a distinctive metrical style, but it is misleading to suggest that Chaucer's is a different species from the others. In this book *decasyllabic* will be used without any suggestion that it refers to a verse different in any important way from iambic pentameter.

CHAPTER 2

1. This chapter will use the following abbreviations for Chaucer's works: *GP* for the "General Prologue" to *The Canterbury Tales,* and *TC* for *Troilus and Criseyde.* For important criticism of Chaucer's prosody, see Baum, Mustanoja, Robinson, Southworth, Ten Brink, and Woods.

2. See the section on Sidney in Chapter 4. Some later examples of expressive spondees: "*Sweet day,* so cool, so calm, so bright" (Herbert, "Vertue," line 1); "And his *gash'd stabs* look'd like a breach in nature" (Shakespeare, *Macbeth,* 2.3.113); "And when I feel, *fair creature* of an hour" (Keats, "When I Have Fears," line 9).

3. Chaucer does make skillful use on occasion of a few monosyllabic adjectives: "He was a lord *ful fat* and in *good poynt*" (*GP,* 200). But the technique, usually limited to staple adjectives like *ful, wel,* and *good,* is emphatic rather than emotional. Much less frequent is the spondee formed by three successive monosyllabic words ("Men *moote yeve silver* to the povre freres," *GP,* 232) and the enclitic adjectival phrase (in which the adjective in stressed position is followed by a noun in unstressed position, resulting in a possible trochee): "The

MILLERE was | a *stout* | *carl* for the nones" (*GP,* 545); "Ther wis|te *no* | *wight* that he was in dette" (*GP,* 280). But see below, Chapter 13, for further discussion of this pattern.

4. See Gower's "Praise of Peace," his only extensive poem in English iambic pentameter.

5. In Fitzroy Pyle's sample (1937), Lydgate does this in 97 percent of his lines.

6. Though he must have had hints from other forms—for example, iambic verse of other line-lengths, including his own—and from similar verse in French and Italian. It is worth noting, too, that Chaucer's couplet verse and his verse in rime royal develop subtle stylistic differences. The stanza requires a more continuous line-flow, which usually involves more extended sentences with a larger number of line-length segments and a periodic organization such that the stanza can achieve an effective rhetorical climax. The open couplet form allows for a looser and more casual accumulation of detail and a more linear organization of its material. I am grateful to my colleague Calvin Kendall for pointing out some of these differences to me. For an excellent analysis of Chaucer's art in writing rime royal stanzas, see Stanley.

7. For a survey of different critical views of Wyatt's meter, see my "Wyatt's Decasyllabic Line." The main views have been: (1) that Wyatt was a peculiarly incompetent metrist when it came to writing poems longer than tetrameter (Saintsbury and others); (2) that Wyatt was writing iambic pentameter of a sort, but the principles of his metrical system are complex and elusive (Foxwell, Padelford, Wright, and others); (3) that Wyatt's line combines two rhythmical phrases that are not necessarily iambic at all (Harding [1946], Southall). The phrasal theory has tempted some scholars (for related views, see Southworth and Robinson on Chaucer, and Bertram on Shakespeare), but it seems anachronistic: could it have been proposed except in an age of free verse? All poets compose in phrases *as well as* in lines. Metrical analysis involves studying the relations between the two, and it solves nothing to decide that a poet like Wyatt cared only about one of them.

Poems cited in this section are quoted from Muir and Thomson's edition of Wyatt, but some lines have been emended on the authority of Harrier, who, along with Mason (1972), has sharply criticized the Muir-Thomson edition.

8. These line-types were long ago recognized by German scholars as the basis of fifteenth-century English decasyllabic verse, and especially of Lydgate's. See Schick, lvi–lx in Lydgate, 1891; and Schipper, pp. 210ff. Schipper's work is a translation of his earlier *Grundriss der englischen Metrick* (Vienna, 1895), which in turn is an abbreviated version of his three-volume *Englische Metrick* (Bonn: Emil Strauss, 1881–1888), from which Schick derived his line-types.

9. Pyle (1937) is especially convincing on this point (41–48). So is Hammond (1925, 129–52); see also the Introduction (17–26) and extensive headnotes to various selections in her anthology (1965 [1927]).

CHAPTER 3

1. The authors of these phrases are, in order: Anonymous, William Webbe, Richard Stanyhurst, Thomas Blenerhasset, Webbe again, and Roger Ascham.

2. Perhaps the most relevant comparison is a modern one. The poets who developed iambic pentameter verse in the sixteenth century, breaking away from the academic tradition of quantitative measure—a measure that by then could appeal only to the learned—bear surprising resemblances to twentieth-century writers of free verse. Poets like Williams

and Pound were angrier, but in their youth they felt a similar exhilaration both in rejecting the academic tradition of iambic pentameter (whose defenders similarly praised its remarkable expressive powers and often declared their disdain or contempt for free verse, in which they could find no form) and in developing formal techniques and rather baffling prosodic apologias to justify their great revolution. One difference, however, is that defenders of iambic pentameter were not defending a foreign verse, though they may have been defending patterns that few people could any longer hear.

3. My only reservation about Spiegel's clear and persuasive account is that he writes as if sixteenth-century poets were trying to create a new meter—iambic pentameter—which needed to assert its independence of the accentual and isochronous native tradition. But iambic pentameter already had a tradition of its own—little understood, to be sure, but vigorously alive in the poems of Wyatt and Surrey most recently, of Lydgate and Hoccleve earlier, and of Chaucer too, however badly misprinted his poems might be. See also Thompson's chapter 3 (1961), 62–87.

4. Although Puttenham's scansion of verse is confusing because he partly adopts Latin criteria for determining whether syllables are stressed, his attitude toward an excess of unstressed syllables is expressed in this passage about dactyls:

> But this advertisement I will give you withall, that if ye use too many *dactils* together ye make your musike too light and of no solemne gravitie such as the amorous *Elegies* in court naturally require, being alwaies either very dolefull or passionate as the affections of love enforce, in which busines ye must make your choice of very few words *dactilique,* or them that ye can not refuse, to dissolve and breake them into other feete by such meanes as it shall be taught hereafter: but chiefly in your courtly ditties take heede ye use not these maner of long *polisillables* and specially that ye finish not your verse with the[m] as [*retribution*] *restitution*] *remuneration* [*recapitulation*] and such like: for they match more the schoole of common players than of any delicate Poet *Lyricke* or *Elegiacke.* (106; brackets in original)

One might think that the wish to increase the variety of iambic pentameter so that it could approach Latin meters in expressiveness would have led some writers of nondramatic verse to admit anapestic variation. Then, after all, the feet in this meter, like those of the revered Latin hexameter, might consist variously of two or three syllables. But the anapest was perceived as opening the door to barbarism, not to elegant variation. Anapests occasionally appear in sixteenth-century songs or lyric strophes, but rarely in lines as long as pentameter.

5. Cf. Freer's discussion, in his chapter 2, of audience expectations and actor skills. Freer notes: "A dead-regular iambic tick-tock was the last thing a good actor was after; ideally he would speak with that ease and grace of modulation that Sidney refers to as 'slidingness of language'" (42).

6. Thompson (1961, 73) was probably the first to point out this important principle of Gascoigne's metrics.

7. Sidney, however, uses *naked* as a monosyllable in *A and S,* 82:4 and 65:5, and Greville rhymed it with *awaked* in "Caelica," XXII, lines 17–18.

8. We find it, for example, in Dryden ("As Hannibal *did* to the altars come," "Macflecknoe," line 112), Gray ("But Knowledge to their eyes her ample page / Rich with the spoils of time *did* ne'er unroll," "Elegy Written in a Country Churchyard," lines 49–50; see also lines 94 and 122), and Coleridge ("In Xanadu *did* Kubla Khan / A stately pleasure-

dome decree," "Kubla Khan," lines 1–2; see also "The Rime of the Ancient Mariner," lines 69, 120, 123, 125, and passim).

9. Representative examples:

There mark what ills the scholar's life assails

> (Johnson, "The Vanity of Human Wishes," line 159)

To her fair works did Nature link
The human soul that through me ran

> (Wordsworth, "Lines Written in Early Spring," lines 5–6)

A mouth that has no moisture and no breath
Breathless mouths may summon

> (Yeats, "Byzantium," lines 13–14)

I was neither at the hot gates
Nor fought in the warm rain
Nor knee deep in the salt marsh, heaving a cutlass,
Bitten by flies, fought.

> (Eliot, "Gerontion," lines 3–6)

10. Gascoigne's essay has often been praised for the insight it shows into both the English language and English metrics, even though no precise descriptive terms were available to so early a metrist. One measure of his acuteness in discussing these matters is given by the fact that some modern linguists have confirmed his view that the binary system of English iambic poetry relies on a language system with three degrees of stress. Tarlinskaja, for example, in her formidable account of *English Verse: Theory and History,* distinguishes three levels of stress, each of which includes two "sub-degrees," and she discusses the middle level ("accentually variable") very much in Gascoigne's way, though with far more sophisticated means of describing grammatical categories and degrees of stress. The whole discussion (76–82) is an important one: she shows, in effect, that monosyllables normally strong in stress may have that stress diminished, that monosyllables normally weak in stress may have that stress strengthened, and that an intermediate class of syllables may function in either strong or weak positions. Gascoigne, of course, restricts his variable syllables to a list of particular words.

CHAPTER 4

1. For a sensitive and discriminating analysis of the subtle movement and "sweet diversity" of Spenser's stanzas and sentences, see Alpers, chapters 2 and 3, 36–106. See also Empson, 33–34, who gives what Alpers calls "the most perceptive account we have of the stanza of *The Faerie Queene*" (39); and Woods' careful analysis (in chapter 5) of Spenser as a "master of line rhythms and stanzaic construction" (159).

2. Quotations, here and elsewhere, are from William A. Ringler's edition of Sidney's poems, but I have usually modernized the spelling.

3. The spondee formed from a repeated monosyllable is common among the Elizabethans. Gascoigne, for example, in his satirical "The Steele Glas," uses "Pray, pray" several times as a directive to priests: "Pray, pray (my priests) that neither love nor mede . . . / Pray, pray that you, and every one of you . . . / Pray, pray (my priests) for these" (*Works,* vol. 2, 167–68). Sackville writes: "Cum, cum, (quod she)" ("Induction," in *Mirror,* line 149),

and Marlowe begins lines with such combinations as "He, he," "Spread, spread," "See, see," and "Blush, blush" (493, 497, 325, 100). Shakespeare's early plays, to go no further, present such series as:

Aye, aye	See, see	Down, down	Hark, hark	Cease, cease
Nay, nay	Die, die	Well, well	Here, here	Mount, mount
Go, go	Tut, tut	Thus, thus	Lord, lord	Fool, fool
No, no	Sir, sir	Come, come	What, what	Sans, sans
	Out, out		Arm, arm	

All of these appear in the first feet of their lines, though some appear elsewhere as well. Probably "Mark, Marcus, Mark" (*Titus Andronicus*, 3.1.143) is intended as a witty echo of this pattern. In all these cases, the pattern being unequivocally iambic, we are probably still meant to hear the second word as stronger than the first; but the first is strong enough to make us feel that what we have in such a foot is a spondaic iamb, and an effective, an expressive, one.

4. Many years ago, around the turn of this century, some academic prosodists—mainly Bright's students—thought that one test of a poet's skill lay in the deftness with which he placed the same (usually monosyllabic) word in different metrical positions—as Sidney does here with "do" and "not." Melton calls this feature "arsis-thesis variation of the same word or words in the same line, or in close proximity" (106) and makes it the focus of his book on Donne's rhetoric. Licklider devotes to it a sixty-page chapter (162–222).

5. The most eloquent and influential statement of this position is John Thompson's in *The Founding of English Metre*. Thompson rightly sees Gascoigne's metrics as "always in touch with speech" (82), regards Spenser's metrical experiments in *The Shepheardes Calender* as hardly "the record of a great deliberate poetic achievement" because they "do not really add up to anything coherent" (126–27)—a judgment with which Woods sharply disagrees (137–144)—and enthusiastically claims: "In Sidney's poetry the metrical system of modern English reaches perfection for the first time" (139).

Thompson's account of the movement toward a mature iambic pentameter is, in general and in many particulars, persuasive. But his reading of this verse is sometimes troubling, for two reasons. First, by ignoring the fifteenth-century history of iambic pentameter and its development of those deviant lines we have noticed in poets from Lydgate (or even Chaucer) to Wyatt, he makes Wyatt's verse sound more baffling than it needs to. Second, his analysis of meter and language is much influenced by structural linguistics, and he adopts the linguists' counterpoint theory of meter, that lines of verse should be read as if they were prose or speech, and then the metrical paradigm should be held up to them like a grid to see how the "counterpoint" between the two works out. (See the discussion of Counterpointers above, p. 11, and below, pp. 186–88.)

Rudenstine's sensitive treatment of Sidney's metrical technique properly emphasizes the significant change from the relatively tame meters of *Arcadia* to the more expressive ones of *Astrophil and Stella*. (See chapter 6, "Style as Convention," esp. 95–103.) Woods contrasts the "graceful unobtrusiveness" (175) and variety of Spenser's "aesthetic" meter with Sidney's more "mimetic" rhythms, which give us "the natural voice of a real personality in a variety of moods" (138). See her chapter 5, 137–82.

6. This is the often-cited view of Ezra Pound: "nothing that you couldn't, in some circumstance, in the stress of some emotion, actually say" (49).

CHAPTER 5

1. See my article on "Shakespeare's Poetic Techniques," 364–65, for further discussion of Shakespeare's formal artistry in these narrative poems.

Shakespeare's minor poems raise no crucial metrical questions. The rime royal stanzas of "A Lover's Complaint" may have prepared the way for *The Rape of Lucrece*. The poems of curious meter in "The Passionate Pilgrim" may not be Shakespeare's; the same is true of "Shall I die . . . ?" and its cretic meter (see Wright, 1986). "The Phoenix and Turtle," in trochaic tetrameter with catalexis, and rhyming *abba,* manages to make that normally spirited meter sound portentous and strange. But if some of these poems show Shakespeare's metrical agility, none of them advances his mastery of the heroic line, which is our main subject here.

2. Cf. Saintsbury (vol. 2, 61): "Shakespeare seems here to have had for his object, or at any rate to have achieved as his effect, the varying of the line with as little as possible breach or ruffling of it. He allows himself a flash or blaze of summer lightning now and then, but no fussing with continual crackers. All the prosodic handling is subdued to give that steady passionate musing—that 'emotion recollected in tranquillity'—which is characteristic of the best sonnets, and of his more than almost of any others."

3. As Heather Dubrow has shown, critics too readily call the *Sonnets* dramatic even though almost all of them lack dialogue, setting, "temporal perspective," narrative incidents, or other normal features of drama. Most of the sonnets, she argues convincingly, should be read as "internalized monologues" (62), in which the concluding couplet frequently compounds or embodies the speaker's "repeated attempts to lie to himself" (65).

4. See Ferry for perceptive studies of the advancing innerness in Elizabethan poetry and, ultimately, in Shakespeare's drama.

The last pages of this chapter are adapted from my essay on "Shakespeare's Poetic Techniques."

CHAPTER 6

1. Even Eliot critics and scholars have a hard time following his directions for reading the verse of his later plays. Eliot's view was that the verse aspect of a play should be taken in subliminally and that the business of the poet was to make sure the audience was entertained while the subliminal verse was doing its work.

2. John Bernard, in his *Prosody of the Tudor Interlude,* includes a little table called "A Chronological Table of Metres" (214), arranged according to the dates when Tudor interludes began and ceased to use various measures. The last half of this table shows graphically how, during the years of Shakespeare's childhood and youth, other meters disappeared in favor first of rhymed couplets (of different lengths and variously iambic or tumbling) and then of blank verse and prose:

1569	Inception of heptameter couplets, inception of poulter's measure, end of ballad-eight.
1573	End of poulter's measure.
1576	End of rime couée.
1577	End of ballad-six.
1582	End of heptameter couplets.
1588	End of rime royal; inception of blank verse and prose.

1590   End of quatrains.

1593   End of tetrameter couplets.

3. By Shakespeare's time, prose had long been a possible medium for a stage play. It had seeped into earlier productions, taken a major role in some, and, as we see here, become the mode of utterance for an entire play in Gascoigne's *The Supposes*. Although a few plays of the 1590s and later (including some of Shakespeare's) admit no prose, many of them mix prose and verse, and they do so in the freely varying proportions we find in Shakespeare's own work. See Chapter 7 for further discussion.

4. So the printer of the second edition of Surrey's translation of the *Aeneid* (Book IV) called it on the title page (T. Brooke, 187).

5. O. B. Hardison makes the point (1984, 254–55) that although blank verse before Milton was usually thought of as a dramatic meter, it had been used in heroic, elegiac, and satiric poems of some importance. Hardison draws another telling distinction between blank verse intended for recitation and blank verse intended for dramatic performance (268–71), and his summary of the history of sixteenth-century blank verse is especially helpful.

6. Still, the segments of Marlowe's sentences often seem cooped up in his lines, as if each line were separately composed to treat a certain portion of what needs to be said, not as if the sentence unrolled "naturally" through lines that were "inevitably" iambic. The sentence-power we may hear through his lines results more from the hypnotically strong semantic interest of what the characters are sometimes saying than from the subtle segmentation of his lines. For Shakespeare's different procedures, see Chapter 14.

7. I have mainly followed the punctuation and wording of the Second Quarto.

8. See Tarlinskaja's claim (1987, chapter 1) that English iambic pentameter is much looser than Russian but not nearly so loose as Italian. The evidence on which this claim rests is described in much more detail in the same author's "Vertical Parameters of Meter . . ."

CHAPTER 7

1. See Vickers (1968) for an extended account of how this works in all the plays; and Barish (1960) for a splendid analysis of prose uses in Jonson and often in Shakespeare as well.

2. Hal's last ten words are usually printed as one line and Falstaff's speech as prose. The word "yet" (from the Quarto) is usually also added to line 43 (before "unreveng'd") even though it is omitted in the First Folio and renders the line difficult to scan. Such printing lets Hal's noble speech trail off confusedly. Hal's reply to Falstaff in 48–49 ("He is indeed, and living to kill thee. I prithee lend me thy sword") is also usually printed as prose, though the first sentence is arguably iambic pentameter. Falstaff's lines, in any case, sound unmistakably iambic as well as probably pentameter, and on the stage the sound is what counts.

3. During the 1984 annual meeting of the Shakespeare Association of America, a seminar devoted to "Shakespeare's Prose: Its Infinite Variety" and well organized and conducted by Ellen M. Caldwell included several papers that illuminated the distinctions between verse and prose in Shakespeare's plays. One by Jonas A. Barish, "Mixed Prose-Verse Scenes in Shakespearean Tragedy," was especially helpful for its discussion of "in-

determinate" passages that fell between prose and verse. Papers by Brian Vickers (1986) and Jane Donawerth threw light on this topic, too.

4. Still, as Barton suggests, "a Shakespearean song or piece of music must always be treated as part of the action of a scene" (160).

5. To read Kent's lines as doggerel also obviates the frequent criticism that, taken as iambic pentameter, they seem pat and lifeless.

CHAPTER 8

1. See E. K. Chambers, vol. 2, 400, 404. I have excluded his figures for *Edward III,* which few scholars now attribute to Shakespeare.

Chambers' figures are probably conservative. He derived them largely from tables originally prepared by F. G. Fleay in 1874. (See also Fleay, 1970 [1876].) Fleay used the Globe edition, whose editorial procedures in respect to short lines have been questioned by Fredson Bowers (see note 8, below), but on grounds that, if anything, would justify a larger number of short lines. Since early editions of Shakespeare do not join together in one line complementary half-lines spoken by different characters, the original texts of Shakespeare's plays show a far greater number of short lines than Chambers reports.

On Virgil's use of short lines, Sparrow writes: "An examination of the hemistiches themselves in detail reveals that while most occur in contexts where they have no artistic effect, and many in contexts which definitely suggest that they are incomplete, there are some which occur in such contexts as we should expect if Virgil used the half-line as a metrical device—in spoken passages, where the utterance is passionate, disjointed, rhetorical" (45). See also Maxwell.

2. The standard form of English blank verse or couplet verse through most of its history is the block verse paragraph, which begins and ends with full verse lines. However much enjambed, the nondramatic stichic verse of *Paradise Lost* and *Paradise Regained,* and of Dryden, Pope, Thomson, and Akenside conforms almost absolutely to this rule. Cowper has two shared lines in "Table Talk," Young uses three in *Night Thoughts,* and Goldsmith has a few, but only in his dramatic verse. In the nineteenth century, Wordsworth and other poets learned to close some verse paragraphs with a short line, which concludes with the opening phrase of the next paragraph:

> While with an eye made quiet by the power
> Of harmony, and the deep power of joy,
> We see into the life of things.
>   If this
> Be but a vain belief . . .   ("Tintern Abbey," lines 47–50)

This effective way of achieving a somewhat informal air is certainly learned from Shakespeare and his younger contemporary playwrights. Here the metrical line is shared not by two characters, by two dramatic speeches, but by two verse paragraphs, by a tone of pithy conclusion and accomplishment and a tone of earnest resumption.

3. See Flatter, whose discussions of the stage business implied by short lines are variously perceptive and bizarre; and see also note 5, below.

4. Carol Sicherman has also noted the special relevance of *Julius Caesar* to any study

of short lines in Shakespeare. The section that follows, which takes a somewhat different view from hers, was written before her article appeared in *SQ*.

After Shakespeare's earliest plays, which show only a sparing use of short lines (see Appendix C), the next plays he wrote that are set in Italy record a surprising increase in the proportion of short and shared lines to total blank verse lines: an average of 7.44 percent in *TS, TGV, RJ, MV, MA*, and *JC*, as opposed to 4.79 percent in all the others of the same period, from *R3* to *H5*. The memory of Virgil's short lines may have led Shakespeare to experiment with them in these plays, especially in *JC*, the first mature play set in ancient Rome, which shows a huge rise both in the numbers and in the proportion of short and shared lines.

Shakespeare apparently did not hear in Virgil's short lines—not, at least, this early in his career—"the recurring note of weariness and pain" which Stephen Dedalus recalls that Cardinal Newman had heard "in the broken lines of Virgil 'giving utterance, like the voice of Nature herself, to that pain and weariness yet hope of better things which has been the experience of her children in every time'" (Joyce, *Portrait*, 164).

5. Flatter and Sicherman, among others, claim that often the rest of a short line actually *does* materialize, in the form of a "metrical pause." This seems a likely enough view when the line is missing only a single syllable or so (see below, Chapter 12). But to imagine that we tick off stage silences precisely for several feet at a time, especially when the silences occur at the beginnings of speeches, as Sicherman suggests (1982, 1984), strains our credulity. Besides, to pretend that short lines are really normal lines despite their being partly silent is to minimize their main feature. The notable thing about short lines is that they are short. They may indeed suggest a pause or a gesture, as some of the examples I cite apparently do; but beyond the duration of one or two syllables the pause will not be measured in the theater and therefore cannot be metrical. Unlike short rests in musical performances, silences in the theater almost immediately fall out of count into unmeasured duration; iambic pentameter, inconsistently isochronous and metrically irregular, does not set a strict enough time to govern the silences for very long.

6. Some readers may wonder whether more stress should be given to "not" in lines 32 and 34, and I have heard actors accent this word heavily. But this reading ignores the clear metrical direction of stress to "are." In my own English, a sharp stress on "are" is a perfectly normal way of marking strong negative meaning in such a phrase. Cf. the similar exchange in *The Winter's Tale* (5.1.204–5):

> *Leontes.* You are married?
> *Florizel.* We are not, sir, nor are we like to be.

To put the stress here on "not" ("We áre | nót, sir") quite unsettles the rhythm. The metrical reading will convey Florizel's feeling: "We áre | nót, sìr, | nor áre | we líke | tŏ bè." The first "are" seems one of the two words in stressed position that attract strongest stress.

Still, in the short line (34) from *Julius Caesar*, one might plausibly argue for a changed tune: "Ĭ ám. | Ĭ sáy, | yŏu áre nót."

7. In studying Shakespeare's style, we should remember that his diminished use of certain techniques does not usually mean a complete abandonment of them. If in his later work he preferred to use more weak or light endings, that does not mean he abandoned the more normal strong endings of lines; if he used a larger proportion of lines that break their phrasing after the sixth or a later syllable, he did not stop breaking lines after the fourth syllable. The normal patterns found in the early plays, including rhyme, persist in the later

verse, but they are not quite so numerous there and Shakespeare has found many other interesting sorts of lines to complement them.

8. Abbott's term for the middle line of a squinting construction is "amphibious section" (513–14); Mayor calls it a "common section" (168–70); and Jespersen comments cogently on this line-type (265–66), noting that "Shakespeare was thinking of the stage only and was not interested in the way his plays would look when they were printed" (265).

The most detailed study of Shakespeare's short lines is Fredson Bowers' long and thoughtful essay. (See also Abbott.) Bowers' essay is rich with insights into Shakespeare's way of disposing metrically incomplete segments of iambic pentameter. But in all his talk of Shakespeare's intentions about how half-lines were to be joined in a written text, he seems not to have considered how extremely likely it is that Shakespeare never thought much about a written text, except as a script from which the play could be performed. Thus, *in the theater* one does not choose between hearing a line-segment as short and hearing it joined to another. One hears, rather, a continuous iambic current, usually embodied in full lines, sometimes in segments that together seem to constitute a pentameter even though the second of two segments may appear to make a pentameter with a third. While listening to the play, one cannot possibly stop to sort out these overlappings, for the play goes on and one has to attend to the lines that follow, to pick up again the pattern of full pentameters when it can again be discerned. Of course, this makes an extremely sticky problem for an editor, who *must* make decisions about which half-lines should be printed in such a way as to form one metrical line and which should stand alone as short. But if readers were alerted to the possibility that half-lines may combine to form full ones, Bowers is right in suggesting (74–75) that the best way to print the plays would be to indent no half-lines but to count on the reader's ear and eye to join segments when it seems useful to do so.

9. *Troilus and Cressida* contains a large number of short lines that occur in bursts between iambic pentameter lines: for example, 2.2.99, 100, 103; 2.3.236–39; 4.5.201, 207–8. Some scholars have suggested that Shakespeare may have written this play, or at least some part of it, earlier than its currently assigned date (1601–1602), which would place it closer in time to *Julius Caesar,* that other play of this period in which Shakespeare was experimenting with short lines.

10. In Donawerth's analysis, Lorenzo and Jessica achieve a love supported by irony and "listen in the moonlight to the music that is only an imperfect realization of the heavenly music, which earthly lovers cannot hear" (213). I would add that their own verse fits this description; like all iambic pentameter, its variant and deviant lines never achieve that transcendent metrical pattern which is to be found only in the imagination of academic metrists.

CHAPTER 9

1. The text is that of Q1. The Folio text lacks Anne's last line, which is essential to the effect described here.

2. See also Abbott, 397–401. If we realize, for example, that "never" is frequently monosyllabic in Shakespeare, we need not treat the following line as hypermetrical:

I ne|ver spáke | wĭth hér, | sáw hĕr, | nŏr heárd | frŏm hér

(*Measure for Measure*, 5.1.223)

Instead, we can take "never" as a monosyllable and recognize that not only metrical stress but a natural speech stress can fall on such syllables as "with," "nor," and "from."

Ĭ nevèr | spăke wìth | hĕr, săw | hĕr, nòr | heàrd fròm hĕr

The disposition of modern metrists and readers to insist on the same kind of congruence between textbook phrasing and metrical foot (shades of Gascoigne and Tichbourne) has helped to render us deaf to the more interesting metrical arrangements of the best earlier poets, who constantly cut across the correct phrasing to give us lines that are both natural and metrical and that have far more energy than lines that look better-behaved.

See Chapter 10 for further examples of lines that look as if they had too many syllables but, with the help of Shakespeare's characteristic practice of elision and syncopation, turn out to be standard (at least, Shakespeare's standard) iambic pentameter.

CHAPTER 10

1. Books on Shakespeare's pronunciation can be helpful but not decisive in settling questions of meter in Shakespeare. See Kökeritz's monumental work on the subject (1953), and the more narrowly focused volume by Sipe. A. C. Partridge's careful study of Shakespeare's orthography and the evidence it provides about Shakespeare's versification is indispensable to the understanding of Shakespeare's syllable. The most recent scholarly study, by Fausto Cercignani, is sharply critical of Kökeritz's methods and of his conclusion that Shakespeare's pronunciation was close to that of contemporary speakers of English.

2. Shakespeare, like other poets of this period, evidently enjoyed using the same word in different metrical contexts. See above, Chapter 4, note 4. In the following two lines, for example, he treats the last two syllables of *Imogen* in three metrically different ways:

My queen, my life, my wife! O Im|ŏgĕn,
Ímŏ|gĕn, Ím|ŏgĕn!
     Peàce, | my lord, hear, hear—   *(Cymbeline, 5.5.226–27)*

The first of these lines ends with a pyrrhic foot; the second begins with a trochee; the third *Imogen* is syncopated (*Im'gen*). Yet only the rarest of theatergoers would be able to discern any difference in pronunciation in the three occurrences of *Imogen*. Only the rarest of actors would permit such differences to be faintly heard.

3. Whether such words were actually pronounced as the abbreviated forms indicate remains uncertain. They are not implausible in rapid speech, even today. (A woman I know named Florence pronounces her name as a monosyllable.) Kökeritz notes that since the omission of the medial vowel is not always indicated by an apostrophe, "our only guide is the scansion of the line" (283). But our guide to what? To the way the line is to be pronounced, or was pronounced, or to contemporary English pronunciation, or to the metrical value of the syllable? If we understand, as Kökeritz does (1953, 276–77), that a syllable erased from the meter by syncope, apocope, synaeresis, or synaloepha may still be *sounded,* then neither the apostrophe nor the scansion may determine our pronunciation so much as our feeling for the English rhythmic phrase. Metrical indications of this sort, in other words, are not wholly reliable guides to English pronunciation of the period. But see the further discussion of syllabic value below.

4. On *-ed,* see Chapter 3, above; on *-es,* see Dam and Stoffel, 5, 7.

Any reader of Shakespeare's plays needs to know also that the accent on some words has changed since his time—for example, in such words as *revénue, advértise, envý,* and *triúmph*—and that in some words the stress was variable: *cháracter* or *charácter, cómfort* or *comfórt.* Such changes do not normally affect the number of syllables in a line, but they may affect our metrical reading of a sequence of syllables.

5. A similar case might be made for contracting the first "I had" instead of the second, but here, too, the contraction need not be complete:

Ĭf Ī had | săid Ī | hăd sĕen | him do | you wrong?

It somewhat complicates the matter to know that both Folio and Quarto place "What" in the following line, so that lines 23–24 read as follows:

Iago.   Ay; what of that?
Othello.   That's not so good now.
Iago.   What if I had said, I had seen him do you wrong?

Editors have understandably been tempted to place "What" at the end of line 23. It finishes that line and makes for the interesting structure of line 24 that has been discussed above. But even if we accept the original reading, the problematical character of phrases like "I had" is borne out by great numbers of similar lines. See, for example, a similar line in *Coriolanus:* "Yŏu ănd | your crafts! | Yŏu have cráft|ed fair! | Yŏu have broúght" (4.6.118). And from *Othello:* "I do not know; | Ī am súre | Ī am | none such" (4.2.123).

6. Jonsonian elision has been studied by W. W. Greg (216–17) and A. C. Partridge (1964), among others. It designates "a combination of two words in which elision of a vowel is intended and indicated by an apostrophe, though graphic suppression does not actually take place" (Partridge, 1964, 35n.).

7. Although the case seems strong for hearing in many of Shakespeare's lines additional sounds that are not quite syllables, I agree with Ramsey that most Shakespearean elision is genuine elision, phonetic as well as metrical. There remains, in my view, a significant residue of sounds *in the plays* that contribute to the effect I have tried to describe. An alternative view is that even if Ramsey's strict syllabism applies to the plays as well as to the *Sonnets,* the frequency with which such elision occurs in certain passages requires the actors to speed up their lines and to make them sound more intense, fervid, excited, as the syllables hurry each other through their moment of vocal presence.

CHAPTER 11

1. See Schoenbaum for a judicious discussion of the perils of numerical analysis in attribution studies.

2. See chapter 5, "Line Endings: Accentual and Syllabic Structure," in Tarlinskaja (1987).

3. The use of the quotation from *Hamlet* in this section was suggested by Philip W. Timberlake's old book on feminine endings (1931), a fruitful source of information on plays up to 1595, though any modern student of the subject will need to consult Tarlinskaja (1987) and her more sophisticated tables and insights.

4. See the analysis of heavy endings in the chapter cited in note 2.

5. Chambers reports none in *The Comedy of Errors* and *Love's Labor's Lost,* but here are instances. From *The Comedy of Errors:*

Horn-mad, thou vil*lain!*
          I mean not cuckold-mad   (2.1.58)

If it were chain'd tog*ether,* and therefore came not.   (4.1.26)

Haply in pri*vate.*
          And in assemblies too.   (5.1.60)

From *Love's Labor's Lost:*

And shape his ser*vice* wholly to my device   (5.2.65)

Their purpose is to par*ley,* to court, and dance   (5.2.122)

The fourth example is unusual only in having no punctuation at the break, but the line's sound conforms to the epic caesural pattern.

    Chambers' figures cover blank verse only, and the last line above is rhymed. If other rhymed lines show this pattern, the figure of 1,655 epic caesuras for all of Shakespeare's plays (a figure derived from Chambers' tables) will be too low.

    6. Tarlinskaja notes, however (1987, chapter 5), that the use of line-final polysyllables whose relatively unstressed last syllable falls in the final stressed position is characteristic rather of late Elizabethan than of Jacobean drama. The triple ending is a different way of treating the polysyllable's final unstressed syllables, a way that more accurately reflects their throwaway status in actual speech. When Shakespeare accords the same metrical treatment to two- and three-word groups, he implies that they, too, are often compressed or slurred in speech.

    7. I have found only two examples, both doubtful, of double onset after an enjambed line with a feminine ending. The first is from *Othello* (1.3.68–69):

You shall yourself read in the bitter letter
After your own sense; yea, though our proper son

That "After your" may have been reduced to two syllables ("Aft'your") is suggested by a similar line in *Richard II:* "After your late tossing on the breaking seas" (3.2.3). The other example might be taken to exhibit Shakespeare's late verse style:

Do anything but this thou doest. Empty
*Old recep*tacles, or common shores, of filth   *(Pericles,* 4.6.174–75)

But the Quarto, our only source for this play, prints this passage as prose; and, although some parts of it seem metrical, attempts to interpret the speech as verse are questionable.

    8. A few lines combine the anapestic variation with a double onset (1, 2), with an epic caesura (3, 4), or with another anapest (5):

    1. *The nobi*|lity are vexed, | *whom we see* | have sided   *(Coriolanus,* 4.2.2)

    2. *Let me see,* | *let me see;* | is not the leaf turn'd down   *(Julius Caesar,* 4.3.273)

    3. Wherein *I* am false, | *I* am hon*est;* | not true, | *to be true*   *(Cymbeline,* 4.3.42)

    4. But wel|*come, sweet Clarence,* | my daughter shall be thine   *(3 Henry VI,* 4.2.12)

The last and most unusual example occurs in *The Merry Wives of Windsor* (4.4.11) between lines that are perfectly regular:

5. Be not | *as ĕxtrḗme* | *ĭn sŭbmĭs|sĭŏn ăs ĭn* | offense

Its three anapests can perhaps be accounted for if we understand that Page, who speaks them, is eager to get on to another topic.

CHAPTER 12

1. This is the Folio punctuation, seldom adopted by editors but metrically and rhetorically more coherent than the usual punctuation that divides the line into two equal lumps ("Hear, Nature, hear; dear goddess, hear") instead of into three segments each of which begins with "hear." The Folio punctuation is consistent with Percy Simpson's rule: "*Vocative followed but not preceded by a comma*" (1969 [1911], 20); and with an implied rhetorical habit, frequent in Renaissance prose and verse, of sweeping through a series of words toward the one that denotes the person addressed. Examples: "Ah my good friend, what cheer?" (*Timon of Athens*, 3.6.40); "As gaming my lord" (*Hamlet*, 2.1.24).

2. One line that perhaps comes close to this pattern is

Sŏft, | so busily she turns the leaves   (*Titus Andronicus*, 4.1.45)

But probably this line is more plausibly read as headless.

Appearing in a metric that so often uses a trochaic first foot, some headless lines may strike us as missing an unaccented *second* syllable: "Then [comes] the whining school-boy with his satchel" (*As You Like It*, 2.7.145)—or even an unaccented *third* syllable: "Witty [and] courteous, liberal, full of spirit" (*3 Henry VI*, 1.2.43). This is not to suggest that the lines came into being when the poet struck out the bracketed words, only that if he had cared to make these headless lines normal, he could have done so by adding a second or third syllable rather than by adding an initial one. This observation, however, does cast some doubt on the analytical procedures used here and by other metrists. Just as in over-crowded lines it is hard to say exactly what is extra, so in lines shorter than the norm it is sometimes not easy to say exactly what is missing. The lines are what they are and, short or long, realize the metrical form in their own way.

3. One passage from *Tamburlaine*, Part I, appears to make effective and deliberate use of three headless lines:

ᴧBarbarous and bloody Tamburlaine,
   Thus to deprive me of my crown and life!
ᴧTreacherous and false Theridamas . . .
ᴧBloody and insatiate Tamburlaine!   (2.7.1–3, 11)

Cosroe's fury at being cut off before he has a chance to rule is well conveyed in these similarly shortened lines. Marlowe can also use a broken-backed line effectively, as in Tamburlaine's angry command to Bajazeth:

Stoop, villain, stoop. | ᴧStoop, for so he bids
That may command thee piecemeal to be torn   (Part I, 4.2.22–23)

Since in both these passages the names traditionally given to the lines fit their content, it is worth noting that one of Marlowe's occasional headless lines begins with the very word: "Headless carcasses pil'd up in heaps" (*Dido, Queen of Carthage*, 2.1.194). Was the term used this early? (The *O.E.D.* ignores this meaning of the word.)

4. See Freer, chapter 2, for a discussion of how important it was for the audience to *listen* to the plays they attended. Donawerth points out that Elizabethans characteristically spoke of going to "hear" a play, not to see it (13).

CHAPTER 13

1. Quoted in Adler (1972, 102).

2. See Chapter 1, above, p. 11 and note 6. Among linguistic analyses of meter, Tarlinskaja's (1987) is unusual in declining to make large claims about counterpointed rhythms. Still, her method, though splendidly useful for helping us understand the relations between phrases and meter, has to depend for its knowledge of stress on categorical rules (words of such-and-such a category receive stress, words of another category do not or do not normally), and so she does not, in my view, sufficiently recognize (1) rhetorical reasons for stressing minor words, (2) the slight differences between stressed and unstressed syllables in this kind of verse, and (3) the uneven nature of stresses in iambic pentameter. Subjective scanners make lots of misjudgments, but their method is essentially truer to the material they are dealing with, because it gives *discretion* a central role in the reading process.

3. See, for example, Attridge (1982, esp. 172–93).

4. See Bolinger for a discussion of the increasing use of phrasal verbs in English. The phrasal verb is flexible and expressive, can register many shades of meaning, and develops the metaphor of motion with greater variety and apparent precision than the unencumbered verb. For calling my attention to this linguistic pattern, and for her own insights into its use, I am grateful to Elizabeth Baldwin. On stress given to particles in phrasal verbs, see Beaver: he notes that in Sonnet 15:14, "*from* receives primary stress, as is the usual case with particles in verb-particle construction" (266n.).

5. On enclitic phrases, see Tarlinskaja (1987, chapter 6).

6. Not syllables but syllabic positions, since some positions may be occupied by two syllables.

7. But Bright and his group of turn-of-the-century prosodists took the view that the ictus is always *heard,* even when it violates speech-stress patterns in lines like "Păcīng, păcīng away the aching night" or "Ĕvĕr the snare was set, ĕvĕr in vain." (These examples are given by Bright's student Licklider [142, 151].) Bright (1901): "In the true reading of poetry one must approximate the exaltation of the poet" (33).

8. Tarlinskaja (1987) notes that most displacements of stress are phrase-initial.

9. Attridge argues in effect (1982, 175–84) that it is best to take the "trochee" as representing a stressed syllable and a compensatory extra syllable that follows later in the line. But his analysis of this metrical figure, as of the pyrrhic-spondee combination, seems unsatisfactory, because it reads iambic pentameter as an accentual five-beat line. In doing so, it ignores or misrepresents some principal features of the iambic pentameter that Shakespeare and his contemporaries used—in particular, the way successive segments of the line affect one another.

10. Halle and Keyser, fathers of generative metrics (1966, 1971), consider double and triple trochees "unmetrical," not because they sound unmetrical to anyone's ears but because they violate one of the rules they claim generate this meter. Their view seems mistaken on several grounds. First, as we see clearly in Chaucer, Wyatt, Shakespeare, and Donne, to go no further, no standard model of iambic pentameter coerces all the poets.

Many English poets prefer not to use double and triple trochees, but that does not make them unmetrical. For many poets do use them:

How many bards | gĭld thē | lăpsēs | of time   (Keats)

Ĭn thў | dĕvăs|tătĭng | omnipotence   (Shelley)

Lắrchĕs, | scắttĕrĕd through pine-tree solitudes   (Browning)

Tĕll thĕm, | dĕar, thăt | if eyes were made for seeing   (Emerson)

Ŏne bў | ŏne hĕ subdued his father's trees   (Frost)

I found, | drŏppĭng | sĕa-fŏam | on the wide stair   (Yeats)

Tŭrnĕd, frŏm | Bŏcă|fŏli's | stark-naked psalms   (Browning)

My first | ĭmpŭlse | wăs tŏ | gĕt tŏ | the knob   (Frost)

I have found at least thirty-four such lines in about 140 pages of Frost's *Collected Poems*. Surely readers do not think "Unmetrical!" when they read such lines. (See above, p. 70.)

But Halle and Keyser's finding of unmetricality is based on their technical analysis of what they call the "stress maximum." Lines of iambic pentameter are supposed (under penalty of being declared unmetrical) to avoid placing strong syllables in weak positions surrounded by weak syllables in strong positions. Since that happens to the third syllable of a double trochee, a line which includes this pattern is regarded as violating the rule. But, of course, what is here exposed is the inadequacy of the rule, not that of the line.

11. Howarth's unusual and attractive essay sensibly maintains that the metrical pattern of a Shakespearean line often gives us the key to its emphasis. He goes on to make the special claim, maintained above, that "Shakespeare often demands a stress on prepositions" (212). In following this principle, I would keep the iambic stress even in some of the lines Howarth offers as examples of variation. (For other comments on straddling trochees, see Jespersen, 262–63; Dam, 206; and Hayes, 362; also Hascall [1971]; and Beaver.)

12. Pyrrhic and iambic feet can also link separate phrasal components of a line. The pyrrhic link hurries us on from the first phrase to the next: "In fair round bel*ly, with* good capon lin'd" (*As You Like It*, 2.7.154); "My shames redou*bled. For* the time will come" (*1 Henry IV*, 3.2.144). The iambic link may be somewhat less usual (the spondaic rare), but it serves the same purpose: "That we remem*ber. There* is our commission" (*Measure for Measure*, 1.1.13); "The pine and ce*dar. Graves* at my command" (*The Tempest*, 5.1.48).

The patterns described here encourage a fairly continuous stage delivery, one that tolerates hesitation but not a long pause. Still, Shakespeare's audience may have been capable of waiting rather long to hear some lines completed. A character's line may be suspended at midpoint almost indefinitely while we attend to entrances and exits, sword fights, dances, deaths, or even musical or vocal business: drums, alarums, voices or cries offstage, or an extended silence. See, for example, *Macbeth*, 5.5.7 and 5.8.8; *Pericles*, 2.3.106; *Coriolanus*, 1.4.15 and 5.3.182; *Romeo and Juliet*, 2.2.151; and *King Lear*, 5.3.312.

Jespersen's claim (263) that we should pause in the middle of a straddling trochee is obviously at variance with the view proposed here.

13. As usual, Milton is a special case. He uses straddling trochees often enough in his early work but rarely in *Paradise Lost*. He too may have come to feel that this metrical figure involved uncomfortable theoretical problems.

14. Rudenstine accurately notices some examples of what he calls "italic stress," but these include specially stressed syllables in stressed positions as well as unstressed (100–103). He also cites Puttenham's interest in disyllabic words in which the normal accent is displaced by contrastive stress:

> Prove me (Madame) ere ye reprove
> Meeke minds should excuse not accuse (Puttenham, 111)

Puttenham thought the last syllables of *reprove* and *accuse* became short, but they probably retain enough weight to anchor the foot they appear in. In his essay on "Contrastive Accent and Contrastive Stress" (1965, pp. 101–17), Bolinger treats this kind of accent-shift with his usual acuteness.

Beaver's article on contrastive stress lumps contrary stress with other promotions of stress for emphatic purposes, including the promotion of stress on minor words in stressed positions. Besides, his aim is not to explore expressive metrical devices but only to investigate that bugbear of generative metrics, "metricality," by deciding whether contrastive stress helps to make lines "metrical" rather than leave them "unmetrical." As with other theorists of this school, for Beaver the fact that competent poets have written such lines under the impression that they were metrical is not enough to establish their metricality. So he decides that lines of his Group V, which corresponds to my contrary stress (along with some of Group VI), since they do not change the metricality of lines, are of little importance. (See above, note 10.)

15. Another pattern frequent in Shakespeare, Donne, and certain other poets involves the use of trisyllabic compound words which in our speech (and probably in theirs) have a stress pattern of ⌣⌣ : godfather, stepfather, grandfather, bedfellow, yoke-fellows, archbishop, gunpowder, alms-houses, and so on. These words occur almost always in Strong-Weak-Strong positions in the line and if pronounced normally would result in some unlikely and undramatic trochees, especially in the fifth foot. Probably the last two syllables were pronounced lightly enough to pass for a pyrrhic foot (⌣⌣ or else ⌣⌣). (See Kiparsky [1975, 589–91; 1977, 220–23]; Koelb; and Suhamy [181–85].)

> And every godfather can give a name. (*Love's Labor's Lost*, 1.1.93)
>
> Lady, were you her bedfellow last night? (*Much Ado about Nothing*, 4.1.147)
>
> A hundred alms-houses, right well supplied (*Henry V*, 1.1.17)

Some modern poets apparently rely on the reader's willingness to suppress the secondary or tertiary stress on the second syllable of such combinations: "And news|papers | from vacant lots" (Eliot, "Preludes"); "Bring flowers in last month's news|papers" (Stevens, "The Emperor of Ice Cream").

If stress on the middle syllable of such compounds is not suppressed, the meter will limp. In fact, Latin poetry included a meter known as *limping iambics* which after five iambic feet deliberately reversed the iambic pattern in its sixth foot and so provided in its last three syllables a pattern that would accommodate just such compounds:

> at tu, Catulle, destinatus obdura

of which a stress-equivalent translation might read:

> But you, | Catul|lus, stay | as you | must, ob|*durate*.

But if the Romans heard this metrical reversal, they heard it not as a reversal of stress but as a reversal of quantity (see above, Chapter 3). In English the effect of any prolonged use of this meter is grotesque. When W. H. Auden cast a poem about the cellar of his house in limping iambics ("Down There," 525), he made the piece as casual and conversational as he could, but the result is still metrically amusing, as he meant it to be:

The rooms | we talk | and work | in al\|ways look | injured
When trunks are being packed, and when, without *warning,*
We drive up in the dark, unlock and switch *lights on,*
They seem put out: a cellar never takes *umbrage;*
It takes us as we are, explorers, home*bodies,*
Who seldom visit others when we don't *need them.*

CHAPTER 14

1. Poets, of course, do not compose poems by combining metrical formulas. As Paul Fussell sensibly reminds us (1974): "The fact that metrical variations . . . can be illustrated by scansion and analyzed dispassionately should not cause the reader to believe that, from the point of view of the poet (at least the good poet), they are anything but instinctual. Many poets whose work can be analyzed metrically according to the foot system would be astonished to be told that they have indulged in 'substitution'; the genuine poet composes according to the rhythms which his utterance supplies, and, although these rhythms frequently turn out to consist of 'normal' and 'substitute' feet, they do not necessarily begin that way" (500–501).

2. Oras's work is breathtakingly exhaustive. He treated poets from Chaucer to Davenant and, unlike most scholars who compile quantitative statistics on verse style (Tarlinskaja is another major exception), Oras did not choose representative passages of the works he surveyed; he counted *all* the interior punctuation in *all* the pentameter lines of a great many poems and plays—virtually the entire work of such prolific poets as Spenser, Shakespeare, and Jonson, along with extremely large portions of Chaucer, Marlowe, Donne, and many other writers. His results, presented in a formidable array of graphs and tables, show clearly where the poets who wrote in this period of about two hundred and seventy-five years preferred to place their marks of punctuation. To be sure, every such mark does not signal a perceptible pause in performance, nor does an absence of punctuation indicate a single, unbroken, line-long phrase. But a count of all the punctuation marks serves as a fairly accurate guide to where the phrase boundaries typically fall, and Oras's figures tell us much about the way Elizabethan and Jacobean poets and playwrights fitted the phrase to the line. The graphs as a group show a remarkable change from the old verse with its fourth-syllable pause in as much as 70 or 80 percent of its lines (74.1 in Henryson, 83.2 in Gascoigne, and figures approaching or exceeding 50 percent for most pre-Shakespearean nondramatic and dramatic verse) to a verse with more broadly distributed pauses, especially after the fourth, fifth, sixth, and seventh syllables.

3. Oras puts it this way (15–16):

A strong pause after the sixth syllable still does not unbalance the pentameter line; the line keeps its self-contained symmetry. Enough space is left for a complete clause to be introduced, a substantial statement to be made, before the end of the line is reached. But when such a pause comes after the seventh, or even the eighth, syllable, the remaining space usually suffices only for a fragmentary statement which needs to be completed in the following line. In other words, very late pauses make for a run-on technique.

4. Oras (17):

> Some attention needs to be paid also to the growing frequency of extra-metrical syllables and feminine endings as Shakespeare's career progresses. Such additional syllables make it possible to crowd more matter into a line, or any part of a line. In Shakespeare's late plays the metrical demand for three or four syllables may in fact be met by some five or six syllables, and more may be said in them than in the corresponding portion of a strictly regular line. Even the last third of a line thus expanded may accommodate as much matter as a full half-line or more. A pause theoretically close to the end of a line may thus actually be removed from it by a considerable number of syllables, all capable of communicating something.

5. When lines in this pattern are rhymed, they frequently end scenes or sections of scenes. Some examples: "O cursed spite, / That ever I was born to set it right" (*Hamlet,* 1.5.188–89); "The play's the thing, / Wherein I'll catch the conscience of the King" (*Hamlet,* 2.2.604–5); "Ever till now / When men were fond, I smil'd, and wonder'd how" (*Measure for Measure,* 2.2.185–86).

6. The passage is perfectly regular—no short lines (until the last decisive one), no alexandrines, no extra syllables of any kind (except feminine endings and a few half-suppressed half-syllables, as in the monosyllabic pronunciation of "heaven-" and "even" in line 52). But the majestic sentences unroll their powerful parallelisms through midline pauses and line-endings of unusually various metrical character. Lines 36 and 53 finish on lightly stressed words ("that") that lead us gently over the line-boundaries; the end of line 35 races past its feminine ending to the light trochee or pyrrhic that begins the next line. Verbs at the end of some lines (41, 47, 51) reach over the line-ending to their object in the next; or objects at one line's end find their verb in the next (46–47, 50–51); and other incomplete forms must voyage past the line to be completed:

>   whose pastime
> Is to make midnight mushrumps, that rejoice
> To hear . . .   by whose aid
>   . . .   I have bedimm'd
>
>   Graves at my command
> Have wak'd their sleepers

As the punctuation makes clear, most of the lines (eighteen out of twenty-four) flow without stop into the next: commas (and a parenthesis) end only six of twenty-four lines; the stronger punctuation (five colons and semicolons, and two periods) places all the most decisive junctures at midline.

CHAPTER 15

1. If so, the line may be an instance of a late epic caesura. See Chapter 11.

2. On vowel sounds, see Macdermott. On sound patterns in Shakespeare, see Booth, Goldsmith, and Masson.

3. Much more might be said on this score, for the manner of this contribution has never been entirely clear. What we probably mean when we say that a device of sound reinforces the meaning of the words is that it intensifies the saying of those words, and that this more intense saying invests their literal meaning with a heightened emotional significance which the words of themselves would not bear. "Go on playing" is flat in comparison with "If music be the food of love, play on"; here, along with the figurative language and the propositional syntax, the spondee quickens the bare request. The trochaic exclamation in "O, it came o'er my ear" seems expressive of a higher degree of emotion than the plain statement, *"That strain came o'er my ear." And some of the hesitation and ambiguity conveyed by the straddling trochee of Orsino's eighth line, " 'Tis not so sweet now, as it was before," would be lost if the line were more regular: *" 'Tis not so sweet this time, as 'twas before."

The theoretical basis of such poetic techniques needs to be explored further, but this is not the place for the extended discussion it would require.

4. See Donawerth (chapter 2) on the growing profundity with which Shakespeare presents the quarrel between passion and reason.

5. Cf. *Coriolanus,* 4.6.89–90:

Menenius.   If Martius should be join'd with Volscians—
Cominius.   *If?*
             He is their god . . .

6. Compare other passages in *King Lear:* Lear's gradual rise to wrath against Kent (1.1.121–22, 143, 154, 157, 159, 161, and 166–79) and against Goneril (1.4.218, 226–30, 232–34, 236, and the series of speeches that culminate in Lear's curse of Goneril in 275–89).

7. One play that sets forth this principle clearly is *Romeo and Juliet,* which moves between sudden, unpredictable flare-ups of hatred and love. Most of the characters are excitable, their dry passions ready to ignite, to the extent that in some parts of the play personages who are themselves excitable (Romeo, Capulet) have the unaccustomed task of quieting the emotions of others (Mercutio, Tybalt). Even the rhetoric of the play is notable for the way it takes off from the merest hint: the Nurse cannot respond to a simple question about Juliet's age without a long self-spreading excursus; by the merest remark Mercutio can be roused to talk fantastically of "dreams." When Capulets and Montagues meet, they burst into flame; when Romeo and Juliet meet, their ardor is instantaneous. The processes of adult rancor and adolescent passion are not so different as at first appears; they all live in the same inflammable world. The oxymorons, therefore, that are so prominent a stylistic feature of this play make this fundamental point: that the human city dedicated to passion must be prepared to see its love destroyed by hate.

8. Barton and his actors of the Royal Shakespeare Company wisely make a point of grounding many of their readings on such "antitheses": "If you stress the antitheses the text will be totally clear" (112; see also 55–56).

9. Such repetitions are common in Shakespeare, and they invite a somewhat different reading of the two similar phrases that compose them. Some examples:

Deso|late, des|olate will | I hence, and die   (*Richard II,* 1.2.73)

Very | like, ve|ry like: | stay'd it long?   (*Hamlet,* 1.2.236)

Dŏ nŏt | weĕp, dŏ | nŏt weĕp: | alas the day   (*Othello*, 4.2.124)

Seize him, aediles!

       Dŏwn wĭth | hĭm, dŏwn | wĭth hĭm!   (*Coriolanus*, 3.1.182)

Othello's "Nŏt ă | jŏt, nŏt | ă jŏt" (3.3.215) is another example, and so is Browning's "Oŭt ŏf | mĕ, oŭt | ŏf mĕ!" ("Andrea del Sarto," 117). John Crowe Ransom's brief paragraph (190) on Milton's "Weep nŏ more, woeful shepherds, weĕp no mŏre" ("Lycidas," 165) touches on some of the main points to be made about this sort of pattern.

CHAPTER 16

1. In analyzing individual styles in various Jacobean plays, Freer, for example, makes rather bold claims for the iambic style of some speeches that seem not notably different in meter from speeches of other characters in the same play.

2. See Doran's revealing studies of other Shakespearean characters' use of language.

3. See Van Laan on disguises, offices, and other circumstances that force characters to adopt different roles.

4. So, when Lear arrives onstage with the dead Cordelia in his arms, the speeches of Kent, Edgar, and Albany (5.3.264–65) add nothing to our understanding of their individual characters:

Kent.	Is this the promis'd end?	
Edgar.	Or image of that horror?	
Albany.		Fall, and cease!

Although each short speech is given to the character who might most suitably speak it, it hardly serves to reinforce our sense of that character.

5. Brashear also maintains that minor syntactical and metrical differences in the speeches of *Measure for Measure* can tell us much about the characters who speak them. But these may be random variations in a standard verse style, may be traced rather to the dramatic context than to the specific character, or may derive, as the argument below goes on to suggest, from the play's need to develop its action in certain ways. Cf. note 1.

6. Imagery and figurative language, as we have seen, work the same way. The conscious use of figures may be a sign of folly or evil, but the speech in which figures come to mind as naturally as leaves to the tree becomes a normal dramatic language, a language which is itself a figure for normal intense speech. Cf. the discussion of Claudio's passionate speech, above.

The analogy with opera is instructive. There, too, song is not a natural speech but an especially expressive language that serves as a figure for emotional speech. Changes from one musical form to another—from aria to recitative, for example—are not chosen by the characters but signal shifts in the style of talk, thought, or feeling.

Donald R. Howard takes a similar view of the verse used by Chaucer's pilgrims, which confers on each tale "an artistry which we cannot realistically attribute to the teller. . . . In its simplest form it is the contingency that a tale not memorized but told impromptu is in verse. The artistry is the author's, though selected features of the pilgrim's dialect, argot, or manner may still be impersonated. In its more subtle uses it allows a gross or 'low' character to use language, rhetoric, or wit above his capabilities" (231).

H. Marshall Leicester, in an engaging article, explores some of the theoretical problems involved in this sensible position, but does not deeply threaten it; and his own complex final view of who or what is speaking in one of Chaucer's tales ("the voice of the poem as a whole" [222], which impersonates each of the pilgrims in turn [221]) is not hard to reconcile with Howard's.

7. Cf. Kermode on "the Globe, which is itself the shadow of the world's substance" (61).

8. Although it strikes me as reasonable to connect a meter in a general way with certain larger attitudes and world-views, Antony Easthope's effort to make specific linkages between meters and social or economic systems seems more questionable. Easthope ties iambic pentameter to "bourgeois liberal capitalism" and accentual meters to collective political economies. As these terms suggest, iambic pentameter is discreditable, accentual verse redemptive. Iambic pentameter "helps to provide a position for the reader as transcendental ego" (158). Free verse depends on "intonational repetition," a view for which Easthope invokes support from sources as different as Pound, Roman Jakobson, and David Crystal, though no one has yet been able to give a satisfactory account of how it works.

Easthope seems to underestimate the discretionary freedom of iambic pentameter and the ideological implications of its being much closer to speech than accentual verse. But there is some tendency in Easthope's school of contemporary Marxist criticism to discredit individual speech as one form of the transcendental ego's decadent affection for private thought and reverie. From the collective point of view, lyric and empathy are suspect; so, ultimately, is free speech; so, one would think, is undisciplined free verse. Perhaps we are meant to suppose that the habit of talk, which iambic pentameter, among all meters, so closely resembles, is merely a relic of bourgeois culture and is, as Easthope imagines the meter to be, "co-terminous" (53) with it.

CHAPTER 17

1. In a series of articles published in the 1940s and 1950s, Arnold Stein described and classified Donne's departures from the metrical norm, and Michael F. Moloney, in a 1950 essay, rightly stressed the importance of elision in Donne's prosody. This section builds on their work but tries to go further in seeing the principles behind Donne's marriage of speech and meter.

2. Following what I take to be Donne's radical elision, I make the following rough count of his deviant lines: eight headless, two or three broken-backed, twenty-three epic caesuras, five short, six to eight nonstanzaic hexameters, thirty anapests, one double onset, two lines with apparent monosyllabic feet, no lines missing stressed syllables, and no split or squinting lines.

3. Page and line numbers in Grierson's edition of Donne: 164:8, 301:6, 251:138, 69 ("Klockius"): 1, 199:4, 283:385, 156:49, 298:7, 223:78 (and 209:51).

4. It is a significant commentary on the character of later iambic pentameter that this pattern is not often found in later poets. After Milton, a different relationship between speech and meter begins to deprive poetry of this speechlike emphasis on whatever word

matters most to the passing phrase, and poets more and more reserve the stress positions for major-category monosyllables, the stressed syllables of major-category polysyllables, or the kinds of weakly stressed syllables that result in pyrrhic feet.

Almost the only later poet to reclaim this metrical technique after it had apparently lapsed forever is Hopkins, who, when his accentual experiments in sprung rhythm had run their course, returned to an iambic pentameter enlivened at moments by just such emphasis on minor words nominated by the meter for stress and seconded by the sentence's rhetorical contrasts. (Quotations, cited by poem numbers and lines, are from Gardner's 1948 edition.)

No worst, there *is* none. Pitched past pitch of grief (65:1)

My *own* heart let me *more* have pity on; let
Me live to my sad self hereafter kind,
Charitable; *not* live *this* tormented mind
With this tormented mind tormenting yet. (71:1–4)

Disappointment all *I* endeavor end (74:4)

Them; birds build—*but* not *I* build; no, but strain (74:12)

Mine, O thou lord of life, send *my* roots rain (74:14)

Or sometimes Hopkins will arrange the sentence and verse to throw especially strong emphasis on nouns or verbs:

With witness I speak this. But where I say
Hours I mean *years,* mean *life.* And my lament (69:5–6)

Oh, the sots and thralls of lust
Do in spare hours more thrive than I that spend,
Sir, *life* upon thy cause. (74:8–9)

As Hopkins realized, when English metrical verse relaxes its ties to impassioned speech and renders most of what it has to say in a neutral, almost official Poetic Voice, its days are numbered.

On the whole, nineteenth-century verse too often renders emotion either by adapting such conventional figures as apostrophe ("O Wild West Wind . . ."), which are no longer so speechlike, or, more successfully, by soaking the phrases in euphonious fountains of symbolic resonance. The art of incising a speaker's feeling in the phrases he utters, by letting the ictus fall on the word most significant here, so that we feel stress as urgent, is lost in later centuries. Three of the most elegant modern writers of iambic pentameter—Yeats, Eliot, and Stevens—rarely use the device I am speaking of here, and the only notable poets who do are Frost and Lowell. Here is Frost:

Because we're—we're—I don't know *what* we are ("West-Running Brook," line 9)

Back out of all this now too *much* for us ("Directive," line 1)

And say no word to tell me who he was
Who was so foolish as to think what *he* thought
("The Wood-Pile," lines 12–13; italics in text)

Frost's verse is probably too much praised for its natural-sounding phrases, which often stand out oddly from the more formal diction of a long speech or passage; but he is one of the few poets since Donne to see the virtue of throwing stress on minor words. (Edwin Arlington Robinson's singsong rhythms and hypnotic rhyming sometimes direct strong stress to important syllables—see "Eros Turannos," lines 8, 24—but he does not risk it on minor ones.)

5. It is hard for me to resist connecting this early success with the same pattern in *1 Henry IV* (1596–1597), in which a young man of unpromising parts, at home in both low and high places, manages to survive his more formidable rival and to assume his rightful role as heir apparent. But I suggest no more than that this story's reflection of Shakespeare's own career enabled him to present Hal's with considerable insight and gusto.

6. Most of Donne's *Songs and Sonets* are composed partly in pentameters and partly in shorter or longer lines. Except for Sidney, Donne is the first English poet to make a common practice of writing stanzas composed of such interwoven lines. In all of Shakespeare's songs, to go no further, there is not a single pentameter line. It looks as if poets realized instinctively what it has taken literary critics much longer to see, that pentameter is different from other line-lengths and that whenever it dominates a stanza or a poem, its strength and heft make for a significantly different kind of verse from that which we find in lyrical forms written in other line-lengths. (Halpern may have been the first to make this point, but see also Attridge [1982]; and above, Chapter 1, note 4.)

Donne used the stanza of mixed line-lengths to combine feelings of very different sorts into poems of remarkably complex, often mercurial, tone. These different feelings proceed from the lines' different structures and the different relations between phrase and line that those structures entail. Usually the line of two or three feet will consist of a single phrase; the tetrameter is variable, but if it contains two phrases, it will often divide in the middle. The pentameter must be made up of at least two phrases or its single phrase must be developed with greater complexity, and it cannot divide in the middle. The shorter lines are less open to metrical variation; hence, both metrically and syntactically, the pentameter line makes for complexity, and it offers room for the more subtle development of an idea or an image. The constant movement that we sense in most of Donne's lyrics proceeds not only from his lively syntax and vigorously prosecuted images, but from the mixture of lines that in their very lengths convey feelings, and even attitudes toward experience, of very different sorts. These feelings and attitudes are not easily characterized, but, in general, the shorter lines tend to emphasize the quick, light, fast-moving, and relatively uncomplicated, even comic, exploration of a subject; the long ones tend to deepen, intensify, and complicate it, to slow it down and make it more serious, more problematical. So brief a summary seems much too formulaic. Obviously, Donne's lyrics do not change their tone abruptly from line to line. Nevertheless, again and again they broach in short lines a subject that at first seems frivolous but is gradually given amplitude and gravity through a series of more expansive pentameter lines, which, as it were, raise the subject to a higher level of serious meditation. See, for example, "The Triple Foole," "The Sunne Rising," and "Loves Infinitenesse."

CHAPTER 18

1. See Donawerth (chapter 2) for a perceptive account of how Elizabethans changed their views of poetic language and its powers and purposes during the course of Shake-

speare's career. In particular, she shows how playwrights—especially Shakespeare—originally content to show passionate feeling in their dramatic figures, increasingly aimed first at a stricter imitation of character and later at language and gestures that can represent more significant idealized human personages. The same stages are probably evident in Shakespeare's versification.

2. A welcome exception is the article by Russ McDonald.

Main Works Cited or Consulted

Abbott, E. A. *A Shakespearean Grammar.* London: Macmillan, 1879.

Adams, Joseph Quincy, ed. *Chief Pre-Shakespearean Dramas.* Boston: Houghton Mifflin, 1924.

Adler, Jacob H. "Notes on the Prosody of *The Vanity of Human Wishes.*" *Studies in the Literary Imagination* 5 (1972): 101–117.

——. *The Reach of Art: A Study in the Prosody of Pope.* Gainesville: Univ. of Florida Press, 1964.

Alpers, Paul J. *The Poetry of The Faerie Queene.* Princeton: Princeton Univ. Press, 1967.

Aristotle. *Nicomachean Ethics,* trans. W. D. Ross. In *Introduction to Aristotle,* ed. Richard McKeon, pp. 308–543. New York: Modern Library, 1947.

Attridge, Derek. "The Language of Poetry: Materiality and Meaning." *Essays in Criticism* 31 (1981): 228–245.

——. *The Rhythms of English Poetry.* London: Longman, 1982.

——. *Well-Weighed Syllables: Elizabethan Verse in Classical Metres.* Cambridge, England: Cambridge Univ. Press, 1974.

Auden, W. H. *Collected Poems,* ed. Edward Mendelson. New York: Random House, 1976.

Bailey, James. *Toward a Statistical Analysis of English Verse.* Lisse, The Netherlands: Peter de Ridder Press, 1975.

Baker, Howard. *Induction to Tragedy.* University, Louisiana: Louisiana State Univ. Press, 1939.

Baldi, Sergio. *La poesia di Sir Thomas Wyatt: il primo petrarchista inglese.* Florence: Le Monnier, 1953.

Baldwin, T. W. *William Shakspere's Small Latine & Lesse Greeke.* 2 vols. Urbana: Univ. of Illinois Press, 1944.

Barish, Jonas A. *Ben Jonson and the Language of Prose Comedy.* Cambridge, Mass.: Harvard Univ. Press, 1960.

——. "Continuities and Discontinuities in Shakespearian Prose." In *Shakespeare 1971,* ed. Clifford Leech and J. M. R. Margeson, pp. 59–75. Toronto: Univ. of Toronto Press, 1972.

Barton, John. *Playing Shakespeare.* London: Methuen, 1984.

Bathurst, Charles J. *Remarks on the Differences in Shakespeare's Versification in Different Periods of His Life and on Like Points of Difference in Poetry Generally.* New York: AMS Press, 1970 [1857].

Baum, Paull F. *Chaucer's Verse*. Durham, N.C.: Duke Univ. Press, 1961.

Bayfield, M. A. *A Study of Shakespeare's Versification*. Cambridge, England: Cambridge Univ. Press, 1920.

Beaver, John C. "Contrastive Stress and Metered Verse." *Language and Style* 2 (1969): 257–271.

Beckerman, Bernard. *Shakespeare at the Globe, 1599–1609*. New York: Macmillan, 1962.

Beckett, Samuel. *Three Novels: Molloy, Malone Dies, The Unnamable*. New York: Grove Press, 1965.

Bentley, Gerald Eades. *Shakespeare and His Theatre*. Lincoln: Univ. of Nebraska Press, 1964.

Bernard, J. E., Jr. *The Prosody of the Tudor Interlude*. Hamden, Conn.: Archon Books, 1969 [1939].

Bertram, Paul. *White Spaces in Shakespeare: The Development of the Modern Text*. Cleveland: Bellflower Press, 1981.

Bethell, S. L. *Shakespeare and the Popular Dramatic Tradition*. London: Staples Press, 1944.

———. "Shakespeare's Imagery: The Diabolic Images in *Othello*." *Shakespeare Survey* 5 (1952): 62–80.

Blake, N. F. *Shakespeare's Language: An Introduction*. New York: St. Martin's Press, 1983.

Bolinger, Dwight. *Forms of English: Accent, Morpheme, Order,* ed. Isamu Abe and Tetsuya Kanekiyo. Cambridge, Mass.: Harvard Univ. Press, 1965.

———. *The Phrasal Verb in English*. Cambridge, Mass.: Harvard Univ. Press, 1971.

Boomsliter, Paul C., Warren Creel, and George S. Hastings, Jr. "Perception and English Poetic Meter." *PMLA* 88 (1973): 200–208.

Booth, Stephen. *An Essay on Shakespeare's Sonnets*. New Haven: Yale Univ. Press, 1969.

Bowers, Fredson. "Establishing Shakespeare's Text: Notes on Short Lines and the Problem of Verse Division." *Studies in Bibliography* 33 (1980): 74–130.

Brashear, Lucy M. "Character and Prosody in Shakespeare's *Measure for Measure*." Ph.D. diss., Univ. of North Carolina, 1969.

Bridges, Robert. *Milton's Prosody*. Oxford: Oxford Univ. Press, 1921.

Bright, James W. "Concerning Grammatical Ictus in English Verse." In *An English Miscellany,* pp. 23–33. Oxford: Clarendon, 1901.

Bright, James Wilson, and Raymond Durbin Miller. *The Elements of English Versification*. Boston: Ginn and Company, 1910.

Brogan, T. V. F. *English Versification, 1570–1980*. Baltimore: Johns Hopkins Univ. Press, 1981.

Brooke, Nicholas. "Language Most Shows a Man . . . ? Language and Speaker in *Macbeth*." In *Shakespeare's Styles,* ed. Philip Edwards et al., pp. 67–77. Cambridge, England: Cambridge Univ. Press, 1980.

Brooke, Tucker. "Marlowe's Versification and Style." *Studies in Philology* 19 (1922): 186–205.

Brown, John Russell. *Shakespeare's Dramatic Style*. London: Heinemann, 1970.

Browning, Robert. *Poems and Plays*. 5 vols. London: Dent, 1906.

Brubaker, E. S. *Shakespeare Aloud: A Guide to His Verse on Stage*. Lancaster, Pa.: Published by the author, 1976.

Cable, Thomas. "Timers, Stressers, and Linguists: Contention and Compromise." *Modern Language Quarterly* 33 (1972): 227–239.

Calderwood, James L., and Harold E. Toliver, eds. "Prosody" (essays by several authors). In *Perspectives on Poetry,* ed. Calderwood and Toliver, pp. 133–190. New York: Oxford Univ. Press, 1968.

Cercignani, Fausto. *Shakespeare's Works and Elizabethan Pronunciation.* Oxford: Clarendon, 1981.

Chambers, David L. *The Metre of "Macbeth": Its Relation to Shakespeare's Earlier and Later Work.* Princeton: Princeton Univ. Press, 1903.

Chambers, E. K. *William Shakespeare: A Study of Facts and Problems.* 2 vols. Oxford: Clarendon, 1930.

Chatman, Seymour. "Mr. Stein on Donne." In *Perspectives on Poetry,* ed. James L. Calderwood and Harold E. Toliver, pp. 177–183. New York: Oxford Univ. Press, 1968.

———. *A Theory of Meter.* The Hague: Mouton, 1965.

Chaucer, Geoffrey. *The Works of Geoffrey Chaucer,* ed. F. N. Robinson. 2d ed. Boston: Houghton Mifflin, 1957.

Chisholm, David. "Generative Prosody and English Verse." *Poetics* 6 (1977): 111–154.

Clemen, Wolfgang. *English Tragedy before Shakespeare: The Development of Dramatic Speech,* trans. T. S. Dorsch. New York: Barnes and Noble, 1961.

———. "Shakespeare and Marlowe." In *Shakespeare 1971,* ed. Clifford Leech and J. M. R. Margeson, pp. 123–132. Toronto: Univ. of Toronto Press, 1972(a).

———. *Shakespeare's Dramatic Art: Collected Essays.* London: Methuen, 1972(b).

Cooper, Sherod M., Jr. *The Sonnets of Astrophil and Stella: A Stylistic Study.* The Hague: Mouton, 1968.

Crystal, David. "Intonation and Metrical Theory." In *The English Tone of Voice: Essays in Intonation, Prosody, and Paralanguage,* pp. 105–124. London: Edward Arnold, 1975.

Daalder, Joost. "Wyatt's Prosody Revisited." *Language and Style* 10 (1977): 3–15.

Dam, B. A. P. Van, and C. Stoffel. *William Shakespeare: Prosody and Text.* London: Williams and Norgate, 1900.

David, Richard. *The Janus of Poets.* New York: Macmillan, 1935.

Davies, Sir John. *The Poems of Sir John Davies,* ed. Robert Krueger. Oxford: Clarendon, 1975.

Dobson, E. J. *English Pronunciation, 1500–1700.* 2d ed. Oxford: Oxford Univ. Press, 1968.

Doebler, John. *Shakespeare's Speaking Pictures: Studies in Iconic Imagery.* Albuquerque: Univ. of New Mexico Press, 1974.

Donawerth, Jane. *Shakespeare and the Sixteenth-Century Study of Language.* Urbana: Univ. of Illinois Press, 1984.

Donne, John. *The Poems of John Donne,* ed. H. J. C. Grierson. London: Oxford Univ. Press, 1933.

Doran, Madeleine. *Shakespeare's Dramatic Language.* Madison: Univ. of Wisconsin Press, 1976.

Downer, Alan S. "The Life of Our Design: The Function of Imagery in the Poetic Drama." In *Shakespeare: Modern Essays in Criticism,* ed. Leonard F. Dean, pp. 19–36. New York: Oxford Univ. Press, 1957.

Drayton, Michael. *Poems of Michael Drayton,* ed. John Buxton. 2 vols. London: Routledge and Kegan Paul, 1953.

Dubrow, Heather. "Shakespeare's Undramatic Monologues: Toward a Reading of the Sonnets." *Shakespeare Quarterly* 32 (1981): 55–68.

Easthope, Antony. *Poetry as Discourse.* London: Methuen, 1983.

Eliot, T. S. *The Complete Poems and Plays, 1909–1950.* New York: Harcourt, Brace, 1952.

———. *On Poetry and Poets.* New York: Noonday, 1961.

———. *The Sacred Wood: Essays on Poetry and Criticism.* London: Methuen, 1920.

———. "Shakespeares Verskunst." *Monat* 2, 20 (1950): 198–207.

Empson, William. *Seven Types of Ambiguity.* New York: New Directions, 1947.

Evans, Ifor. *The Language of Shakespeare's Plays.* London: Methuen, 1964.

Evans, Robert O. "Some Aspects of Wyatt's Metrical Technique." *JEGP* 53 (1954): 197–213.

"Extract from Unsigned Review of Tillyard's Edition of Wyatt's Poems." From *TLS,* 19 September 1929. Quoted in Thomson, 1974, pp. 167–172.

Faure, G., D. J. Hirst, and M. Chafcouloff. "Rhythm in English: Isochronism, Pitch, and Perceived Stress." In *The Melody of Language,* ed. Linda R. Waugh and C. H. van Schooneveld, pp. 71–79. Baltimore: University Park Press, 1980.

Ferry, Anne. *The "Inward" Language: Sonnets of Wyatt, Sidney, Shakespeare, Donne.* Chicago: Univ. of Chicago Press, 1983.

Fish, Stanley. *Surprised by Sin: The Reader in* Paradise Lost. Berkeley and Los Angeles: Univ. of California Press, 1967.

Flatter, Richard. *Shakespeare's Producing Hand.* London: Heinemann, 1948.

Fleay, F. G. "On Metrical Tests as Applied to Dramatic Poetry." *The New Shakspere Society's Transactions,* pp. 1–72. London: Alexander Moring, 1874.

———. *Shakespeare Manual.* New York: AMS Press, 1970 [1876].

Fowler, Roger. "'Prose Rhythm' and Meter." In *Linguistics and Literary Style,* ed. Donald C. Freeman, pp. 347–365. New York: Holt, Rinehart, and Winston, 1970.

Foxwell, A. K. *A Study of Sir Thomas Wyatt's Poems.* New York: Russell and Russell, 1964 [1911].

Fraser, G. S. *Metre, Rhyme and Free Verse.* London: Methuen, 1970.

Freeman, Donald C., ed. *Linguistics and Literary Style.* New York: Holt, Rinehart, and Winston, 1970.

Freer, Coburn. *The Poetics of Jacobean Drama.* Baltimore: Johns Hopkins Univ. Press, 1981.

Fried, Debra. "Spenser's Caesura." *English Literary Renaissance* 11 (1981): 261–280.

Frost, Robert. *The Poetry of Robert Frost,* ed. Edward Connery Lathem. New York: Holt, Rinehart, and Winston, 1969.

Frye, Northrop. *Anatomy of Criticism: Four Essays.* New York: Atheneum, 1966.

Frye, Roland Mushat. *Shakespeare: The Art of the Dramatist.* Boston: Houghton Mifflin, 1970.

Fussell, Paul. "Metrical Variations." In *Princeton Encyclopedia of Poetry and Poetics,* ed. Alex Preminger et al., pp. 500–501. Enlarged edition. Princeton: Princeton Univ. Press, 1974.

———. *Poetic Meter and Poetic Form.* Rev. ed. New York: Random House, 1979.

———. *Theory of Prosody in Eighteenth-Century England.* New London: Connecticut College Monograph No. 5, 1954.

Gascoigne, George. *Certayne Notes of Instruction* (1575). In *Elizabethan Critical Essays,* vol. 1, ed. G. Gregory Smith, pp. 46–57. London: Oxford Univ. Press, 1904.

———. *The Complete Works of George Gascoigne.* 2 vols. Cambridge, England: Cambridge Univ. Press, 1907, 1910.

Gaylord, Alan T. "Scanning the Prosodists: An Essay in Metacriticism." *Chaucer Review* 11 (1976): 22–82.

Giamatti, A. Bartlett. "Italian." In *Versification: Major Language Types,* ed. W. K. Wimsatt, [Jr.], pp. 148–164. New York: New York Univ. Press, 1972.

Goldsmith, Ulrich K. "Words out of a Hat? Alliteration and Assonance in Shakespeare's Sonnets." *JEGP* 50 (1950): 33–48.

Gombrich, E. H. *Art and Illusion: A Study in the Psychology of Pictorial Representation.* Princeton: Princeton Univ. Press, 1960.

A Gorgeous Gallery of Gallant Inventions, ed. Hyder E. Rollins. Cambridge, Mass.: Harvard Univ. Press, 1926.

Gower, John. *The Complete Works of John Gower,* ed. G. C. Macaulay. Oxford: Clarendon, 1901.

Granville-Barker, Harley. *Prefaces to Shakespeare.* 4 vols. Princeton: Princeton Univ. Press, 1946.

Granville-Barker, Harley, and G. B. Harrison, eds. *A Companion to Shakespeare Studies.* New York: Macmillan, 1934.

Greg, W. W. "Some Notes on Crane's Manuscript of *The Witch.*" *Library* 22 (1942): 208–219.

Greville, Fulke. *Selected Poems of Fulke Greville,* ed. Thom Gunn. London: Faber and Faber, 1968.

Gross, Harvey, ed. *The Structure of Verse: Modern Essays on Prosody.* Greenwich, Conn.: Fawcett Publications, 1966.

Halle, Morris, and Samuel J. Keyser. "Chaucer and the Study of Prosody." *College English* 28 (1966): 187–219.

———. *English Stress: Its Form, Its Growth, and Its Role in Verse.* New York: Harper and Row, 1971.

Halliday, F. E. *The Poetry of Shakespeare's Plays.* Cambridge, Mass.: Robert Bentley, 1954.

Halpern, Martin. "On the Two Chief Metrical Modes in English." *PMLA* 77 (1962): 177–186.

Hamer, Enid. *The Metres of English Poetry.* London: Methuen, 1930.

Hammond, Eleanor Prescott. *English Verse between Chaucer and Surrey.* New York: Octagon Books, 1965 [1927].

———. "The Nine-Syllabled Line in Some Post-Chaucerian Manuscripts." *Modern Philology* 23 (1925): 129–152.

A Handful of Pleasant Delights, ed. Hyder E. Rollins. Cambridge, Mass.: Harvard Univ. Press, 1924.

Hapgood, Robert. "Hearing Shakespeare: Sound and Meaning in 'Antony and Cleopatra.'" *Shakespeare Survey* 24 (1971): 1–12.

Harbage, Alfred. *Theatre for Shakespeare.* Toronto: Univ. of Toronto Press, 1955.

Harding, D. W. "The Rhythmical Intention in Wyatt's Poetry." *Scrutiny* 14 (1946): 90–102.

———. *Words into Rhythm.* Cambridge, England: Cambridge Univ. Press, 1976.

Hardison, O. B., Jr. "Blank Verse before Milton." *Studies in Philology* 81 (1984): 253–274.

———. "Speaking the Speech." *Shakespeare Quarterly* 34 (1983): 133–146.

Harrier, Richard. *The Canon of Sir Thomas Wyatt's Poetry.* Cambridge, Mass.: Harvard Univ. Press, 1975.

Hascall, Dudley L. "The Prosody of John Lydgate." *Language and Style* 3 (1970): 122–146.
———. "Trochaic Meter." *College English* 33 (1971): 217–226.
Häublein, Ernst. *The Stanza*. London: Methuen, 1978.
Hayes, Bruce. "A Grid-based Theory of English Meter." *Linguistic Inquiry* 14 (1983): 357–393.
Hebel, J. William, and Hoyt H. Hudson, eds. *Poetry of the English Renaissance, 1509–1660*. New York: Appleton-Century-Crofts, 1929.
Heine, Ingeborg. "The Metrical Intentions of Wyatt's Sonnets. . . ." *Kwartalnik Neofilologicny* 25 (1978): 407–420.
Herbert, George. *The English Poems of George Herbert*, ed. C. A. Patrides. London: Dent, 1974.
Hibbard, G. R. *The Making of Shakespeare's Dramatic Poetry*. Toronto: Univ. of Toronto Press, 1981.
Hollander, John. "The Metrical Emblem." *Kenyon Review* 21 (1959): 279–296.
———. *Vision and Resonance: Two Senses of Poetic Form*. New York: Oxford Univ. Press, 1975.
Hopkins, Gerard Manley. *Poems*, ed. W. H. Gardner. New York: Oxford Univ. Press, 1948.
Howard, Donald R. *The Idea of the* Canterbury Tales. Berkeley and Los Angeles: Univ. of California Press, 1976.
Howarth, Herbert. "Metre and Emphasis: A Conservative Note." In *Essays on Shakespeare*, ed. Gordon Ross Smith, pp. 211–227. University Park: Pennsylvania State Univ. Press, 1965.
Ing, Catherine. *Elizabethan Lyrics: A Study in the Development of English Metres and Their Relation to Poetic Effect*. London: Chatto and Windus, 1951.
Ingram, R. W. "Music as Structural Element in Shakespeare." In *Shakespeare 1971*, ed. Clifford Leech and J. M. R. Margeson, pp. 174–89. Toronto: Univ. of Toronto Press, 1972.
Jespersen, Otto. "Notes on Metre" (1900). In his *Linguistica: Selected Papers*, pp. 249–272. Copenhagen: Levin and Munksgaard, 1933.
Jonson, Ben. *Selected Works*, ed. Harry Levin. New York: Random House, 1938.
Joseph, B. L. *Elizabethan Acting*. 2d ed. Oxford: Oxford Univ. Press, 1964.
Joseph, Sister Miriam. *Shakespeare's Use of the Arts of Language*. New York: Hafner Publishing Company, 1947.
Joyce, James. *A Portrait of the Artist as a Young Man*. New York: Viking, 1956 [1916].
———. *Ulysses*. New York: Modern Library, 1961 [1922].
Keats, John. *The Poems of John Keats*, ed. Jack Stillinger. Cambridge, Mass.: Harvard Univ. Press, 1978.
Kennedy, Andrew K. *Dramatic Dialogue: The Duologue of Personal Encounter*. Cambridge, England: Cambridge Univ. Press, 1983.
Kermode, Frank. *Forms of Attention*. Chicago: Univ. of Chicago Press, 1985.
Kiparsky, Paul. "The Rhythmic Structure of English Verse." *Linguistic Inquiry* 8 (1977): 189–247.
———. "Stress, Syntax, and Meter." *Language* 51 (1975): 576–616.
Koelb, Clayton. "The Iambic Pentameter Revisited." *Neophilologus* 63 (1979): 321–329.
Kökeritz, Helge. "Elizabethan Prosody and Historical Phonology." In *Approaches to En-*

glish Historical Linguistics, ed. Roger Lass, pp. 208–227. New York: Holt, Rinehart, and Winston, 1969.

———. Shakespeare's Pronunciation. New Haven: Yale Univ. Press, 1953.

Kyd, Thomas. The Spanish Tragedy, ed. Thomas W. Ross. Edinburgh: Oliver and Boyd, 1968.

Leicester, H. Marshall, Jr. "The Art of Impersonation: A General Prologue to the Canterbury Tales." PMLA 95 (1980): 213–224.

Lewis, C. S. English Literature in the Sixteenth Century, Excluding Drama. Oxford: Clarendon, 1954.

———. "The Fifteenth-Century Heroic Line." Essays and Studies by Members of the English Association 24 (1938): 28–41.

———. "Metre." Review of English Literature 1 (1960): 45–50.

Lewontin, R. C. "Darwin's Revolution." New York Review of Books 30, 10 (16 June 1983): 21–27.

Licklider, Albert H. Chapters on the Metric of the Chaucerian Tradition. Baltimore: J. H. Furst Company, 1910.

Lord, John B. "Some Solved and Some Unsolved Problems in Prosody." Style 13 (1979): 311–333.

Lydgate, John. Siege of Thebes, part 2, ed. Axel Erdmann and Eilert Ekwall. London: Oxford Univ. Press, 1930.

———. Temple of Glas, ed. J. Schick. London: Kegan Paul, Trench, Trubner and Co., 1891. [Early English Text Society edition.]

Lynn, Karen. "Chaucer's Decasyllabic Line: The Myth of the Hundred-Year Hibernation." Chaucer Review 13 (1978): 116–127.

McAuley, James. Versification: A Short Introduction. East Lansing: Michigan State Univ. Press, 1966.

Macdermott, M. M. Vowel Sounds in Poetry: Their Music and Tone-Colour. London: Kegan Paul, Trench, Trubner and Co., 1940.

McDonald, Russ. "Poetry and Plot in The Winter's Tale." Shakespeare Quarterly 36 (1985): 315–329.

Mahood, M. M. Shakespeare's Wordplay. London: Methuen, 1957.

Malof, Joseph. "The Native Rhythm of English Meters." Texas Studies in Literature and Language 5 (1964): 580–594.

Marker, Lise-Lone. "Nature and Decorum in the Theory of Elizabethan Acting." In The Elizabethan Theatre II, ed. David Galloway, pp. 87–107. [Canada]: Archon Books, 1970.

Marlowe, Christopher. Complete Plays and Poems, ed. E. D. Pendry. London: Dent, 1976.

Mason, H. A. Editing Wyatt: An Examination of Collected Poems of Sir Thomas Wyatt, Together with Suggestions for an Improved Edition. Cambridge, England: Cambridge Quarterly Publications, 1972.

———. Humanism and Poetry in the Early Tudor Period. London: Routledge and Kegan Paul, 1959.

Masson, David I. "Free Phonetic Patterns in Shakespeare's Sonnets." Neophilologus 37 (1954): 277–289.

Maxwell, J. C. "Virgilian Half-Lines in Shakespeare's 'Heroic Narrative.'" Notes and Queries 198 (1953): 100.

Mayor, Joseph B. *Chapters on English Metre*. 2d ed. New York: Greenwood Press, 1968 [1901].

Mehl, Dieter. "Visual and Rhetorical Imagery in Shakespeare's Plays." *Essays and Studies* 25 (1972): 83–100.

Melton, Wightman Fletcher. *The Rhetoric of John Donne's Verse*. Baltimore: J. H. Furst, 1906.

Middleton, Thomas, and William Rowley. *The Changeling*, ed. N. W. Bawcutt. London: Methuen, 1958.

Miles, Josephine. *Eras and Modes in English Poetry*. Berkeley and Los Angeles: Univ. of California Press, 1957.

———. *Poetry and Change: Donne, Milton, Wordsworth, and the Equilibrium of the Present*. Berkeley and Los Angeles: Univ. of California Press, 1974.

———. *Style and Proportion: The Language of Prose and Poetry*. Boston: Little, Brown, 1967.

Milton, John. *Poetical Works*, ed. Douglas Bush. London: Oxford Univ. Press, 1969.

The Mirror for Magistrates, ed. Lily B. Campbell. New York: Barnes and Noble, 1938.

Mitchell, Jerome. *Thomas Hoccleve: A Study in Early Fifteenth-Century English Poetic*. Urbana: Univ. of Illinois Press, 1968.

Moloney, Michael F. "Donne's Metrical Practice." *PMLA* 65 (1950): 232–239.

Muir, Kenneth. *Life and Letters of Sir Thomas Wyatt*. Liverpool: Liverpool Univ. Press, 1963.

———. *Shakespeare's Sonnets*. London: George Allen and Unwin, 1979.

Muir, Kenneth, and S. Schoenbaum, eds. *A New Companion to Shakespeare Studies*. Cambridge, England: Cambridge Univ. Press, 1971.

Mukarovsky, Jan. "Intonation as the Basic Factor of Poetic Rhythm." In *The Word and Verbal Art*, ed. and trans. John Burbank and Peter Steiner, pp. 116–133. New Haven: Yale Univ. Press, 1977.

———. "Standard Language and Poetic Language." In *A Prague School Reader on Aesthetics*, ed. Paul L. Garvin, pp. 17–30. Washington: Georgetown Univ. Press, 1964.

Mustanoja, Tauno F. "Chaucer's Prosody." In *A Companion to Chaucer Studies*, ed. Beryl Rowland, pp. 58–84. Rev. ed. New York: Oxford Univ. Press, 1979.

Nashe, Thomas. *The Works of Thomas Nashe*, ed. Ronald B. McKerrow. 3 vols. Oxford: Basil Blackwell, 1958.

Nelson, Thomas E. "The Syntax of Sidney's Poetry." Ph.D. diss., Ohio Univ., 1975.

Ness, Frederic W. *The Use of Rhyme in Shakespeare's Plays*. New Haven: Yale Univ. Press, 1941.

Newton, Robert P. "Trochaic and Iambic." *Language and Style* 8 (1975): 127–156.

Ogle, Robert B. "Wyatt and Petrarch: A Puzzle in Prosody." *JEGP* 73 (1974): 189–208.

Oras, Ants. *Pause Patterns in Elizabethan and Jacobean Drama: An Experiment in Prosody*. Gainesville: Univ. of Florida Press, 1960.

Ornstein, Robert. "Character and Reality in Shakespeare." In *Shakespeare 1564–1964: A Collection of Modern Essays by Various Hands*, ed. Edward A. Bloom, pp. 3–18. Providence: Brown Univ. Press, 1964.

Padelford, Frederick Morgan. "The Scansion of Wyatt's Early Sonnets." *Studies in Philology* 20 (1923): 137–152.

The Paradise of Dainty Devices, ed. Hyder E. Rollins. Cambridge, Mass.: Harvard Univ. Press, 1927.

Partridge, A. C. *John Donne: Language and Style*. London: Andre Deutsch, 1978.
————. *The Language of Renaissance Poetry: Spenser, Shakespeare, Donne, Milton*. London: Andre Deutsch, 1971.
————. *Orthography in Shakespeare and Elizabethan Drama*. London: Edward Arnold, 1964.
Pearsall, Derek. *John Lydgate*. London: Routledge and Kegan Paul, 1970.
The Phoenix Nest, ed. Hyder E. Rollins. Cambridge, Mass.: Harvard Univ. Press, 1931.
Pirkhofer, Anton M. "'A Pretty Pleasing Pricket'—On the Use of Alliteration in Shakespeare's Sonnets." *Shakespeare Quarterly* 14 (1963): 3–14.
Pope, Alexander. *The Complete Poetical Works of Pope*, ed. Henry W. Boynton. Boston: Houghton Mifflin, 1903.
Pound, Ezra. *The Selected Letters of Ezra Pound, 1907–1941*, ed. D. D. Paige. New York: New Directions, 1950.
Prince, Alan S. "Relating to the Grid." *Linguistic Inquiry* 14 (1983): 19–100.
Prince, F. T. *The Italian Element in Milton's Verse*. Oxford: Clarendon Press, 1954.
Princeton Encyclopedia of Poetry and Poetics, ed. Alex Preminger et al. Enlarged edition. Princeton: Princeton Univ. Press, 1974.
Puttenham, Richard. *The Arte of English Poesie*. London, 1589. Reprinted Amsterdam: Da Capo Press, 1971.
Pyle, Fitzroy. "Chaucer's Prosody." *Medium Aevum* 42 (1973): 47–56.
————. "The Pedigree of Lydgate's Heroic Line, with a Note on His Use of the Line-Types." *Hermathena* 25 (1937): 26–59.
Ramsey, Paul. *The Fickle Glass: A Study of Shakespeare's Sonnets*. New York: AMS Press, 1979.
Ransom, John Crowe. "The Strange Music of English Verse." In *Perspectives on Poetry*, ed. James L. Calderwood and Harold E. Toliver, pp. 184–190. New York: Oxford Univ. Press, 1968. [Excerpted from *Kenyon Review* 18 (1956): 460–477.]
Redgrave, Michael. "Shakespeare and the Actors." In *Talking of Shakespeare*, ed. John Garrett, pp. 127–148. London: Hodder and Stoughton, 1954.
Robinson, Edwin Arlington. *Collected Poems*. New York: Macmillan, 1954 [1937].
Robinson, Ian. *Chaucer's Prosody: A Study of the Middle English Verse Tradition*. Cambridge, England: Cambridge Univ. Press, 1971.
Rosenberg, Marvin. "Elizabethan Actors: Men or Marionettes?" *PMLA* 69 (1954): 915–927.
Rudenstine, Neil L. *Sidney's Poetic Development*. Cambridge, Mass.: Harvard Univ. Press, 1967.
Rylands, George. "The Poet and the Player." *Shakespeare Survey* 7 (1954): 25–34.
Saintsbury, George. *A History of English Prosody from the Twelfth Century to the Present Day*. 3 vols. London: Macmillan, 1923 [1906–1910].
Salgado, Gamini, comp. *Eyewitnesses of Shakespeare*. London: Sussex Univ. Press, 1975.
Schipper, J. *A History of English Versification*. Oxford: Clarendon, 1910.
Schoenbaum, Samuel. *Internal Evidence and Elizabethan Dramatic Authorship*. Evanston, Ill.: Northwestern Univ. Press, 1966.
Schwartz, Elias. "The Meter of Some Poems of Wyatt." *Studies in Philology* 60 (1963): 155–165.
Sedlak, Werner. "Blankversveränderungen in Shakespeares späteren Tragödien: eine In-

terpretation von *Othello, King Lear, Macbeth* und *Antony and Cleopatra.*" Ph.D. diss., Univ. of Munich, 1971.

Shakespeare, William. *Coriolanus,* ed. Philip Brockbank. London: Methuen, 1976. [Arden Edition.]

————. *Cymbeline,* ed. J. M. Nosworthy. London: Methuen, 1955. [Arden edition.]

————. *The First Folio of Shakespeare,* prepared by Charlton Hinman. New York: Norton, 1968. [Norton Facsimile Edition.]

————. *The Riverside Shakespeare.* Boston: Houghton Mifflin, 1974.

————. *Shakespeare's Plays in Quarto,* ed. Michael J. B. Allen and Kenneth Muir. Berkeley and Los Angeles: Univ. of California Press, 1981.

————. *Shakespeare's Sonnets,* ed. Stephen Booth. New Haven: Yale Univ. Press, 1977.

Shapiro, Karl, and Robert Beum. *A Prosody Handbook.* New York: Harper and Row, 1965.

Sicherman, Carol M. "Meter and Meaning in Shakespeare." *Language and Style* 15 (1982): 169–192.

————. "Short Lines and Interpretation: The Case of *Julius Caesar.*" *Shakespeare Quarterly* 35 (1984): 180–195.

Sidney, Sir Philip. *The Poems of Sir Philip Sidney,* ed. William A. Ringler, Jr. Oxford: Clarendon, 1962.

Simpson, Percy. "The Rhyming of Stressed with Unstressed Syllables in Elizabethan Verse." *Modern Language Review* 38 (1943): 127–129.

————. "Shakespeare's Versification: A Study in Development." *Studies in Elizabethan Drama,* pp. 64–88. Oxford: Clarendon, 1955.

————. *Shakespearian Punctuation.* Oxford: Clarendon, 1969 [1911].

Sipe, Dorothy L. *Shakespeare's Metrics.* New Haven: Yale Univ. Press, 1968.

Skelton, John. *The Complete English Poems,* ed. John Scattergood. New Haven: Yale Univ. Press, 1983.

Smith, Barbara Herrnstein. *On the Margins of Discourse: The Relation of Literature to Language.* Chicago: Univ. of Chicago Press, 1978.

————. *Poetic Closure: A Study of How Poems End.* Chicago: Univ. of Chicago Press, 1968.

Smith, G. Gregory, ed. *Elizabethan Critical Essays.* 2 vols. London: Oxford Univ. Press, 1904.

Southall, Raymond. *The Courtly Maker: An Essay on the Poetry of Wyatt and His Contemporaries.* Oxford: Basil Blackwell, 1964.

Southworth, James G. *The Prosody of Chaucer and His Followers.* Oxford: Basil Blackwell, 1962.

————. *Verses of Cadence: An Introduction to the Prosody of Chaucer and His Followers.* Oxford: Basil Blackwell, 1954.

Sparrow, John. *Half-Lines and Repetitions in Virgil.* Oxford: Clarendon, 1931.

Spenser, Edmund. *The Complete Poetical Works of Spenser,* ed. R. E. Neil Dodge. Boston: Houghton Mifflin, 1936.

Spiegel, Glenn S. "Perfecting English Meter: Sixteenth-Century Criticism and Practice." *JEGP* 79 (1980): 192–209.

Sprott, S. Ernest. *Milton's Art of Prosody.* Oxford: Basil Blackwell, 1953.

Stack, Richard Catesby. "From Sweetness to Strength: A Study of the Development of Metrical Style in the English Renaissance." Ph.D. diss., Stanford Univ., 1967.

Stanley, E. G. "Stanza and Ictus: Chaucer's Emphasis in 'Troilus and Criseyde.'" In

Chaucer und seine Zeit: Symposion für Walter F. Schirmer, ed. Arno Esch, pp. 123–148. Tübingen: Max Niemeyer, 1968.

Stein, Arnold. "Donne and the Couplet." *PMLA* 57 (1942): 676–696.

———. "Donne's Harshness and the Elizabethan Tradition." *Studies in Philology* 41 (1944[a]): 390–409.

———. "Donne's Prosody." *PMLA* 59 (1944[b]): 373–397.

———. "Meter and Meaning in Donne's Verse." *Sewanee Review* 52 (1944): 288–301.

———. "Structures of Sound in Donne's Verse." *Kenyon Review* 15 (1951): 256–278.

———. "Structures of Sound in Milton's Verse." *Kenyon Review* 15 (1953): 266–277.

Stein, David Neil. "On the Basis of English Iambic Pentameter." Ph.D. diss., Univ. of Illinois, 1975.

Stevens, John. *Music and Poetry in the Early Tudor Court.* Cambridge, England: Cambridge Univ. Press, 1961. [Reprinted with corrections, 1979.]

Suhamy, Henri. *Le vers de Shakespeare.* Paris: Didier-Erudition, 1984.

Surrey, Henry Howard, Earl of. *The Poems of Henry Howard, Earl of Surrey,* ed. Frederick Morgan Padelford. Seattle: Univ. of Washington Press, 1920.

Swallow, Alan. "The Pentameter Lines in Skelton and Wyatt." *Modern Philology,* 48 (1950): 1–11.

Sypher, Wylie. *Four Stages of Renaissance Style: Transformations in Art and Literature, 1400–1700.* Garden City, N.Y.: Doubleday Anchor, 1955.

Tarlinskaja, Marina. "Aspects of Meter (Phonological and Grammatical Aspects; the General Rule and the Poets' Style)." In *Proceedings, Stanford Metrics Conference 1984.* New York: Academic Press (forthcoming).

———. *English Verse: Theory and History.* The Hague: Mouton, 1976.

———. "Evolution of Shakespeare's Metrical Style." *Poetics* 12 (1983): 567–587.

———. "Rhythm-Morphology-Syntax-Rhythm." *Style* 18 (1984): 1–26.

———. *Shakespeare's Verse: Iambic Pentameter and the Poet's Idiosyncrasies.* New York: Peter Lang, 1987.

———. "Vertical Parameters of Meter . . ." In *Proceedings, Stanford Metrics Conference 1984.* New York: Academic Press (forthcoming).

Ten Brink, Bernhard. *The Language and Metre of Chaucer,* trans. M. Bentinck Smith. 2d ed. New York: Haskell House, 1968 [1901].

Tennyson, Alfred, Lord. *The Complete Poetical Works of Tennyson.* Boston: Houghton Mifflin, 1898.

Thompson, John. *The Founding of English Metre.* New York: Columbia Univ. Press, 1961.

———. "Linguistic Structure and the Poetic Line." In *Linguistics and Literary Style,* ed. Donald C. Freeman, pp. 336–346. New York: Holt, Rinehart, and Winston, 1970.

Thomson, Patricia. *Sir Thomas Wyatt and His Background.* London: Routledge and Kegan Paul, 1964.

Thomson, Patricia, ed. *Wyatt: The Critical Heritage.* London: Routledge and Kegan Paul, 1974.

Thomson, Virgil. "Music Does Not Flow." *New York Review of Books,* 17 Dec. 1981: 47–51.

Timberlake, Philip W. *The Feminine Endings in English Blank Verse.* Menasha, Wisc.: George Banta Publishing Company, 1931.

Tottel's Miscellany (1557–1587), ed. Hyder E. Rollins. Vol. 1. Cambridge, Mass.: Harvard Univ. Press, 1928.

Turner, Frederick, and Ernst Poppel. "The Neural Lyre: Poetic Meter, the Brain, and Time." *Poetry* 104 (1983): 277–309.

Van Laan, Thomas F. *Role-Playing in Shakespeare.* Toronto: Univ. of Toronto Press, 1978.

Vickers, Brian. *The Artistry of Shakespeare's Prose.* London: Methuen, 1968.

———. "Rites of Passage in Shakespeare's Prose." *Jahrbuch* (Deutsche Shakespeare-Gesellschaft West) (1986): 45–67.

Walker, William Sidney. *A Critical Examination of the Text of Shakespeare with Remarks on His Language and That of His Contemporaries, Together with Notes on His Plays and Poems.* 3 vols. London: John Russell Smith, 1860.

———. *Shakespeare's Versification and Its Apparent Irregularity Explained by Examples from Early and Late English Writers.* London: John Russell Smith, 1854.

Waller, Edmund. *The Poems of Edmund Waller.* New York: Greenwood Press, 1968 [1893].

Watkins, Ronald. "The Only Shake-Scene." *Philological Quarterly* 54 (1975): 47–67.

Weismiller, Edward R. "Blank Verse." In *A Milton Encyclopedia,* ed. William B. Hunter, Jr., et al., vol. 1, pp. 179–192. Lewisburg: Bucknell Univ. Press, 1978.

———. "The 'Dry' and 'Rugged' Verse." In *The Lyric and Dramatic Milton,* ed. Joseph H. Summers, pp. 115–152. New York: Columbia Univ. Press, 1965.

———. "Studies of Verse Form in the Minor English Poems." In *A Variorum Commentary on the Poems of John Milton.* Vol. 2, Part 3: *The Minor English Poems,* pp. 1007–1087. New York: Columbia Univ. Press, 1972.

Wellek, René, and Austin Warren. *Theory of Literature.* 3d ed. New York: Harcourt, Brace, and World, 1956.

Wells, Stanley. *Modernizing Shakespeare's Spelling.* Oxford: Clarendon, 1979.

Welsh, Andrew. *Roots of Lyric: Primitive Poetry and Modern Poetics.* Princeton: Princeton Univ. Press, 1978.

Williams, William Carlos. *Interviews with William Carlos Williams,* ed. Linda W. Wagner. New York: New Directions, 1976.

Wimsatt, W. K., Jr. "The Rule and the Norm: Halle and Keyser on Chaucer's Meter." *College English* 31 (1970[a]): 774–788.

Wimsatt, W. K., Jr., ed. *Versification: Major Language Types. Sixteen Essays.* New York: New York Univ. Press, 1970(b).

Wimsatt, W. K., Jr., and Monroe Beardsley. "The Concept of Meter: An Exercise in Abstraction." *PMLA* 74 (1959): 585–598.

Winters, Yvor. "The Audible Reading of Poetry." *The Function of Criticism: Problems and Exercises,* pp. 79–100. Denver: Alan Swallow, 1957.

———. *Forms of Discovery: Critical and Historical Essays on the Forms of the Short Poem in English.* [Denver]: Alan Swallow, 1967.

Woods, Susanne. *Natural Emphasis: English Versification from Chaucer to Dryden.* San Marino, Calif.: Huntington Library, 1985.

Wordsworth, William. *The Poetical Works of William Wordsworth,* ed. Thomas Hutchinson. London: Henry Frowde, 1906.

Wright, George T. "The Meter of 'Shall I Die?'" *Eidos* 3 (1986): 6, 11–12.

———. "The Play of Phrase and Line in Shakespeare's Iambic Pentameter." *Shakespeare Quarterly* 34 (1983): 147–158.

———. "Shakespeare's Poetic Techniques." In *William Shakespeare: His World, His Work,*

His Influence, ed. John F. Andrews, vol. 2, pp. 363–387. 3 vols. New York: Scribner's, 1985(a).

————. "Wyatt's Decasyllabic Line." *Studies in Philology* 82 (1985[b]): 129–156.

Wyatt, Sir Thomas. *Collected Poems of Sir Thomas Wyatt,* ed. Kenneth Muir and Patricia Thomson. Liverpool: Liverpool Univ. Press, 1969.

Yeats, W. B. *The Poems: A New Edition,* ed. Richard J. Finneran. New York: Macmillan, 1983.

Index

225, 242; verse style, personal, 249, 250, 261; verse style, reflective, 89

Pericles, 193, 312, 315

Richard II: endstopping, 214–15; epic caesura, late, 167; lines, broken-backed, 176; lines, headless, 175; lines, long, 143, 147, 148; lines, missing a stressed syllable, 180; lines, short, 126; phrase and line, 212, 214–15, 220; prose, absence of, 109; repeated phrases, meter of, 319; stress on minor words, 191, 193, 212; syllabic ambiguity, 156; syllabic compression, 312; syllabic expansion, 153; trochees, 186; trochees, straddling, 200, 201; variety, metrical, 55; verse style, personal, 250; verse style, reflective, 89

Richard III: contrary stress, 203, 204; double trimeters, 144; endstopping, 214; epic caesura, 166; hexameters, 144, 309; lines, headless, 175; lines, short and shared, 308; phrase and line, 214, 242; stress on minor words, 192, 194; trochaic rhythm, 212; verse style, angry, 242; verse style, declamatory, 89; verse style, natural, 48, 230; verse style, personal, 249, 250

Romeo and Juliet: contrary stress, 203; flare-ups of passion in, 243–44, 319; lines, headless, 175; lines missing a stressed syllable, 182, 183; lines with monosyllabic feet, 178; lines, short, 126–27; lines, short and shared, 308; midline pause, extended, 315; Queen Mab speech, expressiveness of, 60–61; reference to two-hour play, 189; stress on minor words, 191; trochee, double, 198; trochee, straddling, 200; verse style, formal, 93, 114, 139–40; verse style, natural, 230; verse style, personal, 249, 250

Sir Thomas More, 196

The Taming of the Shrew, 114, 118, 144, 171, 173, 180, 308

The Tempest: Auden's commentary on, 261; contrary stress, 205–6; epic caesura, late, 167; line-endings, weak and light, 318; lines, deviant, 101; lines, short and shared, 119; lines, symmetrical, 5; midline break, late, 209, 221, 318; phrase and line, 16, 209, 217, 221, 226–28, 315, 318; polyphonic rhythm, 227–28; Prospero's abjuration speech, analysis of, 226–28, 318; punctuation, 318; pyrrhic, 318; stress on minor words, 192; themes, 223; trochees, 318; trochees, straddling, 200, 202; verse style, personal, 261

Timon of Athens: lines, broken-backed, 177; lines, short and shared, 119; line missing a stressed syllable, 182; line with monosyllabic feet, 178; punctuation, 313; trochee, 186, 188; trochee, double, 198; trochee, triple, 199; verse style, late, 220–23

Titus Andronicus, 55, 197, 200, 304, 313

Troilus and Cressida: date, 309; epic caesura, 134–35; line missing a stressed syllable, 182; lines, deviant, 101; lines, long, 136, 148; lines, problematical, 112; lines, shared, 133–36; lines, short, 121–22, 131, 133–36, 286, 309; lines, squinting, 134–35; prose, 133–36; repeated phrases, meter of, 247–48; trochees, 195; trochees, straddling, 202

Twelfth Night: anaptyxis, 238; contrary stress, 203; epic caesura, 169; feet, variant, 231–32, 234; lines, long, 145; lines, problematical, 112–13; lines missing a stressed syllable, 182; midline break, 209; Orsino's speech, analysis of, 231–32, 234–35; sound effects, 231–32, 234–35, 319; stress on minor words, 192; syllabic expansion, 154; trochees, straddling, 201, 319; two extra syllables at midline, 169; verse style, angry, 242; verse style, personal, 231–32, 234–35, 250; verse style, reflective, 89

Two Gentlemen of Verona, 114, 148, 172, 174, 180, 308

The Winter's Tale: amphibrachs, 163; double onset, 170; enjambment, 163; epic caesura, early, 167; feminine endings, 163; flower passage, analysis of, 223–26; lines, long, 143; lines with monosyllabic feet, 178; phrase and line, 141, 220–25; phrasing, 225, 230;

Shakespeare, William, works (*continued*)
    prose, iambic rhythm in, 112; punc-
    tuation, 223–25; sound devices, 225;
    stress on minor words, 191, 193; syl-
    labic compression, 308; themes, 223;
    trochees, 163, 195; trochees, strad-
    dling, 202; verse style, late, 220–23
Shelley, Percy Bysshe, 19, 315, 322
Shirley, James, 274
Sicherman, Carol, 307, 308
Sidney, Sir Philip: feminine endings, 55, 161;
    iambic regularity, 67–68, 71, 72, 79, 158,
    207; influence on Shakespeare, xi; as
    marking a literary epoch, 23, 40, 55, 70, 93,
    207; meter, expressive, 18, 56, 66–76, 288;
    metrical development, 304; metrical varia-
    tions, 35, 36–37, 54; pronunciation, 302;
    quantitative verse, 41; spelling, xiii, 303;
    varied line-lengths in stanza, 323
—works
    Arcadia, 304
    Astrophil and Stella: double feet, 68–71;
    feminine endings, absence of, 161;
    iambic regularity, 67–68, 71, 72; influ-
    ence on Shakespeare, 76, 78, 82; meter,
    mimetic, 76, 78, 304; metrical devel-
    opment, 304; metrical system, 304;
    metrical variations, 65–73, 209, 300;
    passionate speech and meter, 66, 67,
    72–73, 73–74, 76, 78, 82, 304; punc-
    tuation, 76–77; sonnets compared
    with Shakespeare's, 76–78; syntactical
    inversions, 72; verbal patterning, 73–
    74, 304
Simpson, Percy, 313
Sipe, Dorothy, 156–57, 310
Sir Gawain and the Green Knight, 41
Skelton, John, 29, 30
Smith, G. Gregory, 39, 49, 53, 60
Southall, Raymond, 31, 299, 301
Southwell, Robert, 4
Southworth, James G., 299, 300, 301
Sparrow, John, 116, 307
Spenser, Edmund: different from Sidney, 56,
    65–66, 72; dragons, 14, 234; influence on
    Keats, 19; influence on Milton, 52; influ-
    ence on Shakespeare, xi; knights, 38, 66;
    panoramic tableaux, 66; punctuation, 317;
    quantitative verse, 41, 61; spelling, xiii;

syntax, controlled, 14, 62–63; syntax, in-
verted, 51–52, 61, 62, 63; syntax, pleo-
nastic, 51, 62
—verse, qualities of: elegance, 56, 264; expres-
siveness, 18, 64; forward movement, 14,
56, 62–63, 65, 72, 303; melodiousness, 14,
56, 61, 82, 210, 288, 303, 304; smoothness,
14, 17, 61, 65, 238, 304
—verse techniques: elision, 158; endings in *-e,
-es, -ed,* 51; endstopping, 14; feminine
endings, 161; metrical experiments, 304;
metrical underlining, 65; metrical varia-
tions, 55, 61–62, 63–65, 82, 83; midline
break, 46, 62, 210, 211, 288; phrase and
line, 14, 46, 48, 210, 211, 223; regular
meter, 63, 101; sound patterns, 63; stan-
zaic art, 61–63, 65, 91, 238, 303
—works: *Amoretti,* 48, 51; *The Faerie Queene,*
7, 14, 51–52, 55, 61–65, 91, 274, 303; *The
Shepheardes Calender,* 46, 61, 304
Spiegel, Glenn S., 42, 302
Sprott, S. Ernest, 275–76
Stanley, E. G., 301
Stanyhurst, Richard, 301
Stein, Arnold, x, 271, 321
Stein, Gertrude, 289
Stevens, Wallace: accentual five-stress line, 6,
178; iambic pentameter, 17, 18, 263, 322;
"The Emperor of Ice-Cream," 316
Stoffel, C., 310
Suhamy, Henri, xi, 191, 316
Surrey, Henry Howard, Earl of: blank verse,
58, 97, 288; circumflex words, 58; deviant
lines, scarcity of, 281; elegiac quatrains,
59; enjambment, 58, 59; feminine endings,
infrequency of, 55, 161; influence, xi;
as marking a literary epoch, 28, 40, 44,
150, 281; metrical regularity, xi, 57–58,
150, 158, 207, 300; metrical variation, ex-
pressive, 56, 57–59; metrical vigor, 302;
midline break, 45, 58; phrase and line,
58–59, 207; syntax, energetic, 59; *Aeneid,*
translation of, 57–59, 97, 306; other
poems, 45, 59
Sypher, Wylie, 253, 276

Tarlinskaja, Marina: book on Shakespeare's
meter, xi; chronology of Shakespeare's
plays, 293; Donne's "transitional" verse,

Compositor: G & S Typesetters, Inc.
Text: 11/14 Granjon
Display: Granjon
Printer: Braun-Brumfield, Inc.
Binder: Braun-Brumfield, Inc.